The Renaissance, known primarily for the art and literature that it produced, was also a period in which philosophical thought flourished. This two-volume anthology contains forty new translations of important works on moral and political philosophy written during the Renaissance and hitherto unavailable in English. The anthology is designed to be used in conjunction with *The Cambridge History of Renaissance Philosophy*, in which all of these texts are discussed.

The works, originally written in Latin, Italian, French, Spanish, and Greek, cover such topics as: concepts of man; Aristotelian, Platonic, Stoic, and Epicurean ethics; scholastic political philosophy; theories of princely and republican government in Italy; and northern European political thought. Each text is supplied with an introduction and a guide to further reading.

These readable and fully annotated versions of a wide range of texts will enable serious students of the history of philosophy to gain first-hand access to the ethical and political thought of the Renaissance.

Cambridge Translations of Renaissance Philosophical Texts

Cambridge Translations of Renaissance Philosophical Texts

VOLUME I: MORAL PHILOSOPHY

Edited by

JILL KRAYE

The Warburg Institute

CAMBRIDGE
UNIVERSITY PRESS

PUBLISHED BY THE PRESS SYNDICATE OF THE UNIVERSITY OF CAMBRIDGE
The Pitt Building, Trumpington Street, Cambridge CB2 1RP, United Kingdom

CAMBRIDGE UNIVERSITY PRESS
The Edinburgh Building, Cambridge CB2 2RU, United Kingdom
40 West 20th Street, New York, NY 10011-4211, USA
10 Stamford Road, Oakleigh, Melbourne 3166, Australia

First published 1997

Printed in the United States of America

Typeset in Times

Library of Congress Cataloging-in-Publication Data
Cambridge translations of Renaissance philosophical texts / edited by
Jill Kraye.
p.   cm.
Includes bibliographical references and index.
"Originally written in Latin, Italian, French, Spanish, and
Greek" – p.
Companion vol. to: The Cambridge history of Renaissance
philosophy.
Contents: v. 1. Moral philosophy – v. 2. Political philosophy.
ISBN 0-521-41580-2 (v. 1). – ISBN 0-521-42604-9 (v. 1 : pbk.). –
ISBN 0-521-58295-4 (v. 2). – ISBN 0-521-58757-3 (v. 2 : pbk.)
1. Ethics, Ancient. 2. Man. 3. Political science – Philosophy –
History. I. Kraye, Jill. II. Cambridge history of Renaissance
philosophy.
BJ161.C36   1997   *v. 1*
190'.9'031 – dc20   96-35176
                                                         CIP

*A catalog record for this book is available from
the British Library.*

ISBN 0 521 41580 2 hardback (volume 1)
ISBN 0 521 42604 9 paperback (volume 1)
ISBN 0 521 58295 4 hardback (volume 2)
ISBN 0 521 58757 3 paperback (volume 2)
ISBN 0 521 59208 9 hardback (set)
ISBN 0 521 59772 2 paperback (set)

Contents

PART I. CONCEPTS OF MAN

PART II. ARISTOTELIAN ETHICS AND THE SUPREME GOOD

PART III. ARISTOTELIAN ETHICS AND CHRISTIANITY

PART IV. PLATONIC ETHICS

PART V. STOIC ETHICS

PART VI. EPICUREAN ETHICS

Translators

Martin Davies, Incunabula, British Library, London

Luc Deitz, Alexander von Humboldt Fellow, University of Heidelberg

Eleazar Gutwirth, Department of Jewish History, Tel Aviv University

Neil Kenny, Churchill College, Cambridge

Jill Kraye, Warburg Institute, London

John Monfasani, Department of History, The University at Albany, SUNY, Albany

Adelheid Wiehe-Deitz, Free-lance language teacher and translator, London

Ronald G. Witt, Department of History, Duke University, Durham, North Carolina

Robert V. Young, Department of English, North Carolina State University, Raleigh, North Carolina

Preface

The Cambridge History of Renaissance Philosophy (*CHRP*), published in 1988, aimed to put the study of the philosophical works produced from the fourteenth to the sixteenth century on a new, more solid footing. The editors (Charles B. Schmitt, Quentin Skinner, Eckhard Kessler and myself), along with those who contributed to the volume, sought to demonstrate that the philosophy of this period was worthy of the attention not only of historians and Renaissance specialists, but also of philosophers – at least those interested in the history of their own discipline. While a significant amount of ground has been covered, the goal of placing the philosophy of the Renaissance on the same level as that of the Middle Ages or seventeenth century has by no means been achieved: witness the fact that the Renaissance has no established place in the philosophy curriculum and makes only occasional appearances in university teaching of subjects such as intellectual history.

One reason why Renaissance philosophy has been neglected in the United States and Britain is that a relatively small number of works have been translated into English. The great majority of Renaissance philosophical texts remain, in consequence, inaccessible to students and non-specialists. The present volume, it is hoped, will help to improve this situation by providing twenty-three new translations of works discussed in my chapter on 'moral philosophy' in *CHRP*. In order to increase the amount of primary source material available to an Anglophone readership, an attempt has been made to select texts which have not previously been translated into English. This has meant, inevitably, that the most famous works (for instance, Giovanni Pico della Mirandola's *Oration on the Dignity of Man*) have been left out in favour of texts which, though interesting in themselves, have not yet reached a wide readership. A bibliography of Renaissance moral philosophy texts available in English has been provided so that readers can readily locate published translations.

As in *CHRP*, a broad view of Renaissance philosophy has been taken in this volume. Scholastic as well as humanist works have been included, vernacular texts as well as Latin ones, commentaries and textbooks as well as treatises, dialogues and letters. In this way, readers can gain an appreciation of the variety and richness of Renaissance moral philosophy. Although many texts have been translated in their entirety, it was not possible, due to constraints of space, to have complete versions of all the works in the volume. Where it has been necessary to translate only selected portions of a particular text, priority has been given to those passages which are discussed in *CHRP*. Each translation, as well as being annotated, has been supplied with a brief introduction and a list of further reading, so that the book, although intended primarily as a companion volume to *CHRP,* can also be used on its own.

It may well be true that every translation is an act of betrayal ('traduttore traditore', as the Italian proverb goes); nonetheless, there are different ways of committing such verbal treachery. The policy followed by all the translators in this volume – in some cases, after a good deal of prodding from the editor – has been to avoid literal renderings and to produce versions which, while capturing the sense of the original, read well in English. Since the *ad sententiam,* as opposed to *ad verbum,* technique of translation was one of the innovations of the Renaissance, it seems appropriate to adopt this method for a collection of translations of Renaissance texts. It is, of course, extremely difficult to preserve the stylistic differences between authors writing in the same language – style, like poetry, is what gets lost in translation – but an effort has been made to make the somewhat stiff and laboured Latin of scholastic authors, such as the Coimbra commentators, readily distinguishable from the elegant classical Latin of humanists such as Angelo Poliziano. Where a particular word or phrase has proved especially hard to translate or the translation chosen might be regarded as controversial, the original is given afterwards in square brackets. Insertions on the part of the translator are also placed in square brackets; omissions are indicated by an ellipsis. For quotations from the Bible, the Revised Version has been adopted (as has its numeration of chapters and verses), on the grounds that its strangely familiar yet old-fashioned language resonates in modern ears in the same way that the Latin Vulgate would have done for Renaissance readers.

This volume is a work of collaboration and, accordingly, I am much indebted to my collaborators. Often they were faced with intractable texts, many of them in uncritical and unannotated editions not reprinted since the Renaissance. Drawing on their philosophical and historical knowledge, as well as their linguistic skill, they sorted out innumerable textual problems and produced concise and learned annotation wherever it was called for. I am especially grateful to them for the good grace with which they endured the exacting demands of a highly interventionist editor. It will not, I trust, seem invidious if I single out one translator, my husband Martin Davies, for particular thanks. Not only was he responsible for two translations of his own: he was always available for editorial consultation about tricky bits of Latin and provided a steady stream of sound advice about matters of English style.

Part I.
Concepts of Man

1

Anselm Turmeda

NEIL KENNY

Introduction

Anselm Turmeda (c. 1352–c. 1423) was an extraordinary figure who straddled the worlds of Christianity and Islam. Born in Majorca, he became a Franciscan and studied theology at Bologna but then went in the late 1380s to Tunis, where he remained for the rest of his life and, at some point, was converted to Islam. His treatise *The Gift* (1420), written in Arabic, is a Muslim refutation of Christianity; but the *Disputation of the Donkey* (1417–18), like his *Book of Good Advice* (1398), is a Christian text written in his native Catalan. This duality enabled both Muslims and Christians of subsequent centuries to claim Turmeda as their own. The intersection of the two religions in Turmeda is illustrated by the fact that the *Disputation of the Donkey* is an adaptation (and in places a translation) of a Muslim work, a tenth-century Arabic fable which is one of the fifty-one epistles constituting an encyclopedia composed by a heterodox fraternity collectively known as 'The Brethren of Purity and True Friends'.

The *Disputation of the Donkey* takes the form of a debate on the question whether humans are more noble than animals. Friar Anselm produces many traditional arguments in favour of human superiority, but all are demolished by his interlocutor, a donkey. Only the nineteenth argument forces the donkey to admit defeat: Christ took on human form. This reassuring use of the incarnation to prove human dignity was not unusual in the Renaissance. Nevertheless, the text has an overall unsettling effect thanks to the donkey's eighteen convincing, anti-anthropocentric ripostes, some of which, in attacking man's ill treatment of animals, have a surprisingly modern ring.

The *Disputa de l'ase* was published in Catalan in 1509 in Barcelona but survives only in a French translation that was first published in Lyons in 1544. The 1544 French text, including the headings and subheadings, is published in Anselm Turmeda, *Dispute de l'âne,* ed. A. Llinares (Paris, 1984); the passages translated are at pp. 39, 45, 47–50, 54, 56–7, 79–82, 87–9, 90–2, 117–19, 121, 138–9.

Disputation of the Donkey: Selections

The disputation of a donkey with Friar Anselm Turmeda, on the nature and nobility of animals. Composed and structured by the said Friar Anselm in the city of Tunis in 1417. In this disputation Friar Anselm uses many lively proofs and arguments to prove that the children of our father Adam have greater nobility and dignity than all the animals of the world.

3

Friar Anselm Speaks[1]

'The sight of the world being spurred on to all kinds of wickedness and of everyone living in debauchery made me think it would be appropriate to relate to you an adventure which befell me one day when I was out in the countryside. My debate will make you see that worthless man would be inferior to brute beasts if the divinity had not clothed himself in our infirmity. . . .

'I found myself quite close to a garden in which shade was provided by an infinite number of flowers and fruits of all kinds. . . . In a word, as I beheld this place I was convinced that it was earthly paradise itself or, at the very least, the splendid, beautiful and fruit-laden garden of the Hesperides. . . . I then sat among the flowers, in the shade, the better to inspect this most divine handiwork. But I suddenly began to slumber while I was gazing at this spot, which was so magnificent, and in my sleep I had the strong impression of a vision in which I had a perfect view of the brute beasts of the whole world arriving at this spacious and beautiful place. . . .'

Prologue:
In Which the Reason for So Many Animals Gathering Together Is Stated

The gathering together of so many animals at this time had been caused and occasioned by the death of their king. He had been a noble lion of great wisdom and justice as well as physical courage and bravery. . . . And because of the strong, supreme affection in which they had held this king, they had all assembled in order to elect one of his relatives as king with the consent of all the animals.

End of Prologue

Here One of the Former King's Counsellors, a Great Handsome Horse, Begins to Speak

Then a gracious horse called 'The Bay' got up; he was very wise, experienced and well-spoken. He uttered the following words, speaking loftily and with fine eloquence: '. . . in the name of almighty God, I hereby declare that the long-tailed Lord Tawny Lion, son of the cousin of our lord, the deceased king, is elected, appointed and confirmed as our king and sovereign. And I hold him to be our true lord and protector for the rest of his life.'

When these words had been spoken, the animals shouted out very loudly with one voice, expressing their agreement, saying that this choice was to their liking and great satisfaction since the lion deserved it in terms of both justice and his own worth.

Of the celebrations which the animals held for their new king

. . . their loud songs, noise, uproar and pandemonium woke me from my sleep, and once awake I was as amazed as I would have been if I had strayed outside my own body. And I heard the following words:

The Rabbit Speaks

'O most great and powerful lord, the son of Adam sitting under that tree is a Catalan born in the city of Majorca. His name is Friar Anselm Turmeda, and he is highly learned in all branches of knowledge, exceptionally so in astrology. He is the chief customs official in Tunis, serving the great and noble Maule Bufret,[2] who is king and lord among the sons of Adam. He is also Master of the Horse to the same king. . . .'

After hearing the rabbit, the king said to him: 'Tell me, rabbit, is this the Friar Anselm whose arrogance and high opinion of his own learning lead him to state, preach and hold the opinion that the sons of Adam are more noble and excellent, greater in dignity than we animals? I have heard that he goes even further, stating and asserting that we were created only to serve them, that they are our lords and we their vassals. And he says many other fantastic and ridiculous things, preaching against us without providing any proofs or just arguments. And the sons of Adam take his word for it, firmly believing that what he says against us is the truth.'

The Rabbit Answers the King by Saying

'My lord, this is the man who says all the things you have heard about . . . '

The King Addresses His Barons and Attendants

When the rabbit had said this, the king turned to the great barons and servants who were around him and said to them: 'What do the rest of you think of this dim-witted beast, Friar Anselm, and his ridiculous, mad notions?'

At this, all of the king's barons and servants answered of one accord: 'My lord, what he says and preaches against us can be put down either, on the one hand, to extreme madness or crude reasoning powers, or else to great arrogance and rashness on his part. However, my lord, you know better than we do how it often happens that when people speak ill of someone they are bearing false witness against a person who is in fact innocent, not guilty. If it so pleases you, my lord, let him be summoned immediately to appear before your royal presence and supreme majesty, and let him be questioned about these points. If he accepts that all that has been said about him is true, then let him be asked to furnish proofs for his arguments. After all, when man seeks to prove something, it is not enough (as logicians point out) simply to say "This is so"; rather, we believe that man must sometimes furnish proof in order to prove the truth of what he says about us . . .'

How the donkey was delegated to dispute against Friar Anselm

[Friar Anselm is summoned and the king says to him:] '. . . in order for you to know clearly that we animals have greater nobility and dignity than you humans, that reason and justice require us to be your lords and you our subjects and subordinates, we will leave aside many noble and sharp-witted animals who would need only two or three words to render you as silent as a dumb person. Instead, we desire and hereby decree that the mangy donkey who has had his tail cut off should answer you, although he is the most wretched and miserable animal in our court. Address yourself to him all the same; put all your arguments to him and prove the truth of the assertions you have made against us.'

So I turned round and saw beside me a vile and miserable donkey, his coat abraded all over, snotty-nosed, mangy, without a tail; in my view he would not have fetched a penny at the Tarragona fair. And I considered myself ridiculed; I could see clearly that they were mocking me. . . .

Here Begins the Debate between Friar Anselm and the Donkey

'My lord donkey, the first proof and argument showing that we sons of Adam have greater nobility and dignity than you animals is our beautiful form and appearance. For the parts of our body are well made and put together, and they are all well arranged according to beautiful matching proportions: thus, tall men have long legs, long arms and all the other parts of their body are similarly in proportion with its length; and small men have short legs and arms. So all people are proportioned in accordance with the overall size of their body. And this is the opposite of the way in which you animals are built, since there is no proportion between the parts of your bodies. I mean to tell you this in no uncertain terms.

Of proportion in animals: first, the elephant

'The elephant, as you can plainly see, has an extremely large body, big wide ears and small eyes. The camel has a large body, a long neck, long legs, small ears and a short tail. Oxen and bulls have long hair, long tails and no teeth at the front of their jaws. Sheep have long hair, long tails and no facial hair. Rabbits, despite being small animals, have bigger ears than camels. And so it is that you will find a great – almost infinite – number of animals whose bodies are distortions of the correct proportion that should exist between their different parts. For this reason it is evident that we sons of Adam are more noble than you animals.'

The Donkey's Reply

'Friar Anselm, you sin gravely by speaking of animals so scornfully. You are not so innocent as to be unaware that whenever someone scorns or criticizes any handiwork, the scorn or criticism reflects on the owner and author of that handiwork. Are you then criticizing the creator of animals? Your feeble understanding causes you to do so; indeed, you do not even understand my question. Know that the lord God created all the animals which you have named most accurately and wisely. And Moses testifies to this in Genesis [1:25], where he says that God saw all that he had made, and it was very good, in other words, it was without fault.

'I would also like you to know that God gave the elephant big wide ears so that they could be used to brush flies away from its eyes and mouth. It keeps its mouth open all the time because of its large projecting teeth, which God gave it for the defence of its body. And as for your claim that the elephant's eyes would be larger if they were in proportion with its body, I would like you to know that however small they may seem to you, their visual power is so perfect and sharp that it can extend to 250 miles if the elephant is on some high mountain. So does it strike you that such extended eyesight is in proportion with the elephant's extended body? This is unquestionably the case. I would also like you to know that every animal in the world with large bulbous eyes protruding from its head has poor, weak vision, while those with small eyes have good, sharp vision.

Of proportion in the camel

'Since the camel has long legs and yet must live off the plants of the earth, almighty God gave it a long neck so that it can reach down to the ground and can also scratch its extremities with its teeth. Almighty God created in similar fashion all the parts of the bodies of the animals which you mentioned, catering for their needs in their every activity. . . .

Friar Anselm Says to the Donkey

'Most worshipful donkey, the argument which proves that we have greater nobility and dignity than you animals and that it is right for us to be your lords is that we sell and buy you, feed and water you, protect you from the cold and heat, from lions and wolves, prepare medicine for you when you are ill. We do all this out of pity and compassion for you. And such works of charity are commonly performed only by lords towards their subjects and slaves.'

The Donkey Answers Friar Anselm

'Friar Anselm, your argument has little worth. For if we must be your subjects and slaves, and you our lords, simply because you buy and sell us, then both Christians and Moors must be in a similar position. But such dominion is gained only by force and usurpation, and where force rules, there is no room for either justice or equity. As for what you say about your feeding and watering us, protecting us from the cold and heat and from all ills, you only do this for your own gain, for you profit by our welfare and lose out if we are harmed. And you do none of this out of pity or compassion for us, but you do it for fear that we should die, since by our death you lose the pennies with which you bought us. And without our help you would drink no milk, eat no cheese, butter or cream. You would have no wool to make cloth, nor any lambskins to make furs, but would perish of cold. You would travel on foot and would also carry loads slung over your neck, like porters.

'As for what you say about taking pity on us, in fact you take lambs and kids and shut them away, separating them from their mothers and letting them die of thirst so that you can drink and turn into cheese the milk which God provided for their sustenance. You do this despite the fact that you have extremely good water and many different kinds of wine which you can drink. Friar Anselm, have you ever seen any of us animals drink milk once we have been weaned and are no longer being suckled? But your gluttony and greed are beyond all words and measure. You are old and yet you still consume milk.

'Besides, worse still, you take calves, kids and lambs and kill them. And then you skin them and chop them up; you fry their innards, boil their flesh in a pot and roast it in front of their fathers and mothers, whom you treat similarly, roasting them in front of their children. And they remain silent and endure with great steadfastness all that affliction and cruelty. Where, then, is the pity and compassion which you say you have for animals?

'The more you speak, the more you err and cover yourself in shame; for you are held by people to be wise and experienced, but when they hear your words, they consider you mad and ignorant. Therefore, if you have another argument, state it and you will receive an adequate answer, one that will perhaps make you keep your peace and fall silent.'

Friar Anselm Says to the Donkey

'My lord donkey, another argument and proof that we sons of Adam have greater dignity and nobility than you animals is that we are very clever at building houses, towers and palaces in which to live, constructing them in numerous styles: round, square and in every other shape and size. And this we do through the great cunning and practical wisdom of our minds. All of this is lacking in you animals. And whoever can do all those things is worthy of being a lord. On the other hand, justice and equity demand that whoever cannot do such things should be a subordinate and a vassal.'

The Donkey Answers Friar Anselm

'Friar Anselm, the more you speak the more you go astray, it seems to me. You think you have considerable knowledge, but you are completely devoid of it. For if you had any reason or discernment, you would plainly see the great folly of your praise of skill; your mind genuinely strikes me as being dull and feeble. And this is clear to everyone because of your foolish praise of your own building activities, since a comparison of all of your works with ours makes that praise look ridiculous.

How the donkey uses nimble arguments to prove precisely the opposite case

'Friar Anselm, don't you see how bees are governed by a king under a good system . . . and how with precise measurements they make and build handsomely their fine houses, some with six sides, others with eight, some triangular, others square and others with more or fewer sides, according to their needs. And they construct these with a single material, wax, whereas men never use just one material for their dwellings, nor could they: they need sand, lime, earth, water, stone, wood, iron and plaster. And even when they have all these materials, they also need hammers, pickaxes, rulers, saws, hatchets, squares, files, tracing-lines and other measuring devices and tools without which they could not construct and erect those dwellings. Bees, on the other hand, do not use any of these things, such is their skill and wit; and there is no man on earth who could build dwellings as pretty and as precisely proportioned as those which the bees make out of a single material.

'Spiders too make their dwellings and palaces entirely out of a single material: beautiful thread. These constructions are woven in various ways; they are finer than silk, transparent, long, square, triangular, round, resembling crêpe. They have many cords and threads, yet they require no spindle, distaff, spool, yarn-winder, carder, tailor or weaver, whereas the sons of Adam lack the ability and knowledge to make a yard of cloth or linen without these instruments. A similar example is provided by the swallows' construction of their dwellings, and by the other birds which make their nests in high places, so aptly that they appear to have been planned with sound geometry and measurements.

'Well, Friar Anselm, who are more ingenious in their works, the sons of Adam or animals? Truly, unless you are out of your mind, you will see very clearly that we animals are far more ingenious than men.

'I will now be silent, for fear of incurring the displeasure of our sire, his highness, our mighty king. So look for another argument; think hard to find proof that your false opinion is right.'

Friar Anselm Says to the Donkey

'Sir donkey, without having to think I will prove to you that we sons of Adam have greater dignity and nobility than you animals. The reason is that we eat the animals of the earth, sea and sky, in other words, birds of many different kinds. It is therefore evident and certain that the eater is more noble than the thing eaten. So we are obviously more noble than you.'

The Donkey Replies

'"No fly enters a closed mouth,"[3] Friar Anselm. Good God, it would be better for you to keep your mouth closed than to speak foolishly. For if one accepted the force of your argument, worms would be your lords, since they eat you. Lions, vultures and all the other animals and birds and fish of the sea would also be your lords, since they eat you. Wolves, dogs and many other animals would be your lords. And worse still, lice, fleas, bugs, nits, mites and suchlike would be your lords, since all of these eat your flesh. So tell me, in all honesty, whether your case is convincing, given your inability to provide or set out any arguments in favour of it?'. . .

Friar Anselm Reflects . . .

. . . I began to sweat, such was the mental anguish and distress which I was suffering because of my inability to challenge or refute his arguments. . . .

Friar Anselm Says These Words

. . . 'My lord donkey, the reason for our superior dignity and nobility is that our soul does not die with our body. We are resurrected and enter paradise, where we enjoy infinite glory. And none of this happens to you animals, for when your body dies your soul dies together with it, and you enjoy neither resurrection nor glory. This shows that we have the high place of honour and the dignity of lords. So my opinion is obviously true, not false.'

The Donkey Answers Friar Anselm

'Friar Anselm, a bad listener turns words on their head. That is what you are doing: for you read the Scriptures without understanding them. After all, Friar Anselm, as wise Cato says: "To read without understanding is not to read; it is to be neglectful of something valuable."[4] As you know, Solomon, the wisest son of Adam there has ever been, says in his Ecclesiastes, chapter 3[:21]: "Who knoweth the spirit of man whether it goeth upward, and the spirit of the beast whether it goeth downward?"; he seems to mean that no one knows except he who created them. I assure you, Friar Anselm, that for this reason you have not spoken wisely. Do you wish to resolve a matter over which Solomon, speaking wisely, casts doubt? And as for your statement that you will enter paradise once resurrected, in fact most of you will go to hell and its eternal, everlasting fires; there the fires will never stop burning and the living will never die, as Scripture says. You will wish you had died in your mothers' wombs, and few of you will go to paradise, for that is what is stated in St Matthew's Gospel, chapter 20: "Many are called but few are saved."[5] And the prophet David says in Psalms 15[:1–2]: "Lord, who shall sojourn in thy tabernacle?" God answers: "He that walketh uprightly," in other words, without sin, like us. So if you have any argument to prove that your false opinion is true, put it to me, and you will receive an answer to silence you.'

Friar Anselm Says to the Donkey

'My lord donkey, another reason why we have greater nobility and dignity than you is that, unlike you, we are made and created in the image and likeness of God. And that gives us a great and supreme place of honour, in the light of which it is just and holy for us to be your lords and for you to be our subjects and vassals.'

The Donkey Answers the Friar

'. . . Don't you know that your sins are producing these words? Good God, do you sons of Adam believe that God is made in your likeness? God forbid! For God has neither head, eyes, mouth, hands nor feet. And what is more, he is not corporeal. But you, Friar, you base your argument on the authority of Genesis [1:26], which presents God as saying: "Let us make man in our image, after our likeness." And there is no doubt that this is the unquestionable truth. But you do not understand it; you do not know how it should be understood. Although I have studied neither in Paris nor in Bologna as you have, I will now explain it to you in the clearest terms, if your dull mind has the knowledge or capacity to understand. So open your ears now, heed my words and you will see how that authoritative text should be understood.

The donkey explains that in man's body there are twelve orifices which are made in the likeness of the twelve [zodiacal] signs

'Know, Friar Anselm, that the philosophers state and maintain that man should be called the little world; that is what they call him in their books. This is because, as they point out, man contains everything that is in the great world, in other words, in the heavens and on earth. For just as there are twelve signs in the heavens, so in man you will find twelve orifices: two in the ears, first of all, then two in the eyes, two in the nose, one in the mouth, two in the breasts, one in the navel and two in the lower parts.

Here the donkey speaks of the four elements

'Just as in the great world there are four elements – namely, fire, air, water and earth – so in the little world of man there are four prime organs: the brain, the heart, the liver and the lung. And in the same way that the whole of the great world is ruled and governed by the elements, so the whole of the little world, in other words, the body of man, is ruled and governed by those four organs. . . .

The donkey explains what the front part of man's body corresponds to

'Moreover, the face and front part of man's body is like the populated and inhabited parts of the great world, for just as those parts are populated by towns, villages and castles, so the front part of man's body is populated and inhabited by the nose, mouth, breasts, navel, along with the lower parts, the hands and the feet.

What the rear part of man's body corresponds to

'The spine and the rear part of the little world, of man's body in other words, is like the parts of the great world that are neither populated nor inhabited. In addition, the front part of man's body is like the east, and the rear is like the west. The right hand is like the south and the left like the north. Sneezes, shouts, coughs and the sound and noise made by the bowels are like thunder. . . . And tears, saliva and urine are like rain. Laughter is like daylight, weeping is like the darkness of night. Sleep is like death, being awake is like life. Childhood is like spring, adolescence like summer, youth like autumn, old age like winter. And moreover, just as the great world is ruled and governed by our lord God, so the little world, man's body in other words, is ruled, governed and lorded over by the intellective soul, which does whatever it pleases with that body. When the soul wants the body to stop, it stops immediately, in that very instant and hour; when the soul wants the body to get up, it gets up in that very instant. Also, in general, when the soul wants to make any movement in the body, such as stretching or closing the feet and hands at the same time, closing or opening the eyes, jumping or running, or some greater or smaller movement, then it is performed immediately, without it being necessary for the soul to confer with the body or to give it a signal or sign; rather, in the very instant and moment when the soul wants any of these movements to be made, desire and action are the same thing. So much so that there is no need for the soul to say "Close" to the eyes or "Run" to the legs or "Do such and such" to the other parts of the body. Instead, as I have already said, desire and action are the same thing.

The donkey explains how that authoritative text is to be understood

'The instant and moment that almighty God wills and desires for something to be done in the greater world, in other words, in the heavens or on earth, then immediately it is done and performed in that same instant and moment, without it being necessary for him to say: "Let such a thing be done"; instead, the moment he wills and desires that something should be done, then it is done and performed in that same instant and moment, so much so that desire and action are the same thing. The intellective soul does the same in this smaller world, that is, in man's body, and that is how we should understand the authoritative text: "Let us make man in our image, after our likeness." For he is talking about the soul, meaning that just as God does anything he pleases in the greater world of the heavens and earth, the soul acts in similar fashion in the smaller world of man's body. Indeed, your intellective soul is constituted as follows.

The Donkey Explains That in the Intellective Soul There Are Three Powers,
Which He Compares to the Holy Trinity. The Comparison Shows, He Says,
That This Soul Is Created in the Image and Likeness Of Our Lord God

'Friar Anselm, since I get the impression that you do not sufficiently understand my explanation of this authoritative text, I will explain it to you in another way, so heed my words. According to the philosophers and certain doctors of medicine, man's soul consists of nothing but three powers, namely memory, understanding and will.[6] These three powers make up a soul. And just as the Son is born of God the Father, and the Holy Spirit proceeds from the Father and Son in equal measure, so in the same way understanding is born of memory, and the will proceeds from memory and understanding in equal measure. And just as the Father's person is not that of the Son, the Son's person not that of the Holy Spirit and the Holy Spirit's not that of the Father or Son, so the act of memory is not understanding, nor is the act of understanding will; nonetheless, these three powers together constitute an intellective soul. See, Friar Anselm, how the intellective soul is made in the image and likeness of God. That is how we should understand that authoritative text: "Let us make man in our image, after our likeness."

'Besides, Friar Anselm, if you were not arrogant, you would think a little before you speak (using that power of reason which I mentioned) and reflect on the fact that you are made in the image and likeness of God. I intend to prove to you that we animals legitimately have greater dignity and nobility than you sons of Adam. Whereas you say that you are made in the image and likeness of God, we can truthfully say that not only God but also the saints are made in our image and likeness; and you cannot challenge or refute this. For you sons of Adam depict almighty God through the likeness of a lamb; you depict the evangelists, your foremost saints, through likenesses of our animals, depicting St Luke as an ox or bull, St John as an eagle and St Mark only as a "victory";[7] and at Easter you sing a text which states that Jesus Christ rose with great power and that through his magnificent victory the lamb that he had been became a lion. Who then seems to you, Friar Anselm, to have greater nobility and dignity: you who are made in the image and likeness of God, or we who are in the likeness of God and the saints, as is made clear by your own singing at Easter and by the paintings in all churches? Truly, unless you are out of your senses, you will understand clearly that we have greater dignity and nobility than you. So look for another argument to prove that your false opinion is true.' . . .

Friar Anselm Speaks to the Donkey

' . . . I still intend to prove to you that we sons of Adam have greater nobility and dignity than you animals. And this is because we have natural intelligence and an intellective soul, whereas you only have a little natural discernment.'

The Donkey Answers Friar Anselm, Telling Him about the Nature of Animals and Situating Each Animal within Its Nature

'Friar Anselm, I get the impression that you are a little weak in the head. Dear God, to make you see clearly that we animals have natural intelligence and an intellective soul that is equal, indeed superior, to yours, I'll describe to you certain actions performed by our animals. These will show you plainly that what you say is wrong.

'See, Friar Anselm, how the chicks of hens and partridges run after their mother the moment they have hatched. And when they see their mother fleeing with fear, they also flee immediately, keeping to the route taken by their mother, and straightaway they are able to find food for themselves. If they happen to get lost and hear their mother's voice, they run towards it immediately and come to the place where the mother is.

'Furthermore, in the case of horses, mules, oxen, sheep, goats, cats and similar animals, see how, as soon as the time has come for them to give birth, the females produce their male and female offspring without pain or labour; the offspring need neither a midwife, nor a woman to wash them, nor someone to cut the umbilical cord, and immediately they search for food. They also take the teat straight away and suck. Moreover, with what discernment and attentiveness do cats and dogs carry their young from one place to another with their teeth, so gently and smoothly that they do not hurt them at all. Whereas when you humans are born, Friar Anselm, far from knowing how to take the nipple, you would die of thirst if your mother did not put it in your mouth; lacking the capacity and the knowledge to eat any food, you continue to live on milk alone for five or six months. After that, your fathers and mothers chew your food for you, so it is already chewed when you eat it. And if your fathers or mothers flee because they are terrified for some reason, you stay in the cradle, lacking the knowledge or capacity to flee after them, in contrast with the chicks of hens and partridges. Besides, your females give birth in great pain and labour; they need midwives and others to cut your children's umbilical cords, and very often they die giving birth. That is because of the curse which God put on them. What's more, once the females of our animals are big-bellied, they would not go near the male for anything in the world, since they know that God's purpose in bestowing the congress of male and female has thus been fulfilled. Yet your women are different, Friar

Anselm. The disposition of our females is not at all to their liking. On the contrary, once they are pregnant, they seek out men more than before.

'Friar Anselm, what do you think of the true love of the turtle dove for its male? When he has died she goes into deep mourning, never rests on a green tree, avoids drinking water that is clear rather than murky, and if she cannot find any murky water, she uses her foot to make the water murky before drinking. And then she remains a widow for the rest of her life, not wishing to take another husband. Whereas your women, Friar Anselm, look for other husbands straightaway, with their husband barely rotting in his grave and his bristles still good for a sauce. And it often happens, Friar Anselm, that they will kill their husbands, getting them to eat medicine and poison, so that they can take as husbands men with whom they are in love. See what a difference there is between these two kinds of love. . . .

'What do you think of the intelligence of the beaver in knowing, when it sees hunters intent on catching it, that they only want it for its genitals, which are used in many medicines? If it realizes that it will not be able to escape without being caught, then with its teeth it rips off its genitals itself and throws them to the hunters, preferring to lose them than to die and lose its life. . . .

'So, do these actions which I have described seem intelligent and reasoned to you? That is certainly what they are. And if you wish to speak the truth, you will agree with me that these animals have intelligence and an intellective soul that is equal, indeed superior, to yours. And I will not even go into the many animals, including some beetles, which, fearing some harm when they see sons of Adam approaching, pretend to be dead, bending their feet and hands so that you would take them for dead; afterwards, when they perceive that there is no longer anyone there, they get up and go about their business.' . . .

Friar Anselm Says

'My lord donkey, here for sure is another argument to prove the truth of my opinion that we sons of Adam have greater nobility and dignity than you animals: almighty God chose to take on human flesh, to put his lofty divinity together with our humanity, to become man. He did not assume your flesh or likeness, but for a long time became our brother, became a son of Adam, just like us on his mother's side, so that our flesh is now placed up there, in the highest heaven. St John said of this in chapter 1[:14] of his Gospel: "The Word became flesh, and dwelt among us." Upon which St Augustine commented: "The Word of the Lord is the Son of the Father,"[8] that is, Jesus Christ, who is the Son of the Father eternally and of his mother temporally. This dignity of ours surpasses all other dignity and honour. Holiness and justice therefore demand that we should be your lords and you our vassals and subjects. That is why the great prophet King David said: "Thou has put all things under his feet: all sheep and oxen, yea, and the beasts of the field; the fowl of the air, and the fish of the sea."[9] The same royal prophet also says in his eighth Psalm: "thou hast made him but little lower than God, and crownest him with glory and honour. Thou madest him to have dominion over the works of thy hands."[10] It is therefore manifestly plain and clear that, for all these reasons, we have greater nobility and dignity than you and that we are legitimately and justly your lords and you animals our vassals, slaves and subjects.'

The Donkey Answers

'In the words of the proverb, Friar Anselm, the harm that a man fears is the one from which he perishes. And that is what has happened here. For I swear it is true that each time you said to me that you had another argument to prove the truth of your opinion, I almost perished, fearing that you would utter the argument which you have just now uttered and set out, since I knew that argument well, together with many others which I know to be more authoritative and pertinent than all of those which you have used. Yet you do not remember these, so long is it since you have looked at or read anything in certain books of Holy Scripture. There is, for example, that authoritative passage in chapter 1[:28] of Genesis which states that almighty God said to Adam and Eve: "Be fruitful, and multiply, and replenish the earth, and subdue it; and have dominion over the fish of the sea, and over the fowl of the air, and over every living thing that moveth upon the earth," and many other things, which I will pass over, for fear of speaking for too long.

'Therefore, most venerable master, since I am neither able nor willing to offer resistance or to challenge the truth, I concede to you that the sons of Adam have greater nobility and dignity than we animals, that almighty God created us to serve you, that he thereby bestowed great honour on you and did us no wrong or injury, for all his works are right, just and true.' When the donkey had uttered these words, the king of the animals spoke as follows.

The king of the animals speaks to Friar Anselm, conceding victory to him on the question debated

'Friar Anselm, before we were acquainted with you, when we heard about your knowledge and acute mind, we believed part but not all of what we heard. But now we see that the account of your knowledge and sharp wits that spread throughout the world was entirely true. Hence your equitable and truly just victory over us in winning the debate on this question. Both we and all the venerable barons of our court concede the truth of your opinion that you sons of Adam have greater nobility and dignity than we animals, that you are our legitimate lords and we your vassals. And that is the pure truth, a sun that cannot be blocked out by any screen. We beseech and entreat you, with all our might, to be so gracious as to teach, tell and exhort the sons of Adam to take good care of our poor animals, since they will be rewarded for this by him who lives and reigns for ever and ever.'

Having spoken these words, he left the garden with all the animals. And I rode off home on my horse, full of joy and delight at having won the debate.

Thanks be to God. Amen.

Translator's Notes

1. This opening speech is in verse in the 1544 French translation.
2. A translation of 'Moulay Bouferiz', the name by which the Hafsid ruler Abu Faris was known in Christian documents. See Anselm Turmeda, *Dispute de l'âne,* ed. A. Llinares (Paris, 1984), pp. 3, 32 n. 14.
3. A French proverb; see Turmeda, *Dispute,* p. 143 n. 42.
4. A quotation from the preface to the *Disticha Catonis,* a collection of proverbs, attributed to Cato the Censor, but in fact dating from imperial times.
5. In fact, the quotation is from Matthew 22:14.
6. Cf. Augustine, *De trinitate* X.11.
7. An allusion to the winged lion. St Matthew is not mentioned because he is normally depicted as a man.
8. See St Augustine, *In Iohannis evangelium tractatus* X.1.
9. Psalms 8:6–8.
10. Psalms 8:5–6.

Further Reading

Calvet, A., *Fray Anselmo Turmeda, heterodoxo español . . .* (Barcelona, 1914)
CHRP, pp. 308–9
Goodman, L. E., *The Case of the Animals versus Man before the King of Jinn: A Tenth-Century Ecological Fable of the Pure Brethren of Basra* (Boston, 1978)
Guy, A., *Philosophes ibériques et ibéro-américains en exil* (Toulouse, 1977), pp. 11–56

2

Poggio Bracciolini

MARTIN DAVIES

Introduction

Poggio Bracciolini (1380–1459) was born in Terranuova, a small town in the upper Arno valley some thirty miles from Florence. Near the end of the fourteenth century he moved to Florence and qualified there as a notary in 1402. He is said by Vespasiano da Bisticci to have supported his studies by copying manuscripts, and his formal bookhand of the early fifteenth century is among the first, and certainly the most influential, examples of the new humanistic script. By this time he was a protégé of the humanist chancellor of Florence, Coluccio Salutati (see Chapter 16), and with Coluccio's support he found a place at the court of Rome, as a writer of apostolic letters and papal secretary, from 1403 onwards. He held this post, with interruptions, for half a century until he in turn became chancellor, and ultimately historian, of Florence, where he spent his last years.

Apart from his public career (which included an unhappy five years in England), Poggio made a name for himself in two distinct but connected fields of humanist enterprise. The two decades to about 1425 were marked by a prolonged, systematic and very successful search for older, better or more complete manuscripts of the Latin classics, hitherto unknown or unavailable. The search was one for which his position at the centre of the Church and his travels to ecclesiastical councils offered ample opportunity. He rescued in this way from the 'northern dungeons' Lucretius and Silver Latin poets, unknown speeches of Cicero, Petronius and a complete copy of Quintilian – the last a find of incalculable interest and significance to early humanists as they began to come to grips with classical rhetoric.

The moral writings of Poggio are centred on the idea of the instability of human affairs, usually seen as the playground of a malevolent fortune. The role of fortune had been extensively treated by him several times when he came to write towards the end of his life his last major work, *On the Misery of the Human Condition* of 1455. It sums up themes that had played an important part in a long career of reading and writing as well as of direct experience of a violent and divided world. As he grew older and less adaptable to change, Poggio was increasingly struck by the depth of human misfortune at all levels of society, individual, institutional and national. Here he attacks targets familiar from earlier works – avarice, ambition, hypocrisy, sensuality, above all the fruitlessness of human endeavour in the face of the vagaries of a Fortuna acting independently of God.

Individual and collective misery is the common lot of mankind; nations as well as individuals are subject to evil destinies; the classical past often looked to for example was no better than present wretchedness – a notable admission for a humanist schooled in the classics. In the end Poggio comes to the Stoic-Christian view that we must free ourselves from human passions and their objects before we can be exempt from the blows of fortune. These passions give rise to human iniquity, which is the true cause of all misfortune: the remedy lies within ourselves. All this is spread out on a dense texture of ancient and modern *exempla*.

The ostensible occasion of the work was the recent fall of Constantinople to the Turks (1453), an event shocking to many besides Poggio. Personal circumstances too played a part.

17

His return to Florence as chancellor at the end of 1453 turned out to be a great disappointment, both for Poggio and for the Florentines, and he was effectively relieved of his post within a year or two. His natural pessimism was accentuated by tax difficulties with the Florentine authorities and a continuing series of personal attacks by humanists of a younger generation, as his own friends died off. We may also see in it a reaction (strongly felt, no doubt, not merely rhetorical) to a renewed humanist stress on the 'excellence and dignity of man'. Optimistic works of this sort, taking up a Petrarchan lead, had been written in the years immediately preceding Poggio's work by Bartolomeo Facio and Giannozzo Manetti.[1] Poggio returned to an older and more widespread vein of pessimism which ultimately derived from the Church Fathers and which had found its most notable expression in the well-known work of Pope Innocent III (early thirteenth century) with the same title as the present work, *On the Misery of the Human Condition.*

The work is formally a dialogue, dedicated to the condottiere prince of Rimini, Sigismondo Malatesta, in expectation of princely reward (another disappointment here). Poggio and his fellow Florentine humanist Matteo Palmieri, author of *Civil Life,*[2] take the part of exponents of human misery against a rather feeble defence of human dignity by Cosimo de' Medici. The structure is very loose and rambling, with frequent *longueurs* and repetitions of the same material and themes. This combined with the dialogue's unrelieved gloom does not make for easy extended reading.[3]

For the Latin text of *De miseria humane conditionis* see Poggio Bracciolini, *Opera omnia,* ed. R. Fubini, 4 vols. (Turin, 1964–9), I, pp. 86–131; the translated passage (the dedication and the first third of Book I) is at pp. 86–95.

On the Misery of the Human Condition: Selections

Dedication to Sigismondo Pandolfo Malatesta, Prince of Rimini

Of the various writers who have examined diverse subjects, none seem to me more useful to human society than those who have devoted their efforts to restraining our excessive desires, and to reining back ambition and that truly vain passion for fortune's gifts, which are so injurious to mankind. We really are best served by those who set before readers the wretchedness of the human condition and teach us that since all our unhappiness derives from the gifts of fortune, we must set a limit to our desires. Men will inevitably repress and restrain those idle passions in which we are caught up once they see that fortune's offerings, which are sought with so much eagerness, in fact lie at the origin and heart of our troubles, and constitute the very seat of human misery. In reality, all our anxieties, all of life's difficulties, all our spiritual ailments come from fortune's gifts. They have a specious attractiveness, which tempts men to seek them out, little knowing what sorrows they will suffer when they possess them and what afflictions they will bring in their train. Though in our blindness of spirit and ignorance of what the future holds we strive with might and main to obtain them, yet we will surely retreat from the course we have taken once warned that no trust or certain hope can be placed in those things under the sway of fortune, which twists and turns everything at will.

One man will bend all his efforts to accumulating wealth, unaware of the hole he is digging himself into. Another finds prosperity and comfort, which cannot but arouse envy, and he is tortured by the need to protect them by daily labour and sleepless nights. A third might seek high political office, as though he were looking to attract both hatred and exile. Some labour to impose tyranny on their cities in ignorance of the fact that such men rarely escape a violent death. Others seek a wife or children; but only those who have experienced these burdens can say how great and how many are the cares and anxieties they bring with them. Many take pleasure in bodily strength or beauty; but these are things of brief endurance which the slightest mishap can destroy. We know that the highest positions – principalities, kingdoms and empires – are nothing more than the blandishments of fortune: the number of people who have been abandoned, mocked and ruined by them forms no small part of the record of human misery, as we read in books and have seen for ourselves. We should therefore think of those who try to root out these excessive desires from our minds, and teach us to have as little as possible to do with fortune's gifts, as making the greatest contribution to the two things which, rightly viewed, are to be preferred to all others: bodily peace and tranquillity of mind.

I have here written two books to try to add to the sum of useful human knowledge with my thoughts on these matters. They show, as far as my limited abilities are able, the full wretchedness of the condition into which we are born, and how far men are cheated of their hopes, so that, when the frailty of human nature is exposed, they may recognize that chance decides the lot of those who trust too much to fortune's arbitrary power, and may find for their own longings some quieter haven from which they can contemplate, as from the safety of a watchtower,[4] the storms that beset those who have entrusted themselves to the squalls of fortune.

I am fully aware that I have taken on a subject which requires great intellectual powers, wide-ranging learning and profound eloquence. But we can ask of ourselves no more than what it is in our power to give. However readers may judge it, the task has certainly been undertaken with a view to the common good of all. I have dedicated this little work to you, illustrious prince, in the knowledge that following in the steps of your famous princely forbears you too take pleasure in the exercise of learned men's minds and are happy to read whatever I write. Though I am sure that your mental balance and moderation will ward off any hint of unhappiness, I think there may nevertheless be some profit to be had from its perusal, both in helping to guard against the snares of fortune which batten on our wretched lives, and in adopting safer courses of action. For when you have seen mirrored here the sport that fortune has had with so many men, as if to entertain the masses, and observed how great her influence is in time of war, you will yield to her power with all the more caution and take her gifts with ever more reluctance. Your great virtue has brought you the highest glory in war and peace alike, and that should be not just preserved but augmented. I urge you to trust rather to the protection of the virtues which are needed in a general – which you have in outstanding measure – than to the favour of fortune, which the sages tell us it is rarely safe to enjoy.

BOOK I

At the age of seventy-three I returned to Florence from the papal court, where I had spent almost fifty years, summoned by public invitation to take up the office of chancellor of the republic. I then resumed my old habit of paying frequent visits to that famous and good man Cosimo de' Medici, who was not only a most eminent citizen but thoroughly devoted to the study of the humanities – at that time he was laid up at home for several months with an attack of gout. We used to talk on a variety of matters, concerning our common studies or on questions where the state had as usual sought his opinion.[5]

On one occasion it happened that a number of people were there talking about the course of the current war, and some of them brought up the already worn topic of the lamentable fall of Constantinople, complaining of the monstrous cruelty that the Turks had shown in their bloody slaughter of Christians. Some speakers dwelt at length on the calamity the Christian world had suffered and expressed fears for its future safety unless other strategies and other resources could be brought to bear against such a holocaust. One and all in the end came to the conclusion that no previous century had ever witnessed such a terrible and dangerous fall of a city. Such was the wound inflicted on the Christian faithful that they doubted whether we could avoid the most fatal consequence of all, that of giving the Turks a gateway, as it were, from which to launch the occupation of the other nations of Europe, especially in view of the discord among Christians themselves.

No Christian realm was at peace, practically no people or region was untouched by war. Those whose efforts had in the past been devoted to restraining and crushing the power of the barbarians were now occupied with internal dissension. Italy, which might on its own have the land and sea forces to put the barbarian threat to flight, was riven by a number of wars. The depression brought about by the collapse of Greece was matched by fear for Italy's own collapse, since all those who might have helped to hold back the enemy's onslaught were themselves seen to be ever more weakened.

After these views had been expressed, they all went away except Matteo Palmieri, a very learned man of outstanding qualities. Cosimo began to enquire what we thought of this dreadful conquest, which everyone had deplored and elaborated on at such length that it seemed to be settled opinion that nothing worse had ever befallen Christendom, with the accompanying complaint of the instability of the times and the harshness of fortune, as though nothing more savage or atrocious had been known for many centuries.

Matteo replied: 'I think simple humanity demands our sympathy at the fall of such a city. But if you consider the nature and customs of the Greeks, their treachery, idleness and avarice, it seems to me they deserved their punishment. As to the first, their nature and manner of life are sufficiently explained in Cicero's speech for Flaccus.[6] As to their trustworthiness and devoutness, the attitude they have always taken towards Christians is made clear above all by the destruction of Christian armies which Greek treachery wiped out as they made their way to recover the Holy Land. They have twice now abjured professions of Catholic faith made in church councils.[7] They have such a powerful combination of sloth and avarice that though they had silver and gold in abundance, they spent not a penny on the defence of their own city. And that I think was calculated to leave the Turks a richer prize, since there is a reliable report that a vast treasure was found there, above and beyond what people had generally thought. They were forever imploring the popes for assistance in their hour of need: the help they could very easily have given themselves they sought of others, with the result that the disaster seems to have taken place not through chance but by divine judgement.

'But I must confess that however much they were at fault in the destruction of their city, the cruelty of the barbarians was truly deplorable. The terrible fall of such a city is to be taken very seriously, and I by no means make light of it. But these things are not so surprising as are commonly thought when you consider the role that fortune's arbitrary power is accustomed to playing in human affairs, and the random way she gives and takes away wealth, princedoms, empires and kingdoms. This is not the first time she has shown her strength in overturning cities, peoples and entire provinces. It is her old game of making the mighty quake, raising up one man and casting down another, making a king of a slave and a slave of a king.[8] The record of great cities being laid low is so common that it comes as no surprise when fortune aims her lightning bolts at the higher reaches and demolishes the topmost pinnacles. Constantinople is not alone in being taken and destroyed by enemies; we find many other mighty cities documented in history (as I shall later mention) which the enemy's savagery has wiped out in disasters even bloodier than hers.

'Their wretchedness would indeed be cause for grief and lamentation were there not an even greater store of misery — and fear of worse to come — to which, it seems, some law of nature subjects us as our common lot. We should then have to mourn not the ruin and desolation of a single city but of the whole world — a desolation which has spread so far among all of us and has so gripped the human race that no powers of utterance could find the eloquence to match the degree of misery we share. You see that the universal law which nature has instilled in our minds was established by the sins of our first father. From him derives all our unhappiness, from him originate the mistakes and vices and crimes of mankind which increase the wretchedness of this life. It is from him that we take the possibility and occasion and means of sinning and falling away from virtue.

'And it is fairly obvious that these things would induce in us deep depression if we had leisure to rehearse and grieve for each and every one of our misfortunes. What is our life but a pilgrimage of toil, full of mistakes and foolishness? It was reflecting on these facts that brought the philosopher Heraclitus to look on men's foolishness and wretchedness with incessant weeping.[9] That wise man was saddened at the foolishness of our lives. He grieved that the human race, having lapsed into madness, should be subject to endless woes — spurning just counsel, neglecting virtue, pursuing vice with might and main, hating the good and approving the bad, always recklessly and perversely seeking those very things which vex our minds with the utmost distress and with trouble and disturbance of all sorts.'

'How very much better', said Cosimo, 'was the attitude of Democritus, who viewed the follies of mankind with laughter rather than tears. Nothing could suit a wise man less than to waste tears on something that cannot be mended, and become pointlessly distressed over what cannot be changed. For my part I would rather set a limit on our afflictions than have them multiplied in talk. We might at least look into how they can be alleviated. The human condition is difficult and insecure enough as it is, even once we've resolved to face up to our troubles, without our adding to their crushing weight by letting our thoughts dwell on them or by remembering past woes.

'It is true that life presents us with a great many difficulties and that humankind is very weak in the face of them. I admit that we are exposed to a great many buffets of fortune and that we are by nature fragile creatures. Yet we have been given a great many advantages and ready help for protecting ourselves against fortune's threats and what you call the misery of the human condition. Nature has bestowed on us many delights; she has allowed us many honourable pleasures and diversions to mitigate the burden of misery. She gave us besides wives and children, grandchildren and great-grandchildren, in which we can see, as in a mirror, the very image of ourselves. On top of that we have been given long ancestry, wealth and riches, positions of prestige and honour, magistracies, military commands, the highest offices of state. All of these soothe us by giving us some occupation, as it were, and by taking our mind off our troubles they lead us to calmer thoughts.

'What is most important, however, is that God the creator of everything has granted us the supreme gift of reason, something to which we may turn as to an inviolate fortress. With the support of reason, and obedient to its counsel, we may set a measure on things and not allow our desires to outstrip the limits it has laid down. Those prescriptions will guide us to the perfect life and rescue us from every onset of misery. And if you do but harken to her, reason will indeed enable you to face fortune both good and bad with a firm and constant spirit. You will be able to meet everything that befalls you with equanimity; unmoved and self-possessed, you will have no need to fear onslaughts of grief. No fears will terrify you; your moral liberty will protect you from any of fortune's attacks, steadfast in face of present ills and fearless of the future.

'But since the common folly of mankind means that few cultivate virtue, there is ample scope for fortune, as well as for vice, to throw our lives into turmoil with all sorts of ailments and passions. We have neglected reason (and virtue is no more than right reason) and enslaved ourselves to a host of passions wholly contrary to it. The consequence is that we have lost the right path and found no haven of peace – we are anxious and harassed wanderers, restlessly driven hither and thither by lust, with no end laid down to our desires. So it is that we ourselves cause our own afflictions. All we do is undertaken at fortune's whim and arbitrary power – the power that dominates the lives of the common people and fools above all. It's no surprise, then, if the human condition seems inevitably to involve great misery. And that is certainly our fault, and not nature's: she has given us the means to live well, which we have corrupted by our depraved characters and turned to our own destruction. We have become fortune's slaves when we could be free.'

At this point I said: 'I'm sure Matteo will pardon me if I reply briefly to what you have said, Cosimo. I think you hold these views because you reckon that other people are perhaps just as you are, in terms both of mental gifts and of integrity, good faith and steadfastness of life. But not everyone brings the same intelligence, wealth or resources – in short, the same endowments of nature – to warding off the problems of life. The only difficulty we see you having to face is the gout. For the rest, God has heaped up for you in profusion all that men most want – a great many mental and natural gifts can well make up for that one bodily defect. But what about the others? One man may be afflicted by extreme poverty, another by the great misfortune of stupidity, another by lack of children, another by blindness. Some may be weak in body, others may suffer the misfortunes of prison or their country's ruin, others again may be so hard pressed by wild and savage nature that they would spontaneously proclaim their misery.

'All these men would take a different view from yours and would quote those words of Terence: "you'd think differently if you were in my shoes."[10] So I am by no means surprised that you regard human misery so lightly and do not realize it is spread so wide that all mortals are its slaves. Someone who lacked all your assets would think quite differently about the matter, bringing up the old proverb that it is easy for a full stomach to discourse on hunger. By their own example, they would declare that nothing is more wretched than poverty for a pauper, nothing more unfortunate than exile for one who has been expelled from his country, nothing worse than contempt for one of low birth, nothing harder than blindness for one lacking the use of his eyes, nothing more miserable than illness for one sick in body. (Fools, on the other hand, never complain about their foolishness, for no one would grumble about his own stupidity or bemoan the fact that he is wanting in wisdom.)

'A good many people under the strain of their various hardships would take issue with your views, and they could find good evidence to back their assertion that nothing is more miserable or harder or more difficult than this life of ours. Good fortune reaches few, they would say, and remains with even fewer. Bad fortune plays its game on a broad and well-trodden field, while good fortune's is narrow and cramped. This life is not only all too short but also subject to the cruel whims of fortune, which weighs men's deeds in unequal scales. Fortune is adverse to the good and the brave above all: these are the ones that fall prey to her arbitrary attack, especially the virtuous. We are all subject to her recklessness, more in thrall to her random violence than to the voice of reason. What is more, they continue, the reason which you say is outside fortune's grasp is rendered insensible, so to speak, and forced to yield to the blows she deals out and to shrink before her obstinacy. This is the position taken by that arbiter of morals, Seneca, when he says that we have reached the hard and invincible realm of fortune, destined to suffer good and ill alike according to its whim.[11] It practises cruel and shameless abuse on our bodies without restraint – some it burns with fire, others it drives naked through uncertain seas.

'And so it turns out, they say, that our whole life is mere punishment, a vale of tears, a life that is hateful and full of misfortune. As for your assertion that reason is given us as a means of weakening fortune's strength, I admit that that is true as far as the mind is concerned, as long as one can freely exercise it; yet there are still a great many obstacles and hard barriers placed in the way of our attaining virtue. Mother Nature has granted us reason as the one bulwark we have to enable us to stand up against the attack of fortune, but she has at the same time weakened it with a host of potent enemies. Nature has provided not only battle-hardened soldiers who seek to sack the citadel of reason in unceasing warfare but also machines of war and instruments of torture. You see the nature and scale of the battalion – or rather the army – of vices that assails us on all sides, vices that encourage the growth of the mental infirmities which fight against reason. You see again how the mighty ranks of evil rise up against virtue, how wisdom is assaulted by stupidity and the great crowd of madmen that support it. You have only to consider the strength of all these enemies of reason and virtue to see how very difficult it would be for reason to carry the day by itself in such a hard and hostile line of battle, brought low as she is in this struggle against so many attackers.

'Reason's bitter combatants and persecutors are avarice, prodigality, extrava-gance, fear, foolhardiness, lust, envy, pride, ambition and a thousand other powerful agitations of the mind besides, which are opposed to, and in fact loathe, rational thought. Few men have yet appeared who can overcome the power of these vices by dint of reason – the greater part of mankind, indeed, they easily seduce and use as they will. How few good, honest and moderate citizens are to be found, even in well-ordered states, who can shield themselves from the stain of vice, and even from utter servitude to it. "They are all gone aside," says the prophet, "they are together become filthy; there is none that doeth good, no, not one."[12] If no one does good, if all have fallen by the wayside, certainly the fall has been in the direction of evil. Since we know that those who are evil and disreputable are wretched, it follows that all lives are consumed by wretchedness. What can this life offer that is more wretched or unfortunate than to lack virtue entirely, to be enslaved to vice, to fail to listen to reason? And if any man (or animal, rather) is bereft of these things, he cannot but be a fool and an imbecile – and there is no greater evil, no greater misfortune than stupidity.

'Let it be granted, then, that since everyone is evil, everyone must also be wretched. You regard the possession of wives and sons and grandchildren and the rest as putting the miseries of life to flight; but you should consider whether they are not rather invitations to those very miseries, and whether the things you think bring pleasure and succour to our lives may not carry with them ample scope for misfortune.

'All those goods are granted to us by fortune as a loan, so that she can with absolute justice demand them back at any time. The more we are decked out with fortune's gifts, the more we should fear her power and fickleness. As Terence's young man says: "fortune – you never stay good forever!"[13] And the tragedian too: "Fortune rules human affairs arbitrarily, scattering its gifts with a blind hand, always favouring the worse."[14] How few it smiles upon for any length of time, how inconsis-tent it is, is shown by the example of the many it has deluded. This much all agree on, that there is more pain in being deprived of her benefits than pleasure in their possession. Wife, children and grandchildren do indeed afford the highest pleasure if they are granted long life and good character. But every man is held in suspense and great uncertainty of mind as he fears his wife's death or his son committing a crime or his daughter's illness; as Terence says: "You see the desolation of all those whom fortune has raised to wealth and position."[15] You see one man who mourns for the death of his fine children, another who mourns that his continue to live. You see how much better it would have been for many men never to have had children at all or to have taken a wife. You have heard of a great many men who have died to get riches, and others again who have been driven from their cities on account of their political ambitions.

'We know that each of the goods I mentioned before (if goods they are) is intermixed with its own evil, each has some calamity woven into it. Poverty – worst of all tortures – follows close upon wealth, and want upon plenty; riches are followed by destitution and abandonment; disease treads on the heels of health; the world's contempt sits next to honour and position; bereavement succeeds the birth of children. Supreme power turns at times to enslavement. I pass over the fact that the very things you consider to be productive of happiness are often in reality the instruments of vice – invitations to desire, snares of pleasure, strong incitements to lust. Where there is freedom to sin it is difficult indeed to keep to the good. As the tragedian says, the wealthy and those bolstered by political authority always seek more than is right – men who have too much power always seek to do what they cannot.[16] All this leads me to think that misery is such a universal bane of mankind that no one can be free of it.'

At this juncture, as I seemed to be on the point of finishing, Matteo said: 'If I may add a little something off my own bat, as they say, I think Nature herself supports your case, for she has laid down that the first signs of life of a new-born infant will be tears and tantrums. It is as if Nature foresees the vast and boundless sea of troubles to which she is exposed and laments that she is caught up in them at the very outset. Already at this first step in life she grieves to see that the foundations have been set firm of everything that is to come. It seems that a new-born baby who knows nothing of good or evil will yet envisage the calamities that lie in the future and will sense by some natural instinct the disadvantages of mortal life: disease, poverty, exile, the death of those dear to us, defects of body and soul and all the other drawbacks of human frailty.

'The course our lives take is uncertain too, and made more so by the arbitrary whims of fortune, so that no one can bank on any period of security in his life. I'm afraid that if we were told before birth what the nature and condition of human life really is, we should simply refuse to set out on this vast and stormy sea in such a small vessel and so avoid the reefs on which we could see nothing but the certain prospect of shipwreck. Just think of Virgil – what a desirable and pleasant prospect he holds out to those beginning life! Listen and see if you can deny that they are bound to be wretched:

> Before the entrance, at the very jaws of Hell,
> Grief and avenging Cares have made their beds,
> And there abide pale Disease and sad Old Age,
> Fear too and Hunger that drives men to wrong
> And shameful Poverty – shapes terrible to look upon –
> And Death and Toil and Death's own brother, Sleep,
> And the mind's evil Joys. In the doorway opposite sits death-dealing War
> And the Furies in their iron chambers and raving Discord.[17]

Or do you really believe that when such fine companions are given us at the very outset of life we can somehow avoid this throng of miseries by our own efforts? We are assailed by a vast mass of them, Cosimo, a great host of foes, huge cohorts of misery. I cannot see any method or indeed any possibility of avoiding the difficulties that spring into life as we ourselves are born.'

At this point, Cosimo said: 'Let's look a little closer at what we've just been saying and broaden the discussion of your lines of argument – though whether they are right is for those better versed in the realms of learning to say. I for my part shall say what comes into my mind extempore, and let the rest look after their own views.

'I agree that fortune, that is the grace of God, has looked with favour on me personally and that I have been given, as you say, some moderate mental aptitudes. Yet history records both in our own time and earlier many men of this city whose old age, right to the end of their days, was attended by the utmost felicity. Everyone would say that those cases must be exempted from what you call our common misery.'

Matteo rejoined: 'We know indeed, Cosimo, that your own father,[18] a fine man and notably pious, is himself to be excluded from that company; him apart, however, there is no one who has not been wanting in much of what makes up felicity. But your father was an exceptionally humane and generous man and one endowed with great goodwill, who seems to have lacked none of the elements by which human happiness may be attained. In the goods that fortune bestows, in goods of body and spirit, he outstripped the men of his age.'

Cosimo replied: 'Let us put aside talk of my family, in case it looks as if I were indulging in self-praise, which may perhaps seem invidious. But this I can say with truth, that many of our fellow citizens have departed this life in a similar state of felicity, though to avoid the censure of the fickle crowd I shall pass over them. Our talk should rather centre on reviewing the men of antiquity who gained renown for learning or practical achievements. I shall not speak of the barbarians, who preferred to be tyrants rather than kings. But it does seem foolish to regard as wretched those whose lives are commonly thought to have been wholly successful – the wise men of Greece such as Lycurgus,[19] Solon,[20] Aristides,[21] Lysander,[22] Socrates and Plato and all those other eminent thinkers who ignored the gifts of fortune and gave themselves over to the study of philosophy, or those great Greek generals such as Alexander,[23] Miltiades,[24] Agesilaus,[25] Themistocles[26] and Epaminondas.[27] On our own Roman side we can count Brutus,[28] Fabricius,[29] Publicola,[30] Coruncanius,[31] Camillus,[32] the Catos,[33] the Laelii,[34] the Scipios,[35] Rutilius,[36] Cicero and dozens of others whose outstanding merit left them untouched by any stain of wretchedness. They are held to have been wise and just and to have lived virtuous lives which kept all misery at bay. It is not the case, then, that your miserable condition of human existence applies to all men alike, but only to fools and cowards and the uneducated masses – those who have no resources of reason or prudence or virtue but are driven like cattle by the needs of their senses alone and the sudden impulses of the appetites. By extending their hands towards the goods of fortune they expose themselves and their families to the miseries of this life here below. You remember Aristotle's dictum that fortune lords it over the people and has most power where there is least wisdom.[37] And it is from her that all occasions of unhappiness arise. . . . ' . . .

Translator's Notes

1. See Giannozzo Manetti, *On the Dignity of Man,* in *Two Views of Man,* trans. B. Murchland (New York, 1966), pp. 61–103.

2. For a translation of Book II of Palmieri's *Civil Life* see J. Kraye, ed., *Cambridge Translations of Renaissance Philosophical Texts,* II: *Political Philosophy* (Cambridge, 1997), ch. 11.

3. For a translation of another of Poggio's works, *In Praise of the Venetian Republic,* see Kraye, ed., *Cambridge Translations,* II: *Political Philosophy,* ch. 10.

4. Reading *specula quadam* instead of *speculo quodam;* cf. Cicero, *Epistulae ad familiares* IV.3.1.

5. See F. Ames-Lewis, ed., *Cosimo 'il Vecchio' de' Medici: Essays in Commemoration of the 600th Anniversary of Cosimo de' Medici's Birth* (Oxford, 1992).

6. Though Cicero was himself a Philhellene, it suited his defence of Flaccus (*Pro L. Flacco,* of 59 BC) to pander to Roman prejudice by attacking the moral character of the Greeks.

7. The Eastern Orthodox Church never accepted the Union with the Western Catholic Church proclaimed at both the Council of Lyons (1274) and the Council of Florence (1438–9).

8. See Seneca, *Epistulae* XLIV.4, quoting Plato, *Theaetetus* 174E.

9. The Greek thinkers Heraclitus and Democritus (mentioned later) were traditionally known as the 'weeping' and 'laughing' philosophers.

10. Terence, *Woman of Andros* 310.

11. Seneca, *Consolatio ad Marciam* 10.6.

12. Psalms 14:3.

13. Terence, *The Mother-in-Law* 406.

14. Seneca, *Phaedra* 979–80.

15. Terence, *Phormio* 244.

16. Seneca, *Phaedra* 214.

17. Virgil, *Aeneid* VI.273–80.

18. Giovanni di Bicci de' Medici, died 1429.

19. Lycurgus was the traditional founder of the Spartan constitution and military system.

20. Solon was an Athenian statesman and poet of the sixth century BC.

21. Aristides (b. c. 520 BC or earlier) was an Athenian statesman and soldier.

22. Lysander (d. 395 BC) was a Spartan general and statesman.

23. Alexander the Great (356–323 BC), King of Macedon, was the perhaps greatest general of antiquity.

24. Miltiades (c. 550–489 BC) was the victorious Athenian general at the battle of Marathon (490).

25. Agesilaus (444–360 BC) was a Spartan king.

26. Themistocles (c. 528–462 BC) was an Athenian statesman.

27. Epaminondas (d. 362 BC) was a Theban general and statesman.

28. Marcus Junius Brutus (c. 85–42 BC) was a Roman statesman, famed for his involvement in the assassination of Julius Caesar (44).

29. Gaius Fabricius Luscinus was a third-century BC Roman general and statesman, hero of the war with Pyrrhus.

30. Publius Publicola Valerius is reputed to be one of the earliest Roman consuls in 509 BC; in Plutarch's *Lives* he is paralleled with Solon.

31. Lucius Coruncanius was killed on an embassy, with his brother Gaius, to the Illyrian queen Teutra in 230 BC; his death led to the First Illyrian War.

32. Marcus Furius Camillus was the saviour and second founder of Rome after the Gallic invasion (387/6 BC).

33. The Roman statesman and author Cato the Censor (234–119 BC) was the grandfather of Cato of Utica (95–46 BC), known for his defence of old Roman virtues.

34. Gaius Laelius the Elder (c. 235–c. 160 BC) was a Roman statesman and general; his son Gaius (c. 190–after 129 BC), aside from participating in politics, was a noted orator and is the central character in Cicero's *De amicitia.*

35. Scipio Africanus the Elder (236–184/3 BC) was the Roman hero of the Second Punic War; Scipio Aemlianus Africanus (185/4–129 BC), a Roman statesman and leader of a literary and intellectual circle in Rome, appears as an interlocutor in several of Cicero's works.

36. Publius Rutilius Rufus was a late second-, early first-century BC Roman solider, statesman, jurist and orator.
37. Aristotle, *Magna moralia* II.8 (1207ª4–5); this chapter of the *Magna moralia,* along with *Eudemian Ethics* VII.14, circulated widely in the Middle Ages and early Renaissance under the title *De bona fortuna.*

Further Reading

Bisticci, Vespasiano da, 'Poggio Fiorentino', in *The Vespasiano Memoirs: Lives of Illustrious Men of the XVth Century,* trans. W. George and E. Waters (London, 1926), pp. 351–7

CHRP, pp. 49, 63–4, 81, 91, 103, 117, 119, 307, 321, 332, 361, 380, 389, 421–3, 427–8, 434–5, 447, 451, 647–8, 728, 784, 833

Davies, M., 'Promoting Poggio in the age of reform: correspondence of Tommaso Tonelli and William Shepherd', *Italian Studies,* 48 (1993), 44–61

Gordan, P. W. G., trans., *Two Renaissance Bookhunters: The Letters of Poggius Bracciolini to Nicolaus de Niccolis* (New York, 1974)

Innocent III, *On the Misery of Man,* in *Two Views of Man,* trans. B. Murchland (New York, 1966), pp. 3–60

Kajanto, I., 'The idea of fate in Poggio Bracciolini', *Arctos: Acta philologica fennica,* 22 (1988), 59–73

Poggio Bracciolini and Classicism: A Study in Early Italian Humanism (Helsinki, 1987)

Poggio Bracciolini 1380–1980: nel VI centenario della nascita (Florence, 1982)

3

Marsilio Ficino

LUC DEITZ

Introduction

The Florentine philosopher Marsilio Ficino (1433–99) was the most significant figure in the Renaissance revival of Platonism and Neoplatonism. He produced Latin translations of all Plato's dialogues (first published in 1484), making the complete corpus accessible to Western scholars for the first time. In addition, he translated a number of Greek Neoplatonic works, including the *Enneads* of Plotinus, as well as the group of writings attributed to Hermes Trismegistus. He wrote extensive commentaries on several of the Platonic dialogues, most notably the *Symposium* (1469), where he presented his influential theory of Platonic love as an attraction which moves from a physical to a spiritual plane, ultimately leading the lover to God. He was ordained a priest in 1473 and in the next year completed his *Platonic Theology,* which set out the Platonic arguments for the personal immortality of the soul (see also Chapter 13). Committed to the view that Plato's doctrines were essentially (though by no means completely) compatible with Christianity, he dedicated himself to the uphill task of placing Platonism, rather than Aristotelianism, at the centre of the philosophical curriculum. Aside from his philosophical and religious works, Ficino also wrote *Three Books on Life* (1489), a very popular treatise dealing with a wide range of medical, astrological and occult topics.

The theme of the two chapters from the *Platonic Theology* translated here is the role of man's rational soul as the *vinculum mundi,* the link which unites the universe, establishing a connection between the intelligible and material worlds. Ficino's argument, which added philosophical weight to the Renaissance glorification of human dignity, is based on the metaphysics of the Neoplatonists, in particular their conception of reality as divided into a hierarchically arranged series of hypostases, or realms of being. As part of his Christianizing of this system, Ficino altered the terminology somewhat: One and Mind, the first two levels of the Neoplatonists, in his scheme are called God and Angel. In this section of the *Platonic Theology* Ficino uses a five-tiered ontological scheme – God, Angel, Soul, Quality and Body – which derives from Proclus's interpretation of Plato's *Parmenides,* a key text for Neoplatonic metaphysics. But later on in the treatise and in other of his works, such as his commentary on Plato's *Symposium,* the schemes adopted by Ficino are either tetradic (God, Angel, Soul and Body) or hexadic (God, Angel, Soul, Sensation, Nature and Body). This lack of consistency is characteristic of Ficino's philosophizing: he tended to use whatever doctrine served his particular purpose at the time, without worrying overmuch about the coherence of his system as a whole. The five-tiered ontological scheme, in which Soul occupies the central position, was admirably suited to his aim in this chapter, which was to stress the human soul's essential function as the knot which ties together the various levels of being in the universe.

For the Latin text of the two chapters from the *Theologia platonica de immortalitate animorum* translated here, see Marsilio Ficino, *Théologie platonicienne de l'immortalité des âmes,* ed. R. Marcel, 3 vols. (Paris, 1964–70), I, pp. 38–9, 137–43.

The Platonic Theology: Selections

Book I, Chapter i

If the Soul Were Not Immortal, Man Would Be the Unhappiest of Creatures

Since human beings have such restless souls and such feeble bodies, and since they are in need of everything, they live in greater hardship on earth than the beasts. If, therefore, nature had confined man's existence to the same boundaries as that of other living beings, he would be the unhappiest of creatures. But this cannot be: man, who worships God and therefore comes closer to Him, the source of all happiness, than any other mortal being, cannot be the most wretched of all creatures. Since, on the other hand, he can only attain to a greater state of happiness after bodily death, the conclusion seems unavoidable that some dim ray of light should be left to our souls on leaving this prison.[1] But the human mind never pays heed to its own light, 'pent up, as it is, in the gloom of its dark dungeon',[2] which is why we are often led to distrust our own divine nature. Therefore, I implore you, you heavenly souls who are desirous of regaining your heavenly home, let us remove our earthly chains and fetters as soon as possible, so that we may soar more freely under the guidance of God on Platonic wings[3] towards that ethereal abode where we will contemplate straightaway, in a state of blessedness, the excellence of our nature.

For the rest, in order that it may become clear which means best enable the human mind to draw back the bars of mortality, to become aware of its own immortality and to reach the state of eternal bliss, I will try to prove in the ensuing disquisition as well as I can that, besides our dull corporeal mass, to which the followers of Democritus, Aristippus and Epicurus confined their speculations,[4] there exists a kind of active Quality and a power, which was at the centre of the investigations of the Stoics and the Cynics. We will also try to prove that, beyond Quality, which becomes divided and completely altered when it enters into contact with extended matter, there exists a kind of form superior to it which, although it somehow changes, nevertheless does not admit of division in the corporeal world.[5] It is in this form that the ancient theologians[6] placed the rational Soul, and it is to this level that Heraclitus, Marcus Varro and Marcus Manilius were able to rise.[7] We shall then try to prove that, beyond the Rational Soul, there exists an Angelic Mind, which is both indivisible and immovable. It is at this level that Anaxagoras and Hermotimus apparently stopped.[8] We will finally try to prove that, superior to this eye of the mind, which yearns after the light of truth and is able to receive it, is the divine Sun, towards which our dear Plato has commanded, taught and entreated us to direct the purified vision of our mind. When we have reached that level, I will compare the five levels which form the whole of reality – Body, Quality, Soul, Angel and God – with one another. Because the genus of the rational soul, which occupies the middle position of these five degrees, seems to be the link which connects the whole of nature, because it rules over qualities and bodies, and because it unites itself to Angel and God, I will show that it is completely indissoluble, since it joins together the levels of nature; that it is the most excellent genus, since it presides over the fabric of the universe; and that it is the most blessed genus, since it penetrates into the realm of the divine. That this is the true nature and condition of our soul will be proved in the following way: first, by general reasons; second, by particular arguments; third, by signs; fourth, by responding to objections which might be raised.

BOOK III, CHAPTER 2

Soul Is the Intermediate Degree of Being and Connects All the Degrees Superior and Inferior to It into One through Its Ascent towards the Higher Degrees and Its Descent towards the Lower Ones

Let us now finally come to the goal we have in mind, and let us once again sum up the whole universe in five degrees. We place God and Angel on top of nature, Body and Quality at the bottom of it. Soul, however, stands in the middle of these highest and these lowest parts, and therefore, following Platonic usage, we rightly call it a third and intermediary essence,[9] since it occupies the middle of the universe and ranks third from wherever one starts to count. Descending from God, you will find it at the third degree of your descent; ascending beyond Body, you will also find it at the third degree of your ascent. We consider an essence of this kind to be absolutely indispensable in the fabric of nature. Angel, as the Platonists say, truly *is,* that is, it is always at rest; Quality *becomes,* that is, it sometimes moves. Therefore, Quality has nothing in common with Angel: Quality moves, whereas Angel remains the same; Quality sometimes becomes, whereas Angel always is. Consequently, there must be a middle term that is partly related to Angel and partly related to Quality. What will that be? Perhaps something that sometimes *is,* that is, that sometimes remains intrinsically the same? No! For such a thing does not exist: whatever remains intrinsically the same by its own nature or comes very close to remaining the same by its condition will always remain the same. The middle term, therefore, will be something that is always becoming, that is, that always moves. It agrees with Angel inasmuch as it exists always, and it agrees with Quality inasmuch as it moves.

It follows from this that there must be a third essence situated in between that is always in movement and alive and whose movement causes life to be diffused among bodies. The Platonists rightly assert that that which is everlasting is superior to that which only lasts for a while, that that which is eternal is superior to that which is everlasting and that eternity is beyond that which is eternal.[10] But between those things that are exclusively eternal and those that are exclusively temporal, there is a soul, they say – a connecting link, as it were, between the two.[11] In this respect, the main parts of the body of the universe are to some extent similar to it. There are also authors who, considering that the Empyrean is absolutely fixed, place it in eternity, assigning the remaining spheres both to eternity and to time, and composite beings to time only. They likewise assign pure intellects to the first degree, animal intellects to the second and embodied souls to the third.[12]

But let us now return to our main subject. Every piece of work which is a compound of several parts is most perfect when its constituent parts cohere in such a way that it is one in all respects, in accord and harmony with itself, and not easily broken apart. Corporeal nature shows this clearly in the mixture of the four elements, in which earth and fire, being at opposite ends, are connected by air and water. In order that the product of the one God should be one as well, it is even more important that we assume such a connection of parts to exist throughout God's entire handiwork. God and Body are the outermost boundaries of nature and have nothing whatever in common. Angel does not link them together, since it is entirely intent on contemplating God and is indifferent towards bodies. It stands to reason that the most perfect creature and the one closest to God becomes wholly divine and is transformed into God. Nor does Quality connect the extremes, because it inclines towards Body, abandons higher things and leaves behind whatever is incorporeal in order to become corporeal. Up to this point, everything is an extreme; higher and lower things flee from one another because they lack a connecting link. The third essence that is intermediate between them, however, is of such a nature that it holds fast to higher things without leaving behind lower ones, thus connecting the former with the latter in itself. For it is at rest and it is in motion as well, rest agreeing with higher beings and movement agreeing with lower ones. If it agrees with both, it strives after both. Therefore, it is by a sort of natural impulse that it ascends towards higher things and descends towards lower ones. When it ascends, it does not leave the lower parts behind. And when it descends, it does not abandon the higher parts. For if it were to leave behind either of these, it would incline towards the opposite extreme and would cease to be the true connecting link of the universe. Indeed, the soul's role is comparable to that of air, which, being placed in the middle of fire and water, is akin to fire with respect to its heat and to water with respect to its moisture. On its upper border it is always hot under the influence of fire; here below it is always moist under the influence of water. There it is always rarefied and shines like fire; here, on the contrary, it becomes opaque like water. To give a better analogy, the soul acts in the same way as the light of the sun. The light descends from the sun to fire and fills fire without leaving the sun. It always inheres in the sun and always fills fire. It brings air to its perfection and is not itself tainted by the tainted air. In the same way, the third essence must inhere in the divine and fill whatever is mortal at the same time. While the soul inheres in the divine, it knows this realm, because it is spiritually united with it and spiritual union produces knowledge. While it fills bodies, it bestows life on them, because it moves them from within. Thus, it is the mirror of the divine, the life force of mortals and the connecting link between the two.

But how is it joined to bodies? Should we say, for example, that it touches one particular point when it enters a body and that this is how its union with bodies comes about? Surely not, for it would then be united to this particular point rather than to the body, and it would not animate the whole body, but only one point; the body as a whole would be devoid of life. If it were to remain united like this to itself, eternally concentrated in one point, it would be identical with Angel, which is far removed from Body, or at any rate it would inhere in the divine in that way and leave bodies behind. Therefore, it is not united to one part of Body only, but to several, and in this way it fills the parts of Body. But does it exist in bodies in the same way as whiteness exists in white skin or any other quality in its own peculiar matter? Not at all, for then it would be identical with Quality: abandoning the divine, it would completely incline towards Body. Whiteness exists in the entire skin in such a way that it is coextensive with it and can be divided into many parts: according to natural philosophers, there is one part of whiteness in each part of the skin – a larger portion of whiteness in a larger portion of the skin, and a smaller portion in a smaller one. Whiteness has thus become corporeal. The same fate would befall what we consider to be the third essence if it were spread throughout Body in the same way as Quality: it would be drawn towards the other extremity of nature, and it would cease to be the connecting link of the universe. Therefore, when it enters Body, it is wholly present in every single one of its parts, and it is not divided or dispersed in order to be present in those parts of Body that are far from each other. For it is by means of its indivisible power that Soul touches Body, not by means of its quantitative size. Remaining therefore integral and simple, it is wholly and without division present in every single part, just as the word 'house' and its meaning are somehow wholly present in every single one of its parts, since it is heard and understood in its entirety almost simultaneously in each of its parts.

Moreover, it is not impossible that this essence, despite being indivisible and subsisting by itself, should be present in the vast bulk of Body in this way. On the contrary, it is precisely because it is indivisible and not confined in space that it is capable of completely penetrating and encompassing whatever is in space. For wherever quantitative extension is to be found, no such power or presence is possible; so, a quantitatively extended thing cannot completely and simultaneously exist in a plurality of things. Even if we assume that such a thing is indivisible, it will still be attached to corporeal quantity in some place or other, just as the point that is singled out as the limit of a line is still part of that line. A quantitatively extended and completely indivisible thing cannot simultaneously be present in every part of Body, just as a point that is marked somewhere on a line of a circle is neither present in all the other lines nor spread over the entire line or the entire circle. The point, on the other hand, that constitutes the centre of the circle does not belong to any line in particular: it is somehow found on all the lines that are drawn from the centre to the periphery. And while no point which is marked on the periphery faces the whole circle equally, the centre, which is not attached to any part of the periphery in particular, surveys the entire circle equally. Therefore, a divisible thing cannot be completely and simultaneously present in a plurality of things, nor can a thing which, though indivisible, nevertheless occupies a particular place in another thing which is divisible.

But the third essence is neither extended (for then it would be Quality), nor located somewhere in extension (for if it did not subsist by itself, it would not move freely and by its own power). Therefore, it is like a point that lives in itself and is completely without quantity or position. This is why it evenly encompasses every position occupied by Body, and when it enters Body, it is not confined to any one single point of corporeal quantity because it is not itself a particular quantitative point. Since it lies outside the genus of quantity, it is not destined to touch any one single quantitative point: like the centre, it is in all the lines and in the entire circle. This also explains why this essence is simultaneously divisible and indivisible. It is divisible because it sheds its vivifying shadow through the division of Body while communicating itself to the different parts of Body. It remains indivisible because its presence is at the same time complete and unqualified. It is divisible, in point of fact, because its shadow is present in the whole of divisible Body. It is indivisible because it is itself wholly present in every single part of Body in an indivisible way. It is also indivisible because it has a stable and unified substance. It is divisible because its activities are subject to movement and time: while it acts, it is divided between a plurality of things. It is thirdly indivisible because it looks up to the higher realms, which are completely unified. It is divisible because it inclines towards the inferior realms, which are extremely divided. A nature of this kind seems to be absolutely necessary in the order of the universe: below God and Angel, who can be divided neither with respect to time nor with respect to space, and above Body and qualities, which are dispersed in both time and space, there must be a corresponding intermediary that is somehow capable of division in time without being divided in space. On the other hand, it must not remain eternally wrapped up in its own nature as do the former essences, nor must it be scattered as are the latter ones; rather, it must be undivided and divided at the same time. This is the very essence which Timaeus Locrus and Plato in his book on the universe said consisted of an indivisible and divisible nature.[13] This is the very essence that mingles with mortal beings without becoming mortal itself, for in the selfsame way in which it mingles with mortal beings – that is, integrally and not scattered about – it withdraws from them – that is, integrally and not scattered about. While it governs bodies, it remains attached to the divine realm; it is therefore the ruler of bodies, not their companion.

This is the greatest miracle in nature, for all other things beneath God are each one single being, whereas Soul is everything at once. It possesses in itself images of the divine things on which it itself depends, and concepts and exemplars of the lower things which it itself somehow produces. And since it is at the centre of everything, it possesses the faculties of everything. Consequently, it passes into everything. And since it is itself the true connecting link between all things, it does not abandon one thing while it moves on to another, but rather it goes into individual things while always preserving everything. Therefore, it can rightly be called the centre of nature, the middle of all things, the chain that fastens the world, the mirror of everything and the knot and link of the universe.

The nature of this third essence has now, I think, been explained in sufficient detail. That it is the particular seat of the rational soul as well can be gathered very easily from the definition of the rational soul, which runs as follows: a life force that understands discursively and animates the body in time. This is exactly the condition of the third essence: it is alive, has understanding and bestows life upon Body. That it is alive is evident from the fact that we call those things on earth alive that, by some kind of inner power that is entirely their own, are able to move in all directions – upwards, downwards, forwards, backwards, to the right and to the left. This is the way plants and animals move. So, wherever there is a common inner movement, there is life; and by life I mean the presence of an inner power of movement. This power is particularly present where the source and origin of every activity, as well as the first movement, are to be found, for the common inner movement is greatest where it begins. We have seen that the beginning of movement is placed in the third essence, and it is there, consequently, that life is to be found. Life, to be sure, of such a kind that it is by participating in it that bodies live and move, for life is naturally closest to bodies. We have thus shown that the third essence is a life force that animates bodies.

It also has understanding. If a perfect movement exists somewhere, it must be most perfect where it begins, because there can be no perfection in secondary movements unless it is derived from the first one. Therefore, the movement of the third essence is the most perfect of all movements: it is the one which least departs from its source, that is the most closely linked to its foundation, that is one and uniform in the highest degree, that is self-sufficient and that imitates the most perfect figure – that is, the circular movement, as everyone knows, which is also the only movement that is eternal. All other movements reach an end beyond which no progress is possible, since infinite space does not exist anywhere. Circular movement, however, begins another round when it has completed the first, and then a third and a fourth and a fifth in the same way. Its end is identical with its beginning; whenever it seems to come to an end, it starts afresh. We can therefore conclude that eternal circular movement belongs to the third essence in particular: it returns, moving in a circle, to itself. It is proper that, if it is at the origin of its movement, it should also be at its end, for where there is a beginning of motion, there must also be an end – if it is true to say, that is, that the cause of motion somehow produces movement for its own sake. Therefore, this essence starts its movement from itself and eternally revolves around itself, as it unrolls its powers from the highest beings to the lowest, passing through the middle ones, and similarly rolls back its powers from the lowest beings to the highest, passing through the middle ones. If this is so, it is aware of itself and of everything it possesses inside itself. If it is aware, it knows with a certain knowledge. This knowledge is the result of understanding, which is itself the recognition of the spirituality of its essence and its independence from the limitations of matter; for knowledge of such things is properly called understanding. We see that, inside ourselves, knowledge is nothing other than a spiritual union with a spiritual form. Vision comes about through the union of the visual spirit with the spiritual image of colours. No vision is possible through union with matter, which becomes evident if one places a solid body in front of the pupil of the eye. Even our reason understands things themselves by being spiritually united to their incorporeal forms and their concepts. The same holds true for the third essence, which is itself spiritual: when it is united to itself, its self-awareness becomes knowledge and understanding in a spiritual way. It even understands the divine things with which it is in closest contact in a spiritual way. It also understands the corporeal things towards which it is naturally inclined. Its knowledge, indeed, is the result of discursive reasoning in time because its activity implies motion.

From all this we conclude that this must be the definition of the third essence: a life force that naturally animates bodies. It also knows itself, as well as divine and natural things, discursively. Anyone who does not see that this is also the definition of the rational soul does not have a rational soul himself. Therefore, the rational soul has its seat in the third essence; it occupies the middle region of nature and connects everything together into one.

Translator's Notes

1. For this image, see Plato, *Gorgias* 493A, *Cratylus* 400C and *Phaedrus* 250C.
2. Virgil, *Aeneid* VI.734; H. R. Fairclough's translation (London, 1920).
3. See Plato, *Phaedrus* 251A–C.
4. Democritus of Abdera, a fifth-century BC Greek atomist, and Aristippus of Cyrene, a contemporary of Socrates and putative founder of the hedonistic Cyrenaic school, were both regarded as predecessors of Epicurus (341–270 BC), whose philosophy was characterized by atomism and hedonism.
5. For the background of this doctrine, see Plato, *Timaeus* 35A, as well as H. R. Schwyzer, 'Zu Plotins Interpretation von Platons Timaeus 35A', *Rheinisches Museum,* 84 (1935), 360–8.
6. See D. P. Walker, *The Ancient Theology* (London, 1972).
7. The early Greek philosopher Heraclitus came from Ephesus and flourished about 500 BC; he was noted for his obscure style and his belief in the unity of opposites. Marcus Varro (116–27 BC) was a prolific Roman author, who wrote on a variety of subjects, including the Latin language, agriculture and antiquarianism. Marcus Manilius was a Roman poet who wrote under the emperors Augustus and Tiberius; he was the author of the *Astronomica,* a didactic poem on astrology.
8. The early Greek philosopher Anaxagoras of Clazomenae (c. 500–428 BC) apparently produced only one work, which contained a complete account of the natural world. Hermotimus, also from Clazomenae, was a legendary Greek philosopher of uncertain date who believed that the soul could leave the body.
9. Plato, *Timaeus* 35A.
10. See Proclus, *In Platonis Timaeum commentaria,* ed. E. Diehl, 3 vols. (Leipzig, 1903–6), I, p. 277, line 33–p. 278, line 11.
11. Proclus, *In Platonis Timaeum commentaria,* I, p. 278, lines 14–24.
12. Proclus, *In Platonis Timaeum commentaria,* II, p. 57, line 9–p. 58, line 9.
13. See Pseudo-Timaeus Locrus, *De anima mundi et naturae* 18 (95E); Plato, *Timaeus* 35A.

Further Reading

Allen, M. J. B., 'Ficino's theory of the five substances and the Neoplatonists' *Parmenides*', *Journal of Medieval and Renaissance Studies,* 12 (1982), 19–44

CHRP, pp. 67–70, 79–81, 83, 88, 99, 107, 134–5, 237–42, 246, 255, 257–8, 265–7, 270, 272, 274–85, 287–9, 293–6, 299, 398, 312, 377, 428, 461, 469, 498, 500, 568–81, 583–4, 650–1, 673–5, 738, 769, 772, 775, 783–8, 817

Hankins, J., *Plato in the Italian Renaissance,* 2 vols. (Leiden, 1990), I, pp. 267–359

Kristeller, P. O., *Eight Philosophers of the Italian Renaissance* (Stanford, Calif., 1954), ch. 3 ('Ficino')

The Philosophy of Marsilio Ficino (Gloucester, Mass., 1964), esp. ch. 6

4

Fernán Pérez de Oliva

ELEAZAR GUTWIRTH

Introduction

Born around 1494 in Cordova, Fernán Pérez de Oliva began his studies at the age of fourteen in Salamanca and after three years attended the recently founded Complutensian University in Alcalá. In 1512 he left for Paris, and at the Sorbonne was the pupil of Juan Martínez Guijarro Siliceo. Three years later he was taken to Rome by an uncle who was in the service of Pope Leo X. In 1518 he went back to Spain but later returned to Paris, where he stayed for three years, studying Aristotle's *Nicomachean Ethics* among other works. In 1524 he returned once again to Spain, residing until 1526 in Cordova and then transferring to Salamanca. In 1529 he was elected rector of the University of Salamanca and, the next year, he obtained the chair of theology. He died on 3 August 1531.

Best known for his historical works on the discovery of America, Pérez de Oliva also produced (rather free) translations of the tragedies of Euripides, as well as treatises on scientific topics and moral philosophy. His *Dialogue on the Dignity of Man* purports to record an argument between two friends: Aurelio, who gives a relentlessly negative account of human life, and Antonio, who exalts man's dignity. The work needs to be seen within the context of what recent studies have identified as the particular flourishing of the dialogue in sixteenth-century Spanish literature, though it has to be said that Pérez de Oliva's work is notably lacking in narrative movement and dramatic tension. The dialogue format does, however, allow him to contrast the two major traditions concerning the nature of the human condition. Aurelio gives voice to the pessimistic view that man's life is full of pain and misery. This ancient theme, laid out in great detail by Pliny the Elder, found many exponents in the Middle Ages, including St Bernard, in Book III of his *Meditations,* and, most famously, Pope Innocent III, in his *On the Misery of the Human Condition;* Poggio Bracciolini's dialogue of the same title demonstrates that this point of view was still to be found in the fifteenth century (see Chapter 2). Through Antonio, who wins the debate, Pérez de Oliva enumerates the arguments, many of which were also of ancient lineage (Cicero and Lactantius are key sources), for man's uniquely favoured condition and status. Giannozzo Manetti's *On Man's Dignity and Excellence* and Giovanni Pico della Mirandola's *Oration on the Dignity of Man* are the two most important fifteenth-century representatives of this tradition.

The *Dialogue* was first published in Alcalá de Henares in 1546. Its relatively limited diffusion in Spain is probably due to its inclusion, for reasons which still remain unclear, in successive editions of the Index of Prohibited Books from 1632 onwards. As late as 1787 an application made by the Real Compañía de Filipinas for an export licence for the book was delayed for two years by the Inquisition. One of the censors excused himself from the task of reading and passing judgement on it 'because his head was in a delicate state'. A copy in the Biblioteca Nacional of Madrid bears a seal stating 'forbidden by the government in 1863'.

The *Dialogue* was translated into Italian by Alfonso de Ulloa and published anonymously in Venice in 1563; a revised edition, with substantial additions by the translator, was printed in

Venice in 1564 and 1642. The French version by Hièrosme d'Auost, published in Paris in 1586, was made from the Italian translation rather than the original Spanish.

A new edition of the Spanish text has recently been published: Fernán Pérez de Oliva, *Diálogo de la dignidad del hombre; Razonamientos; Ejercicios,* ed. M. L. Cerrón Puga (Madrid, 1995). This edition, containing valuable information about the author's life, works and sources, replaces the earlier one (Madrid, 1982) by the same editor; the passages translated are at pp. 123–7, 145–53. There is another modern edition of the work, edited by J. L. Abellán (Barcelona, 1967). I would like to thank Dr Alejandro Coroleu, of the University of Nottingham, who read over the translation and made helpful suggestions for improving it.

Dialogue on the Dignity of Man: Selections

Book I

Aurelio: . . . Let us first consider the universe and our place in it. We will see the heavens, which are the dwelling place of happy beings and which are luminous and adorned by twinkling stars, many of which are bigger than the earth. Things there are not mutable, nor is there anything to cause them harm; on the contrary, everything in heaven continues in an undeviating state, free from change.[1] Below this is the realm of fire and air, limpid elements, which receive the light of the heavens.

We are located here in the dregs and depths of the world, living among beasts and covered in darkness. We are inhabitants of the earth, where everything is in flux. We are confined in a space so small that it seems a mere point when compared to the whole universe.[2] And we do not even have free reign over all of the earth. The cold prevents us from living beneath the zones which are surrounded by sky. In many areas it is the heat and, even more so, the water, and also the sterility which create vast solitary spaces. Elsewhere it is the unfavourable climate that prevents areas from being inhabited. So, for all the world's great size, we are restricted to a very small space, in the most contemptible part of it.

There we are born, unprovided with all the gifts granted by nature to other animals.[3] Some of these nature covered with hair, others with feathers, others with scales, still others are enclosed within shells. Man, however, is so unprotected that the first natural gift which the cold and heat run up against is his flesh. Thus, he comes into the world as if it were a foreign place, crying and moaning like someone signalling the miseries he is about to endure. Other animals, only a short time after leaving their mother's womb, go about the fields, graze on the grass and take pleasure in the world after their own fashion, as if they had arrived in their proper and natural place. Man, by contrast, even many days after his birth, lacks the ability to move and does not know where to find sustenance, nor can he endure the changes of climate. Everything must be learnt through lengthy discourse and through the acquisition of habits. It seems as though the world is almost forced to receive him and that nature gives man a place in life almost against her own wishes. Even then she sustains him by means of the most contemptible things. Those animals which are by nature domesticated eat herbs, seeds and other clean foodstuffs. Man, on the other hand, feeds on blood, becoming a tomb for other animals.

And if we consider nature's gifts, we find that most of them are granted to other animals. Many have bigger bodies than man's, where their souls can reign. Bulls are stronger. Tigers are swifter. Lions are more dextrous. Crows live longer. From these examples and similar ones, it would seem that man is the least worthy of animals. This is why nature hates him and does not provide for him. And since she is the guardian of the world and secures the universal good, it seems likely that, if it would have contributed to the well-being of the world, she would not have left man so unprotected from all these dangers. Those things which are of value she put in safe places, where they would not be harmed. Look at where she put the sun, the moon and the other celestial lights by means of which we see. Look where she put fire, the most noble of the elements.

As for other animals, if she did not give them better locations, at least she armed them against the dangers encountered on the earth. She gave wings to birds so that they can flee from these dangers. Animals were given weapons for their defence: some have horns, others nails, others teeth. Fish were given great freedom to flee through the water. Men are the only ones who have no natural defence against the earth's dangers. They are slow to run away and have no weapons to lie in wait. Moreover, nature created a thousand poisons and venomous animals to kill man, as if she had repented for having created him. . . .

Book II

Antonio: . . . Anyone who speaks ill of human beauty should take care not to offend God by making him guilty of a crime for having created a piece of work which he judged worthy of being preserved at the cost of such perseverance and so much suffering. For the things which you, deceived by your own guilt, scorn in man are in fact, as you shall now see, made more out of love than gratitude.

The human body, which you, Aurelio, deem to be such a vile and contemptible thing is in truth made with such skill and proportion that it certainly seems as if God created something magnificent when he made it. The proportion of man's face is equal to that of the palm of his hand; his palm is a ninth of his entire stature, his foot is a sixth of it and his elbow a fourth. His navel is the centre of a circle which reaches the ends of his hands and feet when he is lying down flat with open arms and legs.[4] Such an arrangement and such proportions, which are not to be found in other animals, show us that the human body was created according to a higher reason.

God created man to stand erect, on feet and legs which are handsomely and conveniently shaped, so that he would be able to contemplate the heavenly mansions for which he was created.[5] Other animals were created of short stature, facing towards the ground, in order to search for pastures on which to graze and fulfil the one concern they have: feeding their stomachs. Although God covered their entire bodies with fur and wool, in the case of man the one thing he covered was his head, showing that it is only reason, which dwells there, that needs protection. Once reason is provided for, it will sufficiently provide for the rest.

Let us now examine the excellence of man's face.[6] What a majestic forehead, on which the soul represents its changes and affections! How beautiful! How striking!

Beneath it are placed the eyes, like very high windows in the castle of our soul; through them, it gazes on the outside world. His eyes are not flat and sunken but round and prominent so that they can move in different directions and thus receive all images from wherever they come. Man's ears are placed on both sides of his head in order to receive sounds from all over. His nose is located in the middle of his face. This is very necessary to its beauty: for man breathes through it and thus avoids the ugly spectacle of a gaping mouth. Through the nose we receive odours, and it is the nose which tempers the organ of the voice. Underneath it is the mouth which, between red lips, shows white teeth within. This mixture of colours is very beautiful. The mouth is the door through which enters our life, that is, the food which sustains us; and it is the door through which our soul's messages exit, published by our tongue, which dwells in our mouth – a house, as it were, in which it has all that it needs. There the voice comes up from the chest; and once the voice arrives, it has teeth, lips and other instruments with which it can be shaped. Who could explain with sufficient clarity the excellent deeds which the tongue performs in our mouth? Sometimes it governs the voice by means of musical harmony with such sweetness that I cannot imagine what other legitimate human pleasure could be a greater delight. At other times it reveals the reasons behind things with such force that it goads ignorance, reforms evil, subdues anger, reconciles enemies and brings peace to things which were in furious commotion. How great are the miracles worked by the tongue! Even on its own it would be sufficient to bring honour to man's body.[7]

But let us now speak of the other parts of man's body so that we may grant all of them the dignity which is their due. His chin and cheeks are not only there for the sake of firmness and in order to contain what is in them but also on account of the singular beauty which they bring to his face. His neck, as we can see, is flexible, so that his head can turn around and consider all the parts of the body which are near to it. His chest is located below and is broader than that of other animals, as if it were capable of greater things. God not only worked on it in order to provide for natural needs but also to produce beauty. In the male, he put a little nipple on each side of the chest, for no other reason than to adorn it.

From the upper sides of man's chest, his arms extend, and at the end of them are located his hands. They, on their own, are more valuable than those organs which nature gave to other animals. In man they are very obedient servants of both art and reason, doing any task which reason presents to them by means of an image which it constructs. Although they are soft, they can mould iron and make from it weapons which are better for self-defence than the nails or horns of any animal. They can also turn iron into instruments for compelling the earth to provide us with sufficient sustenance or into other tools for opening things which are unyielding and turning them to our own use. It is man's hands which clothe him, not with a covering which is rough and ugly, as is the case with other animals, but with whatever apparel he chooses. They construct dwellings which are well defended from damage caused by the weather and also ships to cross the seas. They build roads through rugged terrain and turn the whole world into flat ground. They tame brave animals, transforming mighty bulls into man's servants, with their necks bowed under a yoke. They make wild horses do our work for us. They load cargo on to elephants. They kill lions. They lasso clever animals. They bring up fish from the depths of the sea, and they strike birds which fly high above the clouds. They have so much strength that there is nothing in the world sufficiently powerful to defend itself from them. Nor is their appearance less impressive than their deeds.

Now, if you consider the matter thoroughly, you will see that man is composed of noble and excellent bodily parts. No one can judge whether their artificer put more effort into making them convenient to use or into making them beautiful. This is why wise painters believe that man is never portrayed as more beautiful than when he is naked. Similarly, nature brings man forth from the womb naked, as if she eagerly wished to display such an excellent piece of work without any covering.

If man comes into the world weeping, it is not because nature hates him or because this world does not serve him well, but rather, as you correctly stated, Aurelio, because he is not in his true homeland. For what native of heaven could feel well anywhere else, no matter how good the treatment he received there? Man is a native of heaven; so do not be surprised to see him weep when he is far from home.

Nor must you think that he is less well constructed on the inside than on the outside. On the contrary, his internal parts are even better designed [than his external ones]. I shall not speak of them now, however, for fear that philosophy might lead me away from my purpose. But I will at least say, in response to the issue you raised,[8] that there is not as much danger as you claim in the battle between opposing qualities, nor in the multitude of our veins or the fragility of our bones; or, if there is, it shows how much God cares for us, since he preserves us for such a long time amid so many inevitable dangers. And, as for your view that, in order to survive, we have to place everything under compulsion, this is an empty quibble; for all worldly things come into our service not through force but on account of the obedience which is our due. Have you not heard the songs of David, in which, speaking with God about man, he says: 'Thou madest him to have dominion over the works of thy hands; Thou hast put all things under his feet; All sheep and oxen, Yea and the beasts of the field; The fowl of the air, and the fish of the sea'?[9] This is what David says; and God, as the lord of the universe, was able to give his creatures to us. Having been given to us to make use of them, as required by our needs, they are not injured when they are slaughtered in order to sustain man's life; rather, they strive to attain the goal for which they were created. From what I have said, you can see, Aurelio, that man has not been left without protection by the ruler of the world, as you have claimed; on the contrary, he is better provided for than any other animal, since he was given not only reason and hands, in order to be self-sufficient, but also everything in abundance which he needs to maintain himself.

Now I want to reply to your claim that it would be better if man were able to attain these things without having to work so hard and without having to search for them with such effort and guard them with such care.[10] If you consider this carefully, you will find that these needs are precisely the ones which cause men to live together in a community. You can see for yourself how much delight and benefit derive from this. It gives rise to friendships among men and pleasant conversations. It is because of this that one man teaches another and the efforts of one person are shared by everyone. And if our natural needs did not make us unite in cities, you would see how solitary men would wander about with no cares, no learning, no virtue. They would scarcely be any different from brute animals. The divine part of man, which is reason, would almost be lost, since there would be nothing to occupy it. So what appears to be a fault of nature is in reality a guide which leads us to our perfection.

Furthermore, even if we attained these goods without the spur of natural necessity, men have such diverse wills that it would not have been convenient for God to have given them more [bodily] instruments, so that each one could provide himself with things according to his appetite. Thus, the indeterminate condition in which God placed man corresponds to the freedom of his soul. Some desire to wear woollen clothing, others prefer linen and still others want to dress in furs. Some love eating fish, others meat, still others fruit. God wanted to fulfil everyone's desires by so constructing them that they would each be able to make their own choice. And since this is the case, we must not think it harsh that this was granted to us by God in the manner of a father who gives gifts to his spoilt children. Now tell me, Aurelio, if God had made you with the horns of a bull, with the teeth of a wild boar, with the claws of a lion and with woollen skin, does it not seem to you that, having been provided with what you praise in other animals, you would be so unprovided in relation to your own will that, even having these things, you would desire nothing other than death? If this is so, do not complain about human nature, which imitates all things and surpasses them in perfection.[11]

The one thing I can see that man is unable to imitate are the wings of birds. It seems to me that this was forbidden to us with great providence; for the harm which could be wreaked by evil men through the use of wings would far exceed the benefit they would bring to good men. There is nothing for us to do in the air. It is quite sufficient that we have the entire earth, which we inhabit, to walk about on and that we are able to cross those seas which cut off the roads.

Man is a great and admirable thing. God therefore wished him to bide his time for a long while after birth, in order to make clear what a magnificent piece of work he was creating in him. We see that great buildings are begun in one age and finished in another. In the same way, God brings man to perfection only after many long days, although he could do it in a moment. This is so that we come to know this work of his, just as we come to know those things which we make with our own hands.

To see this clearly, it is time that we entered inside of man in order to consider the soul which dwells within this corporeal temple. God is everywhere, but he selected the heavens as the dwelling place to display his glory; and he identified it as his own abode, as he showed us in the prayer 'Our Father which art in heaven . . .' From heaven, he sends forth angels and governs the world. This is also the case with our soul, which imitates him in all things. Although it lives in the body, ruling and maintaining everything, it has its principal seat in the head; and it is there that it achieves its most excellent actions. From there, it sees and understands and rules. From there, it sends out subtle spirits to the body in order to give it sensation and movement. And it is there that the nerves have their origin; they are like the reins with which the soul guides the parts of the body. I am well aware that the brain, where the soul primarily resides, is corruptible like the other parts of the body and receives wounds, as you, Aurelio, have shown us.[12] But this is not a fault in the soul; on the contrary, it is for its own good, for by means of these corruptions it can separate itself from these bodily parts in order to fly away to heaven, which is its natural home. Let us now speak about reason,[13] which you condemn so strongly. I find it to be an admirable thing, when I consider that although we live here, as you say, in the dregs of the world, by means of reason we go everywhere. We travel around the earth; we chart the seas; ascending to the heavens, we view their magnitude and we calculate the movements; and we do not stop until we reach God, who does not hide himself from us. Nothing is so shrouded, so distant, so obscure as to escape human reason. In order to arrive at the world's secrets, reason uses well-known paths, which are the intellectual disciplines by means of which it travels everywhere. The body's sloth is no match for the agility of reason, nor is it necessary to walk on our feet in order to see with our soul. . . .

Translator's Notes

1. This is a standard Aristotelian account of the heavens; see, e.g., *De caelo* I.9.
2. Cf. Macrobius, *Commentarium in Somnium Scipionis* I.16.6–7 and 10.
3. The main classical source for this line of argument is Pliny the Elder, *Natural History* VII.1.1–5.
4. For this famous 'Vitruvian figure', as drawn by Leonardo da Vinci and others, see R. Wittkower, *Architectural Principles in the Age of Humanism* (London, 1949), pls. 2–4.
5. For the topos of man's erect posture see Plato, *Cratylus* 399C; Aristotle, *De partibus animalium* IV.10 (686a27–8); Ovid, *Metamorphoses* I.84–6; Cicero, *De natura deorum* II.56; Silius Italicus, *Punica* XV.84–7; Manilius, *Astronomica* IV.905–8; Lactantius, *De opificio Dei* 8.1–3 and *Divinae institutiones* II.1; Boethius, *De consolatione philosophiae* V.m.5; Peter Lombard, *Sentences* II.16; Giannozzo Manetti, *De excellentia et dignitate hominis*, ed. E. R. Leonard (Padua, 1975), pp. 5 (I.1), 12 (I.14).
6. The catalogue of man's bodily parts which follows is based on classical and patristic sources, especially Cicero, *De natura deorum* II.54–8, and Lactantius, *De opificio Dei* 8.5–15.6; see also Book I of Manetti, *De excellentia*, pp. 5–33.
7. Cf. Erasmus's treatment of the same topic in his *Lingua*, first published in 1525; for an English translation see Erasmus, *Collected Works* (Toronto, 1974–), XXIX, pp. 249–412 ('The Tongue', trans. E. Fantham).
8. For the two arguments of Aurelio which are refuted in this paragraph, see Pérez de Oliva, *Diálogo*, pp. 126–7.
9. Psalms 8:6–8.
10. Pérez de Oliva, *Diálogo*, p. 132.
11. This paragraph seems to be based on Giovanni Pico della Mirandola's *Oration on the Dignity of Man;* see the English translation published in E. Cassirer, P. O. Kristeller and J. H. Randall, Jr., eds., *The Renaissance Philosophy of Man* (Chicago, 1948), pp. 223–54, at 224–5.
12. Pérez de Oliva, *Diálogo*, p. 128.
13. For the praise of man's reason see, e.g., Cicero, *De natura deorum* II.59, and Lactantius, *De opificio Dei* 2.1–3.2.

Further Reading

Atkinson, W., 'Hernán Pérez de Oliva: a biographical and critical study', *Revue hispanique,* 71 (1927), 309–484

Bono, D. M., *Cultural Diffusion of Spanish Humanism in New Spain: Francisco Cervantes de Salazar's 'Diálogo de la dignidad del hombre'* (New York, 1991), esp. pp. 53–5

CHRP, pp. 306–16

Gómez, J., *El diálogo en el Renacimiento español* (Madrid, 1988)

Rico, F., *El pequeño mundo del hombre* (Madrid, 1972) p. 135

'"Laudes litterarum": humanisme et dignité de l'homme dans L'Espagne de la Renaissance', in A. Redondo, ed., *L'Humanisme dans les lettres espagnols* (Paris, 1979), pp. 31–50

Solana, M., *Historia de la filosofía española: época del Renacimiento (siglo XVI),* 3 vols. (Madrid, 1941), II, pp. 49–64

Sozzi, L., *La 'Dignité de l'homme' à la Renaissance* (Turin, 1982)

Part II.
Aristotelian Ethics and the Supreme Good

5

Donato Acciaiuoli

Jill Kraye

Introduction

Donato Acciaiuoli (1429–78) was a Florentine humanist and statesman with a keen interest in Aristotelian philosophy. Having received training in classical Latin literature and language in his youth, he began to learn Greek in his twenties; his interest in ancient history led him to compose lives of Hannibal and Scipio Africanus the Elder. In addition, he studied logic both privately and at the University of Florence, and became familiar with the major scholastic philosophers of the Middle Ages (e.g., Thomas Aquinas, Albertus Magnus and Walter Burley) and the Renaissance (e.g., Gaetano da Thiene and Paul of Venice). Between 1457 and 1461 he attended lectures on Aristotelian philosophy given by the Byzantine scholar Johannes Argyropulos (c. 1415–87) at the University of Florence. His surviving lecture notes, covering the *Physics, De anima* and the *Nicomachean Ethics,* are extremely detailed and appear to be almost verbatim records of Argyropulos's classes. On the basis of such notes, Acciaiuoli produced commentaries on the *Ethics* (1464) and the *Politics* (1472). After 1461, he became actively involved in political life, serving the Medici-dominated government in a variety of diplomatic posts, both within Italy and abroad.

Acciaiuoli's commentary on the *Ethics* was written at the request of Cosimo de' Medici and was dedicated to him. In the preface, he heaps praise on Argyropulos and makes it clear that the purpose of the commentary is to make his teaching available to a wider audience. Surprisingly, given the strong humanist inclinations of both Argyropulos and Acciaiuoli, the commentary is largely scholastic in both form and content. Philological considerations play little or no part in the exposition of Aristotle's text, and the only classical author who is cited with any regularity is Cicero. The Latin style, though accurate and clear, bears hardly any traces of humanist eloquence, while scholastic philosophical terminology is very much in evidence. Although the *quaestio* format favoured in scholastic treatises is not adopted, some traditional questions are addressed; and medieval authors, though not frequently referred to by name, have clearly left their mark on the interpretations presented.

Essentially, the work is a literal commentary, going through Aristotle's text sentence by sentence and presenting his arguments in the form of syllogisms. Acciaiuoli explicitly states in the preface that the happiness discussed by Aristotle concerns only the present life, and in general he leaves aside theological questions (such as the issue of the superiority of the intellect or the will). Nevertheless, he is willing to cite Augustine and Jerome as authorities, and he provides an elaborate philosophical proof for the immortality of the soul.

For the Latin text see Donato Acciaiuoli, *Expositio libri Ethicorum Aristotelis* (Florence, 1478), sigs. I4^v–9^r. The commentary was reprinted at least eighteen times during the sixteenth century: Venice, 1535, 1565 and 1576; Paris, 1541, 1542, 1555 and 1560; Lyons, 1544, 1553, 1554, 1559, 1560, 1561, 1567, 1588, 1592 and 1598; and Geneva, 1588.

Commentary on the Nicomachean Ethics

BOOK X, CHAPTER 7

[If] happiness consists of an activity in accordance with virtue, it is reasonable that it should be in accordance with the most excellent virtue. . . . . Aristotle, after having declared [at the end of the previous chapter] that in general happiness is an activity which is desired for its own sake and which is in accordance with virtue, now deals with speculative happiness, which in his opinion is the highest of all human goods. The definition of happiness will be complete if a clause is added to it specifying that it is an activity in accordance with the best virtue, which is the virtue belonging to that which is best and most excellent in man.

This chapter is divided into four parts, which will be disclosed [at the appropriate places]. In the first part Aristotle states – as if narrating, since it does not seem to require proof – that if happiness is an activity in accordance with virtue, it is fitting that it is in accordance with the best virtue. That virtue will belong to the best and most excellent faculty and to its activity as well; for the most excellent disposition and the most excellent activity must be attributed to the most excellent faculty, whether that part – that is, that faculty – is the mind and the intellect or whether there is something else which is the principal element in us, which bears a similarity to divine entities and which by nature dominates our irrational faculties, as Aristotle shows in the *Politics* [VII.13 (1334ᵇ17–28)]. The activity of the best element in us, in accordance with its proper virtue, will constitute human happiness; and later on he shows that this activity is contemplation and speculation in accordance with wisdom, which in Book VI [chapter 7] he attributed to the speculative part of the mind.

It should be noted that the rational faculty – and the intellect itself as a whole – fulfils three conditions of nobility, among others. It fulfils the first condition because, by nature, it rules the lower and more ignoble faculties: the irascible, concupiscible and such like.[1] The second condition relates to perception. Although other faculties of the soul, such as the sensitive, also perceive, they do not do so in the same way as the mind, which perceives universals – intelligible ideas which are entirely separable from matter. In addition, it deals with the most noble objects, perceiving them as far as it is possible to do so. It fulfils the third condition because, according to some, Aristotle holds that the mind, on account of its apparent conformity with separate substances,[2] is not extended in the extension of its subject [i.e., the human body] and its activity is not located in a bodily instrument.[3] Aristotle says that it is the most divine thing in us.

Let us put aside in the present context the question of whether the will or the intellect is the principal faculty in us. Our religion holds that our soul is indivisible and that it is not extended in the extension of its subject, but rather is present in its entirety throughout the entire [body] and also in each part [of the body].[4] The human soul has many faculties, the most excellent of which is without doubt a rational faculty;[5] but since there is a great dispute as to whether the most excellent faculty is the will or the intellect, let us, as I said, put the matter to one side for now and refer it to the theologians.[6]

It is reasonable that it should be an activity in accordance with the most excellent virtue. This is the second part of the chapter, in which Aristotle proves that the best activity of the mind, that is, contemplation, constitutes the highest and most complete human happiness. It has already been stated, as he himself says,[7] that this activity is contemplative. He proves this conclusion by means of six proofs. The first proof is: the most perfect activity of man is his ultimate and supreme happiness; contemplation is the most perfect activity of man; therefore, contemplation is his ultimate and supreme happiness. Aristotle demonstrates this partly in terms of the faculty, that is, the mind itself, and partly in terms of its object, because the highest and most perfect activity is the most perfect activity of our most perfect faculty directed towards the most perfect object. Contemplation is such an activity, for the mind deals with universals and separate substances. Since the mind is the most noble faculty and these are the most noble objects, such an operation is deservedly the most noble and the most perfect. This proof seems to be entirely valid.

In addition it is the most continuous activity. The second proof is: that human activity which is most continuous constitutes the most perfect and the ultimate human happiness; contemplation is such an activity; therefore, contemplation constitutes the most perfect and the ultimate human happiness. The more continuous a good is the better and more desirable it is; and we can contemplate, as Aristotle says, more continuously than we can do anything else. By means of these arguments, he shows that contemplative happiness is nobler by far than active happiness. It should be noted that activities are interrupted on account of the exhaustion which arises in us, so they do not seem to be continuous. Therefore, those activities which are more continuous are more noble. The more an activity is in need of bodily instruments – as are, for instance, the activities of the sensitive soul – the greater the exhaustion; and the more material the instruments are, the more exhausting the activity. This is because the spirit [*spiritus*] in [bodily] instruments is of a fixed quantity, so that when it is severely depleted, humans cannot be further exhausted, and it is necessary for it to be generated anew.[8] From this it is clear that contemplation is more continuous because it occurs in the mind, which is not located or extended in a bodily instrument, as Aristotle says;[9] for this reason we are able to contemplate more continuously – though not without intermission, because even the mind itself needs and employs things which exist in bodily instruments, such as phantasms.[10] Therefore, contemplation is the most continuous activity in comparison with other human activities. A practical activity can also be continuous, though not as much so as contemplation, because prudence and the active intellect make greater use of instrumental powers than does the speculative intellect. In addition, a practical activity needs a number of means in order to function. Therefore, contemplation and speculation are the most continuous of all human activities, that is, they can be more continuous than other activities.

Moreover, we think that happiness must contain an admixture of pleasure. The third proof is: of those activities concerned with knowledge, the one which is the most pleasant constitutes the supreme and most perfect happiness; speculation in accordance with wisdom is such an activity; therefore, it constitutes supreme happiness. Aristotle explains this proof by stating that while enjoyment is connected to happiness and to an activity concerned with knowledge, it will without doubt be greatest when that activity is contemplation in accordance with wisdom. This is based partly on its purity and partly on its certainty. That activity which is purest and most separated from material circumstances is most enjoyable; contemplation in accordance with wisdom is this type of activity; therefore, it receives very great and exceptionally unadulterated pleasure from its productive cause, which is exceptionally pure and remote from material circumstances. Similarly, an activity which has a greater degree of certainty is exceedingly enjoyable; an activity in accordance with wisdom is such an activity; therefore, it will be the most enjoyable. That contemplation has a greater degree of certainty is clear from the fact that it is concerned with things which are necessary and cannot be otherwise.

Aristotle adduces another reason or ground for preferring contemplation to a practical activity. The activity of those who know is more certain and more enjoyable than that of those who strive to know; those who contemplate in accordance with wisdom know, whereas those who lead an active life strive to know through prudence; therefore, the certainty and, by consequence, the pleasure will be greater in contemplation than in another activity concerned with knowledge, that is, another practical activity concerned with knowledge. The reason for this is that the person who contemplates in accordance with the wise disposition which he possesses functions as someone with knowledge and no longer strives to know; the person leading an active life, on the other hand, strives to know everyday by means of prudence and seeks advice regarding what should be done. He seeks advice as to whether peace and alliances should be made, whether ambassadors should be sent and other matters of this nature. All consultation constitutes an enquiry: those who seek advice strive to know what will lead to the best result; and this is the characteristic of the prudent man. From this it follows that contemplation in accordance with wisdom, on account of its certainty and its purity, is the most perfect and the most enjoyable activity; therefore, it constitutes supreme happiness.

In my opinion, those commentators who say that Aristotle is here comparing the relative merits of different types of contemplative activity – that is, contemplation which occurs after a wise disposition has been acquired with those types of contemplation which precede the acquisition of this disposition – should be given less consideration. For although this position could be true, nevertheless the exposition which I have given seems to be better suited to Aristotle's thought: rather than comparing the relative merits of different types of speculation or contemplation, he is making a comparison between practical activities in accordance with prudence and speculation in accordance with wisdom.

Contemplation has the greatest degree of self-sufficiency. The fourth proof is: that activity which is most self-sufficient and in relation to which there is the greatest degree of self-sufficiency constitutes supreme happiness; contemplation is such an activity; therefore, the activity of contemplation constitutes supreme human happiness. It is stated, in the first place, that something is self-sufficient when it provides a self-sufficient and desirable life; happiness is such a thing. When, however, one compares the contemplative with the active life, the former has the greatest self-sufficiency. Aristotle argues on this basis that it is the greatest and supreme happiness in human affairs.

This is because practical activities require more resources. The just man, for instance, needs men towards whom to behave justly and others with whom he can pursue this activity; likewise, temperate and generous men, as well as various others, are in need of a number of means. The wise man, by contrast, can contemplate on his own. If they are equal in that they both require the necessities of life, the person who leads an active life nevertheless is more in need of resources in order to pursue his activities than the person who leads a contemplative life, for the wise man can contemplate on his own. Even though it is better when there are two people, so that contemplation occurs in the company of a friend, the condition is itself, nevertheless, the most self-sufficient.

Contemplation is loved for its own sake. The fifth proof is: that activity which is most desirable for its own sake constitutes supreme human happiness; contemplation is such an activity; therefore, contemplation constitutes supreme human happiness. Since happiness is the ultimate goal, it must not be desired for the sake of anything else, but rather for its own sake; and this is the case above all with contemplation in accordance with wisdom. By means of a practical action, something is obtained beyond the action itself, whether greater or smaller. For instance, by means of a brave action, victory is obtained; by means of generosity, goodwill; by means of temperance, the calming of passions, emotions and desires. The same is true with other such activities: they are not done merely for their own sake, but rather, in a manner of speaking, on account of something else which is obtained by means of them. In contemplation, however, nothing is obtained beyond contemplation and speculation about the truth. It is evident, therefore, that we contemplate in order to contemplate and in order to speculate about the truth. . . .

Happiness consists of leisure. The sixth proof is: that activity which consists above all of leisure and peacefulness constitutes supreme happiness; contemplation in accordance with wisdom is such an activity; therefore, this activity constitutes supreme happiness. This is clear because its ultimate goal is peacefulness and leisure, that is, a peaceful activity. Practical activities, on the other hand, are especially concerned with military and political affairs. No one desires military actions for themselves – to do so would be excessively cruel and bloodthirsty. Likewise, the action of a man leading a political life involves him in much work and is directed towards the peace and leisure of the community. His aim is honour or dignity or – since neither of these is the ultimate purpose of human life (as I demonstrated in my comments on Book I [chapters 4 and 5]) – his aim is rather happiness for himself and for his fellow citizens: not the political happiness which he already has, but speculative happiness, towards which active happiness is directed as its ultimate goal. Therefore, if we consider these activities successively, we will find that they are related to each other in the following way: political activity is directed towards virtuous practical activity,[11] which is itself directed towards contemplative activity, in which we attain peace and reach our goal, in the most perfect of activities and the final goal of all preceding ones. For why do we acquire virtues? So that we can act in accordance with them. Why then do we do that? So that we can contemplate peace-fully at our leisure. Hence, whatever a person does is directed, by its very nature and essence, towards contemplative activity as its ultimate goal. Practical activity, there-fore, is directed towards contemplation, which is why, in Book VI [chapter 13], when Aristotle compares prudence with wisdom, he says that prudence issues orders in the interest of wisdom, but not *to* wisdom, as is evident.

When practical activity is compared with speculative activity, it seems that spec-ulation is its ultimate and final goal. When, however, practical activities are con-sidered individually within their own genus, the ultimate goal in respect to practical activities and practicable things is an activity in accordance with prudence, which is the ultimate goal within this genus. But when we arrive at this goal and speculative activity is proposed to us, we do not rest but rather proceed on further towards that speculation, as towards that which constitutes our souls' rest and leisure. For this reason many philosophers, according to Cicero, placed the supreme good in knowl-edge, which they referred to as *euthumia* [contentment] and *athambia* [impertur-bability], that is, a sort of tranquillity of the soul.[12]

It should be carefully noted that Aristotle stated earlier [X.6 (1176^{b}34–6)] that rest was not a goal, since it comes about for the sake of an activity; here, on the other hand, he says that happiness consists in leisure. In the earlier passage, he was speaking about repose, that is, the relaxation by which activity is interrupted before the achievement of its goal, on account of the weakness brought about by continuous activity. Here, by contrast, he takes rest to mean an end in itself, which consists in a tranquil and peaceful activity, not something which is directed towards a further goal. According to Aristotle, contemplation is such an activity. In this contemplation our soul is not seeking anything further by means of contemplation, but rather is at rest – as far as this can be attained in human life. I add this proviso because St Augustine says: 'thou hast made us for thyself, and our heart remains restless until it finds repose in thee'.[13]

If therefore politics and war are superior to all other practical activities in excel-lence and importance, they nonetheless involve much work. This is the third part of the chapter, in which Aristotle concludes that perfect human happiness consists of contemplative activity. He does so by rehearsing briefly, in the following way, the proofs which he has already adduced, starting from the final one: military and political actions involve much work, accomplish something beyond themselves and are directed towards leisure and speculative activity; contemplation, on the other hand, is not sought for the sake of something else, but rather for its own sake, is the most perfect and the most continuous activity, has a pleasure peculiar to itself which augments its activity, is self-sufficient and therefore fulfils all the conditions which Aristotle mentioned earlier. It is obvious therefore that perfect human happiness is nothing other than contemplative activity – provided it occurs over a period equiv-alent to a complete lifetime, for everything which is attributed to perfect happiness must be attributed to the man who attains speculative and contemplative happiness. A complete span of time is attributed to him because in Book I [chapter 7 (1098^{a}18–20)], Aristotle adds to his definition of happiness that it must occupy a complete lifetime; therefore, the required duration and a complete span of time must be attributed to the man who attains contemplative happiness. A man must move towards his perfection over a lengthy period of time and then pursue this activity still further in order to become completely happy, for one swallow does not make a spring, nor does one activity make a happy man: it takes a long time. . . .

Such a life will, however, be superior to the human condition. This is the fourth part of the chapter, in which Aristotle, after having declared that contemplation is the highest and most perfect happiness available to man, now confirms this point and goes even further, stating that such a life is superior to that available to man. For contemplative happiness is more excellent than active happiness, and although both belong to man, they belong to him according to different principles, the one active, the other contemplative; therefore, Aristotle shows how contemplative happiness relates to man. And he proves, in the following way, that contemplation is the most perfect human happiness and that it, in a certain sense, transcends the human condition: a life which is superior to that which is lived according to the human condition is man's most perfect happiness; the contemplative life is such a life; therefore, it constitutes the most perfect human happiness and, in a certain sense, transcends the human condition. Aristotle adds that the person who leads such a life, that is, a life of contemplation, does not live according to the human condition, but rather according to something divine which is in him, inasmuch as his intellect bears a likeness to separate substances.[14]

It should be noted that several powers, activities and ways of life belong to man. The human soul has, for instance, a vegetative faculty, which does not belong to man on account of his humanity but rather on account of what he shares in common with plants. Plants do not live a life superior to this; therefore, to lead a vegetative life is to live like a plant. The sensitive life is attributed to man as well. It does not belong to him as his ultimate activity but rather on account of what he shares in common with animals: to lead such a life is to live like an animal or brute beast. The rational life is also attributed to man, because he is said to live not like a plant or an animal but rather to lead a more excellent and superior life. There are two types of rational life: leading one type, he is said to live like a man; leading the other, he is said to transcend the human condition. There is a rational principle in man which is concerned with actions and another which is concerned with speculations: that is, there is an active mind and a speculative mind; the former deals with human actions, the latter speculates about [the nature of] that which exists. When distinguishing man from the beasts, it is more convenient to distinguish him by means of the rational faculty which is closer to the senses than by means of the faculty which is more distant; therefore, he is distinguished from them in the first instance and proximately through his practical rational faculty. Since it is this which distinguishes him proximately from the beasts, this faculty and the practical activity associated with it belong to man on account of his human condition.

It follows from this that active happiness belongs to the man who is living in a human and political condition, not to the one leading a more excellent and superior life, that is, an intellective life; for the other rational principal and other type of life belong to the man who lives above the human condition, leading a life which is similar to that of separate substances, who have no vegetative, sensitive or active faculties of their own. It is for this reason that the moral virtues are said not to occur in them, as Aristotle states later on [X.8 (1178^{b}10–18)], except in a metaphorical sense. They lead instead a contemplative and intellective life, and such a life belongs properly to them. Man, however, is an intermediate being between other animals and separate essences, having similarities and dissimilarities to both in relation to his various faculties and activities. He is similar to animals in his sensitive faculty and its activities; but he differs from them proximately through his mind and his active life. He also differs from them through his contemplative life, but the distance is so great that it does not seem to be proximate. Through his contemplative mind and the contemplative life, on the other hand, he is said to have similarities with separate substances; and it is for this reason that Aristotle maintains that such a life is superior to the human condition. 'In the flesh', says St Jerome, if I remember correctly, 'they are beyond the flesh and seem to live in a heavenly rather than a human manner.'[15] Man differs, however, from separate substances on account of his inferior faculties. . . .

A very fine argument for the immortality of the soul arises from this situation.[16] If the human soul is an intermediate nature between separate substances and those immersed in matter, it is right and fitting that in relation to those conditions which distance it most from substances immersed in matter it is similar to separate substances, and that in relation to those conditions which distance it from separate substances it corresponds to those immersed in matter. Separate substances are said to be characterized by two conditions: they are not produced from matter, and they are not the substantial forms of material beings. Those immersed in matter, by contrast, are characterized by two conditions which are opposite to those belonging to superior beings: they are educed from matter, and they are the substantial forms of material beings.[17]

Therefore, if the human soul, as an intermediate being, differing from both and having similarities with both in diverse ways, has a similarity with substances immersed in matter, it will either be that it is educed from matter or that it is the substantial form of a material being. It is not similar to them in the first manner because if it were educed from matter and were also the substantial form of a material being,[18] it would be entirely the same as substances immersed in matter and would not be an intermediary, as was assumed and stated [earlier]. The remaining possibility therefore is that it is similar to them in that it is the substantial form of a material being; and it differs from substances immersed in matter in that it is not educed from matter.

If the human soul must have a similarity with separate substances, then it will not be in respect to the fact that separate substances are *not* the substantial forms of material beings, because separate substances are in no way substantial forms of material beings, whereas the human soul is the substantial form of the body and is totally in the totality of the body and totally in each part of it. Since the soul differs from separate substances in that it is a substantial form of a material being, the remaining possibility is that it is similar to them in respect to another condition, that is, in respect to the fact that it is not produced from matter nor does it come out of the potentiality of matter. This being the case, it follows straightaway that the human soul is immortal, because all learned men agree that anything which does not come out of the potentiality of matter is incorruptible and immortal; the human soul is such a thing; therefore, the human soul is immortal.

We should not, as some advise, occupy our minds with human matters since we are human, nor mortal matters since we are mortal, but rather we should, as far as possible, make ourselves immortal. After showing that the contemplative life belongs to man in view of something which transcends the human condition, Aristotle now adduces the opinion of some ancients who said that men, since they are mortal, ought to occupy their minds with mortal matters and not immortal ones. Some say this was the opinion of Solon, others of Hesiod, and certain people attribute it to Simonides.[19] Aristotle attacks this view by drawing three conclusions. In the first place, he says that we should take little account of the opinion of those who advise us to concern ourselves with mortal and human matters and that we must instead strive to lead a life which is similar to that of immortal beings and separate substances, pursuing that life which is based on the best element in us, that is, the mind, reason and intellect. Although the mind is small in mass, because it is indivisible, absolutely unmixed and consequently lacks quantity or magnitude, nevertheless it greatly excels [other faculties] in power, because it rules, in the natural order of things, all the inferior faculties that exist within us. It is also of superior worth because it is unmixed and immaterial. Hence Aristotle says that each of us consists of this, that is, a mind and reason, because it is the principal thing in us. The first conclusion is therefore that each creature seems to be, in some sense, that which is most outstanding in it; the mind is that which is most outstanding in man; therefore, each of us seems, in some sense, to consist of a mind. . . .

When a man lives according to his intellect, he leads the life which is most appropriate to him. This is gratifying to him, as Aristotle says in Book IX [chapter 8 (1168b35–1169a4)], because it is that which is characteristic of him in the highest degree. It would therefore be absurd if someone were to neglect that life which surpasses all others, which is more worthwhile and which belongs to him – for that which is the best by nature in each genus is the most appropriate to it – if, I repeat, he were to neglect this life which is more worthwhile and which is similar to that of the gods and turn instead towards mortal matters, as these people advise. From this point Aristotle draws the second conclusion: that which by nature is appropriate to each creature is the best and the most enjoyable for it; intellectual life is by nature appropriate to man; therefore, it is the best and the most enjoyable life.

From this arises the third conclusion: the life which is best and most enjoyable for each creature is also the happiest; a life led according to the mind is this kind of life; therefore, such a life – one which is lived according to the mind and which is entirely contemplative – is the happiest life for man and the most enjoyable, since it is the most appropriate for him. Nor does this contradict what was said earlier, namely, that it is not a human life but one which transcends the human condition. This life does not belong to man in respect to his composite nature (for man's nature does not consist of only one element), but rather it is most appropriate to man in respect to that which is the principal thing in him and which is found most perfectly in superior substances, but only imperfectly in man if compared with them. And although it is small in mass, because it is indivisible, it is more excellent in power and nobility than anything else which is in man.

It is to be noted that nothing which is indivisible has mass, properly speaking. There are many indivisible things which are more imperfect than divisible ones: for example, an [indivisible] point in comparison to a line, which is divisible; and a line in comparison to a surface, where the line, as the boundary of the surface, is indivisible; and a surface in comparison to a body, for a body, which has three dimensions, is more complete than a point, a line and other things of this kind which come before it. But in order to prevent anyone from perhaps feeling scorn for such an indivisible thing, that is, the mind, thinking that such indivisibility indicates a defect in the mind, as it does in many things, Aristotle adds that in power and value it is much more excellent. Therefore, it is clear that contemplation according to the virtue of the mind [i.e., wisdom] constitutes supreme happiness and the greatest happiness which can be attained in this life.

Moreover, if anyone is by chance surprised that Aristotle in Book VII [chapter 1] stated that a certain heroic virtue surpasses the human condition and that here he also says that the contemplative life surpasses, in a manner of speaking, the nature of man and the human condition too, it is to be understood that in Book VII he was speaking of that virtue which, in relation to men's moral behaviour, seems to surpass the common run of human nature, but nevertheless is a mean between two vices: monstrous behaviour which exceeds human nature and monstrous behaviour which falls short of human nature.[20] Here, however, he is speaking about the contemplative life, which is removed from all occupations and is not concerned with men's moral behaviour but rather with speculative and intelligible matters. Because it is conducted by the most perfect faculty of all those which exist within us, it is said, in a certain sense, to transcend human nature, in the way that I explained earlier, that is, inasmuch as such a life is similar to that of separate substances. He also adds that contemplation is directed towards the most noble objects.[21] For these reasons, Aristotle attributed to it the leading position among all types and ways of life and placed supreme happiness in such a life and such an activity.

Translator's Notes

1. The irascible and concupiscible faculties (the seats of anger and appetite respectively) are Platonic, rather than Aristotelian, divisions of the lower soul: see *Republic* IV (439E).
2. Separate substances are immaterial beings, such as Aristotle's incorporeal unmoved movers (*Metaphysics* XII.6–9) or, in a Christian context, God and the angels.
3. See Aristotle, *De anima* III.4 (429a24–7) and the interpretation of this passage in Thomas Aquinas, *In Aristotelis librum De anima commentarium,* ed. A. M. Pirotta (Turin, 1925), pp. 228–9 (Book III, lecture 7, 684–6).
4. See, e.g., Thomas Aquinas, *Summa theologiae* Ia, q. 76, art. 8.
5. The three rational faculties (or divisions of the intellective soul) are intellect, will and memory: see *CHRP,* p. 466.
6. The issue of whether the intellect or the will was the superior faculty was widely debated in the Middle Ages and the Renaissance, with the Dominicans generally supporting the intellectualist position of Thomas Aquinas and the Franciscans adopting the voluntarist

view of Duns Scotus. Unlike Acciaiuoli, both John Case and the Coimbra commentators bring this discussion into their commentaries: see Chapters 6 and 8.

7. Aristotle is perhaps referring to VI.13 (1145ª2–11).

8. See the definition of *spiritus,* used in the medical sense, in D. P. Walker, *Spiritual and Demonic Magic from Ficino to Campanella* (Notre Dame, Ind., 1975), p. 2: 'a corporeal vapour, centred in the brain and flowing through the nervous system; it is the first instrument of the incorporeal soul, an instrument for sense-perception, imagination and motor-activity – the link between body and soul'. See also G. Verbeke, *L'Évolution de la doctrine du pneuma du stoïcisme à S. Augustin* (Paris, 1945); M. Fattori and M. Bianchi, eds., *Spiritus: IVº colloquio internazionale, Roma . . . 1983* (Rome, 1984).

9. See n. 3.

10. Phantasms are mental images of particular material things, stripped of their matter in the process of perception and stored in the imagination, which Renaissance thinkers believed to be located in the brain; though not themselves the objects of intellection, phantasms were regarded as indispensable to it.

11. That is, activity involving honour and dignity.

12. Cicero, *De finibus* V.29.87.

13. Augustine, *Confessions* I.1.

14. On separate substances see n. 2.

15. Jerome, *Commentarii in Amos* II.4.12.

16. On the issue of the immortality of the soul in the Renaissance see *CHRP,* pp. 485–534.

17. According to Aristotle, every body is a composite of matter and form; it is the form which gives actuality or actual existence to the potentiality of the matter. A substantial form is what gives an individual thing its essence and effects its existence within a species: the substantial form of an axe, for instance, is that which makes it an axe and without which it would cease to be an axe: see Aristotle, *De anima* II.1 (412ᵇ12–15).

18. Acciaiuoli assumes, as becomes clear in what follows, that the human soul is the substantial form of the human body. This position was based on Aristotle's statements in *De anima* II.1, as interpreted by influential commentators such as Thomas Aquinas: see his *In librum De anima commentarium,* pp. 81–2 (Book II, lecture 1, 220–6); *Summa theologiae* Ia, q. 76, art. 1; and *Summa contra gentiles* II.70; see also N. Kretzmann, 'Philosophy of mind', in N. Kretzmann and E. Stump, eds., *Cambridge Companion to Aquinas* (Cambridge, 1993), pp. 128–59.

19. Modern editors cite Pindar, *Isthmian Odes* V.20; and Sophocles, *Tereus* fragment 590 (531): see *Tragicorum Graecorum fragmenta* (Göttingen, 1977), IV: *Sophocles,* ed. S. Radt, pp. 441–2.

20. In other words, it belongs to the category of moral virtue, which Aristotle defines (II.6) as a mean between two extremes: one of excess, the other of deficiency. For Renaissance discussions of this doctrine of moral virtue see *CHRP,* pp. 339–42.

21. X.7 (1177ª22).

Further Reading

Bianchi, L., 'Un commento "umanistico" ad Aristotele: l' "Expositio super libros Ethicorum" di Donato Acciaiuoli', *Rinascimento,* 30 (1990), 29–55

Bisticci, Vespasiano da, *The Memoirs,* trans. W. George and E. Waters (London, 1926), pp. 276–93

CHRP, pp. 328–9, 423, 806

Field, A., *The Origins of the Platonic Academy of Florence* (Princeton, N.J., 1988), chs. 5 and 8

Garin, E., *Medioevo e rinascimento: studi e ricerche* (Rome, 1976), pp. 199–267

Kraye, J., 'Renaissance commentaries on the *Nicomachean Ethics*', in O. Weijers, ed., *Vocabulary of Teaching and Research between Middle Ages and Renaissance. Proceedings of the Colloquium, London, Warburg Institute . . . March 1994* (Turnhout, 1995), pp. 96–117

Lohr, C. H., 'Medieval Latin Aristotle commentaries: authors A–F', *Traditio,* 23 (1967), 313–413, at 400–1

6

John Case

JILL KRAYE

Introduction

John Case (1546–1600) was the most important English Aristotelian of the Elizabethan era. Born in Woodstock near Oxford, he spent his whole life associated with the university. He received his BA and MA from the newly founded St John's College, where his education combined the old scholasticism and the new humanism. In 1572 he took up a fellowship at St John's, which he lost two years later when he married. For the next fifteen years he engaged in private teaching of Oxford students at his home and published a series of textbooks on subjects ranging from logic to moral philosophy. These went through many editions in England and Germany, the latest in 1629, and were printed more often than almost any other sixteenth-century British philosophical works. Many of his books were dedicated to figures such as Robert Dudley, Earl of Leicester, who were involved in the world of Elizabethan court patronage.

Case's logic textbook, the *Summa veterum interpretum* (1584), is a beginners' manual, oriented towards the essentially rhetorical task of persuasion, rather than the more technical problems of demonstrative inference explored by Italian philosophers, who were more concerned with the application of logic to natural philosophy. His commentaries, such as those on the *Politics* (1588), *Magna moralia* (1596) and *Physics* (1599), were aimed at an undergraduate audience and his intentions were primarily didactic. Nevertheless, he produced works of respectable scholarship based on an unusually wide range and number of sources: ancient, medieval and contemporary. His Protestantism did not prevent him from making extensive use of Catholic works, above all, those of Thomas Aquinas, the author whom – after Aristotle – he cites most frequently. He also made use of Walter Burley, Duns Scotus and other scholastic authorities. Nor was he averse to quoting from contemporary Catholic commentators, such as the Jesuits of Coimbra (see Chapter 8). But he combined this scholastic perspective with a more humanist orientation, reading and interpreting philosophical works, at least partially, in a humanist framework and adopting humanist translations of Aristotle, such as Leonardo Bruni's version of the *Nicomachean Ethics,* in his commentaries. Despite his firm commitment to the Peripatetic approach to philosophy, he remained open to different strains of thought, bringing in Platonic or Neoplatonic material where it seemed relevant, to supplement the basic Aristotelian structure of his textbooks. In addition, he believed that there was much common ground between Peripatetic and Christian ethics: even on the very difficult and controversial issue of the immortality of the soul, Case argued (in the first of the chapters translated here) that Aristotelian doctrine was fundamentally in agreement with Christian dogma.

Case's *Mirror of Moral Questions on the Whole of Aristotle's Ethics* (1585) is essentially a commentary on Aristotle's *Nicomachean Ethics,* structured, as the title indicates, around a series of questions. The manner in which the questions are presented is closer to the simple catechistic format which had been a popular pedagogic tool since the late Middle Ages than to the complex and elaborate *quaestiones* found in scholastic commentaries. Another device regularly employed by Case is the so-called Ramist table. This method, associated with Petrus

Ramus's recent attempts to reform logic and quite fashionable in England at the time, entailed presenting material in lists, often according to either/or alternatives, in order to clarify and simplify the basic structure of an argument. It is characteristic of Case's eclecticism that he uses new-fangled Ramist tables in conjunction with some traditional features of the philosophical commentary, such as the exploration of dubious points (*dubia*) and the raising and resolution of possible objections.

For the Latin text see John Case, *Speculum questionum moralium in universam Aristotelis philosophi summi Ethicen* (Frankfurt am Main, 1594), pp. 624–39.

A Mirror of Moral Questions on the Whole of Aristotle's Ethics

BOOK X, CHAPTER 7

[1] Is the mind the subject of contemplative happiness?
[2] Is the happiest life that which is guided solely by the mind and by wisdom?

Even if Aristotle had written only this brief treatise, in which he discusses the immortality of wisdom and the excellence of the intellect in an almost religious manner, it would be sufficient in my view to weaken and entirely destroy the opinion of those who imagine that the immortality of the mind cannot be proved on Aristotelian grounds. For here he calls the mind a divine entity five times;[1] here he confirms that it is the subject of eternal, unmixed and divine beatitude [*beatitudo*]; here he acutely demonstrates that it renders us immortal and wise, and that we live the happiest life on the basis of it; here and at the end of chapter 8 he shows with great learning that it is in our minds that we most resemble God, and that it is in our minds, when they are rightly disposed, that we are most dear to God. Is the mind a divine entity, yet does it nevertheless die? Is it the subject of unmixed, eternal and divine beatitude, yet does it nevertheless perish? Is the happiest of lives located in it, yet does it nevertheless cease to exit? Is it both the likeness and delight of God so that it can disappear entirely or turn into dust? I cite here nothing from *De mundo,* nothing from Book I of *De caelo,* nothing from Book III of *De anima,* nothing from the *Metaphysics.*[2] It would be irritating if I were to adduce this material, as if I were picking at a sore.

Why then do I say these things? Certainly, so that you, the diligent reader, will understand that the topic for discussion at this point is contemplative happiness [*felicitas*]; and you will not be able to attain a correct view of what that is if you do not know beforehand about the divine and immortal mind, which is its seat and subject. I will rehearse in a clear and orderly fashion the conclusions to be found in Aristotle concerning this matter. The first is that contemplative happiness is an internal action of that part of the soul which governs the other parts and faculties, and which embraces the science of virtuous and divine matters; the mind, which is granted to man by God, is with doubt that part of the soul; therefore, contemplative happiness is located in this part.

The second conclusion is that the truest happiness is that which is concerned with speculation. Aristotle confirms this conclusion by means of six arguments. The first is from the dignity of the subject; the second from the uninterrupted duration of the action; the third from the adjunct of happiness; the fourth from the essence of happiness; the fifth from its special property; and the last from its effect or result. The argument from the dignity of the subject runs as follows: the intellect is the most divine thing in us; contemplation is the action proper to the intellect; therefore, the happiness located in the intellect must be contemplation. The argument from the uninterrupted duration of the action goes thus: the action in which true beatitude consists must be continuous; only mental contemplation is continuous; therefore, only mental contemplation is complete beatitude. The argument from the adjunct takes this form: unmixed and true happiness must be adjoined to unmixed and continuous delight, which must be in accordance with the most perfect virtue; this is found only in contemplation and wisdom (which, as Aristotle says here, produce astonishing delights); therefore, the truest happiness consists only in contemplation. The argument from the essence of happiness is demonstrated by this type of syllogism: the beatitude regarded as the most true is that which is large enough in itself and is, as the ancients say, the most self-sufficient; the beatitude which is found in the mind of a wise man is large enough in itself and is the most self-sufficient; therefore, the beatitude which is found in the mind of a wise man is to be regarded as the most true. Here is the reasoning behind the argument from special property: nothing should be sought in true happiness except happiness itself; nothing is sought in true contemplation except contemplation itself; therefore, true contemplation is happiness. This is how the final argument, from effect, is constructed: happiness consists above all in peace and tranquillity; of all human activities, contemplation is the most peaceful and tranquil; therefore, absolute happiness consists in contemplation.

In Aristotle's text, the minor premise of the last syllogism is proved by means of similarities and examples: just as we undertake business in order to have leisure and just as we wage wars in order to live in peace, so we devote our energies to the difficult practice of political virtue in order to arrive triumphantly in the haven and repose of contemplative happiness. From this Aristotle infers that the political life is toilsome: one is always on the move and practically breathless. If this is true – and it is very true – it follows, as set out in the final argument, that the happiest of lives is that which is guided solely by the mind and by wisdom. But this type of life, as Aristotle says here, is too good for man to attribute it to himself; for he lives this life not because he is a man, but rather because there is a certain divine entity enclosed within him (by this he means the mind) which excels what is made of solid matter (say, the body) to the same extent that a mental action surpasses one which issues from the will. Can anyone read this and not admit that Aristotle knew about the immortality of the soul? But he adds the following points. He says that just as the mind is a divine entity, so that life which corresponds to it is also divine. We must all therefore strive, as far as we are able, for immortal glory and take pains to accomplish everything so that we lead a life based on the developed intellect, which is the most outstanding thing in us.

He says that it is unworthy for someone to live the life of another rather than his own life, as if he were saying that the life which is above all to be spoken of is that which is in accordance with the form of man, that is, his mind, and that therefore only the man who lives according to his mind seems to be alive. I wish that the banqueters of our own times, those who live their lives governed by common sense, appetite and will, would listen to this precept from the pen of a pagan. Did I say *their* lives? No, I mean the lives of others, for the only life which belongs to us is that which is governed by the mind and by wisdom. Even if we do not perfectly attain such a life in our brief time on earth, Aristotle here persuades us that we should nevertheless exert ourselves day and night so that, although we are human beings, by means of our minds we can nevertheless contemplate not human but divine matters, not mortal but immortal things.

The structure of the first question is sufficiently clear. Here is an outline of the second question. The life of the mind is the happiest because

the mind is the most divine part
the mind is guided by wisdom
the mind is unchangeable and eternal
God, who is infinite, is its objective material, which is proved in the next chapter.

Objection [*arising from the first question*]: The will is nobler than the intellect; therefore happiness, which is the most noble object, is placed not in the intellect but in the will. The major premise is proved because Aristotle defines the will as the queen of all the faculties in the soul.[3]

Reply. Happiness is considered

either actively, under the name of the supreme good, and thus is in the will alone;
or contemplatively, under the name of the supreme truth, and thus is located in the mind alone.

Another objection: Active happiness does not differ from contemplative happiness in essence; therefore, they should not be placed in different subjects. The preceding premise is proved because both in essence are goods of the soul.

Reply: Just as will, intellect and memory, the three faculties of the soul,[4] are in essence one soul, so the two types of happiness according to their nature constitute one happiness. And just as these three faculties are distinct in their activities and duties, so the two happinesses are distinct in their principles and subjects. This happens when they are considered according to their differences.

Objection arising from the second question: Aristotle encourages us at the end of this chapter always to contemplate divine and immortal matters; but this cannot happen while we remain human beings; therefore, he stirs us to do something impossible, which is absurd.

Reply: He encourages us, not because he thinks that immortality exists in this life, but so that on our way to the grave we ennoble that part of our soul which will not feel the voracity of time nor the teeth of decay. This part is the mind, as he says in Book III [chapter 5] of *De anima*,[5] which is uncreated, eternal and separable from matter.

A doubtful point arising from the third argument of the second conclusion: Does the greatest and most perfect enjoyment of which human nature is capable come from the mind? Mental enjoyment is

either unmixed and thus is most perfect because
    its material, that is God, is eternal
    its action is unchangeable and continuous
    its virtue, namely wisdom, is enjoyable;
or mixed, when it arises from the same object which the senses enjoy; and it is also more

perfect because
the mind is a more powerful faculty
the mode of perception in the mind is simpler
its comprehension is clearer
mental delight itself is more continuous.

Another objection: Something is regarded as more natural when it is suitable for more people according to nature; corporeal pleasure is suitable for more people than is mental pleasure; therefore, corporeal pleasure is more natural than mental pleasure, which is nevertheless denied by Aristotle in the chapter.

Reply: Although corporeal pleasure is suitable for more people than is mental pleasure and appears to be sweeter, this applies only to those who have not tasted mental pleasures. Therefore, just as everyone desires by nature to know, though few attain knowledge, because they flee from the difficulty of acquiring it, so everyone seeks the delightful life of the mind, but few attain it, because they do not learn the laborious method of contemplation at a tender age. But those who have once tasted the nectar and ambrosia of pleasures which come from true mental contemplation are carried away by such a passion for the good that, always flying on high with the eagles, they look with wide-open eyes at that sun from which all goods radiate. Picture in your mind, if you can, how great and how incredible this mental enjoyment is.

CHAPTER 8

[1] Is the contemplative life better than the active?
[2] Does an abundance of possessions hinder those who are truly happy?
[3] Does God behave morally?
[4] Is he concerned about human affairs?
[5] Does he take pleasure in those who are fond of learning and happy?

You are too concerned about your possessions, Crassus.[6] Why do you torture yourself? Why do you fret beyond measure if everything does not turn out well? You certainly live a miserable life. Now listen to me, the riches of Croesus did not make him happy. If you trust Aristotle, learn this one sentence: having adequate resources does not depend on an abundance of all things, nor do judgement or action: those who do not rule on land or at sea can do great things which are full of dignity. The person who has a moderate and modest amount of wealth can not only do but also excel in everything which is virtuous, since private men cultivate virtue no less, and in fact much more, than those who are engaged in public office. This is what Aristotle says.

You can see from this what that wise man is aiming at: to teach you to live the happiest of lives and to have contempt for the trifles and nonsense of fortune. Locating the happiest of lives in the unmixed and eternal contemplation of God, he compares it in this chapter with the political life, concluding that it is infinitely preferable. I will list the main points, reducing to summary headings material which could flow out and pour forth from here into an ocean of discourse. First, Aristotle prefers the speculative and contemplative life because it strives solely through wisdom towards divine matters; the political life is led towards human matters by prudence. Moreover, the contemplative life, which is located in the mind, deals only with exalted, internal and divine objects; the political life is situated in the will, and treats things which are human, external and subject to change. Next, the contemplative life is eternal; the political, by contrast, coincides with our mortal life. Furthermore, the enjoyment which comes from contemplation is superior to all pleasures which derive from action and from the active life. Add to this the fact that the contemplative life requires fewer things than the active life; it is more self-sufficient and content with its aggregate of goods. In addition, this type of life involves greater mental repose and peace; for the active life is vulnerable to the passions. You will be on the right track if you consider also that the contemplative life makes us similar to God and dear to him, whereas the active life reconciles men to each other. Finally, the contemplative life in man, as Aristotle says in this chapter, is modelled on the very life and activity of God, who lives and acts for eternity. He is not like Endymion sleeping on a mountain in Lydia, but is rather a watchful governor, observing and taking care of everything from on high. Good heavens, how brightly the light of nature shines in Aristotle, who knew these things which many illuminated by the light of grace do not understand!

If I were to speak about the individual gradations of this comparison, step by step and item by item, this discussion would never come to an end. But if you do not mind, I will write a bit more concerning various points. Aristotle teaches in this comparison that an abundance of external possessions hinders to some extent those who have achieved contemplative happiness. But why does he say this, I wonder? It is certainly because possessions distract the human mind from true contemplation: a person who is anxious about worldly things looks downwards to the centre [of the earth] rather than upwards to the heavens. Another question is: does God behave morally? This doubt arises because Aristotle in the chapter maintains that the duties of justice, courage and magnificence do not exist in God. This is indeed very true if you understand these to be acquired dispositions. All these things are, however, attributed to God in the highest degree of perfection and of essence. I say in the highest degree of perfection and of essence because, according to Aristotle in the *Metaphysics* [XII.6–7], there is nothing imperfect in God, nothing changeable, nothing which is not unmixed, eternal and essential. Likewise, there is this question: is God concerned about human affairs? Aristotle says that he is concerned because he holds human beings dear. But I will say more about this matter, with God's help, in my metaphysical questions, when the subject to be discussed will be providence, which is, so to speak, a singular arrangement, order and concern for all things. The final doubtful point is this: does God take pleasure in those who are fond of learning and happy? Listen, please, to what Aristotle has to say: the man who follows reason as the guide of his life and actions and whose soul is in the best state is most dear to God; for if God cares about human affairs (as he surely does), it is appropriate that he takes pleasure in those who live the life of the mind and of wisdom and who pursue right actions.[7]

Outline of the First Question

The contemplative life is superior to the active on account of

the excellence of the subject, namely the intellect, in which it is located
the divinity of the object, namely God, with which it deals
the eternity of the contemplation, by which it is perfected
the purity of the enjoyment, by which it is maintained
the superiority of the delight, on account of which it is sought for its own sake
the continuousness of the peace, in which it is enjoyed
the absence of the emotions, from which it is freed
the nobility of the wisdom, by which it is guided
the affinity and love, by which it is united to the infinite God.

Outline of the Second Question

An abundance of possessions hinders those who are truly happy because

it distracts them from contemplation of eternal matters and pulls them towards human affairs
it exerts pressure on the human soul through emotions and cares.

Outline of the Third Question

Virtues are considered

either in a moral sense, as they are acquired through effort and thus do not exist in God;
or in their essence, as they come together by nature, and thus God is said to act justly,
   courageously and kindly with us.

Outline of the Fourth Question

God is concerned about human affairs because he regards mankind with

infinite gentleness, with which he takes pleasure in everything
infinite wisdom, with which he perfects everything
infinite providence, by which he rules everything.

Outline of the Fifth Question

God is said to take pleasure in those who are happy

because they live the life of the mind, by which we are made similar to God
because they cultivate wisdom, which is discerned above all in God
because they are inclined towards God, who is said to be the true object of the mind.

Objection arising from the first question: that life which unites man more closely
to God is the more excellent life; man is more closely united to God by the active life;
therefore, the active life is more excellent. The minor premise is proved because love
[*charitas*] is a virtue of the will, not of the intellect, and it is by means of love that we
cling to God, who is the supreme good.

Reply: Love, that is the love belonging to the will, serves the wisdom of the mind;
for wisdom prescribes as the master, while love obeys as the servant.

Another objection: The active life is led to its object by virtue of something better
than that which leads the contemplative life; therefore, it is better. The preceding
premise is proved because the active life is led to God by virtue of the good, whereas

the contemplative life is led [to him] by virtue of the true; and the good is superior to the true.

Reply: In God the good and the true are equal, since both in their essence are appropriate to God. That life, however, is said to be better which is purer and therefore freer from commerce with perishable things. Contemplation is located in such a life.

Another objection: Contemplation is useful only to itself; therefore, the contemplative life is not more excellent.

Reply: It is not useful only to itself; for it is dear to God, as Aristotle says. Therefore, the man living the contemplative life is often more useful to a republic than the one leading an active life in the glare of publicity and in the midst of bystanders. Although God is not swayed[8] by an army composed of a thousand cohorts, he is often won over by the prayer of one poor man.

Another objection: The active life is more necessary to the community, which without it would fall into ruin; therefore, it is more excellent.

Reply: The argument does not follow, for what is being discussed here is not necessity but dignity. To be a philosopher, says Aristotle in Book III [chapter 2 (118ᵃ10–11)] of the *Topics,* is better than to possess a fortune in riches; nevertheless, for a man oppressed by poverty, it is better to gain wealth, if one considers the necessity of the moment and not the dignity of the thing.

Objection arising from the final question: God is in himself sufficient in every good; therefore, it seems absurd for Aristotle to say in this chapter that it is fitting for him to take pleasure in those who are fond of learning and happy. This is to detract somewhat from his divine majesty.

Reply: When Aristotle says that it is fitting for God to take pleasure in those who live the life of the mind and of wisdom, he is not imposing any necessity on God, for in Book VII [chapter 1] of the *Physics,* he says that God is entirely free from all efficient causes.[9] What he means is that God, who is concerned about human affairs, takes pleasure above all in those who especially venerate his divinity with a pure and sincere mind, not under compulsion, but of their own free will, not because they cannot do otherwise, but voluntarily, because they do not wish to do otherwise. In this way human souls are not dragged to their eternal and immutable good.

Translator's Notes

1. Aristotle, *Nicomachean Ethics* 1177ᵇ15, 1177ᵃ16, 1177ᵇ28, 1177ᵇ30, 1177ᵇ31.
2. These were the texts most frequently cited in discussions of the compatibility of Aristotelianism and Christianity. On *De mundo,* now generally regarded as a pseudo-Aristotelian treatise, see J. Kraye, 'Aristotle's god and the authenticity of *De mundo:* an early modern controversy', *Journal of the History of Philosophy,* 28 (1990), 339–58.
3. Aristotle never says this; indeed, the concept of the will, as used here by Case, did not exist in Greek philosophy; it was invented by St Augustine: A. Dihle, *The Theory of the Will in Classical Antiquity* (Berkeley, 1982). This did not, however, prevent some medieval and Renaissance thinkers from reading their own Christian notion of the will back into Aristotle.
4. See Augustine, *De trinitate* X.11.
5. Reading *De anima* instead of the *Physics.*

6. For all his immense wealth, the first-century BC Roman general and statesman Marcus
   Licinius Crassus Dives ultimately failed to achieve his aims in both war and politics.
7. See *Nicomachean Ethics* 1179ª23–9. Note that Case changes Aristotle's 'gods' [*theoi*] into
   the singular God [*deus*] and transforms Aristotle's cautious statement about the existence of
   divine providence ('as is generally believed') to the more definite 'as he surely does'.
8. Reading *flectatur* instead of *flectantur.*
9. That is, he is an unmoved mover.

Further Reading

CHRP, pp. 231, 327, 331, 343, 801, 813

Lohr, C. H., *Latin Aristotle Commentaries* (Florence, 1988–), II, pp. 85–6

Schmitt, C. B., *John Case and Aristotelianism in Renaissance England* (Kingston, Ontario,
    1983)

    'John Case and Machiavelli', in S. Bertelli and G. Ramakus, eds., *Essays Presented to
        Myron P. Gilmore,* 2 vols. (Florence, 1978), I, pp. 231–40

    'John Case on art and nature', *Annals of Science,* 33 (1976), 543–59

7

Francesco Piccolomini

JILL KRAYE

Introduction

Francesco Piccolomini (1523–1607) studied at the University of Siena, where he also began his distinguished career as a professor of philosophy (1546–9), before moving on to teach first at Macerata (1549–50) and then at Perugia (1550–60). For almost forty years (1560–98) he taught at the University of Padua, the most important centre of Aristotelian studies in Italy, attaining the senior chair in natural philosophy in 1565. Through his courses on the *Physics, De anima, De caelo* and *De generatione et corruptione,* he achieved considerable eminence and renown (not to mention a salary higher than that paid to any previous philosophy professor). His fame attracted students from outside Italy, though the bulk of his audience was composed of young men from the Venetian patriciate. Torquato Tasso, who heard Piccolomini lecture at Padua, described him as 'a veritable sea and ocean of all learning'. Surprisingly, the first work to be published under his name, *A Comprehensive Philosophy of Morals,* appeared when he was sixty years old and dealt with a subject, ethics, on which he never lectured. In 1596 he published an equally encyclopedic work in his own field of natural philosophy, followed in 1600 by a philosophical dictionary, containing some 120 terms. After his retirement in 1598, he returned to Siena, where he continued to produce works on Aristotelian philosophy; his commentaries on *De generatione et corruptione* and *De anima* came out in 1602, and on the *Physics* in 1606, the year before his death.

Piccolomini's lifelong commitment to Aristotelianism was combined with a firmly held devotion to Catholic dogma and a wide-ranging interest in other ancient philosophical systems, especially Platonism and Stoicism. By focusing primarily on the this-worldly issues dealt with by Aristotle, he largely avoids areas of conflict between Peripateticism and Christianity. He sometimes makes the claim that Aristotle is broadly in agreement with Catholic theologians, but more commonly points out the similarities between Platonism and Christianity, while stressing the vague, shadowy and derivative nature of Plato's vision of the afterlife. Piccolomini's eclecticism is apparent in the impressive array of classical, medieval and Renaissance philosophers he cites and in the serious attention he gives to positions, such as the Stoic view of the supreme good, which run counter to those of Aristotle. As far as possible he tries to resolve disagreements between different philosophical schools by emphasizing their common ground. In the end, however, his moral philosophy remains fundamentally Aristotelian.

Although the subjects he treats in *A Comprehensive Philosophy of Morals* are taken from the *Nicomachean Ethics* and *Politics,* the work is not a commentary and is closer in format (though far longer and more detailed) to the type of textbook which became the main vehicle of philosophy instruction in seventeenth-century universities. Instead of following Aristotle's order of exposition, Piccolomini organizes the work into ten levels, each covering an area of moral philosophy: the passions of the soul; the principles of virtue; the semi-virtues; the moral virtues; the intellectual virtues; the heroic virtue; friendship; the instruments of virtue; the supreme good; the political context and application of virtue.

Francesco Piccolomini's *Universa philosophia de moribus* was first published in Venice in 1583; a second, revised edition came out, also in Venice, in 1594. This edition was twice reprinted in Frankfurt (1595 and 1601) and once in Geneva (1596). Around 1603 Piccolomini produced an Italian summary of the work entitled *Compendio della scienza civile,* dedicated to the grand duchess of Tuscany; this treatise remains unpublished. The translation is made from the 1594 Venice edition, pp. 400–1, 410–13, 434–5.

A Comprehensive Philosophy of Morals

LEVEL IX: THE SUPREME GOOD, SELECTIONS

Chapter 1: The Purpose of the Virtues, Namely, the Supreme Good

I know for certain that everyone, on account of a certain stirring of nature within them, desires happiness; but as of yet I have not come across anyone in this world of mortals who is happy. Those who are commonly said to be happy or fortunate are so far from true happiness that they are judged by the wise to be the most unhappy of all. Therefore, it is right that we should be puzzled and that we should make the utmost effort to investigate happiness, so that when we come to know about it, we may discern whether it is a universal human good which we are destined to acquire, or whether our soul's inclination towards it is futile; and also so that when we get to know what happiness is, we may in an appropriate manner discover and marshal those things which lead towards it; and, finally, so that when we perceive what happiness is like, day by day we may more and more be directed and predisposed towards its investigation. Knowledge of happiness is so appropriate to man and is such a powerful force in instructing us how to live well that without it not only do we not know where we are headed, we do not even deserve to be regarded as human beings or to be considered of sound mind. Both its excellence and its utility are so obvious and are implanted so deeply in our souls and appetites that nothing clearer can be said to make these qualities any more conspicuous. Therefore, leaving aside an explanation of these points, and with the help of that immense good, without which we lack the strength to say anything good concerning it, I shall begin my discussion of the supreme good. You happy minds, who, separated from the shadow of the body, constantly inspect the essence of the good, deign to rouse the eye of the soul[1] – the offspring of the supreme good and therefore connected to you by a bond of affinity – to an investigation of the good which has been prepared for it; and when it has been roused, elevate it; and when it has been elevated, turn it towards the parent of us all.

Chapter 2: The Terms by Which the Supreme Good Is Known

On account of its various conditions and its different relationships, the supreme good has been designated by various terms, especially by the Greeks. Although these terms have frequently been confused, they nevertheless have distinct and specific meanings. The general term is *to agathon;* hence, it is called the good, the good itself and the supreme good. The reason for this name is obvious. In addition, it is called *eudaimonia,*[2] a term which is more specific to it. Therefore, Aristotle says in *Nicomachean Ethics* I.4 [1095ª17–19]: 'as for the name, almost everyone is in agreement: for both the multitude and learned men call it *eudaimonia*'. The reason for this name is explained in this opinion of Aristotle; not to mention the fact that the prudence which leads to the supreme good is each person's good [*eu*] daemon [*daimōn*].[3] Moreover, in Aristotle's view, the best daemons are separate minds. There is also a certain outstanding condition of the human mind by which it is elevated to the divine and whose perfection is called *eudaimonia.* Aristotle says this in Book II [chapter 6 (112ª37–8)] of the *Topics,* citing the opinion of Xenocrates that a diligent soul is each person's daemon. For this reason Porphyry, according to the account of Iamblichus in *De mysteriis* IX.8, thought that the highest part of the soul, that is, the mind, was a tutelar deity or daemon; and he said that the happy person was one who possessed a wise mind. In Plato's view, the supreme good could be called *eudaimonia,* in that he thought happy individuals were ruled and guided by the best daemon, for there is frequent mention in Plato of daemons who show human beings the way.[4]

A third term for the supreme good is *makarismos* or beatitude. It is called that because of the joy which accompanies it: according to the ancients, the derivation of *to makarion,* 'that which has beatitude', is *apo tou malista chairein,* 'from very great rejoicing', as Aristotle asserts in *Nicomachean Ethics* VII.11 [1152ᵇ7–8]. These Greek words are especially appropriate to God and in a secondary way are suited to those men who emulate God. Thus, Aristotle says in Book I, chapter 12 [1101ᵇ23–5] of the *Ethics:* 'we speak of gods as *makarizomen kai eudaimonizomen* [enjoying beatitude and happiness] and of especially godlike men as *makarizomen*'. Nevertheless, the term *makarismos* is more appropriate to God and *eudaimonia* to men when they are elevated above the common level of human nature; for God is located above daemons. Archytas the Pythagorean, in his book *On the Good and Happy Man* (cited by Stobaeus in the first section of his *Anthology*),[5] laid down this scheme: in the first place a man acquires probity through the virtues, and to him belongs praise; *makarismos* arises from an abundance of the goods of fortune, a condition which he called *eutuchia; eudaimonia* is constructed from *makarismos* and probity; therefore, if the goods of fortune and nature are taken away from him, his probity is preserved but not his *makarismos* nor his *eudaimonia.* Let us, however, put Archytas aside.

The fourth name for the supreme good is *eutuchia,* that is, favourable and very prosperous fortune, the opposite of which is *dustuchia,* that is, adverse fortune. In Book II [chapter 6 (197ᵇ3–4)] of the *Physics,* Aristotle says that *eutuchia* is either the same thing as happiness or close to it. The reason for this name is either that some people place the supreme good in an abundance of the goods of fortune; or that, at least in Aristotle's view, the goods of fortune are the instruments without which a man cannot be happy;[6] or, finally, that, as Simplicius noted in his commentary on *Physics* II [chapter 6 (198ª10–13)], where there is room for distinction, participation and acquisition, fortune is also taken into account,[7] and for this reason the acquisition of the supreme good can be called *eutuchia.*

Fifthly, happiness is called *eupraxia,* that is, virtuous action,[8] as Aristotle testifies in *Physics* II [chapter 6 (197ᵇ5)]. The reason is that the supreme good is located in the virtuousness of the action, as Aristotle says in Book I [chapter 8] of the *Ethics.* Sixthly, it is called *euzōia* in *Ethics* I.8 [1098ᵇ21–2], in other words, rectitude of life and a life well lived, since virtuous action is the best life for man. Therefore, Plotinus, in *Enneads* I.4,[9] concludes that happiness belongs only to human beings because a full and complete life is suited to them alone among all mortal creatures.

These are the most important terms for happiness. The very learned Marsilio Ficino, in his epitome of Plato's *Euthydemus,* states: '*eudaimonia* signifies knowledge of the good, *eutuchia* acquisition of the good, *eupraxia* vision of the good'.[10] But he neglects certain of the principal terms and does not explain the reason why *eudaimonia* signifies knowledge rather than possession of the good.

Chapter 3: The Different Types of Happiness

Since happiness has contempt for the entire condition of mortality, only a very narrow part of it is seen by mortals and even then quite dimly. It shines brightly, nevertheless, in its own most resplendent dwelling-place. Therefore, when we examine it, it presents itself to us under many different guises. Occupying the first place, in the natural order of things, is the happiness of God. He alone is happy in his essence and, rather than being blissful, is beatitude itself. As St Augustine says in *De trinitate:* 'God is good without quality, great without quantity, the good not in respect to another good but the good of all that is good.'[11] Next comes the happiness of separate minds; but these are not part of the present consideration, since our discussion will concern the supreme good of man.

The supreme good of man can be considered in two senses: either after death in another, truer life or in this life, which is really a pathway. In addition, if the next life is taken into consideration, it can be considered according to the view of the Platonists, who have lightly sketched, rather than firmly explained, various points concerning the supreme good and the misery of the dead, as can be clearly seen in the *Phaedrus, Phaedo, Gorgias,* the tenth book of the *Republic* and other dialogues. Whatever solid information is to be found in these works was taken from Sacred Scriptures.[12] Either we desire a firm and certain account of this matter, such as only our theologians, by the gift of divine revelation, have fully achieved, in which case we must seek the answer from them; or we can enquire solely about that supreme good of man which is destined to come to him while leading a mortal life and inhabiting this inferior world. This supreme good does not require a more exalted grace but is destined to be acquired by means of powers which belong to us naturally. As this is what the Peripatetics talked about, it is my purpose to discuss only this aspect of the supreme good. It is twofold: one type is political and is dealt with chiefly in the first book of the *Ethics;* the other type is located in contemplation and is the subject of the tenth book. I will discuss both according to the Peripatetic position. . . .

Chapter 12: The Peripatetic Position and the Proofs by Which It Is Confirmed

In his treatment of every subject, Aristotle, who was endowed with acute judgement and an exceptionally perspicacious mind, either came up with new thoughts or at any rate ordered and perfected the ideas of others. Dealing with the supreme good in Book I [chapter 8] of the *Nicomachean Ethics,* he did not regard it as located in virtue alone, but rather in an activity which proceeds from virtue. Various arguments can be adduced to confirm this position, some taken from Aristotle, others of my own devising. First of all, the supreme good is located in something which, when it is present in a man, he is said to be happy, and when it is absent, he ceases to be happy. Virtue, however, does not fit this description. This is shown, first, by the fact that a man endowed with virtue can be asleep or can be doing nothing, in which states he will not be happy. It is correct to say that when asleep a virtuous man cannot be told apart from a wicked one, nor a happy man from an unhappy one; and this is also the case when they are doing nothing. When Aristotle states that they cannot be told apart, he should be understood as saying that they cannot be distinguished by means of a secondary act [i.e., an action]; they can, however, be distinguished in terms of a disposition, that is, a primary act. The same minor premise is demonstrated by the fact that a man endowed with virtue can be oppressed by every sort of calamity and tormented by the greatest adversities of nature and of fortune. The situation of such a person is without doubt not as he would unreservedly wish it to be, and therefore no one can reasonably judge him to be happy.

Second, the supreme good is the final goal, desirable solely for its own sake, and worthy not of praise but of honour. Virtue, however, does not fit this description. This is because virtue is desired for the sake of virtuous actions; for something which has an action exists for the sake of that action, as Aristotle says in *De caelo* II [chapter 3 (286ᵃ8–9)]. In addition, since virtue is a disposition, it is numbered among those things which are worthy of praise, not of honour, as was made clear in the discussion of honour and praise.[13]

Third, the supreme good is said to be self-sufficient and complete in and of itself. Something is complete when nothing can be added to it, as is stated in Book I [chapter 2] of *De caelo* and Book V [chapter 16] of the *Metaphysics*. Virtue, however, does not fit this description. Since it is a primary act, a secondary act can be added to it: that is, since it is a disposition it can be completed by means of an action. And since it includes within it an element of potentiality, it incorporates something imperfect, which through actuality, that is, through an action, can be removed. Eternal things, since they are complete, are never in potentiality but are always engaged in activity; for potentiality, since it is united to privation, lacks final completion.

Fourth, everyone agrees that the supreme good is either located in enjoyment or has enjoyment as a mental condition connected to it; and this is confirmed by Plato in the *Philebus* and Aristotle in Book X [chapter 6] of the *Ethics*. Enjoyment arises not from a disposition but from an action. Enjoyment is defined in Book X [chapter 4 (1174ᵇ23)] of the *Ethics* as the completion of an activity. Since therefore enjoyment is the essence of the supreme good or a mental condition connected to it, and since it is produced by an action and is the completion of an action, it is obvious that the supreme good is located in an action.

Fifth, when investigating that supreme good which man is able to enjoy in this life, we are surely investigating the best and most complete thing that man is able to attain, which is perfect in all respects. It is not virtue, however, but only the action which proceeds from it which fits this description. Virtuous action demands virtue as its starting point; it includes within it the instruments of nature and of fortune as its means; and finally, it adds to this the form of an action, on the ground that it is the application and final perfection of goods. So, from virtuous action alone nothing further can be sought; and the person who perfectly enjoys it will not change places with anyone. It therefore must be regarded as the supreme good.

Is there anyone who would not consider a king to be deprived of his perfection and ultimate dignity if, though highly skilled in the art of ruling, he nevertheless loses his kingdom through a fault of nature or of fortune and is not able to fulfill the function of a king? We are investigating the supreme good of man, not a man located beyond the boundaries of nature, but one in the hands of nature and fortune; not a solitary man, but one living in a community and in the company of other men; and not the supreme good of his soul alone, but of the totality of his composite being. To live such a life happily, without impediment, virtue alone is assuredly insufficient. Therefore, Theages was right when he said that the supreme good must be suited to the entire man, not just to parts of him. Man is composed of a body and a soul; therefore, his supreme good must arise from a harmonious combination of all those things which are conducive to the perfection of his composite being.[14]

Sixth, there is the argument based on the goal of human good. The supreme good is located in that which connects us most closely to God, the goal and origin of our good. We are connected to him most closely through an action, not a disposition; this can be seen in relation to contemplation, for a wise disposition unites us to God through the intervention of contemplation. Hence we say that the supreme good of intellective beings is not located in some virtuous disposition but rather in contemplation. This is also confirmed by the authority of Plato, who in the *Euthydemus* [280B–D], also known as 'The Controversialist', affirms that possession without use is worthless. He therefore concludes that it is necessary for someone who is going to be happy not only to possess good things but also to use them. Possession alone brings no benefit. Plato affirms, for example, that if in constructing some piece of work everything is ready to serve its correct function, but the craftsman does not employ these materials, they will be useless.

Finally, if the supreme good is located in virtue, it is either because virtue produces a happy life or because virtue itself is the essence of happiness. If the former, virtue is connected to happiness as cause to effect, for nothing is able to cause itself. If, however, you think it is the latter, I shall use the argument put forward by Alexander of Aphrodisias in Book II, chapter 43, of his *De anima*:[15] if virtue itself were the supreme good, a man endowed with virtue could not reasonably prefer death and forsake life, for by this splendid action he would destroy a virtuous disposition; and if a disposition is more excellent than an action, it must not be disregarded and destroyed for the sake of a splendid action. Nevertheless, the Stoics claim that a man must sometimes prefer death and inflict it on himself. So, in order to be consistent, they are forced to admit that the supreme good is located in an action rather than a disposition.[16]

Since this is Aristotle's position, he is to some extent in agreement with our theologians, who say that in this journey of life the supreme good comes to a person according to his merits, not as a prize. Merits, as they pertain to us, proceed from our virtuous actions, for faith alone is not sufficient, unless it is given form and life; and this happens when it is accompanied by works. It is not enough to believe in God, but rather we are held to believe in God by obeying his laws.[17] Similarly, the supreme good of the next life is not located in a virtuous disposition but in the contemplation of the supreme good, which is an action. Let us conclude, therefore, with Aristotle that, just as in the Olympic games, it is not those who are the best looking who are crowned but those who fight strenuously (for it is they who win), so in the arena of life, it is not those who are endowed only with a virtuous disposition who are honoured with the crown of the supreme good, but those who undertake splendid tasks of virtue.[18]

Chapter 13: Doubts Concerning Aristotle's Position

Aristotle's position provokes no less serious doubts than those which seemed to call into question the views of the Stoics; indeed, these doubts are perhaps more valid and of greater significance. In the first place, there are those arguments in favour of the Stoic position [that the supreme good is located in a virtuous disposition] which have already been set out.[19] In the second place, someone might object that in common usage we understand the term supreme good to refer to something which, when we have acquired it, accompanies us forever, something which is permanent and cannot be taken away. An action, however, does not fit this description, but a disposition does; for an action is very dependent on other things, and if the instruments of nature and of fortune are lacking, the action is ruined, and we cannot do what we unreservedly want to do.

In the third place, if the supreme good had been situated in an action, the capacity to obtain the supreme good, which is a characteristic [*affectio*] belonging exclusively to human beings, would not follow on from human nature, nor would it flow directly from our internal principles, as characteristics belonging to us must do. For an action does not depend squarely on our internal principles but demands various external things. The capacity to obtain a virtuous disposition does, however, depend on principles belonging to the human species.

In the fourth place, if the supreme good were located in an action, when men who were poor and those who were congenitally unhealthy failed to obtain the supreme good, they could with justification lay the blame for their misery on nature or on their parents, inasmuch as it would be their fault that these people lacked the instruments required for those actions in which the Peripatetics locate the supreme good. This is false, because each of us is responsible for our own misery and our own happiness; and the one thing which nature seems to have placed entirely in our hands is virtue.

In the fifth place, if the supreme good were located in an action, the happy person, like a chameleon, would be subject to various alterations. Human beings frequently move from a state of leisure to one of occupation, from sleep to wakefulness and vice versa; therefore, sometimes they will be happy and sometimes they will not. Indeed, they will resemble a character in a play or a story: one minute they will sparkle, the next minute they will be shrinking violets; and sometimes they will sparkle more brightly, at other times more dimly, for some actions are more illustrious, others less so. Virtuous dispositions alone always remain the same.

In the sixth place, if the supreme good is a virtuous action, either it involves all the virtues at the same time, or it involves one virtue at one time, another at another time. It cannot involve all of them at the same time because man is not able to perform a task involving all the virtues at the same time. If it is an action involving one virtue at one time, another at another time, man will never enjoy the whole, uniform good at the same time, but rather one part of it at one time, another part at another time. Nor will this kind of good stay with him; it will continuously move on and fade away.

In the seventh place, if the supreme good is located in an action, why is Aristotle in doubt, in Book I [chapter 11] of the *Ethics,* as to whether the supreme good of the dead is affected by the prosperous or adverse fortunes of their descendants? The actions of the dead do not live on.

In the eighth place, virtue is an efficient cause, including actions within its power. That which a thing has in the capacity of a cause is said to be more outstanding, more excellent and less dependent than that which it has in the capacity of an effect. Therefore, the perfection of a [virtuous] action is contained in a manner which is somehow more outstanding in the virtue [than in the action]. Indeed, an action is what necessarily follows from a moral virtue, for someone endowed with moral virtue, when the opportunity is offered to him, cannot (unless he fights with himself) fail to act. Consequently, virtue is sufficient to constitute the supreme good.

In the ninth place, virtue is like peace, whereas action is like war. And just as other goods have some application, so the supreme good must have the best application. A [virtuous] action therefore deserves with more justification to be called an application of the supreme good than to be called the supreme good itself. This doubt expresses the view of Aristotle himself and is of the utmost significance.[20]

Chapter 14: Resolution of the Difficulty

Frequently famous men, either because they are using a different method of philosophizing, or because they are considering the same thing from a different angle or are speaking in a different way, put forward views which on the surface seem to conflict with each other. Nevertheless, when these views are examined more closely, they are found to be the same – if not completely, then at least for the most part. I think that this is the case with the difficulty in question, for in many respects those who hold these [apparently differing] opinions seem to be in agreement. They agree, in the first place, that the foundation of the supreme good is virtue. Second, they agree that an action, in the way mentioned earlier – that is, when the opportunity is offered – necessarily follows from moral virtue.

But although they are in agreement on these matters, the supreme good can be considered in two ways: either as a disposition or as an action; either as a foundation or as something which is built on a foundation; either as something which is totally the same and accompanies us without fluctuation, or as something which is subject to a certain degree of fluctuation; and, finally, either as a thing in itself or as an application of a thing. Therefore, while the Stoics, and along with them most Platonists, looked upon the supreme good as a disposition, a foundation and a thing which is always the same, the Peripatetics, by contrast, considered it to be an action, a result and an application, in that it is a final perfection. In addition, the Stoics considered the supreme good in relation to private life – a solitary existence rather than a public one. Aristotle, however, considered it in relation to public life, spent in association with, and in the company of, other people. The Peripatetics proposed for themselves the most exact perfection of the supreme good, arising from a combination of goods of the soul and the gifts of fortune and of nature, so that nothing in this life which might contribute to it was missing. The Stoics, on the other hand, took into consideration only what was most important. Finally, the Peripatetics considered the supreme good insofar as it is without any impediment and is endowed with its own characteristic mental state, composed of gladness and joy. This state is the result of an action that proceeds from a disposition, not of a disposition alone. Thus, depending on the way that it is considered, the supreme good can be regarded as existing in virtue alone or in a [virtuous] action.

Let us conclude, therefore, that the supreme good when considered as a foundation is located in virtue; when considered as a form and final perfection, in a virtuous and perfect action; when considered as a mental state, in the enjoyment which proceeds from a perfect action; when considered as instruments or (as the Stoics call them) conveniences or (as the Peripatetics say) necessities, in the gifts of nature and of fortune; when considered as a distinguishing mark, in honour and glory; when considered as a result, in tranquillity of the soul and a life in harmony with nature; when considered as an object and the final goal which brings us bliss, in the best and greatest God; and, finally, when considered as the culmination of everything that comes together to form the supreme good of this life, in a harmonious combination of all goods. On this basis, the difficulty is resolved. It is clear that there is truth in the arguments put forward by all sides; and it is clear, finally, that the Peripatetic view is nearer to the common manner of speaking and corresponds more closely to our feelings and our experience. . . .

Chapter 31: When a Man Dies, Is His Supreme Good Also Destroyed?

Since we are discussing the supreme good of someone living in the present life, the following doubt arises: does the death of a happy person destroy his supreme good? In the view of both Plato and Christian theologians, we can say that not only is his supreme good not destroyed, it is perfected; for the supreme good of this life is good insofar as it leads us to the supreme good of the next life. As for Aristotle's view, it is more difficult to say. On the one hand, it seems that it must be the case that the supreme good of a dead person is preserved. First, because if it were not preserved, a happy man should not, under any circumstances, make a rational decision to choose death, for in that case he would be choosing the destruction of his supreme good. Second, Aristotle states in Book I, chapter 11, of the *Ethics* that when a happy man dies, events which befall his descendants and friends, if they are of sufficient magnitude, can increase or diminish his happiness. This could not happen unless his happiness was preserved, since what does not exist cannot be harmed. On the other hand, Aristotle's support for the view that the supreme good vanishes after death is apparent, first, in Book XII [chapter 7 (1072^{b}15)] of the *Metaphysics,* where he says that we enjoy the supreme good for only a short period of time; and second, in Book III [chapter 5 (430^{a}20–5)] of *De anima,* where he says that in death knowledge is destroyed, because an animal thinks nothing without the faculty of imagination [*phantasia*].[21] This is confirmed by his statement in Book I [chapter 4 (408^{b}25–9)] of *De anima* that it is not the soul which thinks but the person, not the soul which acts, but the person; hence, when a person dies, the disposition and action in which his supreme good are located necessarily vanish.

The supreme good, however, is said to be preserved in two ways: first, thanks to the memory and collective word of mouth of humanity; second, by virtue of the instruments and certain external elements of the supreme good – or, at any rate, items which accompany it, such as children, relatives, friends, riches spent on magnificent endeavours and other outstanding exploits. These things are so closely connected to the supreme good that they seem in some sense to be a part of it. Therefore, they always exhibit it, in some way, to his descendants; and turning their attention towards these things, they say, depending on the vagaries of fortune, that the happiness of the dead person is now increased, now diminished. And for this reason we see that prudent men dispose, arrange and lay down in their wills and codicils what should be done with their worldly goods after their death, on the ground that this is something which is of concern to them. And those who, in the manner of Diogenes and Socrates, entirely neglect everything to do with corpses, funerals, tombs and other things of this kind, show themselves to be indifferent to public happiness and go against the commonly held opinions of the people, which a man living in a political community must not disregard. Let us conclude, therefore, that, according to Aristotle, the death of a happy man destroys the essence of his supreme good. Only the memory of it is preserved, along with some of the things which accompany it – its instruments and certain external achievements.

But the objection has been raised that if this is so, it will never be possible for a happy man to make a rational choice to end his life. My reply to this is to say that it does not follow: for he must choose death rather than commit some villainous act; but if he were to commit that act, it would completely overthrow his supreme good to such an extent that it would be converted into misery. If, however, he were to put an end to a splendid life with a splendid death, he would embellish his supreme good (as it is permitted to him to do) by means of that splendid action. Another objection which has been raised is that if a man's supreme good were to perish at his death, events which befell his descendants would have no bearing on him, nor would his supreme good be increased or diminished. To this I reply that when the question is asked whether the fortunes of a dead man's descendants have any bearing on him, we should say, with Aristotle, that partly they do, and partly they do not. They have no bearing in that he does not feel them, nor do they alter the essence of his supreme good; therefore, we would not say that, having been happy, he is made unhappy. But they do have a bearing by virtue of those things that survive after his death, which are like the rays and brightness of his extinguished light; for we say that the happiness of the dead person is either increased or diminished on account of what happens to these things.

Speaking of those events which either increase or diminish happiness, they should be placed in the following order: first come those events that happen to the person while he is alive, which have the greatest power to increase or diminish his happiness; second comes what happens to his children and friends while he is alive; and in third place comes what happens to his descendants and friends after his death. I say his friends not because they are still his friends, but because they were his friends before his death; for when one friend dies, the other is no longer his friend, since their reciprocal affection is not preserved. Thus, friendship with fellow citizens who have died is not preserved; however, our affection, memory and concern for those things associated with them are preserved.

Translator's Notes

1. That is, the mind.
2. Although *eudaimonia* is usually translated simply as happiness, it in fact refers to a state of flourishing, well-being, prosperity and good fortune.
3. The Greek term *daimōn* refers to a supernatural being, with a nature intermediate between that of gods and men.
4. Most notably, the daemon of Socrates: see, e.g., *Apology* 31C–D.
5. See Johannes Stobaeus, *Sententiae ex thesauris Graecorum delectae . . .*, ed. C. Gesner, 3rd ed. (Zurich, 1559), p. 13 (section 1: 'On virtue'); for a modern edition see Johannes Stobaeus, *Anthologii libri duo posteriores,* ed. O. Hense, 2 vols. (Berlin, 1894), I, pp. 57–8 (III.1.107); see also B. Centrone, ed., *Pseudopythagorica ethica* (Naples, 1990), pp. 71, 109, 138–40. Archytas of Tarentum was a famous Pythagorean of the first half of the fourth century BC; this work, however, is a Hellenistic forgery, part of a corpus of pseudo-Pythagorean writings: see H. Thesleff, *An Introduction to the Pythagorean Writings of the Hellenistic Period* (Åbo, 1961), pp. 8–11, at 10.
6. See *Nicomachean Ethics* I.8 (1099^a31–1099^b8).
7. Simplicius, *In Aristotelis Physicorum libros quattuor priores commentaria,* ed. H. Diels, Commentaria in Aristotelem Graeca, 9 (Berlin, 1882), pp. 354–61.
8. *Eupraxia* means doing well, as opposed to mere good luck.
9. Piccolomini wrongly cites *Enneads* IV.3.
10. M. Ficino, *In Euthydemum epitome,* in his *Opera omnia,* 2 vols. (Basel, 1576; reprinted Turin, 1959), II, pp. 1300–3, at 1301.
11. See Augustine, *De trinitate* V.1 and VIII.3; Piccolomini wrongly cites III.10.
12. For the Christian tradition that Plato, in his travels to Egypt, gained access to the Old Testament, on which he drew in his works, see A. S. Riginos, *Platonica: The Anecdotes Concerning the Life and Writings of Plato* (Leiden, 1976), p. 65.
13. See *Nicomachean Ethics* I.12.
14. See Stobaeus, *Sententiae,* p. 14, where this statement occurs in a quotation from Archytas, not Theages; a treatise entitled *On Virtue,* attributed to Theages, immediately precedes the selections from Archytas, and Piccolomini presumably failed to notice that a new author was signalled. For a modern edition of the passage see Stobaeus, *Anthologii libri duo,* I,

pp. 61–2 (III.1.112); see also Centrone, ed., *Pseudopythagorica ethica*, pp. 74–5, 111–12, 151.

15. Alexander of Aphrodisias, *Quaestiones naturales et morales et De fato . . . De anima liber primus . . . De anima liber II* (Venice, 1539), fols. 58v–60r (II.43: 'Virtue is not sufficient for happiness') at 58v.
16. The Stoics, in fact, held the opposite view.
17. Piccolomini is endorsing the Catholic position on good works and arguing against the Protestant belief in salvation by faith alone.
18. See *Nicomachean Ethics* I.8 (1099a3–10).
19. See Piccolomini, *Universa philosophia de moribus*, pp. 409–10 (Level IX, ch. 11).
20. See *Nicomachean Ethics* X.7 (1177b4–12).
21. For Piccolomini's views on the process of intellection see *CHRP*, pp. 527–30.

Further Reading

Baldini, A. E., 'Per la biografia di Francesco Piccolomini', *Rinascimento*, 20 (1980), 389–420
  'La politica "etica" di Francesco Piccolomini', *Il pensiero politico*, 13 (1980), 161–85
CHRP, pp. 313, 329, 347, 351, 353, 357–8, 363, 481–3, 527–31, 533–4, 831
Lewis, C. J. T., 'Scotist influence on the natural philosophy of Francesco Piccolomini', in C. Bérube, ed., *Regnum hominis et regnum Dei: Acta quarta congressus scotistici internationalis, Patavii . . . 1976*, 2 vols. (Rome, 1978), II, pp. 291–6
Lohr, C. H., *Latin Aristotle Commentaries* (Florence, 1988–), II, pp. 331–42
Poppi, A., 'Il problema della filosofia morale nella scuola padovana del Rinascimento: platonismo e aristotelismo nella definizione del metodo dell'etica', in *Platon et Aristote à la Renaissance: XVIe colloque international de Tours* (Paris, 1976), pp. 105–37
Santinello, G., *Tradizione e dissenso nella filosofia veneta fra Rinascimento e modernità* (Padua, 1991), pp. 162–6

8

Coimbra Commentators

JILL KRAYE

Introduction

From 1592 to 1606, the Jesuits of the University of Coimbra in Portugal published a course of studies on Aristotelian philosophy, known as the *Conimbricensis Collegii Societatis Jesu commentarii*. The idea was conceived by Pedro de Fonseca, who assigned the project to Emmanuel de Goes, provincial of the Jesuit Order in Portugal. Intended to serve as textbooks in Jesuit universities, the commentaries, which were the work of several authors, combined humanist philological scholarship with traditional scholastic philosophical exegesis. In the *quaestiones* (questions), where most of the philosophical analysis is located, there is often a focus on issues of particular relevance to Christian doctrine, in line with the Counter-Reformation conception of philosophy as an enterprise in the service of Catholic theology. Most of the commentaries were on Aristotle's natural philosophy treatises: the *Physics* (1592), *De caelo* (1592), the *Meteorology* (1592), *Parva naturalia* (1592), *De generatione et corruptione* (1597) and *De anima* (1598); there was also a commentary on Aristotelian logic (1606). All the volumes were frequently reprinted and widely used as university textbooks in the first half of the seventeenth century, gaining considerable popularity even in Protestant northern Europe, despite their strong Catholic associations.

The Coimbra commentary on the *Nicomachean Ethics* (1593) is not a full-scale treatment (it lacks the Aristotelian text and the literal explanations found in the other volumes) but rather a brief compendium, consisting of nine disputations. Each disputation is divided into questions, which are subdivided into articles. Different formats are employed, all of them variations on standard scholastic methods of exposition: from the phrase-by-phrase analysis of an Aristotelian pronouncement (as in article 3) to the elaborate presentation of arguments in favour of or opposed to a proposition, followed by objections and responses to these objections (article 1). The style of writing adopted in scholastic treatises did not change a great deal from the thirteenth to the late sixteenth century: it tends to be formulaic, jargon-ridden, repetitive and rather stilted, but has the virtues of clarity and precision.

The Jesuits were committed by their founder, Ignatius Loyola, to follow Aristotle in philosophy and Thomas Aquinas in theology. This double commitment is reflected not only in the use of Thomas as the prime interpreter of Aristotle, but also in the topics selected for discussion, many of which are taken from the *Summa theologiae* rather than from the *Nicomachean Ethics*. Article 2, for instance, includes a debate on the nature of the supernatural beatitude of the next life: the intellectualist view of Thomas Aquinas, which became the accepted position of the Dominicans, is upheld against the voluntarism of other medieval theologians, especially the Franciscans, and also against those who argued that the intellect and the will are simultaneously involved in beatitude. The selection of sources drawn upon by the Coimbra commentators is wide and eclectic, ranging from the Bible and commentaries on the *Sentences* of Peter Lombard (the most important medieval textbook of theology) to the dialogues of Plato.

The Latin text of the 1593 Lisbon edition is reprinted in *Curso conimbricense* (Lisbon, 1957–), I: *Moral a Nicómaco, de Aristóteles,* ed. A. A. de Andrade; see pp. 118–30 for Disputation III, Question 3. There were frequent editions of the commentary until the 1630s: Coimbra (c. 1594), Lyons (six editions from 1593 to 1616), Venice (1593 and 1616) and Cologne (sixteen editions from 1603 to 1631).

Commentary on the Nicomachean Ethics

DISPUTATION III, QUESTION 3

Whether Happiness Consists in an Activity of the Soul

Article I: Arguments in favour of the proposition
Since happiness [*felicitas*] must be present in the person who is called happy, and since it has already been demonstrated that happiness does not reside in goods of the body,[1] it necessarily follows that it must reside in goods of the soul. Furthermore, speaking in a general manner, goods of the soul are either faculties [*potentiae*], dispositions [*habitus*] or activities [*operationes*]; since faculties and dispositions are directed towards activities, and since happiness is desired for its own sake, we must necessarily assert that happiness consists in an activity of the soul. This is shown by Aristotle in *Nicomachean Ethics* I.7 and X.6, *Politics* II.3 and *Magna moralia* II.10. And it can be confirmed in the following way: happiness is man's ultimate perfection; everything which is perfect exists in actuality [*in actu*];[2] and the final actuality of those things which lay claim to an activity is the activity itself.

Three objections to this proposition might be raised. First, beatitude [*beatitudo*] is defined by Boethius as a condition [*status*] made complete by the accumulation of all goods.[3] Therefore, beatitude does not consist in an activity, but rather in a condition and, so to speak, a disposition. Second, if beatitude consisted in an activity, no one would be called happy unless he produced that activity in actuality. This is absurd since it would mean that the same person would at one moment be happy for a brief time, then at another moment would be unhappy.[4] Therefore, it cannot be so. Third, a disposition is superior to an action; therefore, beatitude must be located in a disposition, not in an action or an activity. That a disposition is superior to an action is proved by the fact that a disposition is the active beginning as well as the end of its action, since the action is brought about by the disposition, and we repeatedly perform the action in order to perfect the disposition. Likewise, as Aristotle states in *Topics* III.1 [116ª13–14], things which are of a more perfect condition are more stable; and dispositions are by definition more stable, since they are permanent, whereas actions immediately fade away.

In reply to the first objection, one can cite St Thomas Aquinas, *Summa theologiae* IaIIae, question 3, article 2, where he maintains that when beatitude is defined as a condition, it indicates simply that the blissful person [*beatus*] is in a condition of perfect good. Therefore, the proposition that beatitude is a condition is not essential or formal,[5] but rather causal, as if it were stated that beatitude was the cause of the condition of perfection, as Cardinal Cajetan notes in his commentary on this passage.[6] The reply to the second objection is that for someone to be called happy, it is sufficient for that person to be engaged in this action as far as reason prescribes and to the extent that is permitted by the condition of this life and by human weakness. As for the third argument, dealing with the question of whether a disposition or an action is more perfect, it should be asserted that, in an unqualified sense [*simpliciter*], an action is superior to a disposition. This is so, first, because whatever is less dependent is by nature more excellent; and an action depends less on a disposition than vice versa, since a natural disposition, which is what we are speaking about, does not exist except because of an action, whereas an action can exist without a disposition. Second, that thing for the sake of which something else exists is more distinguished than the thing which exists for its sake, as Aristotle says in *Physics* II.3 [195ª24–6] and *Magna moralia* I.1; and a disposition exists on account of an action, as if on account of something optimal. Therefore, in *Physics* VII.3 [247ª2–4] Aristotle defines a virtue as a proclivity of that which has been perfected towards that which is optimal. In other words, as St Thomas Aquinas explains in his commentary on this passage, a virtue is a quality by which a subject is appropriately perfected so as to perform an action which in comparison with a virtuous disposition is something optimal.[7] Therefore, it seems that it cannot be denied that an action is superior, in an absolute sense, to a disposition, at any rate in natural things. This is not the place to decide what would be the case for supernatural things – an issue which certain people are in the habit of debating.

It will be easy for someone to refute the objections to our assertion about a natural action by saying that although a disposition is the beginning of an action and its equivocal cause, this does not make it more noble, since it is not the principal equivocal cause but only the instrumental cause.[8] Likewise, although we act in order to perfect a disposition, nevertheless the disposition itself is perfected for the sake of the activity – so that, for instance, we can perform the activity more readily and agreeably; therefore, it remains valid that the end purpose of a disposition is an activity. In reply to the second part of the third objection, let it be said with Richard of Middleton, in his commentary on the fourth book of the *Sentences* (distinction 49, part 1, question 4),[9] that Aristotle's pronouncement [in *Topics* III.1] is to be under-stood with the proviso that all other things are equal, which in the proposition under examination is not the case, as can be seen from what has been said, since an activity in other respects has greater perfection.

Article II: In which activity [of the soul] is happiness located?

In order for us to explain which activity [of the soul] happiness consists in, it must be noted that there are two types of happiness: supernatural and natural. Moreover, both types are further divided into two parts: supernatural happiness is divided into that part which concerns this mortal life and that which concerns the next life; likewise, natural happiness is divided into speculative and practical happiness.

The supernatural beatitude which is attained in the next life consists in an intuitive contemplation of the divine nature, as St Thomas Aquinas maintains in *Summa contra gentiles* III.25–6 and *Quaestiones quodlibetales* VIII, article 19. This position is defended in various places by his followers and by others against John Duns Scotus in his questions on Peter Lombard's *Sentences* Book IV, distinction XLIX, questions

4 and 5,[10] against Henry of Ghent, *Summae quaestionum ordinariarum* article 49, question 6,[11] against Giles of Rome, *Quodlibeta* III, question 19[12] and against many others who assert that the previously mentioned beatitude is located in an act of loving God, after he has been clearly seen. Likewise, [Thomas's view is defended] against St Bonaventure in his commentary on the *Sentences* Book IV, distinction 49, part 1, question 5,[13] against Albertus Magnus in his commentary on the same work, Book IV, distinction 48, article 4,[14] against Alexander of Hales, *Summa theologiae* Part III, question 23, section 1, and Part IV, question 92, section 2, article 4,[15] and against others who place beatitude in both acts, of the intellect and of the will, at the same time, that is, in intuitive contemplation of the divine nature and in love or enjoyment of the same.[16]

The position of St Thomas Aquinas, which his supporters confirm by many arguments, can be briefly explained as follows. Beatitude in the formal sense is nothing other than the acquisition and possession of the ultimate good; and only the clear vision of God lays claim to this; therefore, it alone is beatitude. The major premise is accepted by everyone, as can be seen by these words from I Corinthians 9[:24]: 'So run, that ye may obtain', and from I Timothy 6[:12]: 'lay hold on eternal life'. The minor premise is proved by that fact that the will is not a faculty of apprehension but of desire, and its action is not apprehension but inclination, by which it is pulled towards the love object, according to what St Augustine says in his *Confessions* XIII.9: 'My love is my weight'. The intellect, on the other hand, is a faculty of apprehension, which by means of its particular mode of operating pulls the object towards it, and when it is present and united to it, possesses it. Therefore, beatitude consists in a clear vision of God.

This can likewise be shown by means of the following syllogism: the highest beatitude consists in the most perfect of all activities; the intuitive contemplation of the divine essence is the most perfect of all activities; therefore, the highest beatitude consists in the intuitive contemplation of the divine essence. The minor premise is proved, first, because that faculty by which intuitive contemplation is produced, that is, the intellect, is the most noble of all, as Aristotle shows in *Nicomachean Ethics* X.7–8. It is also proved because an object of the intellect is simpler and more abstracted than an object of the will, since the intellect is carried to a thing by a perfect action, which abstracts the thing from a state of existence. The will, on the other hand, desires nothing by a perfect act except with reference to a state of existence: for example, no one chooses or loves money unless he wants to possess it.

As for the supernatural beatitude which pertains to this life, since this type of beatitude is a tendency towards that supreme happiness which we have just been speaking about, it is certainly necessary that it is contained above all in an action of love [*caritas*],[17] since such a tendency comes into being in particular through meritorious actions, which love partly brings forth and partly exerts control over. For this reason, Christ the Lord, the teacher of the heavenly doctrine, in the Sermon on the Mount, when discussing the beatitudes of this life, decreed that beatitude consists in virtuous actions.[18] Nor is it valid to object that, according to the ranking and order of nature, the will, in which love resides, is less perfect than the intellect; for it is sufficient that the will is more perfect when considered with respect to the task and procedure of striving through meritorious actions towards the celestial homeland and the vision of God, as towards our ultimate end as intellectual creatures.

Therefore, we reject the view of those who place the supernatural beatitude of this life above all in the supernatural cognition of God or in the gift of wisdom. For although this gift and others of its kind, which are infused into our souls, advance us towards the blessed life, that advancement consists particularly in actions of love. We have said actions of love rather than of grace because grace, according to the view of those who distinguish it from love – a view we strongly support – is said not to be, strictly speaking, the beginning of an action or at any rate not the immediate beginning, which is instead love. Since, however, beatitude is located in an activity, it is to be attributed to that disposition from which such an activity immediately arises, as its source and beginning.

Finally, the natural happiness of this life is divided into two types, as we indicated already; and Aristotle shows in *Nicomachean Ethics* X.7 that one type is practical and has the active life as its end, while the other type is contemplative and has the contemplative life as its end. Since practical happiness must of necessity be located in an action of the practical life, it consists in an activity based on moral virtue, above all prudence, which is the regulator of virtues and obtains the highest place amongst them. Contemplative happiness is located in contemplation, especially the contemplation of God and other immaterial substances, since this is the most noble activity of the speculative intellect. And while we remain in this condition (taking no account of the next life towards which we are progressing and in which we hope to attain supernatural beatitude), we do not possess God in a more perfect way through our natural faculties.

Article III: Explanation of Aristotle's definition of happiness
Having reached this point, it will not be difficult to understand the definition of happiness given by Aristotle in *Nicomachean Ethics* I.7 [1098a15–18]: happiness is an activity of the soul based on reason, or not without reason, in conformity with virtue in a complete lifetime.

Happiness is said to be an activity of the soul based on reason or the intellect, that is, an activity produced by the intellective faculty; or not without reason, that is, prescribed and regulated by reason, since human actions are produced either by the intellect or by other faculties which the intellect rules and governs. Happiness is said to be in conformity with virtue because it is necessary for an action in which happiness is located to be honest and in agreement with right reason. The proviso 'in a complete lifetime' is added at the end because just as one swallow does not make a summer, so one day or one activity does not make a man happy. Consequently, for someone to be called happy, it is necessary for that person to pursue this activity for the course of an entire life or for a long period of time.

If this definition is taken in the sense which it plainly conveys, it applies to both practical and speculative happiness, as will be clear to anyone who considers it. But according to Aristotle, who in the passage cited earlier was discussing only active happiness, it applies to active happiness alone; and in accordance with this limitation, only moral virtue is to be understood by the term virtue, for it is in moral virtue alone that active happiness is located.

You should note a few points here. The first is that although in this life, which is so vulnerable to illnesses and discomforts of both body and soul, neither active nor contemplative happiness can be perfectly possessed, and although while we remain in this condition neither can completely satisfy our appetite, let us nevertheless assuage this appetite to some extent; for a prudent and wise person bears with a calm and imperturbable spirit the lack of those things which he is unable to obtain.

The second point is that natural contemplative happiness is not situated in contemplation in the same way that the supernatural beatitude of the next life is situated in the intuitive cognition of the divine nature. For, since meditation on God and separate substances can be found in this life together with depraved morals – though no one with such morals would be called happy – the point must be made that, although the essence of natural contemplative happiness is located, as we have indicated, above all in contemplation, nevertheless it is necessary to include in the definition of such happiness moral probity and virtuous actions, which are not however included in the essence of supernatural beatitude. The reason for this distinction is that it is clear that moral well-being [*sanitas*] does not necessarily accompany the previously mentioned natural contemplation. Moral well-being does necessarily follow, however, from a vision of the divine essence, in which it is in effect contained; and in the very instant that it is brought forth it gives birth itself to rectitude of the will, love of God and the other things which are required for that condition in which all goods are amassed.

The third point is that contemplative happiness is more perfect than active happiness. This clearly emerges from the fact that since contemplation by its very nature is sought for its own sake, it is nobler and more excellent than practical action [*praxis*], as Aristotle showed in *Nicomachean Ethics* VI.13 and X.7, as well as in *Politics* VII.2.

Plato expressed the same opinion in the *Philebus* [33B], in which he says that a life dedicated to contemplation is the most divine of all; and in the *Statesman* [271C–272D], where he lists two kingdoms: one ruled by Jupiter, signifying action, and the other (which he preferred) ruled by Saturn, signifying contemplation. You can find the same view in the second chapter of Alcinous's *Didaskalikos* and in the sixth *Lecture* of Maximus of Tyre.[19]

Translator's Notes

1. In disputation III, question 2.
2. In Aristotelian philosophy the process of change is explained as a transition from potentiality (*dunamis* in Greek), a state in which something is potentially what it might become, to actuality (*energeia* in Greek), a state in which it actually is that thing: e.g., when an acorn becomes a full-grown oak tree, its potentiality has been transformed into an actuality. See *Physics* III.1 ($200^b25–201^a29$).
3. Boethius, *Consolation of Philosophy* III.prosa 2.7–8, quoted from Thomas Aquinas, *Summa theologiae* IaIIae, q. 3, a. 2, cited in the subsequent paragraph.
4. That is, he would be happy only when he was actually in a state of happiness; when he was merely potentially in a state of happiness, he would be considered unhappy.

5. That is, beatitude is not in essence or by definition a condition.
6. Thomas Aquinas, *Prima secundae partis Summae sacrae theologiae . . .* , comment. T. de Vio [= Cardinal Cajetan] (Antwerp, 1576), p. 11: 'when beatitude is said to be a condition made perfect by the accumulation of all goods, the predicate is not essential but causal, so that beatitude is understood as the cause and the condition as the effect'. The Dominican theologian Tommaso de Vio (1469–1534) rose to become general of his order (1508–18) and was created a cardinal in 1517. His commentary on the *Summa theologiae* (written 1507–22) helped to initiate the sixteenth-century revival of Thomism.
7. Thomas Aquinas, *In octo libros De physico auditu sive Physicorum Aristotelis,* ed. M. Pirotta (Naples, 1953), pp. 404–5 (Book VII, lecture 6, 1859–60).
8. In scholastic terminology, a univocal cause is of the same nature as its effect (e.g., human generation), while an equivocal cause is of a superior nature (e.g., generation which occurs through the sun's influence); an instrumental cause is secondary and subservient to a principal cause: e.g., the author is the principal cause of a book, while the pen he uses is the instrumental cause. See R. Goclenius, *Lexicon philosophicum* (Frankfurt am Main, 1613), pp. 356–8; J. Micraelius, *Lexicon philosophicum terminorum philosophis usitatorum . . .* (Jena, 1653), cols. 213, 549.
9. It is disputed whether the Franciscan theologian and philosopher Richard of Middleton (Richardus de Mediavilla) (b. c. 1249) was English or French. His main writings consist of a commentary on the *Sentences, Quodlibeta* and *Quaestiones disputatae.* On a number of issues he abandoned the traditional doctrines of his order, in favour of the teaching of Thomas Aquinas.
10. The Franciscan theologian and philosopher John Duns Scotus (c. 1265–1308) was known as the 'subtle doctor'. In his commentary on the mid twelfth-century *Sentences* of Peter Lombard, he gives primacy to love and the will in contrast to Thomas, for whom reason and knowledge hold first place.
11. Henry of Ghent (d. 1293) was known as the 'solemn doctor'; a member of the secular clergy, he was an influential proponent of Augustinianism.
12. Giles of Rome (Egidio Colonna; 1243/7–1316) was elected general of the Augustinian Order in 1292; though taught by Thomas Aquinas (1269–71) and in agreement with him on some points, he maintained the primacy of will over intellect.
13. The Franciscan theologian St Bonaventure (c. 1217–74) was known as the 'seraphic doctor'. He was elected minister general of his order in 1257. His most extensive work is his commentary on the *Sentences.*
14. The German theologian and philosopher Albertus Magnus (c. 1200–80) entered the Dominican Order in 1223 and held the Dominican chair in theology at Paris (1245–8), where he wrote his commentary on *Sentences.* Thomas Aquinas was his pupil.
15. The English Franciscan theologian and philosopher Alexander of Hales (c. 1186–1245) was known as the 'irrefutable doctor'. His major work, the *Summa theologica,* was left incomplete at his death and continued by William of Melitona and others.
16. For example, the Spanish Jesuit theologian Francisco Suárez (1548–1617) in his *De ultimo fine* (disputation VII, section 1). For a translation of Suárez's *De legibus* III.4 see J. Kraye, ed., *Cambridge Translations of Renaissance Philosophical Texts,* II: *Political Philosophy* (Cambridge, 1997), ch. 3.
17. *Caritas* is a love directed primarily towards God but also towards our fellow human beings as objects of God's love. It is the most important of the theological virtues ('faith, hope, love . . . and the greatest of these is love': I Corinthians 13:13).
18. Matthew 5:3–11.
19. The *Didaskalikos* is an elementary manual of instruction in Platonism, written in Greek in the second century AD; until recently the author, Alcinous, has been identified with the Middle Platonist Albinus: see Alcinous, *The Handbook of Platonism,* trans. J. Dillon (Oxford, 1993), pp. ix–xiii. Maximus of Tyre (c. 125–85) was a Platonizing sophist and author of forty-one extant *Lectures (Dialexeis),* containing low-level, popular philosophy, studded with quotations from Plato and others.

Further Reading

CHRP, pp. 145–6, 229, 327, 512–14, 607, 798, 814

Lohr, C. H., *Latin Aristotle Commentaries* (Florence, 1988–), I: *Renaissance Authors,* pp. 98–9

Schmitt, C. B., *Aristotle and the Renaissance* (Cambridge, Mass., 1983), pp. 41–2, 138

Part III.
Aristotelian Ethics and Christianity

9

Juan Luis Vives

JOHN MONFASANI

Introduction

The Spanish humanist, philosopher and educational theorist Juan Luis Vives (1492–1540) was born in Valencia, the child of converted Jews. After receiving his early humanist training in Spain, he went to Paris in 1509, where he developed a lifelong hatred for the obscurities and complexities of scholastic philosophy. In 1512 he moved to Bruges, where he worked as a private teacher. Transferring to Louvain in 1517, he lectured publicly at the university there for several years. It was in Louvain that he made the acquaintance of Erasmus. The great Dutch humanist commissioned Vives to write a commentary on St Augustine's *City of God,* which was published in Basel in 1522, with a dedicatory letter to Henry VIII. A year later Vives travelled to England, where he established ties with Erasmus's great friend Thomas More and also with Queen Catherine of Aragon. He was hired by Cardinal Wolsey to teach Greek at Oxford and later became personal tutor to Princess Mary, the daughter of Henry VIII and Catherine. In 1528, a few months before Henry divorced Catherine, Vives returned to Bruges, which remained the centre of his activities until his death.

In 1524 Vives's *converso* father, a successful merchant, was arrested by the Spanish Inquisition on the charge of resuming Jewish religious practices. After a trial that lasted two years, he was burned at the stake. Four years afterwards, his mother, who had died in 1508, was posthumously found guilty of having visited the synagogue after her alleged conversion to Christianity; her remains were exhumed and burnt. In the light of these events, it is not surprising that Vives, who had left Spain when he was seventeen, never returned to his homeland.

He wrote a wide range of treatises, dealing with subjects as varied as the education of women, the improvement of the social condition of the poor and the promotion of peace between European states. He also produced humanist textbooks, commentaries on classical and patristic texts and translations of ancient Greek works into Latin. One of his main contributions to philosophy was his attempt to reform logic from a humanist perspective, especially in the treatise *Against the Pseudo-Dialecticians* (1519). He regarded the scholastic logic in which he had been trained in Paris as educationally useless because it was both philologically and historically barren. In his lengthy work *On the Disciplines* (1531), Vives protested that too much time at university was wasted on dialectic. Rejecting the highly technical and non-classical jargon of scholastic logic, he argued, like the Italian humanist Lorenzo Valla, that correct discourse could only be learnt by reading good ancient authors, such as Cicero and Quintilian.

On the Causes of the Corruption of the Arts, which is the first part of *On the Disciplines,* is a thoroughgoing critique of the entire foundation of contemporary education. Vives is extremely critical throughout of the Aristotelian orthodoxy of his day in the various fields of philosophy: metaphysics, physics, logic and ethics. As regards ethics, his main objection to Aristotelianism was its incompatibility with the Christian religion. Vives took the Erasmian view that Christianity was not primarily a collection of dogmas and doctrines, but a programme for moral life – a programme, moreover, which had been revealed to man by God. As such it provided, according to him, a morality which did not need to be supplemented by the merely human ethical doctrines devised by pagans who had *not* received the illumination of the Gospels. While Vives had some sympathy for Stoicism and Platonism, which he believed were broadly in line with Christian morality, he was hostile to Aristotle, especially his this-worldly notion of happiness and of virtue. For Vives, Aristotle's conception of happiness and his account of the virtues were not merely inferior to those promoted by Christianity, they were completely incompatible with them: 'We cannot serve both Christ and Aristotle, whose teachings are diametrically opposed to each other.'

Vives's humanist perspective is apparent in his attack on the ignorance of scholastic commentators on Aristotle, who lacked the linguistic and literary knowledge which he felt were necessary in order to expound the writings of an ancient Greek author. He also condemns their incessant verbal squabbling and their penchant for hairsplitting logic, which he compares unfavourably to the genuinely persuasive and inspiring prose style of classical writers such as Plato, Seneca and Cicero.

For the Latin text, see Juan Luis Vives, *De causis corruptarum artium liber sextus, qui est de philosophia morali corrupta,* in his *Opera omnia,* ed. G. Mayans, 8 vols. (Valencia, 1782–90; reprinted London, 1964), VI, pp. 208–22.

On the Causes of the Corruption of the Arts: Book VI: On the Corruption of Moral Philosophy

CHAPTER I

Who First Cultivated Moral Philosophy, and How Much More Excellent and Noble Christian Ethics Is Than That of the Ancient Philosophers. The Opinion of Aristotle concerning Happiness Is Refuted

The ancients believed the adage 'Know thyself' to be so important for every aspect of life and wisdom that, although it was coined by a wise man, they considered it to be of greater force and weight than human authority could bear. So they attributed it to a god, specifically, to that god whom everyone else conceded was the god of wisdom.[1] There is no doubt that they judged knowledge of the heavens, of the elements and of all things to be superfluous and wrong-headed for those who did not know themselves. That is to say, a man knows what every single thing is; he knows its efficient cause, its end and its capacity; what justification, then, is there for that man not to know these very same things about himself? This was the reason why Socrates, though he was so learned in every branch of philosophy that he was satirized in Old Comedy as an overzealous busybody,[2] nevertheless entirely transferred his attention and thought from all other things to himself, first and foremost. He wanted to take a good look at himself, and, once he had observed and examined himself, to improve himself through the proper disposition of his soul. He also wanted to benefit the general good by making known the principles of this medicine, this cure not only for our private life but also for our common and public life.

This discipline was called 'ethics' or moral philosophy, because through it the mores of men are put in order. Hence, Socrates is said to have brought philosophy down from its lofty wanderings amidst the heavens and primal elements into our homes and cities. There is no conceivable achievement more distinguished than that of Socrates, nor is there anyone else to whom mankind owes greater thanks than to him. In cultivating and acquiring this discipline, Socrates turned inwards upon himself and away from the attitudes and opinions of the populace, whom he always regarded with suspicion. He was in the habit of calling them 'the great teacher of error' and 'the perverse interpreter of truth' because he saw that most often it was the worst things which pleased the multitude. Therefore, drawing on his acute mental powers, he investigated this branch of philosophy by putting his trust neither in the deceptions favoured by the herd, nor in the dreams and insanities of religions fabricated by demented men and accepted by the deluded multitude, but rather in the teaching of God, that is, in the natural light of his [own] mind. In point of fact, there is no one so dim-witted that some light does not shine in his soul as a gift from God. Right behaviour makes this light shine brightly, and it grows even brighter if one commits oneself to it and keeps it uncorrupted and uncontaminated by the ignorance of the people.

Socrates understood that he was following as his guide not men and their depravity, but God, from whom he had received this light. Since he saw that men were blind and in their madness had turned from the truth and that only God was wise and could be called wise, he deemed true education to be the imitation of the deity, so that men might become, as far as possible, like God, as we know him through our reason. Now, because men do not have great faith in other men – to be sure, it is like the blind leading the blind, and the foolish teaching the foolish – he attributed the fact that he knew how to obey the deity to the deity's own signals and admonitions, pretending that the deity was a friend and a companion of his. Similarly, as tradition has it, certain lawgivers, such as Minos and Lycurgus, attributed their laws and precepts to the teaching of the gods.[3]

Furthermore, Socrates strove to impart to his listeners the discipline which, with God's help, he had forged for the common good. He was so effective and persuasive when speaking that he did not merely teach them but rather spurred them on and instilled into them an understanding of what they ought to do, as well as the will to do it, in speeches which were copiously and conscientiously transcribed by his students Plato and Xenophon.[4]

This is the true way of investigating the science of putting our souls in order and also the true way of passing this knowledge on. Those who stray from this path hurl themselves, along with their errors, into the depths of the wilderness. Socrates preferred to believe in God, that is, in the instruction of nature, purified and purged – as far as possible – of the common madness. He persuaded others to believe him by asserting that his discoveries and his teaching came not from himself, but from a certain god who was his guide and teacher and who suggested and indicated virtually everything to him.[5]

But we Christians prefer to believe in men rather than in God. For the philosophy which it is fitting for us to receive from the one God as our teacher, we seek and demand from Plato, Aristotle, Cicero, Seneca, Plutarch and Xenophon. And we do so not so much in order to question their opinions carefully as to find in them the supreme authority for our doctrines and for the rules by which we live our lives. This is in spite of the fact that today we have not merely the very meagre light of nature, not merely some fictive god supposedly sending us signs, but the true God himself openly speaking to us. We have the very sun which has cast its light on this world so that we would no longer wander, uncertain of the path, and waver among human opinions but would rather know through it and in it the sure, right, infallible road, which it alone can show us, as even the pagans themselves understood. How greatly we insult the sun by bringing out small lanterns to supplement the most brilliant and shining of lights!

These philosophers scorned their religions, which were fabricated by men; and they listened to their own intellects, which, to be sure, they considered to be similar to the heavenly mind. We Christians put our faith in these one-eyed and half-blind men, and we ignore the teachings which are without doubt heavenly. And we do this even though, if the doctrines are put to the test, using our entire rationality and intellect, with all authority left aside, ours will triumph over theirs as much as light conquers darkness and wisdom stupidity.

But if we, as we should, favour our own divine philosophy, which we know for certain was given to us by God, what is the point of making decisions about the virtues and the vices based on the hallucinations of pagan philosophers? We would be relying upon philosophers who, in ethical matters, envelop themselves in language which is so obscure that to understand them you have to become a soothsayer. The Stoics are a case in point. This is why so many disagreements arose among them concerning the sect's doctrines. Their arbitrary interpretation of terms provided them with an inexhaustible source of overly subtle arguments, cavils and sophistries. Other philosophers make decisions about virtue on the basis of their own emotions, as Theophrastus said in relation to the sorrow of Callisthenes: 'Fortune rules his life, not wisdom.'[6] Dionysius the Turn-Coat, although he was a Stoic, posited pleasure as the ultimate good because when his eyes began to cause him pain, he did not want to include the suffering he experienced from them among what the Stoics call the *adiaphora* [indifferent things, which are neither good nor bad].[7] Others take the people as their guide, as Aristotle frequently does. Epicurus actually took animals as his guide, though he did not even do that accurately or correctly enough, for which he was thoroughly rebuked by the Stoics; as they said, beasts do not seek pleasure first of all, but rather self-preservation, and then pleasure, as being consonant with self-preservation. There were philosophers who based the rules of virtue on cavils, rhetorical schemata and games, believing something to be well said if it was agreeably or cleverly said.

Into this darkness there also enters the dense fog of ignorance, which prevents us from judging the opinions and conduct of these philosophers. We are not even able to determine from among their conflicting voices which one we should listen to most carefully. How much ignorance has everywhere penetrated into discussions of the virtues and the vices and of the supreme good and evil! On the same issue we take as our guide Plato the Academic, Aristotle the Peripatetic, Seneca the Stoic and Cicero the dilettante! We belong to this sect one day and that sect the next day. Amazed by their disagreement, we strive with great labour and effort to bring them into harmony. We are affable conciliators, drawing not on the writings of the philosophers or on knowledge of antiquity, but rather on our own inept little conjectures. Moreover, of all the pagans, we have chosen to follow Aristotle, either because he alone was left in the schools of logic and philosophy, or because he aptly organized his precepts both for learning and for disputation, distributing the virtues and vices into genera and species. Therefore, I will pass over the other philosophers in silence and talk about him alone, even though St Augustine chose Plato and the Platonists with whom to dispute concerning the Christian religion on the grounds that they were either the most spiritually healthy of all philosophers or the ones who could most easily be cured;[8] and even though Jerome said that the Stoic sect was the one most similar to the Christian religion.[9] I move on now to Aristotle.

Like the Christians who attacked him, such as Origen, Gregory Nazianzenus, Gregory of Nyssa, Ambrose and others, the pagans themselves certainly regarded Aristotle as impious, because he cobbled together his philosophy for training our souls straight out of the errors of the multitude. And, from sheer love of contradiction, he deserted the most holy doctrines of his teacher Plato.

So that you might have some notion of what the totality of Plato's doctrines were like, let me give you a little taste of it from his writings. First and foremost, Socrates, as portrayed by Plato, more than once brings his discussions to the conclusion that man's happiness is not to be sought in this life, but in the next. Socrates argues this in the *Philebus,* in the *Symposium* and again, as he was dying, in the *Phaedo.* Aristotle seeks happiness in this life, leaving nothing to the next. Not only does he locate our ultimate good here on earth, he also places wisdom there. He makes fun of Simonides, a mere poet, who asserted that only God is wise. According to Aristotle, in that case God would be jealous of men, not wanting them to attain wisdom, a good which they particularly desired.[10] Where is that voice full of modesty, maintaining that our minds can only dimly perceive the most obvious things in nature? How much more correctly and religiously did Plato teach that human wisdom is either nothing or very little indeed,[11] and that only God is wise![12]

Aristotle employs another argument as well: can there be anything more unfortunate than man when he seeks and craves what he can never attain?[13] He uses the same weapon to show that man is happy here on earth, namely: what all men desire is natural; but natural things cannot be in vain; all men, furthermore, desire happiness; this appetite would be in vain if no one were ever to find it or have his desire for it satisfied.[14] How well you argue, Aristotle! Approach the issue differently, however, and you will arrive at truth. Convert the argument into a syllogism this way: everyone desires happiness; happiness is therefore a natural appetite; therefore, it is not in vain; but, as experience teaches us, no one attains it here on earth; therefore, it is to be sought elsewhere. This way of thinking led Socrates and your teacher Plato to the truth.[15] Plato establishes that the end and pinnacle of all goods is the love of, and union with, that beauty than which there can be nothing more beautiful, which suffers no interruptions or alternations of its beauty and which will never come to an end.[16] There is nothing more admirable or divine than this statement of Plato.

Aristotle creates three types of happiness. One is impure and, as it were, drawn from the dregs of the mob, who pursue obscene pleasures. Straight off, he casts this happiness aside as more suitable for animals than for men. The second type of happiness is civil; and the third contemplative. He approves of the latter two.[17] But what use are these distinctions between ultimate goals? It is as if the enquiry concerned the ultimate goals of the arts and not of human nature, which is one and the same in everyone. Otherwise, why does he not include the ultimate goal of artisans? Indeed, why does he not discriminate more minutely between the different happinesses of statesmen depending on whether they are in a democracy, an oligarchy or a monarchy? Again, why not the ultimate goal of the householder and then those of the carpenter and the shoemaker? Does anyone enquire into human happiness in this way? Since there is only one happiness, it is the single goal of the various goods.

Aristotle next adds three types of goods based on conventional opinion: goods of the soul, of the body and of life.[18] Both civil happiness and contemplative happiness need these goods, but civil happiness needs them more, and contemplative less. Both require longevity of life for happiness. The happiness of the civil life is to be located in virtue; that of the contemplative life, however, in contemplation, that is to say, in the activity of the divine mind. But both are embellished and increased by prosperity; and both are dimmed, diminished and sometimes even erased by adversity. The Stoics attack this opinion of Aristotle with powerful arguments. They contend that what he calls goods are not in reality such. Furthermore, Aristotle assigns great influence to external goods in the attainment of happiness although he locates the perfection of happiness in the soul.[19] But if the soul has perfect happiness, external things cannot alter this condition, since they do not pertain to the soul; rather, it is the soul itself that sets an appropriate value upon external things. This inconsistency is also to be noted in Aristotle's disciple Theophrastus.[20]

But no one, I think, can doubt that Aristotelian happiness is contrary to our Christian piety and, therefore, to right reason. For Christianity locates our happiness not in this brief life, not in our feeble body, which is vulnerable to chance and misfortune (it would not play such a dirty trick on us!), but in that immortal body of ours, which will be free of all harm and refashioned into something that is immutably durable. This is a most magnificent gift and one plainly worthy of an eternal and almighty God.

Some say that Aristotle was speaking only of the happiness of this world. But even by that standard, has anyone ever achieved happiness? Not those whom the common people take as happy: Metellus,[21] the Curiones,[22] Augustus,[23] Alexander,[24] Agathonius;[25] nor those whom the gods pronounced happy: Pedius and Aglaus;[26] nor those whom the philosophers, with more exacting judgement, call happy: Regulus,[27] Rutilius,[28] Cato,[29] Socrates, Zeno.[30]

Now, let us return to the first difficulty, that our appetite vainly desires what is forever unattainable. Now, what path to happiness is truer than that which marks the beginning of eternal happiness? The Psalmist says of it: 'Blessed are they that are perfect in the way, Who walk in the law of the Lord. Blessed are they that keep his testimonies, That seek him with the whole heart.'[31] Our Lord lists the eight beatitudes of this life,[32] which are very different from Aristotle's; indeed, they are opposed to his. Tell me, Aristotle, which of these would you term affluence: shoemaking and wagonmaking, crafts which invariably provide their practitioners with a miserable and squalid standard of life; or the arts of oratory, civil law, political theory and public administration – skills which bring no income when they are being learned, but once they are mastered provide their practitioners with immense honours and riches?

But, some will say, Aristotle spoke as a pagan and by the light of nature. They are quite wrong. It is obvious that Aristotle's view is not identical to the light of nature because others, such as the Platonists and the Stoics, have proceeded along a more correct path, aided and shown the way by the same light of nature.

But what good is this argument in any case? Do we Christians not enjoy sound spiritual health? Do we not know what true happiness is and how to arrive at it? And yet do we still debate about Aristotelian happiness? Or do we create two happinesses, one put forward by Christ, the other by Aristotle? Look once again how we blasphemously split happiness up into parts, just as we have previously split up the light of nature! If we are supposed to desire Aristotle's happiness in this life, then we ought not to desire Christ's happiness in this life: we cannot long for mutually contradictory things to come about in the very same time and place. If Aristotelian happiness is a fraud, why do we strive to preserve it in some way? Indeed, by the same token, will we allow every insane notion of every philosopher concerning the supreme good into our schools? And will we become accustomed to defending these insanities? Or are we just playing games when we theorize about happiness, that is, about the whole purpose of our life? It is dangerous to stand for falsity against truth. How much more dangerous is it to do so in a matter of such great importance! In a matter of religion! In a matter upon which our whole life depends! If Aristotle's happiness is false, it is neither spiritually healthy nor pious, even for pagans. Let us Christians learn instead to know and defend what is true. But let us move on to the next topic.

CHAPTER 2

The Author Explains and Analyses, in a Truly Remarkable Manner, What Aristotle and Other Philosophers Have Taught concerning the Virtues

Aristotle defines virtue as a disposition, that is, a *hexis*,[33] as if it were not also an *energeia* [activity, force]. Indeed, to be more accurate, virtue is like a drink that imparts health to us – such is its power when it functions and exerts its force [on us]. Furthermore, Aristotle locates virtue in the mean, that is, between two extremes and in opposition to both of them:[34] for instance, a timid man and a rash man are both opposite to a brave one. And acts of one and the same virtue are opposite to acts of its extremes: so, it is the task of bravery to attack the enemy when necessary and, likewise, to retreat and steal away when necessary.

To some degree, Plato agrees with Aristotle on this matter; but Lorenzo Valla rightly criticizes him in Book III of his treatise *On Pleasure,* with the following argument.[35] If I retreat or even flee, I am not brave; nor if I enjoy legitimate pleasures, am I temperate. Rather, there are other names for these things. Nor is one thing contrary to two things, but rather one thing is contrary to one thing, and two things are contrary to two things. The person who does not abstain from illegitimate pleasure is incontinent; the one who abstains is continent and moderate. The person who enjoys legitimate pleasures is civilized, or, as Valla says, merry (although, contrary to what Valla believes, this is not a virtue); the one who does not enjoy legitimate pleasures is not intemperate, but rather inflexible. The same pattern holds true in regard to dangers and to the distribution of money. The person who flees or succumbs to dangers is timid; the one who resists them is brave; the person who avoids them, especially those that are not necessary, is cautious; the one who does not avoid them is rash. The person who gives money when the situation demands is generous; the one who does not give when appropriate is miserly or hard-hearted; the person who spends heedlessly is extravagant or prodigal; the one who gives nothing when there is no need to give is parsimonious or frugal.

Next, Aristotle says that bravery relates to fearful things, but not just any things. For bravery, he says, is not involved in enduring disgrace, penury, *aphilia* [lack of friends] or death, whether on account of illness or by drowning in the sea; rather, it involves the dangers of war.[36] It is impossible to say anything more wrong-headed than this, whether in relation to our religion or to paganism. In the case of our religion, who does not see that no one has ever been more courageous than our martyrs and those saints who have patiently endured everything in the hope of Christ's grace? As for paganism, was Socrates not courageous in jail and in drinking the hemlock?[37] What about Themistocles and Rutilius and Metellus in exile?[38] Regulus undergoing torture?[39] Cato in the desert and in the Syrtes?[40]

Aristotle's doctrine that bravery is ignited and, as the Academics say,[41] set afire by anger as if by a flint[42] has been sufficiently condemned and derided by Cicero,[43] Seneca[44] and the Stoics.[45]

Aristotle defines magnificence as a virtue to be found in great expenditures, such as the building of temples and theatres and the mounting of public games.[46] He also adds a very coarse sentiment: that it is impossible or at any rate difficult '*ta kala prattein achorēgēton*[47] *onta*' [to do noble deeds when penurious].[48] What does he mean by *ta kala*? Things which are good or things which are noble? I find the two to be mixed together in all languages, with one taken for the other or, to make the point even more explicit, joined together, such as *kalos kagathos* [a noble and good man] and *kalokagathia* [nobility and goodness]. But, Aristotle, do you call noble what your senses judge to be noble, as does the mob? Or what your mind judges to be noble, as do the wise? To display what the populace, ruled by the external senses, calls noble is not merely difficult for a pauper, it is utterly impossible, unless he steals the property of others. But if you mean what the wise call noble, what is more noble or excellent than the great feats of virtue which have been performed better and more often by lofty souls having no wealth than by those living in the lap of luxury? Is there anything more noble than what Socrates did, ignoring his own material interests so that he could make others better? Was Scopas more excellent than Callion?[49] Did Xerxes perform more noble deeds than Aristides the *dikaios* [just]?[50] Or any of the richest Romans than Fabricius and Curius in the most modest of circumstances?[51] Note that I am speaking here as much about the man of affairs, living in the midst of the city and the populace, as I am about the contemplative man.

Magnanimity, says Aristotle, is the desire for great honours.[52] The Stoics define magnanimity more correctly and prudently as the knowledge which imparts a loftier character to all those things which can occur equally for good or ill.[53] Plato, Cicero, Seneca and others, however, define magnanimity as consisting more in spurning honours than in the desiring them.[54] Anyone can desire honours, even the most wicked men and the most foolish women. To scorn honours belongs to the greatest soul, a soul of the most generous proportions and with a higher destiny. This is the reason we have such admiration for Cato, who, as Pliny says, rejoiced in honours spurned as if they had been honours gained.[55] Of the same order of magnitude was the dignity of Publius Africanus,[56] Quintius,[57] Verginius[58] and Fabius,[59] all of whom scorned honours, when they could have acquired or retained them.

But perhaps, Aristotle, you call honours not these high-ranking positions, but rather the praise and reverence that come on account of virtue, striving for which you classify as a type of virtue, even if it is *anōnumos* [without a name].[60] Will you, therefore, stir the philosopher whom you have undertaken to educate to strive for this popularity? Do you say that this is the *athlon* [prize] of virtue, the reward, as it were, of victory? Cicero was of the same opinion, though he located this glory not in the schools of the philosophers, but in the company, as he says, of highly learned and civilized men. 'Glory', he claimed, 'is the most honourable fruit of true virtue',[61] which we fish for with a golden hook. As a prize for so excellent a thing as virtue – nothing is nearer to the gods – do you put forward honour, a vain and fickle thing, proffered by the vain and fickle populace?

But perhaps Aristotle and Cicero do not want honour to be expected from just anyone, but instead from good people, as Aristotle states, '*kai tais [megalais] upo tōn spoudaiōn*' [and great honours from those who are worthy].[62] As Naevius says about Hector: 'he rejoices to be praised by a praiseworthy man'.[63] For the same reason, Cicero, speaking as a philosopher and no longer as a senator, defined rightful glory as 'a thing of substance, which is plainly visible and not sunk in shadows. It is the agreed praise of good men, the incorruptible voice of those truly capable of judging virtue; honour re-echoes virtue, as the image of its glory.'[64] But how do you know who is a good man, one truly capable of judging you? For, the more serious and prudent men are, the more prone they are to reserve judgement and to issue rather obscure indications of their opinion. Furthermore, how could you know for sure that someone would judge you with discernment and wisdom when he can scarcely do the same in relation to himself, given that nothing is more difficult than to judge oneself? Is it any less difficult to make judgements about someone else's soul, locked up and hidden under so many layers of covering?

But let us concede that this person is a competent and exacting judge. And let us further concede that he understands you.[65] I doubt that you will expect him [to render a fair judgement of you] when people make way for you, when you are escorted to and fro, when people rise when you enter, when they take off their hats before you, when they address you in magnificent terms. The wise man laughs at, and even flees from, these displays of honour, so far is he from being caught up in such things. Will you acquiesce in these tacit judgements? What then? Will you be satisfied to be judged by another's conscience? Will not your own conscience satisfy you, especially when you are no worse or less wise a man than any judge, and when your conscience knows you much better than anyone else could? Is this the reason why we put so much effort into stern virtue: so that someone passing by us will mumble to himself: 'What a wise and good man'? Since, however, as you yourself teach, honour is not in the hands of the person who is honoured, but of the one who honours him,[66] it will happen that virtue is frequently deprived of its reward and profit. And because the good man gains no profit or recompense when he strives for virtue, then virtue is a purposeless and unprofitable venture, since he has nothing to show for it. How much better is the lesson taught by the poet Claudian than that of the philosopher and the senator![67] He says:

> Virtue is its own reward. Its far-flung splendour alone is
> Secure from the blows of fortune. It is not elated by great offices,
> Nor does it seek to bask in the applause of the rabble.
> It desires no external wealth, nor is it in need of praise
> Since it revels in its own riches.[68]

But if the reward of virtue is honour, and if *'kat'alētheian', hōs phēs, 'ho agathos monos timēteos'* ['in reality', as you say, 'only the good man should be honoured'],[69] why do you link the profit and worth of virtue to things which are not good? For you say that those who have riches along with virtue are more honourable.[70] And you would have any magnanimous and upright man judge for himself what honour he deserves.[71] What am I hearing? Are you permitting each person to decide for himself what honour he merits – in particular, a person who is not familiar with others, despite the fact that most honours are based on comparative merit? Do you believe that everyone will be a fair judge of his own virtue, given that, however honestly a man has observed himself, the better he is, the more tempered his feelings regarding himself will be? Nor is it the same thing to know oneself and to evaluate oneself: it is very different to examine oneself carefully and to compare oneself to another person whom one has not examined. How foreign all this is to true judgement! How foreign, indeed, it is to our religion, where we hear: 'When ye shall have done all the things, say, We are unprofitable servants.'[72] 'Be not highminded, but fear.'[73] 'Happy is he that judgeth not himself in that which he approveth.'[74] Our religion has innumerable other statements of this kind aimed at reducing arrogance.

There is also the fact that, in religion and in everything concerned with true value, the basis on which each person's merit and worth is judged is hidden – not only are we uninformed about others but even about ourselves. That great secret is reserved solely to the divine wisdom. 'The righteous, and the wise, and their works', says Solomon, 'are in the hand of God; whether it be love or hatred, man knoweth it not; all is before them.'[75] Paul expresses the same thought when he says: 'I know nothing against myself; yet I am not hereby justified.'[76]

Just as earlier you fabricated two happinesses, are you now also fabricating two virtues (that is, two courages and two magnanimities), one Christian, the other pagan or rather, to be precise, Aristotelian? It would be shameful for Christians to assert such a thing, unless perhaps Aristotelian virtue is for us false, fabricated and deprived of life; do we then exert ourselves for the sake of mere shadows and cadavers? We cannot serve both Christ and Aristotle, whose teachings are diametrically opposed to each other. Christ brings us to heaven, to God, his Father and, through contempt for this life, to a concern for eternal life. Aristotle urges our soul to cling closely to the body and would have us dedicate our every care and thought to this brief life here on earth. What a great obstacle to piety Aristotelian ethics is for many people! They forget the precepts of Christ and think that by following those of Aristotle they live a sufficiently correct and holy life. They measure human works and actions in accordance with Aristotle's precepts, as if these were a formula for life; and they indulge themselves and others in sin and wickedness by using Aristotle's authority to assign to this behaviour the name of the most beautiful virtues. They do this with anger, ambition, the search for honours, luxury, extravagance and revenge – for even revenge is classified by Aristotle as a virtue![77] But I cannot examine his errors individually. Nor is it necessary here since I have decided to dedicate a separate work to the defence of our religion against every form of human wisdom.[78]

CHAPTER 3

This Chapter Criticizes Aristotle for His Love of Obscurity in Speech and for Being So Inconsistent in His Opinions. [It Also Examines] Why Some Readers Are Pleased by Some of This Philosopher's Writings, While Others Prefer Other of His Works

But let us see how they understand this Aristotle, whom they tenaciously hold on to, clutching and grasping him in their hands. First, it is hard to get at what he means because of the delight he always takes in making his words and notions ambiguous and obscure. Everywhere you look it is the same. Concerning happiness, for instance, how differently he speaks in Book I of the *Ethics* from what he says in Book X. And what he says in Book X of the *Ethics* is not the same as what one finds in Book VII of the *Politics*. His admirers, hardly noticing that he posits a twofold happiness – one for the contemplative man, another for the citizen – confuse the two. Nor do they take into consideration the fact that in Book I of the *Ethics* he makes enquiries and speaks of everything without going into detail, more in the manner of the crowd than following his own procedure, but that in Book X he writes with greater precision. When, however, our contemporary Aristotelians have to speak of Aristotelian happiness, they draw from Book I rather than from Book X. What is to be done with them? Perhaps they have never read as far as Book X. But even in Book X Aristotle is by no means sufficiently clear, nor is he consistent. There, before speaking about the happiness of the private individual and of the man engaged in contemplating the highest matters, he first discusses the virtues; yet throughout the *Ethics* it is the virtues of the citizen [and not the contemplative man] which he has been discussing. Since they do not understand this, they mix up everything and turn it inside out. We should not, however, be surprised at their confusion, given that Aristotle himself published all this in such a confused jumble that it is a labour of the highest order to separate it all out and make the proper distinctions.

Passing on to the next topic: up to the present day, Aristotle has been read by westerners in such incompetent Latin translations that one might easily imagine that they arrived at his meaning either by conjecture or by divination. The Greek names of many virtues and vices have been retained, even though the Latin language has quite apt and completely appropriate terms for them. Greek figures and phrases are also preserved in the Latin. Many things have been erroneously understood by the translators and then erroneously passed on to Latin readers. But even the better translators cannot understand Aristotle unless they are extraordinarily well versed in ancient [Greek] literature and language. Take, for example, Aristotle's assertion: '*dokei gar timē en tois timōsi mallon einai, ē en tō timōmenō*',[79] that is, 'Honour seems to be more in those who honour than in those who are honoured.' From this statement most people would suppose that Aristotle considers honour to be located in the person who confers it, not in the one who receives it; and this is the commonly held opinion. But the expression *einai en tois* signifies 'in the power of' and almost 'in the hands of' rather than 'located in'. What follows makes this clear: '*t'agathon de oikeion ti kai aphaireton einai manteuometha*',[80] that is, 'according to the oracle, the good belongs to its possessor and cannot be taken away'.[81]

Now, Aristotle was very well versed in the poets, orators, historians and all the ancient authorities. Throughout his works he alluded to their sayings, which were then well known, especially in the schools. Frequently, the allusion itself contained the point he wished to make. Who can understand these things? Only someone who is an expert in such matters, which is the kind of learning our scholastics do not encounter even in their dreams. But let me continue with the issue of literary allusions in Aristotle's *Ethics*.

In Book II, he advises us to be on guard against pleasure so that it does not worm its way into our favour. 'And we', he says, 'should have the same attitude towards it as the elders of Troy had towards Helen.'[82] What a load of rubbish has been written about this![83] Were the Trojan elders born yesterday? For the meaning of this allusion, you have to read Book III of the *Iliad*.[84]

Next, in Book VIII, when discussing the advantages of friendship, Aristotle suddenly introduces the phrase '*sun te du' erchomenō*' [two going together], alluding to the words of Diomedes about himself and Ulysses in Book X of the *Iliad*.[85] And a little further on he says: 'they say that all such men are like potters to each other', in an allusion to the line in Hesiod about envy: '*homotechnōn kai kerameus keramei koteei*' [and with those in the same trade, potter envies potter].[86] I have to omit an innumerable quantity of such allusions; but the purpose of those I have cited is simply to serve as examples illustrating my point.

Because there are even more allusions to history, fables, antiquarian lore and the sayings of the ancients in the *Politics* and the *Rhetoric* than there are in the *Ethics,* the scholastics hold on tight to the *Ethics,* regarding the *Politics* and the *Rhetoric* as irrelevant to them. Their ignorant brawls have little to gain from the *Politics,* which demands more intellectual power, judgement and experience than they possess; nevertheless, some scholastics have ventured to try their hand at the *Politics* and have written commentaries on it. But these commentaries are like the ones which they write on all other authors: full of questions and arguments, with the thrust of the entire work directed towards contentious bickering.

What on earth will be the end result of this insatiable mania for disputation? The scholastics have turned the discipline of morals, which aims at action, into mere verbal jousting. They discuss ethics not in order to become better or to make others better, nor in order to determine the truth about the virtues and about life, but rather in order to quibble. And, leaving no indignity against ethics untried, they even import into the discipline the logical puzzles of Swineshead,[87] along with thorny sophisms on the intension and remission of the vices and the virtues.[88] They also introduce dialectics, not however the sort which is relatively sound, but rather the fictions of the *Little Logicals* on ascent, descent, suppositions, ampliations, restrictions and appellations.[89]

What else could these wretched people do? They were only practising what they had been taught. They would put something better forward, if they had it. But their disputations are utterly unsuited either to persuasion or to making men better. Someone who disputes *contra* or who hears a question as if it were a trumpet of war prepares himself continually for the fight, throwing up defences everywhere so that he is not captured or beaten. So averse are they to paying attention to anyone who speaks with them that they ignore what the person is actually saying, even if it is good advice, guarding themselves from him as if he were the enemy. For this reason nothing is as inimical to moral persuasion (which aims not so much to teach as to stir and incite people to action) as verbal squabbling or saying the opposite of one's listener. Worse, unlike the physical sciences, where arguments drawn from knowledge and the judgement of the senses can be adduced, ethics relies completely on the probability of arguments which can be parried or, at all events, ignored by an obstinate opponent. How elegant, how shrewd, how well suited to persuasion and how pleasing are the arguments of Plato, Cicero and Seneca! How easily everyone is persuaded by them! (It may be objected that they by no means persuaded Lactantius, but that was because he read them in a hostile manner.)[90]

Aristotle himself most prudently advises against using dialectics when we wish to stir up people's minds or to calm them down.[91] How ineffective moral philosophy is when argued dialectically! Especially the way it is taught in the schools! Small wonder young people imbibe nothing of moral integrity in the midst of such altercations about ethics and so many shouting-matches about every kind of virtue and every form of good behaviour. Students are not imbued with the discipline through practice, as tends to happen in other disciplines; on the contrary, they are more quickly stained by a multitude of vices. The reason for this is that all these aspects of ethics are taught to them in such way that moral excellence cannot be commended to their souls, nor can the foulness of the vices be made the object of their hatred. How much more courageous in bearing outrageous fortune, how much wiser in managing good fortune and how much better disposed towards all of life, with the soul's tumults and tempests under control, is a reader after finishing a single page of Seneca or Plutarch than someone who reads the entire commentaries of Almain and Master Martin, even though their works are entitled *Morals* and *On Courage* and *On Temperance*![92] Why? Because we become callous when we habitually receive splendid things into our souls without giving them due regard, so that henceforth no exhortation to virtue can penetrate our hardened hearts. Medicine meant for our souls will not help them any more than a drug or a potion can help our bodies if we get habituated to it by taking it when it is not needful and treating it merely as a game.

Translator's Notes

1. 'Know thyself' was one of the exhortations carved on the temple of Apollo at Delphi.
2. Old Comedy refers to the comedies produced in Athens during the fifth century BC. Aristophanes, the major figure in Old Attic Comedy, ridiculed Socrates in his play the *Clouds*.
3. Minos was a legendary king of Crete; Lycurgus was believed to be the founder of the Spartan constitution.
4. Speeches attributed to Socrates are preserved in Plato's dialogues and in Xenophon's *Memorabilia*.
5. Vives is thinking of the famous daemon of Socrates, which from time to time in his life gave him signs and warnings that determined his course of action.
6. See Cicero, *Tusculan Disputations* V.9.25. Callisthenes was the nephew of Aristotle, and Theophrastus (c. 370–288/5 BC) was his successor as head of the Lyceum. According to Diogenes Laertius, *Lives of the Philosophers* VII.144, Theophrastus wrote a book entitled 'Callisthenes, or On Bereavement'.
7. Dionysius of Heraclea (c. 328–248) was given the nickname 'Turn-Coat' because of his abandonment of the Stoics in old age in favour of the Cyrenaics, who placed the highest good in pleasure: see Diogenes Laertius, *Lives of the Philosophers* VII.37, 166.
8. St Augustine, *City of God* VIII.5–11 and *Confessions* VII.9.
9. See, e.g., Jerome, *Commentarii in Isaiam* IV.11, in J.-P. Migne, ed., *Patrologia Latina,* 221 vols. (Paris, 1844–64), XXIV, col. 147D.
10. See Aristotle, *Metaphysics* I.2 (982^{b}28–983^{a}11).
11. Vives seems to be referring to the notion of Socratic wisdom presented in Plato's *Apology,* that is, the idea that Socrates was the wisest of all men because he knew that he did not have wisdom.
12. Vives apparently assumed that Simonides' statement reflected Plato's opinion. Simonides is expressly quoted in Plato's *Protagoras* 339A–340E and *Republic* I (331E), but not this statement.
13. See Aristotle, *Nicomachean Ethics* I (1100^{a}10–^{b}7); but Vives is not accurately portraying Aristotle's position.
14. Though Aristotle often said that nature did nothing in vain and though he posited natural appetites, this particular argument, as formulated by Vives, is not to be found in his writings. It derives instead from the Neoplatonist Marsilio Ficino, who used the argument from natural appetite to prove the immortality of the soul in his *Platonic Theology* of 1474 (for selections from this work see Chapters 3 and 13). The Aristotelian Pietro Pomponazzi tried to refute this argument in his 1516 treatise *De immortalitate animae.*
15. This argument is not to be found in Plato, but comes instead from Ficino; see n. 14.
16. Once again, this argument derives from Ficino, especially his *De amore* (1469), rather than from Plato, who did not make beauty the ultimate end of man, even in his dialogue on love, the *Symposium,* on which Ficino's work is a commentary.
17. Aristotle, *Nicomachean Ethics* I.5 (1095^{b}14–1096^{a}5).
18. Aristotle, *Nicomachean Ethics* I.8 (1098^{b}12–18).
19. Aristotle, *Nicomachean Ethics* I.7 (1098^{a}3–20).
20. See Cicero, *Tusculan Disputations* V.9. 24–5.
21. Quintus Caecilius Metellus Macedonicus (d. 115 BC), whom the Roman historian Valerius Maximus, *Facta et dicta memorabilia* VII.1.1, considered to have enjoyed continual happiness from birth to death.
22. The Roman aristocrats Gaius Curio Scribonius and his son of the same name, both of whom enjoyed notable public careers in the first century BC.
23. Augustus Caesar (Octavian; 63 BC–AD 14), the first Roman emperor.
24. Alexander the Great of Macedonia (356–323 BC).

25. Apparently the Greek poet Agathon, who was known for his exceptional beauty and who is one of the speakers in Plato's *Symposium.*
26. According to Pliny the Elder, *Natural History* VII.46.151, Pedius, a fallen warrior, and Aglaus, a gentleman from Arcadia of temperate desires, were both pronounced the happiest of men by the Delphic Oracle; for Aglaus, see also Valerius Maximus, *Facta et dicta memorabilia* VII.1.2.
27. The celebrated Roman general Marcus Regulus Atilius, who, when taken prisoner and conditionally paroled by the Carthaginians in the First Punic War, returned to his captors to honour his oath and was tortured to death.
28. Publius Rutilius Rufus, a Roman aristocrat and Stoic who in 92 BC disdainfully refused to make a great effort to defend himself against an unjust persecution and went into permanent exile in Asia Minor.
29. Cato the Censor (234–149 BC), a distinguished Roman statesman and author.
30. Zeno of Citium (335–263 BC), the founder of the Stoic sect.
31. Psalms 119:1–2.
32. Matthew 5:3–11; Luke 6:20–3.
33. Aristotle, *Nicomachean Ethics* II.6 (1106^{b}36–1107^{a}3).
34. Aristotle, *Nicomachean Ethics* II.6 (1107^{a}3–8).
35. Lorenzo Valla, *On Pleasure. De voluptate,* trans. A. K. Hieatt and M. Lorch (New York, 1977), pp. 236–51 (III.4). At the start, on p. 237, Valla says that Plato agreed with Aristotle, although this was not, in fact, Plato's position; see, however, Cicero, *Academica* II.44.135, where the 'Old Academy' is said to have endorsed the doctrine of the mean in ethics.
36. Aristotle, *Nicomachean Ethics* III.6.
37. See Plato's *Crito* and *Phaedo.*
38. The statesman Themistocles (c. 528–c. 462 BC) spent his last years in Persia after being ostracized and prosecuted for treason at Athens. For Rutilius see n. 28. Vives seems to have confused Q. Caecilius Metellus Macedonicus (n. 21), who never suffered exile, and Q. Caecilius Metellus Numidicus, who was forced into exile in 100 BC (for praise of his behaviour see Valerius Maximus, *Facta et dicta memorabilia* V.6.7).
39. See n. 27.
40. Vives is apparently thinking of M. Porcius Cato Uticensis (Cato the Younger, 95–46 BC), who committed suicide at Utica on the African coast, after valiantly leading the struggle against Caesar. 'Syrtes' is the plural of 'Syrtis': Syrtis Minor is today the Gulf of Gabes off the coast of Tunisia, while Syrtis Maior is the Gulf of Sidra off the coast of Libya. Seneca, *Epistulae* XCV.69–71, comments on the bravery of Cato Uticensis, who is also one of the heroes of Lucan's *Pharsalia,* especially Book IX.
41. See Cicero, *Academica* II.44.135, and also *Tusculan Disputations* IV.19.43.
42. Aristotle, *Nicomachean Ethics* III.8 (1116^{b}23–1117^{a}9).
43. Cicero, *Tusculan Disputations* IV.19.43, where he criticizes Aristotle from the perspective of the Stoics.
44. Seneca, *De ira* I.92 and XVII.1; see also I.3.3.
45. See n. 43.
46. Aristotle, *Nicomachean Ethics* IV.2 (1122^{a}17–24).
47. Correcting *achorēgton* of the edition.
48. Aristotle, *Nicomachean Ethics* I.8 (1099^{a}32–3).
49. Vives seems to be comparing the famous fourth-century BC sculptor Scopas of Paros to the much earlier and less refined sculptor Callon or Calon (not 'Callion') of Aegina (sixth century BC), mentioned by Quintilian, *Institutio oratoria* XII.10.7; Pliny the Elder, *Natural History* XXXIV.49; and Pausanias, *Description of Greece* II.32.5, VII.18.10.
50. The Persian Emperor Xerxes, who invaded Greece in 480 BC, and the statesman Aristides (b. c. 520 BC), famed for his honesty, who was ostracized from Athens in 483–2 but was called back to be one of the leaders of the Athenian forces against the Persians.

51. It was common practice to cite the third-century BC military heroes Gaius Fabricius Luscinus and Manius Curius Dentatus as examples of the old Roman virtue: see, e.g., Cicero, *Paradoxa* VI.3.50.
52. Aristotle, *Nicomachean Ethics* IV.3.
53. Diogenes Laertius, *Lives of the Philosophers* VII.92.
54. In the Platonic corpus the word *megalopsuchia* (magnanimity) appears only in the spurious *Second Alcibiades* 150C, where it is treated as a sign of foolishness. Cicero nowhere speaks of magnanimity as the scorning of honours. For Seneca, see *De clementia* I.5.3 and *Epistulae* LXXIV.13, which only very distantly correspond to Vives's view of magnanimity. See also R. A. Gauthier, *Magnanimité: l'idéal de la grandeur dans la philosophie païnne et dans la théologie chrétienne* (Paris, 1951).
55. Pliny the Elder, *Natural History* preface 9.
56. Presumably the celebrated Publius Scipio Africanus (236–184/3 BC), who defeated Hannibal in the Second Punic War but withdrew from Rome, at the end of his life, to retirement in Liternum.
57. The Roman hero Lucius Quinctius Cincinnatus, who, according to legend, in 458 BC resigned his dictatorship after sixteen days and returned to his farm.
58. Lucius Verginius Rufus, who twice refused to be hailed emperor: first in AD 68, after he defeated the Germans under Vindex; and then again in AD 69, after Emperor Otho was assassinated.
59. Fabius Maximus Verrucosus, 'Cunctator' (Delayer), whose stubborn dogging of Hannibal made him one of the Roman heroes of the Second Punic War.
60. Aristotle, *Nicomachean Ethics* IV.4 (1125^{b}12–25).
61. Cicero, *Oratio in Pisonem* 24.57.
62. Aristotle, *Nicomachean Ethics* IV.3 (1124^{a}6).
63. Cf. Cicero, *Tusculan Disputations* IV.31.67. Naevius was a third-century BC Roman poet, whose works survive only in fragments quoted by other authors.
64. Cicero, *Tusculan Disputations* III.2.3.
65. See Aristotle, *Nicomachean Ethics* I.5 (1095^{b}28–9).
66. Aristotle, *Nicomachean Ethics* I.5 (1095^{b}24–6).
67. That is, Aristotle and Cicero.
68. Claudian, XVII (*Panegyricus dictus Manlio Theodoro*) 1–5.
69. Aristotle, *Nicomachean Ethics* IV.3 (1124^{a}25).
70. Aristotle, *Nicomachean Ethics* I.8 (1099^{a}31–^{b}8), X.8 (1178^{b}33–1179^{a}13).
71. Aristotle, *Nicomachean Ethics* IV.3.
72. Cf. Luke 17:10.
73. Romans 11:20.
74. Romans 14:22.
75. Ecclesiastes 9:1.
76. I Corinthians 4:4.
77. Aristotle, *Nicomachean Ethics* V.5 (1132^{b}21–1133^{a}2).
78. Vives may be referring here to his treatise *De veritate Christianae fidei* (Basel, 1543), which deals with the relationship between human knowledge and faith.
79. Aristotle, *Nicomachean Ethics* I.5 (1095^{b}24–5).
80. Aristotle, *Nicomachean Ethics* I.5 (1095^{b}25–6). Vives's text has *aphaireton* where modern editions have *dusaphaireton* [not easily taken away].
81. Instead of 'according to the oracle', Vives should have translated the Greek phrase as 'we instinctively feel that'.
82. Aristotle, *Nicomachean Ethics* II.9 (1109^{b}7–11).
83. Vives is apparently referring to those Latin commentators on the passage who did not know what the Trojan elders had said.
84. Homer, *Iliad* III.156–60.
85. Aristotle, *Nicomachean Ethics* VIII.1 (1155^{a}15); see Homer, *Iliad* X.224.
86. Aristotle, *Nicomachean Ethics* VIII.1 (1155^{a}35–^{b}1); see Hesiod, *Works and Days* 25.

87. Richard Swineshead was a famous fourteenth-century English logician and natural philosopher, known as 'The Calculator' because of his major work, the *Liber calculationum* (c. 1350), in which he developed a highly mathematical approach to physics; see the article on him in C. C. Gillispie, ed., *Dictionary of Scientific Biography*, 16 vols. (New York, 1970–80), XIII, pp. 184–213.
88. See E. Sylla, 'Medieval concepts of the latitudes of forms: the Oxford calculators', *Archives d'histoire doctrinale et littéraire du moyen âge*, 40 (1973), 223–83.
89. *Parva logicalia* was the name given to the last six or seven tracts, containing introductory information on the technicalities of scholastic logic, of the *Summulae logicales* of Peter of Spain (d. 1277), the standard university logic textbook. Thomas More claimed that it had received the title *Little Logicals* 'because it has very little logic in it': quoted by C. Fantazzi in the introduction to his edition and translation of J. L. Vives, *In pseudodialecticos* (Leiden, 1979), p. 16 n. 30. On the terminology of scholastic logic see *CHRP*, pp. 143–72.
90. See Lactantius, *Institutiones divinae*, esp. Book III.
91. Cf. Aristotle, *Nicomachean Ethics* I.3 (1094^b23–7).
92. The French scholastic Jacques Almain published a work entitled *Moralia* in 1510; for his *Question at Vespers* see *Cambridge Translations of Renaissance Philosophical Texts*, II: *Political Philosophy*, ed. J. Kraye (Cambridge, 1997), ch. 2. The *Quaestiones morales de fortitudine* of Martin Le Maistre (d. 1483) were printed in 1489 and his *Quaestiones morales de temperantia* in 1490.

Further Reading

Bietenholz, P., and Deutscher, T. B., eds., *Contemporaries of Erasmus: A Biographical Register of the Renaissance and Reformation*, 3 vols. (Toronto, 1985–7), III, pp. 409–13

Fantazzi, C., 'Vives, More and Erasmus', in A. Buck, ed., *Juan Luis Vives. Arbeitsgespräch in der Herzog August Bibliothek Wolfenbüttel . . . 1980* (Hamburg, 1981), pp. 165–76

González y González, E., *Joan Lluís Vives: de la escolástica al humanismo* (Valencia, 1987)

Margolin, J.-C., 'Vivès lecteur de Platon et Aristote', in R. R. Bolgar, ed., *Classical Influences on European Culture* AD 1500–1700 (Cambridge, 1976), pp. 245–58

Noreña, C. G., *Juan Luis Vives* (The Hague, 1970)

 Juan Luis Vives and the Emotions (Carbondale, Ill., 1989)

 A Vives Bibliography (Lewiston, N.Y., 1990)

10

Philipp Melanchthon

John Monfasani

Introduction

The German theologian and educational reformer Philipp Melanchthon (1497–1560) was the chief disciple of Martin Luther. He was born in Bretten (Palatinate), where he pursued his early studies before moving on, in 1508, to the Latin school in Pforzheim. It was at this point that his great-uncle, the humanist Johannes Reuchlin, bestowed on him the name 'Melanchthon', a Greek rendering of his German surname Schwarzerd. He matriculated at the University of Heidelberg in 1509 and obtained his BA two years later. In 1512 he went to the University of Tübingen, receiving his MA in 1514 and then teaching classics for a few years. He was appointed professor of Greek at Wittenberg in 1518 and, after completing his biblical studies, he also gained a chair of theology; he held both positions until his death.

Melanchthon, who became known as 'Praeceptor Germaniae' (the teacher of Germany), made important contributions to the humanistic reform of education. He produced editions of and commentaries on classical authors (e.g., Thucydides, Cicero, Ovid, Quintilian), as well as extremely influential textbooks of Greek and Latin grammar, natural philosophy, rhetoric, logic, psychology and numerous other subjects.

It was primarily due to the efforts of Melanchthon that Aristotle gained a central place in the Lutheran university curriculum. Early in his career, Luther had been extremely hostile to Aristotle, regarding the *Nicomachean Ethics* as a pernicious work which was directly opposed to the Christian doctrine of grace and of virtue. He was eventually won over, however, by Melanchthon, who believed that a Protestant reform of education must be grounded in the systematic philosophy of Aristotle, which was far more useful for didactic purposes than, for instance, the rhetorically superior but difficult, problematic and disturbingly ironic dialogues of Plato.

Aristotle's ethical thought played a central role in Melanchthon's philosophical programme. He wrote a series of commentaries on the *Nicomachean Ethics,* in which he presented clear and readily comprehensible interpretations, free from the hairsplitting complexities of the scholastic commentary tradition. He also produced manuals and compendia in which he distilled the major themes of Aristotelian moral philosophy. One of the most important of these ethical textbooks was *The Elements of Ethical Doctrine,* first published in Wittenberg in 1550 and followed by three further editions (1553–4, 1557 and 1560). In this work Melanchthon deals with a variety of topics, presenting not only Aristotelian views but also those of other ancient philosophical sects, such as the Stoics and Epicureans (to which he was notably less sympathetic than to Aristotle). He constantly draws attention to the distinction between the moral law, embodied in philosophy, and the Gospel, which contains God's message and promise of salvation. Both systems were necessary for mankind corrupted by the Fall; but it was essential to recognize that they operated on completely different principles and were directed towards completely different ends.

For the original Latin text see Philipp Melanchthon, *Ethicae doctrinae elementorum libri duo,* in his *Opera omnia,* ed. C. G. Bretschneider and H. E. Bindseil, 28 vols. (Halle-Braunschweig, 1834–60), XVI, cols. 165–9, 170–5, 189–93.

The Elements of Ethical Doctrine

BOOK I, SELECTIONS

Those who praise the commonly accepted doctrine of the virtues found in the philo-sophical tradition are most often content to say in its justification that it is the norm for human life delivered to us by God for the purpose of regulating our external behaviour, so that those who savagely violate it call down harsh punishments upon themselves and others. But even if this praise is true and by no means to be belittled, nonetheless, whenever one thinks about the value and content of this doctrine, one comes up with other important and weighty justifications which could also be men-tioned. We should therefore keep in mind these four reasons why a knowledge of the virtues is necessary.

First, an awareness of the virtues is a testimony to the existence of God. For the eternal and unshakable distinction in our minds between right and wrong testifies that such a nature cannot have arisen by chance, but must have been designed by the mind of some eternal architect.

Second, it teaches us what God is like. For since we distinguish right from wrong, we understand that God is wise, generous, just, beneficent, chaste, merciful and so on. Indeed, in prayer these characteristics of God ought always to be kept in view so that we pay him due honour and distinguish him from non-living, wicked and unclean spirits who seek to harm us.

Third, it is a testimony to the judgement of God. For God would have established the distinction between right and wrong in our minds to no purpose if he had not added punishment as a consequence of violating that distinction. In addition, it is in the natural order of things that torment invariably afflicts the conscience of evildoers, which is a testimony to divine justice. Furthermore, terrible penalties regularly accompany sins in this life.

When you have considered these three reasons, relating to God, then comes the fourth reason: the doctrine of the virtues is the norm of human life in external actions or discipline. Consideration of these reasons embellishes ethics and leads our mind to the consideration of God and of the creation of man. It also reminds us that men were created in accordance with a marvellous plan: that human nature should be the image of God, in which the rays of divine wisdom and virtues would shine. Such is our infirmity, however, that we disrupt this most beautiful natural order – easily, often, repeatedly and monstrously. So we must ask where this infirmity comes from and what remedies God offers us. Since, however, philosophy has nothing to tell us about the cause of this infirmity or its remedies, we recognize that we require some other doctrine, beyond philosophy, namely, the announcement of promises or the Gospel.[1] And we very much need to keep in mind the distinction between philosophy and the

Gospel, which I shall speak of here and about which it is often necessary to speak. . . .

What is Moral Philosophy?

Moral philosophy is the explication of the law of nature. It assembles, as far as reason is able to determine, demonstrations arranged in the order commonly used in the arts. Its conclusions consist of the definitions of the virtues or the precepts of the discipline which must be maintained amongst all men. These precepts agree with the Decalogue[2] insofar as it deals with external discipline.

Does Moral Philosophy Conflict with the Doctrine God Has Given to the Church?

It is often said that we are greatly in need of the light of Church doctrine in order to become aware of the distinction between the law and the Gospel. The moral law is the eternal and unchangeable wisdom and the rule of justice in God. It distinguishes that which is right from that which is not right and directs its awesome anger at the disobedience that contradicts the norm which it embodies. It was divulged to mankind at the time of creation; and afterwards it was frequently reiterated and declared by divine utterance in order that we might know that there is a God and what he is like. It places all rational creatures under obligation and demands that they conform to it, damning and destroying all those who do not conform, unless they receive remission and reconciliation through the Son, the Mediator.

The Gospel, on the other hand, is the preaching of penance and the condemnation of sins. And it is the promise of the remission of sins and the promise of reconciliation, justice and eternal life freely given through the Son of God. Knowledge of this promise is by no means innate in us, but was instead revealed from the hidden bosom of the eternal Father, beyond and out of the sight of all creatures.

Once we understand this distinction, it is easy to make a judgement about philosophy. Moral philosophy is by no means the promise of the Gospel; rather, it is a part of the law – just like the law of nature – which addresses the issue of discipline. And just as Christians can rightly heed, embrace and approve of the law of nature and the honest laws enacted by governments which are derived from it and can use these to maintain Christian discipline, so too they can rightly embrace and approve of true philosophy and make use of it. Indeed, it is much to be regretted that we have been persuaded by many quite false arguments to hold this discipline in contempt. It is because of this attitude that we are plagued by many public and private calamities.

Since it is obvious that God's law is good, as Paul tells us (Romans 7:12, 16), and that God enjoins discipline with the utmost severity, it follows and is also obvious that we should embrace and approve of philosophical opinions which are true and that Christians can rightly use them, just as we embrace and approve of mathematical doctrine and are permitted to use it. For a doctrine that is universally true is a light which originates in God. To contradict knowingly the truth on any matter is a

violation of the commandment: 'Thou shalt not bear false witness' (Exodus 20:16).
The syllogisms concerning a rightful oath are true: [thus,] we must put the truth
before any physical danger to ourselves; Regulus swore that he would return; he
therefore put his oath before physical danger.[3] [Likewise,] justice means not harming
the innocent; Abel was innocent; therefore, Cain acted unjustly when he killed him.[4]
To deny such syllogisms, since they embody the truth, is an insult to God, the author
of this light.

But the utility of moral philosophy becomes clearer when we begin to control
ourselves through discipline. We also learn from moral philosophy the reasons why
discipline is to be privileged, namely, these four: first, because of God's commandment; second, in order to avoid punishment; third, in order that we may facilitate the
tranquillity of others; and, fourth, because discipline prepares us for Christ, since
God provides no help to those who persist in their sins against their own conscience.
The usefulness of discipline is so great that those of us who belong to the Church are
spurred on to a love of it. . . .

What Is Man's End?

Just as someone who is about to begin a journey thinks at the start about his specific
destination so that he might direct the intervening stages of his journey towards it, so
too in all our actions we must look first to our end. The same, therefore, is true for
moral philosophy: the first question concerns the end which man, according to right
reason, desires above all and which above all he should obtain and that to which all
his actions ought to be referred so that he does not stray from this end.

Now, Church doctrine offers an explanation which is splendid because it leads us
to the acknowledgement of God, to whom above all honour is due and in whom
nature finds repose. In the strictest sense of the word, therefore, our end according to
the law of God is God himself, who communicates his goodness to us when we truly
acknowledge and celebrate him. Those who simply respond that the end of man is the
true acknowledgement and celebration of God are saying the same thing, for we must
be flexible in understanding these modes of speaking.

The Son of God teaches us about our end in the following words: 'Let your light
shine [before men that they] may glorify your Father, which is in heaven' (Matthew
5:16). And in I Corinthians 10:31, it is written: 'do all to the glory of God'. Again, in
Psalms (115:1): 'Not unto us, O Lord, not unto us, but unto thy name give glory.' And
the First Commandment teaches us that this is the end of man, for at the start it
enjoins the acknowledgement and obedience which we owe to God.[5]

This very end is assumed, moreover, in God's purpose in creating man: 'Let us
make man in our image, after our likeness' (Genesis 1:26). God therefore created a
rational creature so that his image might shine forth in it, and this, in turn, would
result in God being acknowledged and in the existence of similar virtues. Since
human nature was created for this purpose, men necessarily desire to acknowledge
and love God truly and also to find their repose in God,[6] who communicates his

goodness to us. These things are obvious to those who have been well educated and who are in harmony with the law of God.

The Gospel leads us to the same end, but it adds the Son as our guide. This doctrine transcends the scope of human reason; and it is in this manner that the famous passage from John (17:3) refers to our end: 'this is life eternal, that they should know thee the only true God, and him whom thou didst send, even Jesus Christ'.

It was necessary to speak first here about our end from the perspective of Church doctrine in order to take account of the difference between the doctrine of the Church and that of philosophy. I shall now explain the philosophical doctrine.

The true light of reason, implanted in man by nature, accords with the law of God. But in the haze of the present life our knowledge of God is rather obscured, in addition to being disturbed by many doubts. Therefore, philosophers, even though they sometimes enjoin us to refer our actions to God, nevertheless more often than not speak only of virtue and say that virtue is our end. Although the Stoics maintained many absurd things, they did get it right when they said that man is the reason why everything comes into being, but God is the reason why man comes into being.

Our conscience attests to the fact that God is our end. Therefore, men grieve in the midst of their evil deeds because, by the light of nature, they perceive and fear the anger of God. On the other hand, our minds are at ease when we do good deeds because we judge that such actions will receive the approval of God, who is both observer and judge. Therefore, according to true philosophy the pre-eminent end of man is either some acknowledgement of God, or else it is God. But philosophers speak in the way I have described: they say that virtue is the end. And when I say this, I include in the meaning of the term 'virtue' the supreme virtue, which consists in acknowledging God and referring all right actions to him.

Since, however, I am about to set forth two contrary opinions – one of Aristotle and the other of the Epicureans – I shall speak in the customary manner. Here is the question: is virtue the end of man or is it, in fact, pleasure? Aristotle says that virtuous activity is man's end. When I say that virtue is the end, I do not mean an inactive disposition; rather, I support Aristotle's opinion,[7] even if, for the sake of brevity, I refer to it simply as virtue, in the manner of Cicero. Let us be done, therefore, with *logomachiai* [battles over words] and clearly establish that Epicurus's opinion is false. He contends that pleasure is our end. It is stated more accurately in philosophy, however, that man's end is virtue, that is, doing what is right even if pain and loss are the consequences. Aristotle confirms this opinion with a brilliant demonstration derived from natural philosophy, which runs as follows:

It is absolutely certain that in any nature whatever the end which is most proper to it is the activity of its own nature; it is proper to it, since its nature was created principally for that activity.
Virtue is the activity most proper to man.
Therefore, virtuous activity is his end.[8]

This demonstration is true even if the Epicureans set against it many plausible arguments, the explication of which will throw a good deal of light on this debate.

But before I get to these arguments, I have to point out that the root of this controversy is the divergence between the laws of nature which are in our minds and the appetites which are in our hearts. The Church teaches us how this divergence began; and for a clearheaded determination of this controversy, it is useful to juxtapose the doctrine which the Church has handed down to us concerning the causes of human misery against the divergence between law and appetite in man, which is, as they say, an evil resulting from original sin. Man was created to obey the law, and in his heart of hearts he would have obeyed with enthusiasm and pleasure if his nature had not been corrupted, for it is just that the good prosper. But after man's nature was corrupted, many confusions ensued, both in us ourselves and in society. The harmony between law and appetite was disturbed; afterwards, external evils were also opposed to virtues, as when wicked citizens envied Camillus.[9] Consequently, enmities, dangers and unjust killings follow upon good deeds. Since many of the grounds I use to disprove the views of Epicurus derive from this source [that is, the divergence between law and appetite], I have provided this reminder before turning to his arguments.

The principal and most attractive of Epicurus's arguments are the following.

First

The end of any nature whatever is that to which it is attracted spontaneously, naturally and with a powerful impulse, not that which it does with difficulty and under external compulsion. The downward motion of a stone, for instance, is natural, whereas its upward motion occurs by violence.

Human nature tends spontaneously towards pleasure. By contrast, it obeys laws only with difficulty.

Therefore, pleasure is man's end.[10]

Here is my response to the minor premise. Those of us who know what caused the harmony in man's powers to be disturbed can easily disprove this argument. The minor premise contains a fallacy of accident, for it is an accident of our nature, due to its corruption, that our bad appetites burn so fiercely that we find it difficult to obey God's law. If, however, our nature were uncorrupted and if God were to suffuse us with his light and the flames of virtue, obedience in all things would be pleasant. This refutation is a perspicuous and useful reminder for those of us in the Church to think about the tragic consequences of this divergence in our powers and to ponder how it came about.

Staying within the realm of philosophy, however, one can respond truthfully and clearly as follows. I deny the minor premise because it contains the fallacy of arguing from what is relative to what is absolute. Not all [of human] nature is attracted to pleasure: the mind, before the actual deed and even after it, is opposed to pleasure, for extremely painful punishments follow misdeeds. Moreover, it is impossible for the end of a nature to be a thing or an action which, after the event, provokes terrible opposition on the part of the entire nature, so that it would prefer not to exist rather than to have to bear the contemplation of that deed. David, for instance, preferred not to exist rather than to bear the thought of the sin he committed.[11] This counter-argument very plainly refutes the Epicureans and shows that not all [of human] nature is attracted principally to pleasure.

Second

Any nature whatever with a right and ordered appetite seeks above all its own self-preservation.

Pleasure entails the conservation of man's nature, while virtue entails its destruction, as is obvious from the example of Socrates and others like him, who were killed because they acted rightly.

Therefore, man's end is pleasure, not virtue.

I deny the minor premise. The reason is that it contains a fallacy of accident, for it is accidental when virtue destroys a nature. When Socrates was killed, the cause was not his virtue, but rather the injustice of his enemies. Similarly, when a highwayman kills a traveller whom he is about to rob, the cause is not the traveller's money, but the evil will of the highwayman. Nor, moreover, would virtue be accompanied by dangers if man's nature were uncorrupted.

Furthermore, virtue is what preserves a nature. God's judgement attests to this since he rewards virtue. Besides, it is universally true that species are preserved by means of virtue. Truth, justice and bravery are advantageous to the whole society, even if an individual is destroyed here and now. It is more important to preserve the whole [species] than a part of it.

A further point: this very destruction and all the calamities suffered by good people are manifest testimony to the fact that men are not born simply for this life, since it is impossible for a nature which understands virtue, along with the rewards of virtue and the penalties [of vice], to come into existence in such a way that there is no difference in the future between those who are good and those who are evil. For then the understanding of virtue and turpitude, of rewards and punishments, would be instilled into that nature in vain.

Now that the minor premise has been refuted, we must also reject the major premise. It is not a true proposition to say that any nature whatever seeks above all its own self-preservation. It is, however, true that all things desire in a well-ordered way to remain unimpaired in the condition for which their nature was created, for in that condition their nature can truly be preserved. But when an appetite wanders without order, it does not follow that it will achieve its end, since an unordered appetite also seeks things which are contrary to its end. Besides, what we can thus refer to as a state of being unimpaired must not entail the destruction either of an individual or of a species. Therefore, even if Nero remains for a time unimpaired, nevertheless the pain of conscience resulting from having committed sins entails his destruction, which will necessarily follow. Even the devil would prefer not to exist than to be as he is – indeed, he suffers terribly because he is not able to put an end to his misery by reducing himself to nothingness. And there is that very tragic statement about Judas (Matthew 26:24): 'good were it for that man if he had not been born'. Since, therefore, the major premise is not true, a false conclusion follows. The major premise should have been framed in this way: any nature whatever with a right and ordered appetite seeks above all its own self-preservation in the condition for which it was created.

But the other refutation, that of the minor premise, demonstrating that pleasure does not preserve a species and that virtue destroys a nature only accidentally, is clearer. Moreover, if human nature were not corrupted, a nature which remained unimpaired would always be accompanied by virtue. . . .

The Final Cause [of Virtue]

It is customary in philosophy to say that virtue is an end in itself and that it is not primarily desired for the sake of something else. But it would be more correct, even according to reason, to add a more powerful end, namely, that virtue is desired for the sake of God. Joseph abstained from another man's wife in order to obey God and to avoid bringing scandal upon his profession and so on.[12]

The standard teaching concerning the distinction between different types of end should be maintained. There can be many ends for one thing, but these are arranged in order: some are primary, others are secondary. Virtue should be desired primarily for the sake of God, but subsequently also on account of present and eternal rewards, for it is absolutely certain that horrendous crimes are punished by horrendous penalties in this life. Jacob says: 'If God will give me bread and water, then shall the Lord be my God, and this stone shall be God's house.'[13] Although the conditional has been inserted into this statement, it does not signify an end or reward, but rather a possibility and a limit (in other words: 'if I live, I shall gather together the Church in this place for the purpose of sacrifice and of preaching', in conformity with Psalms 115:17: 'The dead praise not the Lord'). Nonetheless, the statement is also correctly interpreted to mean that Jacob seeks bodily goods in their place and in the right order, but in such a way that the primary end is given precedence.

Does Free Will Exist?

There is a ready explanation for those seeking the simple truth in this matter. But first we have to draw distinctions between the various actions of the will. Some choices are in the realm of external movements, whether they are concerned with moral actions or with actions involving the making of something or with a person going some place. For example, Scipio can restrain himself from touching the betrothed of another,[14] and Fabricius can restrain himself from accepting the money sent by Pyrrhus;[15] a painter can paint either a head or a chimera; Plato can go to the city from the Academy or not go. In such choices and in all external movements, the human will is free in itself, that is, it can choose to make these movements or it can choose not to make them; it can command its exterior limbs to bring about these movements or not command them; and when it chooses or commands, it chooses or commands of its own accord, without external constraint or coercion. For instance, Eve chose of her own accord and without external constraint or coercion to eat the apple, and she commanded her organs to chew the apple.

That freedom of the will functions in this way is shown by the clear and firm testimony of Paul. He often admits that there is some righteousness of the flesh, that is, there is a discipline by which unregenerate man performs external good deeds, such as when he says to Titus (3:5): 'Not by works done in righteousness which we did ourselves etc.' Since, therefore, there is some righteousness of the flesh, and since men are able to command themselves so that they perform the external works of the law, there is no doubt that the will has some choice and freedom to prefer good works to evil deeds. We should not allow this argument to be foiled by means of sophistic cavils and trickery. We should instead hold on to it with both hands as a true opinion which, for the sake of discipline, is necessary for life.

Next, since it is God's commandment that discipline should be rigorously maintained, concern for the maintenance of discipline must not be driven from our minds; for our determination flags when we think that it is impossible or useless to control morality. That discipline is commanded by God is, however, plain from Paul's statement (I Timothy 1:9): 'Law is made . . . for the lawless and disobedient', that is, in order that they should be coerced and punished when they violate discipline. Again, Romans 13:5: 'ye must needs be in subjection, not only because of wrath, but also for conscience sake'.

Furthermore, the horrible punishments which all nations and families suffer in this life proclaim the wrath of God against those who violate discipline. There is a perpetual, eternal and inflexible rule: dreadful crimes are punished by swift, dreadful punishments in this life, in accordance with the saying (Matthew 26:52): 'all they that take the sword shall perish with the sword'. Again (Hebrews 13:4): 'fornicators and adulterers God will judge'. Again (Wisdom of Solomon 11:16): 'by what things a man sinneth, by these he is punished'.

The advantages of discipline are enormous because it leads to the avoidance of great evils, immediately and for all eternity. Many crimes committed by individuals are punished by both private as well as public penalties; and for as long as these individuals persist in their crimes, God does not operate in them. It is therefore necessary to abandon the intention of acting against one's conscience. To make such a choice is, in some way, within the power of the human will. For these weighty reasons, let us learn to understand discipline, and let us moderate our blind impulses through diligence and impose upon ourselves the reins of discipline.

The second testimony to free will is the very structure of the human body. The human body is constructed in such a way that the muscles are at the service of voluntary motions. When the will commands our locomotive faculty, the muscles obey. To deny this freedom is to reject our unmistakable experience of man's workings.

It is utterly certain, therefore, that in the choice of external actions there is some freedom. But even if this freedom genuinely remains in human nature, it is, nevertheless, impeded by two causes. At times the force of our emotions is so great that our will relaxes its reins over them. It does so, however, willingly. At other times devils drive men to rush headlong into abominable acts of wickedness, as with Nero, who indulged horribly in every kind of wickedness. Such fits of frenzied madness originate with the devil. Nonetheless, this does not mean that there is no freedom, for Nero could have blocked the onset of these fits in some way.

It often happens, however, that even people of outstanding prudence and virtue suffer grievous lapses. This happened to David, to Solomon and to others in order that we might acknowledge the weakness of human nature and, all too late, seek the help which God promised the Church.[16] God wishes and strictly enjoins us to petition him. He eagerly helps us so that his presence in the Church and his mercy might be conspicuous. This is why the Scriptures say (Luke 11:13): 'How much more shall your heavenly Father give the Holy Spirit to them that ask him?'

I have spoken of external discipline, which the human will can achieve in one way or another. Now I shall speak about actions of a different sort, which cannot be accomplished without the promptings of the Holy Spirit: true fear of God, true confidence (which conquers our fears at the time of death and at other moments of great suffering), burning love of God, constancy in confessing the faith (which does not succumb[17] to torture nor to the passions of lust, ambition, jealousy and desire for revenge in great affairs).

We should be aware that internal movements [of the soul] such as these, which are pleasing to God, are not achieved without the aid of the Holy Spirit. Nevertheless, the will is not powerless in these matters, nor does it behave like a statue. Rather, there is a confluence of active causes working together: the Son of God moves the mind by means of his word and the Holy Spirit; the heart becomes inflamed; the mind deliberates; and the will does not resist, but in some way or other heeds the prompting of the Holy Spirit and at the same time asks God for help. Hence, that man who says (Mark 9:24): 'I believe; help thou mine unbelief.' Moreover, those [internal] actions which command our locomotive faculty are in our power: we can command ourselves to read, listen, think about a doctrine, as well as commanding [the movement of] our exterior limbs. I leave aside evil actions which our conscience opposes before they are done. All these things are quite evident.

We also must consider carefully that both the message of repentance and the message of grace are universal. God charges all men with sin in this depraved state of nature. In turn, the promise is also universal, in accordance with what is said in Matthew 11:28: 'Come unto me all ye that labour and are heavy laden, and I will give you rest.' God offers grace to all who take refuge in the Son, the Mediator. Nor is there *prosōpolēpsia* [respect of persons] in God. Nor ought we to imagine that there is any partiality [in the case of grace], as there is with goods which are not necessary. God does not give the strength of Samson to everyone, nor does he make everyone a gifted musician. We must not, however, think that such partiality holds true in the case of salvation. There the promise is universal since it is the supreme good and is necessary for everyone.

Let us look to this promise and not allow its consolation to be cast out from our hearts. It is as true as true can be that this promise is to be judged a reflection of God's will and of his word. It is most truly said (Psalms 119:105): 'Thy word is a lamp unto my feet.' Why therefore do you cast away the universal promise and seek other expectations? Bring your mind and heart back to this promise and gaze upon the Son of God. Listen to his voice. Know that he wishes to be the supreme priest and mediator for you. And do not imagine that there are contradictory wills in God.

Do not, therefore, indulge in misgivings. Do not imagine partiality, as if you were thinking about the strength of Samson or about musicians. Instead heed both messages. Fear the judgement of God. Cast away evil actions, which occur contrary to your own conscience, and look to the promise and to the Son of God. Ask him to help you by means of the Holy Spirit; as he says (Luke 11:13): 'How much more shall your heavenly Father give the Holy Spirit to them that ask him?', that is, not those who ask for help indolently, bitterly or reluctantly, but those who weep and wail with genuine sorrow.

Thus, it is understood that since the promise is universal, there must be some sort of concurrent assent on our part, especially after the Holy Spirit has inflamed our mind, will and heart. This is the message preached by many writers. Augustine frequently says: 'with grace preceding and the will accompanying'.[18] And Chrysostom: 'God draws us, but he draws only those who are willing.'[19] And Basil: 'God cooperates only with the willing.'[20]

It is obvious that we need this consolation in the struggle [of life]. For what can you say to a guilty person, who is already brought to punishment, and who is horribly tortured even by the thought of his own crime? Certainly he must be led to the promise and not to other expectations.

Translator's Notes

1. In the Gospel (in Greek *euangelion*, or good news) divine promises of salvation were given to mankind through Christ, as Melanchthon explains here.
2. That is, the Ten Commandments; see Exodus 20:1–17 and Deuteronomy 5:6–21.
3. The celebrated Roman general Marcus Regulus Atilius, when taken prisoner and conditionally paroled by the Carthaginians in the First Punic War, returned to his captors in order to honour his oath; he was tortured to death.
4. See Genesis 4:8.
5. Exodus 20:7: 'Thou shalt not take the name of the Lord thy God in vain.'
6. Cf. Augustine, *Confessions* I.1: 'For you have created us for yourself, and our hearts cannot find peace until they rest in you.'
7. That is, that virtuous activity, rather than the mere possession of virtue, is man's end; see Aristotle, *Nicomachean Ethics* I.8.
8. See Aristotle, *Nicomachean Ethics* I.7.
9. The great fourth-century BC military hero and 'second founder of Rome', M. Furius Camillus, was fined and exiled about 391. For Camillus as a victim of popular envy see Valerius Maximus, *Facta et dicta memorabilia* I.5.2; cf. Plutarch, *Life of Camillus* 12.
10. See Cicero, *De finibus* I.9.30; Melanchthon seems, in fact, to be summarizing the opening argument of Book I of Lorenzo Valla, *On Pleasure. De voluptate*, ed. and trans. A. K. Hieatt and M. Lorch (New York, 1977).
11. For David's sin (adultery with Bathsheba and murder of her husband Uriah) see II Samuel 11–12; for his repentance see Psalm 51.
12. See Genesis 39:7–10.
13. Cf. Genesis 28:20–2.
14. For P. Cornelius Scipio, who captured the betrothed of Prince Allucius of the Celtiberi and restored her to him still a virgin, see Livy, *Ab urbe condita* XXVI.50.
15. See Plutarch, *Life of Pyrrhus* 20.

16. For David see n. 11; for Solomon see I Kings 11.
17. Reading *quae . . . succumbit* for *succumbere.*
18. For the sentiment, though not the precise words, see Augustine, *Epistulae* CLXXXVI.3, in J. P. Migne, ed., *Patrologia Latina,* 221 vols. (Paris, 1844–64), XXXIII, col. 819; *De gratia et libero arbitrio* chs. 4 and 17, in *Patrologia Latina,* XLIV, cols. 887, 901.
19. Again, for the sentiment, but not the words, see John Chrysostom, *Homilia in Matthaeum* 82(= 83).4, in J. P. Migne, ed., *Patrologia Graeca,* 162 vols. (Paris, 1857–66), LVIII, cols. 742–3; for many other similar statements see C. Baur, *John Chrysostom and His Time,* trans. M. Gonzaga, 2 vols. (Westminster, Md., 1959–60), I, p. 360.
20. See Pseudo-Basil the Great, *Homilia de paenitentia* ch. 3, in Migne, ed., *Patrologia Graeca,* XXXI, cols. 1480D–1481A; the work is now attributed to Eusebius Emesenus.

Further Reading

Aristotle, *L'Éthique à Nicomaque,* ed. R. A. Gauthier and J. Y. Jolif, 2 vols. (Louvain, 1970), I.1: *Introduction,* pp. 165–9

Bietenholz, P., and Deutscher, T. B., eds., *Contemporaries of Erasmus: A Biographical Register of the Renaissance and Reformation,* 3 vols. (Toronto, 1985–7), II, pp. 424–9

CHRP, pp. 46, 71–2, 100–1, 153, 192, 227, 323–4, 328, 344–6, 359, 369, 385, 479–84, 516–18, 530, 621–6, 630, 633, 654, 663, 665, 705, 723, 742–3, 750–1, 756, 797, 826

Frank, G., *Die Theologische Philosophie Philipp Melanchthons (1497–1560)* (Leipzig, 1995)

Kusukawa, S., 'Law and Gospel: the importance of philosophy at Reformation Wittenberg', *History of Universities,* 11 (1992), 33–57

The Transformation of Natural Philosophy: The Case of Philip Melanchthon (Cambridge, 1995)

Lohr, C. H., *Latin Aristotle Commentaries* (Florence, 1988–), II, pp. 254–8

11

Antonius de Waele

John Monfasani

Introduction

The Calvinist theologian Antonius de Waele (Walaeus; 1573–1639) was born in Ghent and received his early education there and in Middelburg. He went on to study Greek, Hebrew and theology at the University of Leiden. After a 'grand tour' of France, Switzerland (including Geneva, where he attended the lectures of Theodore Beza) and Germany, he returned to the Netherlands in 1601. The following year he was called as a minister to Koudekerke, where he remained for three years, after which he returned to Middelburg. He stayed there for several years, also teaching Greek and philosophy at the local Latin school. Sometime around 1611 he became friends with the Dutch theologian, jurist and humanist Hugo Grotius; but the two men parted company after the latter was sentenced to lifelong imprisonment in 1618 on account of his irenical sympathies. De Waele attended the Synod of Dordrecht (1618–19), which condemned the Arminians – who, in reaction against Calvinism, held that human free will was compatible with divine sovereignty and that Christ died for all men, not just the elect – and promoted the strongly Calvinist orientation of the Dutch Reformed Church. In 1619 de Waele was appointed professor in the faculty of divinity at the University of Leiden, which was now purged of all Arminian influence. He remained at Leiden until his death in 1639, a few months after having been appointed rector of the university.

The aim of de Waele's treatise is clearly indicated by its title, *A Compendium of Aristotelian Ethics Accommodated to the Standard of Christian Truth.* All too often, he believed, works on moral philosophy had done precisely the opposite by making Christian theology conform to the standards of Aristotelian ethics. He was also opposed, however, to the approach of those Protestant theologians who had strayed so far from Aristotle and his treatment of the subject that their textbooks were of little value to the moral philosophy curriculum, which was grounded on Aristotle and other pagan authors. Attempting to strike a balance between adapting Christianity to Aristotelian morality, on the one hand, and transforming Aristotelian ethics into a branch of theology, on the other, de Waele based his treatise solidly and closely on the *Nicomachean Ethics,* but he carefully corrected the many errors which had resulted from Aristotle's ignorance of the truths of religion. Aristotle had entirely neglected, for instance, the moral duties which we owe to God and, worse still, he had been unaware of the true purpose of virtue, which was to serve the glory of God and to lead us towards happiness in the next life. In his discussion of the vexed issue of the freedom of man's will, de Waele steers clear of strictly theological questions, but nevertheless demonstrates that the Bible is in fundamental agreement with the best philosophical solutions to this problem. He makes the further point that even the achievement of natural and civic good at times requires divine inspiration.

For the Latin text see Antonius de Waele, *Compendium ethicae Aristotelicae ad normam veritatis Christianae revocatum* (Leiden, 1620), sigs. †2ʳ–8ʳ, pp. 3–4, 6, 10–12, 15, 45–50, 124–38. There were at least eleven more editions before 1686, and the treatise was also published in his *Opera omnia,* 2 vols. (Leiden, 1643), II, pp. 257–92.

A Compendium of Aristotelian Ethics Accommodated to the Standard of Christian Truth: Selections

Dedicatory Epistle

. . . Among all the branches of philosophy, my right honourable and reverend sirs,[1] the one which we call ethical or moral has long been considered – and rightly so – the most useful to mankind. For although the other branches of philosophy which are concerned with the contemplation of things lift our thought up to a level beyond that of the human mind, and although these other parts supply us with a great many items which add to the embellishment and happiness of human life, nonetheless it is ethics alone which adorns human actions with the splendour of virtue. It is ethics alone which prescribes the norms and forms by which human behaviour is clothed with moral goodness within the community, within the family and in private dealings,[2] and by which human society is distinguished from associations composed of beasts and criminals. This is why in former times certain great men, whom God called forth from among the pagans in order to put them to the test,[3] and above all the others Plato and Aristotle in particular, laboured assiduously in this noble branch of philosophy.

Although there are those who think that Plato is as superior to Aristotle in ethics as Aristotle is to him in natural philosophy, the fact nevertheless remains that for several centuries now Aristotle's writings have been preferred to Plato's in schools and universities. I have no intention of entering here into this quarrel [that is, on the relative merits of the two philosophers]. For it is true enough that on some points Plato's doctrine far surpasses Aristotle's. But it is equally true that on other points Aristotle rightly criticizes and corrects Plato.

But though they are head and shoulders above other pagans, both philosophers were deprived of the true light of Sacred Scripture and the Holy Spirit. Accordingly, on occasion they committed egregious errors in their rules and precepts. Therefore, those who in their turn harbour suspicions about the writings of these men and of others like them perform a notable service for Christian commonwealths and churches when, while commending to others what [these pagan philosophers] have to offer that is learned and praiseworthy, they nevertheless do so in such a way that they make use of their rightful and necessary freedom as Christians to call attention to, and to refute, their faulty doctrines.

Otherwise, on account of the authority of [these pagan philosophers], prejudices gradually take shape in the tender minds of the young. Subsequently, when they become adults, these prejudices can scarcely be removed, even with great effort, and they are often the cause of great upheavals in Christian commonwealths and churches, as these men strive to make Christian theology conform to the standards of Aristotelian doctrine rather than accommodating Aristotelian rules to the standard of Christian truth. I could cite many examples of this tendency in our own country and abroad, if I were not intent here on healing wounds rather than reopening them.

For this reason, right honourable and reverend sirs, even before I was assigned the task of teaching this discipline, among other subjects, in your illustrious school, I had planned to write for my students a kind of compendium of ethics based on Aristotle himself, in which, as far as my meagre powers of discernment allowed, I would cull, in a concise and clear fashion, whatever was useful in Aristotle and other philosophers. I did not conceive the compendium with publication in mind; nevertheless, before taking my leave of your school and church in order to go the University [of Leiden], I was so earnestly urged by you to publish it that I could not disregard your judgement and wishes in this matter. After spending a few days in revision, I published it so that those who had previously heard this material in my lectures could refresh their memory of it and so that others could, if they wanted to, use it as a guide to this branch of philosophy, providing them with help and steering them in the right direction.

I am well aware that others before me have engaged in this sort of enterprise; and I in no way wish for my small contribution to detract from their achievement. I would like, however, for Christian philosophers to exercise more freedom when they correct these [pagan] texts, so that young people can approach the sources with less risk. As long as philosophers do not dare to deviate from Aristotle's opinions by even a hair's breadth, they are forced either to do harm to divine truth or to do violence to Aristotle's meaning. Among our theologians, Philipp Melanchthon[4] and [Lambert] Daneau[5] have demonstrated to the churches their diligence in this matter too. But while they made use of only a tiny bit of Aristotle, most of the other material they incorporated into their systems was taken from theological practice. Since the works they constructed clearly belong to a new and different genre, they are not of much use for correctly understanding Aristotle or other pagan moralists. Consequently, I have tried in this modest work to fulfil both aims: first, succinctly imparting in almost the same order as found in Aristotle the substance of his *Nicomachean Ethics,* while also taking some notice of the opinions of other philosophers; and, second, correcting the errors we find in these authors in accordance with the standard of Christian truth. . . . Leiden, 10 September 1620.

Introduction

. . . Active philosophy (*praktikē,* in Greek) is that branch of the discipline which, not content with the contemplation of things, demands that these things are not merely known about but put into action and practice. Ethics belongs to this category of philosophy. The name 'ethics' derives from the Greek word *ethos,* that is, usage or custom, because it concerns men's mores, which is why it is called *scientia moralis* [moral philosophy] in Latin. It can be defined as the practical philosophy of human actions insofar as moral goodness [*honestas*] is relevant to these actions. . . .

Many people regard the emotions or passions as the object of ethics. This opinion is not inappropriate if we understand it as designating the principal object of ethics: the subjugation of the emotions to right reason. Occasionally, however, the emotions cannot be regarded as the entire or adequate object of ethics because this discipline in some way also helps, by means of its precepts, to heal the blindness of our reason and the corruption of our will.

Therefore, it is more appropriate to speak of the adequate object of ethics as human actions – not, however, human actions considered in any way whatever, but insofar as *to prepon* [that which is seemly, fit, proper] or moral goodness is relevant to them and insofar as they are capable of virtue. This is because everything which is treated in ethics can be referred to this end and goal. . . .

In order that you may gain a much better understanding of the true use of this discipline, let me comment briefly on the difference between Christian and Aristotelian ethics.

1. Aristotelian ethics obviously knows nothing of the Gospels and of the virtues which properly belong to the Gospels. Furthermore, it teaches the precepts of the moral law very imperfectly.
2. For Aristotelian ethics has little or nothing to say concerning the precepts set out in the first table [of the Ten Commandments],[6] where, in fact, the most outstanding virtues are contained. Pythagoras and Plato were a bit more fortunate in this respect because they travelled to Syria and Egypt and learnt a great deal from the Hebrew sages;[7] but Aristotle either did not have this information or he chose to ignore it.
3. Aristotle, in addition, skipped over some virtues of the second table [of the Ten Commandments], such as mercy, the obedience owed to superiors and so forth. Indeed, he actually regarded some vices as virtues: for instance, like Cicero, he considered revenge to be praiseworthy.[8] He did not classify the first stirrings of the emotions (or of desire) as vices, although they are prohibited by the Tenth Commandment.
4. Moreover, Aristotle was ignorant of the principles and the end of true virtue. For he derived the origin of all virtuous actions from a virtuous disposition alone, although it is faith in God and love (or reverence for God) which draw forth all truly virtuous actions from virtuous dispositions and direct them towards their proper end. Aristotle established moral goodness as the end for the sake of which virtue is practised; but he was completely silent on the glory of God and our future happiness, to which all things, including moral goodness itself, must be referred.

If, therefore, we wish to study Aristotle's ethics without running the risk of error, it is necessary for us to correct every part of this discipline according to the standard of the Word of God and to use the Word of God to supply whatever is lacking in this discipline. . . .

Man's Supreme Good

What we call man's supreme good is the ultimate end of all human actions. It is also called beatitude and happiness. The Greeks call it *eudaimonia* [good fortune; from *eu* = good, and *daimōn* = a supernatural being] because it makes us similar to the fortunate intelligences. They also call it *eupragia* [well-being] from *eu prattein,* that is, to live well and happily. In addition, they call it *to agathon* [the good] and *to eschaton* [the end]. . . .

From what has been said and discussed so far, we can define the supreme good according to Aristotle as follows. The supreme good is the perfect exercise of the most perfect virtue in a life which is in every way perfect.[9] This virtue suffuses the soul of man with the greatest delight and makes him worthy of supreme honour.

Aristotle splits this virtue which we have termed most perfect into two, that is, into contemplative and active virtue. Contemplative virtue resides in the mind and is called wisdom. Active virtue resides in the will and is called justice. The more perfectly these two species of virtue combine in a man, the happier and the more fortunate he is. Even if it frequently happens that one person excels more in wisdom and another in justice, both of them are to be deemed happy, though they are less than perfectly so. Perfect happiness arises precisely from the combination of both virtues.

Aristotle has a good deal to say about the combination of the two virtues in Book X of the *Ethics*.[10] The debate usually centres on what he means by a 'perfect life'. The most probable interpretation is that he understands a perfect life to be one which lasts for a due period of time and is free throughout its entire course of any depraved deeds.

This opinion of Aristotle, if we have interpreted him accurately, is very imperfect. But if we correct his thinking, without imposing on his words a sense that they cannot bear, then his opinion can be reconciled with the truth.

Man was created by God for this end: that he conforms himself to God by means of virtuous actions, both of the mind and of the will. But here a defect in [Aristotle's] definition arises: the extreme perfection of man is placed in these virtuous actions, although the conformity which is demanded in this life is merely the path or means to eternal happiness in the future. In truth, virtue should not be desired for its own sake in such a way that it is not also desired for the sake of something else which is actually a greater good: that through it we may worship God and pave the way to future happiness.

Plato ascends higher here, for he made the supreme good consist in the vision or fruition of God. He understood the virtues which can be achieved here on earth to be the means [to this end], since they purge our mind and will so that we are better and more readily able to see God and unite ourselves to him. Among the purgative virtues, Plato gave first place to religion and piety towards God, which were simply ignored by Aristotle. As the most eminent Platonists point out, Plato called the vision and fruition of God an idea which our minds ought always to contemplate so that they can always be happy. Consequently, Aristotle's criticisms of Plato concerning the ideas[11] – as if Plato made happiness consist in the contemplation of abstract forms – seem to be a misinterpretation of his intentions, as is readily apparent to anyone who reads Plato's books.

This opinion of Plato agrees beautifully with theological truth, for the Sacred Scriptures affirm that man's supreme good consists in the vision and fruition of God. A true illumination of the mind and purification of the will must precede this vision of God, as Christ says in Matthew 5[:8]: 'Blessed are the pure of heart: for they shall see God.' But Plato erred because he did not know the true cause which purifies and prepares our minds and wills. The true cause of this purification is the grace of Christ alone, gained through faith and its efficacious application to our minds and wills by the Holy Spirit, as Peter testifies in Acts 15[:9], when he refers to 'cleansing their hearts by faith'. The fruit of, and the testimonies to, this grace imparted to us by Christ are the true and Christian virtues. Many of these far exceed the measure of the virtues in Aristotle's *Ethics,* even though we admit that these latter virtues – or, as the Scriptures call them, good works – are the means by which we should strive towards our future celestial happiness.

Freedom of the Will

. . . From the issues which have been discussed so far [that is, the proper object of the will and our powers of deliberation and choice] a celebrated ethical question arises, one which was formerly debated by Aristotle and other pagan moralists and which has now become no less an object of controversy among theologians: do these principles [of deliberation and choice] act freely and are they self-determined, or, instead, do they act under compulsion? Leaving aside the more prolix disputations of the theologians, I shall briefly indicate what a moral philosopher needs to know concerning these things, and then I shall lay out the true Christian position.[12]

Freedom is an equivocal term which is usually understood in a variety of ways. First, whatever is spontaneous is said to be free. This is the freedom that is proper to beasts, for the ox freely seeks his fodder and birds freely fly through the air. Second, any acts of the will guided by reason are called free. Thus, the angels in heaven act freely and yet always correctly; and man's will freely wishes its ultimate end and happiness. Third, we take someone to be free when he is not subject to or dependent on anyone else. According to this definition, only God is free or *autexousios,* that is, he is the absolute master of his own actions. Fourth, the word freedom is taken to mean the power to accept or reject, to seek or avoid a proposed thing.

This fourth form of freedom is determined in two ways: through specification and through exercise. The scholastics define specification as the power of choosing by prior deliberation one thing from among a variety of proposed things. They define exercise as the power of choosing or rejecting a proposed thing; others call it the freedom of contrariety and of contradiction. It is with this fourth kind of freedom that we are concerned.

I am not, however, going to dispute anxiously as to why man, rather than the rest of the animal world, was endowed with freedom. The fact is that it pleased God, the author of nature, to adorn man with these gifts in comparison with the other animals. Nevertheless, we should not disregard what others suggest as a secondary cause, namely, that man was given this freedom because the human mind is not corporeal nor is it necessarily dependent on matter, as are the [substantial] forms of other animals. Since, therefore, the human mind is unfettered and free of corporeal bounds – even though it is connected to matter – it is, accordingly, capable of ruling the body and bodily passions, unless it has surrendered itself in voluntary servitude to the body.

Nor am I going to launch into a lengthy dispute as to which faculty freedom properly resides in, that is, whether it is located in the intellect or the will, since a strong case can be made for either. At times, however, the conventional and more common opinion that freedom resides in the will is better suited to the way the Holy Scriptures speak; for God instilled into the will the ability to turn one way or the other. Yet, even if this is so, the will itself is blind. Consequently, without an indication and judgement from the intellect, the will cannot choose or refuse anything. The neutrality of the intellect (for it extends itself over diverse means) is another reason why the will can vary its actions. We should also take note of the scholastic dictum: freedom is in the intellect radically, but in the will formally.

The difficulty which has to be explored in depth here revolves entirely around the question of the extent to which freedom manifests itself in these principles or faculties of the soul. To resolve this difficulty fully, we have to understand the question in two ways: first, in respect to God and his providence, which transcends our will; and, second, in respect to the objects with which the will is concerned.

We must ask first of all: is the will so free and so much the master of its own actions that in everything it does it is not subject to the will of God and to his governance? Ancient philosophers put forward different opinions in reply to this question. The Epicureans, though they acknowledged some sort of divinity, nevertheless denied its providence and argued that everything comes about by chance and without any purpose. Consequently, they denied that man's will is subject to divine governance. As Horace put it, expressing the Epicurean point of view: 'For I have learned that the gods lead a life free from care.'[13] But the Epicureans are rejected by all other philosophers. Indeed, Cicero rightly comments about them that although they *said* that the gods existed, in actual fact they abolished them;[14] for, without his care and providence, God cannot be understood.

The Platonists and Aristotelians were more sensible. They recognized that God rules over everything and that by his providence he maintains everything in its nature. But they removed from his governance the individual actions of the human will, which, they argued, were *eph'ēmin,* that is, purely within our own power.

The Stoics, by contrast, rightly subjected everything, both universals as well as individuals, to divine governance; but they sinned in the opposite direction, since they abolished the distinction between those causes which act necessarily and those which act contingently. They asserted that everything happens by an inexorable fate and a natural concatenation of causes.

Having dispatched the opinions of the philosophers, we can now turn to the true, Christian position, which is that all human actions, good as well as bad, universal as well as individual, are subject to divine providence and governance and are ruled by it according to the eternal decree and infallible knowledge of God. In addition to Scripture, which clearly attests to this in many places, reason too necessarily forces the very same conclusion upon us. It would follow that those things which do not happen according to God's decree have an existence apart from him; in which case he would either have been ignorant or negligent or unfavourably disposed. None of these states can be ascribed to God without blasphemy. Therefore, he knows, wills and governs everything which happens; in other words, everything happens according to his will and under his direction, by means of which he makes and promotes all that is good. Evil things, however, he justly permits to happen, directing them towards ends which he has foreordained.

First objection. If this is the case, how can man's actions be free? Or, how can he deserve praise for his good actions and punishment for his bad ones?

My reply. This difficulty is so great that some people, unable to reconcile these positions, either deny with the Peripatetics that God governs individual actions or assert with the Stoics that everything happens according to fate. Yet even if this difficulty cannot be removed, we must not deny what is clearly stated in the Scriptures on the grounds that we cannot solve a difficult problem.

Those of a well-balanced disposition seem, however, to be able to find satisfaction in the following way: they say that God's decree concerning the determination of contingent things and of those things which are dependent on man's liberty does not exclude but rather includes freedom and contingency, because God's wisdom is so great that he does not violate the nature of inferior causes by his decree. Consequently, he determined that necessary causes produce their actions necessarily, while contingent causes work contingently and through antecedent choice. Thus, man freely does what he does because God decreed that he should freely perform these actions rather than those.

Second objection. But the decree which determines that the will of man will produce these rather than those actions obviously seems to take away all freedom of the will in producing these actions since the essence of freedom is self-determination and not determination by another.

My reply. I admit that being determined solely by oneself and not by another is the essence of absolute freedom. But this absolute freedom belongs to God alone. It is enough, however, for the freedom of a created being that it determines itself as the proximate cause of its own actions, while sometimes being determined by God as the supreme cause, who also leaves to the created being the motions that are proper to it, as Augustine rightly states in *The City of God* VII.30.

Third objection. But these things can scarcely be understood.

My reply. I admit this freely. The ways and modes of action of a power and a wisdom which are infinite cannot be perfectly grasped by a finite intellect. But it does not follow from this that things are not as we described them. For everyone (unless they are even worse than Turks and pagans) acknowledges that God has had foreknowledge from eternity of the determination of the human will in all its actions. Can any human being understand how God has foreseen that something which is the effect of undetermined causes will definitely happen? Indeed, if anyone can explain to me how God, by the infinite light of his knowledge, has foreseen this without violating human liberty, I will by the same token explain to him how God decreed it from eternity by his supremely wise decree and executed it in time without violating human freedom.[15]

Another question which Aristotle raises at this point in the *Ethics* and which I mentioned earlier is whether by its nature the will has the same power for good as for evil.[16] I am not speaking here about a man regenerated in Christ through the Spirit. It is the task of theologians to discuss such a man's capacity for doing good or ill, since regeneration is a supernatural phenomenon, about which a natural man obviously knows nothing. I am, therefore, referring to a natural man considered outside the state of regeneration, such as were all the pagan philosophers and their disciples. The question thus is whether it is as much in their power to do good as to do evil and vice versa.

Aristotle proves the affirmative against the Stoics and others by means of the following arguments. First, because [if the will did not have the same power for good as for evil] legislators would be wrong to reward those who do good deeds and to punish those who perpetrate evil ones. Second, because [if this were the case] chastisements and criticisms would be employed in vain. Last, because [otherwise] remorse and pain would not follow upon doing evil or peace of mind and happiness upon good deeds.[17]

It is sometimes maintained, however, that those who do wrong out of ignorance, for which they themselves are the cause, or due to an evil disposition, cannot help doing wrong; and yet they are justly blamed and punished because the origin of their ignorance and their wicked disposition lay in their own power and also because individual wicked acts are not necessary in the same way as are the wicked dispositions from which these acts derive.

These arguments have some weight against the Stoics. Nevertheless, in order to understand and resolve this question in a Christian fashion, we need to distinguish between two different goods. One good is supernatural and spiritual; it without doubt has a definite relationship with the future life. It is true repentance, true trust in God through Christ the Mediator, true love for God and men, true hope of eternal life in the future and so on. Plainly, an unregenerate man has no capacity for this good because 'the natural man receiveth not the things of the Spirit of God; . . . and he cannot know them because they are spiritually judged': I Corinthians 2[:14]. Consequently, this good has to be revealed to us by supernatural means; and, once revealed, it must be communicated to us through the grace of Christ.

The other good is natural and civic; it is related to the life of a man living in this world. Man neither properly obeys God within his soul nor provides for his future eternal reward by means of this good; but through it he does exercise the virtues as well as the domestic and civic arts by means of which life on earth and human society are conserved and earthly rewards are provided. I admit that natural man has some residual freedom and capacity for attaining this good, as is attested by the arguments advanced by Aristotle, the example set by many praiseworthy pagans and even the Holy Scriptures, when speaking of the Pharisees.[18]

Sometimes, nevertheless, one must insist on the following point (as Plato, Pythagoras, Plutarch and other pagans are forced to acknowledge): nature is extremely weak in attaining this good and incapable of reaching its more elevated levels without the aid of divine inspiration, which the theologians call a 'special aid'. Sacred history is a witness to this in relation to Saul, who was clothed with the spirit of Jehovah at the start of his reign;[19] and for the same reason Cyrus was called the anointed of Jehovah;[20] and Bezalel and Oholiab,[21] the builders of the tabernacle and the temple, are said to have been peculiarly endowed by the spirit of God for the construction of these things. Consequently, this good too is to be sought from God, and all the more so by Christians who have learned to refer even this natural good to supernatural ends.

Translator's Notes

1. The work was dedicated to various civic and religious officials in Middelburg.
2. This is an allusion to the standard tripartite division of moral philosophy into politics, oeconomics and ethics; see *CHRP*, pp. 303–6.
3. De Waele uses the expression 'ad ipsorum *elenchos* excitavit'.
4. For selections from Melanchthon's *The Elements of Ethical Doctrine* see Chapter 10.

5. Lambert Daneau (1530–95) was a prolific Calvinist theologian; in his *Ethices Christianae libri tres* (Geneva, 1577), he eschewed pagan moral philosophy and constructed his ethical system on the basis of the Ten Commandments.
6. According to the Old Testament, the precepts revealed by God to Moses were engraved on two tables of stone, each containing five commandments. For the text of the Ten Commandments see Exodus 20:1–17 and Deuteronomy 5:6–21.
7. For this widely held belief of Christians see Eusebius of Caesarea, *Praeparatio Evangelica* IX.6.6–8; and Clement of Alexandria, *Stromata* I.15. For Plato, see also A. S. Riginos, *Platonica: The Anecdotes concerning the Life and Writings of Plato* (Leiden, 1976), p. 65.
8. This is not quite accurate; see the discussion of reciprocity in Aristotle, *Nicomachean Ethics* V.5 (1132^b21–30). For Cicero, see, e.g., *De inventione* II.22.66 and II.53.161.
9. Cf. Aristotle, *Nicomachean Ethics* I.7 (1098^a16–20).
10. Aristotle, *Nicomachean Ethics* X.7–8.
11. Aristotle, *Nicomachean Ethics* I.6.
12. For Melanchthon's discussion of this issue see Chapter 10.
13. Horace, *Satires* I.5.101, quoting Lucretius, *De rerum natura* V.82.
14. See Cicero, *De natura deorum* I.12.29, where this criticism is directed against Democritus, not Epicurus.
15. On this issue see *CHRP*, ch. 17.
16. See Aristotle, *Nicomachean Ethics* III.5; see also de Waele, *Compendium,* pp. 120–2.
17. For the first two arguments see *Nicomachean Ethics* 1113^b21–30; the final argument seems to be a very free reading of 1114^a11–15.
18. See, e.g., Acts 5:34–40, where the Pharisee Gamaliel, 'a teacher of the law, held in reputation among all the people', publicly defends the apostles before the Sanhedrin.
19. See I Samuel 12:12–25.
20. Isaiah 45:1.
21. See Exodus 31:1–11 and 6:1; de Waele refers to Oholiab as 'Chira'.

Further Reading

Aristotle, *L'Éthique à Nicomaque,* ed. R. A. Gauthier and J. Y. Jolif, 2 vols. (Paris, 1970), I.1: *Introduction,* p. 203
CHRP, pp. 325, 346, 359, 363–4, 379
Grotius, Hugo, *Meletus sive De iis quae inter Christianos conveniunt epistola,* ed. G. H. M. Posthumus Meyjes (Leiden, 1988), pp. 46–53
Lohr, C. H., *Latin Aristotle Commentaries* (Florence, 1988–), II, p. 489
Lunsingh Scheurleer, T. H., and Posthumus Meyjes, G. H. M., eds., *Leiden University in the Seventeenth Century: An Exchange of Learning* (Leiden, 1975), pp. 94–5, 478
Nieuw Nederlandsch Biographisch Woordenboek, 10 vols. (Leiden, 1911–37), II, cols. 1513–17
Schouten, J., *Johannes Walaeus* (Assen, 1972), pp. 6–8

Part IV.
Platonic Ethics

12

Cardinal Bessarion

LUC DEITZ AND JOHN MONFASANI

Introduction

Bessarion (c. 1403/8–72) was born in Trebizond and educated in Constantinople. Entering the Order of St Basil in 1423, he was ordained a priest in 1431. His philosophical training culminated in his study of Platonism in Mistra under the guidance of George Gemistos Plethon, who was to become notorious when his treatise *The Laws* was posthumously revealed to contain blatantly pagan material. After becoming archbishop of Nicaea in 1437, Bessarion attended the Council of Ferrara/Florence (1438–43), where he was one of the key Byzantine supporters of union of the Greek and Latin churches. Created a cardinal of the Catholic Church in 1439, he took up residence at the papal court in Florence in 1440, subsequently moving with the Curia to Rome in 1443. He became a highly influential member of the Curia and was several times nearly elected pope. He was actively engaged in papal diplomacy and became patriarch of Constantinople in 1463, a decade after the fall of the city to the Turks. His magnificent collection of Greek manuscripts was bequeathed to Venice, where – after decades of neglect – it formed the core of the Marciana Library.

Against the Slanderer of Plato, written in Greek by Bessarion but published in Latin translation (1469), was a reply to the *Comparison of Plato and Aristotle* (1458) of George of Trebizond (1396–c. 1472).[1] George, like Bessarion a Byzantine émigré living in Italy, was a virulent anti-Platonist, who maintained Aristotle's superiority over Plato on all counts – as a metaphysician, as a moral philosopher and, above all, as a Roman Catholic *avant la lettre.*

Bessarion's voluminous apology is far less venomous than George's ferocious attack. Whenever possible, he tries to show that the philosophical differences between Plato and Aristotle are at worst minimal and at best non-existent. There is only one aspect, says Bessarion, in which Plato is constantly and without exception superior to Aristotle: he was much closer to Christianity and anticipated all those truths of the Catholic faith that natural reason, unaided by revelation, could permit a pagan to grasp.

The passages from Book II translated here illustrate both Bessarion's approach to Plato, which was strongly influenced by the ancient Neoplatonist Proclus, and the way in which he continuously reminds his readers that Plato accords much better than Aristotle with the Church.

The Greek and Latin texts of *In calumniatorem Platonis* are published in the second volume of L. Mohler, *Kardinal Bessarion als Theologe, Humanist und Staatsmann,* 3 vols. (Paderborn, 1923–42); for the translated passages see pp. 81–93, 103–7, 139–46, 154. Chapters 1 and 2, and the selections from chapters 5 and 8, have been translated from the Greek text by Luc Deitz. Chapters 3 and 4 have been translated from the Latin version by John Monfasani.

Against the Slanderer of Plato

BOOK II, SELECTIONS

*Chapter 1: Plato's Writings Agree More Readily with the Christian Religion
Than Do Aristotle's*

Although Plato has not provided us with a fully fledged method for understanding the
sciences and the arts, I have shown that he must nonetheless be considered superior
to all other philosophers inasmuch as he wrote the best and wisest books on these
subjects.[2] Now his detractor claims in the second book of his work that the philosopher who comes nearer to the truth of the faith and who is more in agreement with the
teaching of the Church must be held wiser; and he tries to prove that the doctrines of
Aristotle are in tune with those of the Church, whereas the doctrines of Plato are out
of tune with them. I am now going to advance the opposite claim and show with clear
arguments that, if either of them, it is Plato rather than Aristotle who agrees with the
Catholic faith. I do not say this because I would wish Plato rather than Aristotle to
enter the Church by the backdoor; nor do I say it out of contempt for Aristotle: both
are alien to our faith and far removed from it, and both are Greek in origin as well as
religion. Therefore, it is fruitless for the detractor of Plato to praise Aristotle in this
part of his work, and fruitless for him, lacking any genuine praise, to take refuge in
the Church and in the faith, like those who are condemned to death and hide themselves in a sanctuary as if it were a place of retreat. Accordingly, it is not my aim to
enter a pointless competition and to prove, as he did with Aristotle, that Plato was a
Christian; rather, I will try to show that even an enemy of the Church, if he were
looking for assistance and a guide to lead him towards the truth of the faith, should
turn towards the writings of Plato instead of those of Aristotle; and I will also try to
show how such a person can derive the greatest benefit from them.

*Chapter 2: Reply to the Opinion Expressed by the Slanderer of Plato That
One Should Put More Faith in Those Who Have Devoted Themselves to
Particular Sciences Than in Our Church Fathers*

This fine fellow knew full well that the Church Fathers — saintly men, who
distinguished themselves by their knowledge of both Christian and pagan doctrines —
derived greater benefit from Plato's writings than from Aristotle's, and that they
would always invoke Plato as their guide and their witness, but never Aristotle.
Therefore, he sets out to refute the Fathers and to eradicate the esteem we feel in our
hearts for their wisdom by recommending to us that, as far as he is concerned, we
should rely on his judgement in these matters rather than on theirs. Who is he to put
himself above such men? But this comedian's joke does not carry conviction, even if
this is indeed his recommendation.[3] For he says: 'Whatever they have written when
inspired by the Holy Spirit — that is, whatever relates to faith and the salvation of the
faithful — we must believe, but whatever relates to other matters and what they have
said about these matters is not always trustworthy. For in questions related to geome-

try or astronomy, it is the geometer or the astronomer rather than any of our holy Fathers whom we must believe.'[4] Thus, we must believe them in matters related to faith, my dear fellow, since these are the things that have been dictated to them by the Holy Spirit. But if the Fathers employed the writings of Plato in order to expound our faith, then we must believe them in another respect as well – that they considered Plato to be wiser and more consonant with the Church than Aristotle. On the other hand, if the Church Fathers had been nothing more than saints, devoted to God in this particular respect, and if they had tasted from the spring of knowledge with the tips of their tongues only (as the saying goes) in order to be able to explain the general meaning of a doctrine in a simplified way in their own writings, then I would grant you that, just as one should trust a geometer in matters geometrical rather than a saint, one should also trust those who are thoroughly acquainted with philosophy and have mastered all the arts rather than those who are completely uninitiated, even if they are saints. If, however, they have not only attained the summits of holiness and wisdom but have also studied the writings of Plato and Aristotle and become thoroughly acquainted with the doctrines of both – such as, for example, Basil, Gregory Nazianzenus, Cyril and Gregory of Nyssa among the Greeks, or Augustine and Boethius among the Romans, as well as many others who were not only very wise, but had reached the highest degree of wisdom and who never shrank from seeking assistance in the philosophy of the pagans when they were dealing with questions related to faith – how dare you claim that we should abandon their lead and follow you as our sole guide? I will therefore dismiss your claim and follow our Fathers instead, the holiest and wisest of men, in order to prove my thesis.

Chapter 3: *The Author Justifies Himself for Not Wishing to Attack Aristotle*

But now I am in the unpleasant position of having to write what I in no way wish to write. For, though I myself am accustomed to praise Aristotle no less than Plato,[5] my opponent's iniquity towards Plato forces me to write these things so that I do not appear to shirk my duty. My opponent says and, by his lights, proves that Aristotle wrote better than Plato concerning the divine nature because Aristotle posited a divine trinity, while Plato did not; that Aristotle understood heaven and earth to have been produced out of nothing solely by the will of God, while Plato posited prime matter as the origin of the world; that Aristotle also discussed the soul most splendidly, while Plato wrote fictions about it; that Aristotle believed everything to be ruled and governed by God's providence, while Plato subjected everything to fate and necessity. My adversary has framed his argument in such a way that when I strive to demonstrate the contrary, I appear to think better of Plato than I do of Aristotle. I seem thus to be censuring Aristotle, which is not what I intend at all. For I too always speak most honourably of Aristotle. It would be depraved and insolent of me to want to disparage Aristotle in order to defend Plato. May such a notion be banished from my mind! For I consider both to have been supremely wise. I believe that we owe both a debt of gratitude for the good that they have conferred on humankind. This is something that Aristotle himself authorizes us to do. In the book which he calls the *Metaphysics* and which deals with that part of philosophy concerned with divine things, he has this to say: 'It is right to give thanks not only to those who have assiduously handed down to us the precepts of the disciplines, but also to those who have treated these matters superficially or meagrely. They too have done us a service by having us improve our aptitude through exercise. For if there had been no Timotheus, we would not have so many melodies; but if there had been no Phrynis,[6] not even Timotheus would have excelled. We should have the same attitude towards those who wished to investigate the truth. While we have derived certain of our opinions from some of them, the rest were responsible for the views of those who did influence us.'[7]

Therefore, in this comparison of the two philosophers, I shall not praise one to the heavens and heap scorn and abuse upon the other – as my adversary did – for I cherish and venerate both of them. But let those who are capable of carrying on such investigations discover for themselves what Aristotle's opinion was concerning the topics listed here. Let them also discover whether he wrote any of the things, or wrote in the way, my adversary attributes to him. There are many people who can do this: virtually all the philosophically sophisticated Latins of our age are devotees of the Peripatetic sect. They have very diligently studied and comprehended what Aristotle wrote. I certainly shall in no way claim that Aristotle thought or wrote about these matters better here and less well there. It is a waste of time to belabour what is common knowledge. Nor shall I say anything against Aristotle, except to deny that he was a Christian and perhaps to show on occasion, by way of explanation, that Aristotle's words are not to be read in the way that my adversary supposes. I shall not do this in order to accuse Aristotle, but in order to make clear that this slanderer of Plato had no understanding of Aristotle and perverted his ideas.

I shall strive, on the other hand, to expound Plato's opinions with the greatest care, since his views are unknown to virtually all Latins – partly because his writings have not been available in Latin translation, and partly because what translations there are do not accurately express his thought, which is the fault of the translators. For good reason, therefore, Plato's opinions on such divine matters must be explained so that the Latins can also understand how close and almost akin to our religion his opinions are. Conversely, it will also become clear how falsely my adversary has slandered Plato.

For the most part, I shall proceed in the following manner. If I prove the opposite of what my adversary charges against Plato, I shall do so by quoting Plato's own words. But if I also adduce the testimony of the Church Fathers and demonstrate that Plato's views were expounded and approved by these sacrosanct voices, the truth of the matter will surely shine forth all the more, and no one will doubt that Plato thought and wrote, not as my adversary imagines, but as I say. After expounding Plato, I shall refute, in turn, the inept commentary and flimsy arguments of my adversary in relation to Aristotle and show how far his assertions depart from the philosopher's thought and words.

But before I take up Plato, let me make it perfectly clear that I am not defending his doctrine in this way because I endorse it in every respect and consider it comparable with our religion. I approve neither of the pre-existence of souls, nor of the multiplicity of gods, nor of the souls of the heavens and the stars, nor of many other things for which the Church condemns the pagans. Rather, I plan to set forth what the two philosophers believed and what the difference is between them. Both were pagans and foreign to our religion. Nonetheless, if one of them had better beliefs and was more in harmony with our religion, it will be worth saying so. I certainly will not be harming Aristotle if I seem to prefer Plato to him, especially since I have not entered into this comparison gratuitously, but was forced into it by my adversary, who compared the two philosophers in a shameless and ignominious manner. In my opinion, Aristotle ought to be praised both for his learning, in which he above all excelled, and for his scholarly writings, for which he deserves the thanks of mankind.

Chapter 4: What Plato Says in the Parmenides on the First Principle of All Beings

Let us see, therefore, what Plato wrote in the *Parmenides* concerning the first being or rather concerning the first of all beings and the first principle positioned above all beings. I cite, however, just the main points. 'The One', he says – for this is how he refers to the supersubstantial divinity of God,

is not many. Nor is it a part or a whole. Nor does it have a beginning, a middle or an end. It is infinite and without form. It is circumscribed by no place. It never stays still. It has no movement, neither through locomotion or alteration. It is not in any way in the state of becoming. Nor is it the same as, or different from, itself or another. Nor is it equal or unequal, nor old or new, nor in any time, but utterly without time. Consequently, it has never been begotten, nor is it being begotten. Nor has it ever or in any way become, nor is it becoming, nor will it become in the future. Nor will it be begotten. Nor does it participate in a substance. The words 'was', 'was becoming', 'has been begotten' signify past time; 'will be', 'will become' and 'will be begotten' signify future time; 'is' and 'is being begotten', present time. That, however, which is subject to no time, neither was, nor is, nor will be. It therefore follows that we attribute no name to it, nor give it a definition, nor have any knowledge or sensation or opinion of it. Thus, it is neither named, nor mentioned, nor thought, nor recognized, nor perceived by any being.[8]

These are Plato's words in the *Parmenides,* though selectively collected together by me. In his other works, such as the *Phaedrus,* the *Phaedo,* the *Philebus,* the *Timaeus,* the *Sophist,* the *Laws,* the *Republic,* the *Letters,* and in all the passages where he talks about divine matters, he is invariably consistent, speaking the same way about the same points, which is the duty of a learned man and is evidence of true and secure reasoning. For Plato everywhere calls the first principle of all things the One; everywhere he calls it the maker and creator of the universe, everywhere the supreme good, the king and founder of all things. His books are to hand; those who wish can read them and imbibe from the source in its original language what I have translated as best I could. This theology of Plato was so appealing to the most holy Fathers of our faith that whenever they wrote about God, they wanted to use not just his ideas, but also his words.

Take that holy man, Dionysius the Areopagite, who was the first and supreme author of Christian theology and who had no one before him save the apostle Paul and Hierotheus, the pontiff of Athens.[9] They were his teachers, and he was on intimate terms with both of them. In the book he published *On the Divine Names,* he wrote as follows: 'The supersubstantial infinity indeed abides above all substances, and the supermental unity above all minds; and it is unintelligible to all intelligences because the One and the Ineffable transcends every intelligence and because the Good transcends every manner of speaking about it.'[10] Again, he wrote: 'Unifying Unity is the supersubstantial substance of every unity; it is unintelligible mind, ineffable reason, irrationality, unintelligibility, unnameability. It is similar to no being and is the cause of all beings. It, however, is not a being since it is beyond all substance.' Again: 'There is no sensation of it, nor imagination, nor opinion, nor reason, nor knowledge, nor name.' And a little later: 'The supersubstantial divine principle can in no way be understood because it is the superessence of supergoodness. For it is not permissible for anyone who is gripped by the love of the truth which transcends all truth to speak of it as reason or virtue, nor as mind or life or substance. It must instead be understood as transcending utterly every disposition, life, magnitude, opinion, name, reason, mind, intelligence, substance, motion, condition, place, union, end, infinity and, in sum, all things.'[11] Did Dionysius not take these things from Plato and did he not – I ask you before immortal God! – use almost the same words?

What about Gregory the Theologian,[12] who received this cognomen from the Greeks because of the excellence of his theological teaching? Let me quote him. He says in the sermon *On the Resurrection of the Lord:*

Thus, God was and is and will be, or, to speak more correctly, always is. For the words 'was' and 'will be' are particles of our time and of flowing and unstable nature. God, however, is always being, and that is what he named himself when he spoke to Moses on the mountain.[13] For he encompasses in himself his whole being,[14] which neither begins nor ends.[15]

And a little later he says: 'Indeed, God's infinite existence cannot be easily contemplated by reason; this one thing about it is not difficult to grasp: to understand that it is infinite.'[16]

Plato, illuminated only by the light of nature, wrote these things about the One and the first principle of all things and about the simplicity and unity of God. Our most holy and wise Fathers, the leading men of the Christian religion, taught these things by divine inspiration,[17] a fact which would seem to offer sufficient proof that Plato was right to have written and believed these things. If the foremost leaders of our faith believe this, can anyone doubt that other Christian authorities also have the same opinion about Plato? For the sake of brevity, however, I shall pass over them.

But is it possible to get any closer to our religion than what Plato wrote in Book IV of the *Laws*?

God, as ancient opinion has it, encompasses the beginning, the end and the middle of all things. He proceeds in a straight course, traversing everything through the agency of nature. Justice, the punisher of those who have violated the divine law, always comes in his train. Anyone who wants to be happy follows God devotedly, in humility and modesty. God, however, will abandon and leave to wander in miserable loneliness the person who is puffed up with pride or is insolent on account of wealth or honour or physical beauty or youthfulness and who at the same time is so insanely haughty that he has the effrontery to desire to have no prince or leader for himself, as if he himself were able to govern others.[18]

Take note, I beseech you, of the great conformity and similarity of these words [of Plato] with Sacred Scriptures. 'I the Lord, the first', the Scriptures say, 'and with the last, I am he' [Isaiah 41:4]. Plato says:'God encompasses the beginning, the end, and the middle.' The Scriptures say: 'The upright [*rectitudines*] shall behold his face' [Psalms 11:7]. Plato says: 'He proceeds in a straight [*recte*] course.' The Scriptures say: 'The Lord is righteous; he loveth righteousness' [Psalms 11:7]; and: 'Vengeance belongeth unto me; I will recompense saith the Lord' [Romans 12:19]. Plato says: 'Justice, the punisher, always comes in his train.' The Scriptures say: 'You shall walk after the Lord' [Hosea 11:10]. Plato says: 'The person who follows him devotedly will be happy.' The Scriptures say: 'God resisteth the proud' [I Peter 5:5]. Plato says: 'God abandons the proud.' In addition, he says in the *Philebus:* 'Mind is the king of heaven and earth',[19] which he later superbly and beautifully explains at length. Also, in the *Timaeus* he asks what is it that always is and was never begotten. And then he says: 'That which can be grasped by intelligence in conjunction with reason always exists in the same state', and so forth,[20] which he explicates in that passage with supreme wisdom.

Plato, therefore, has received the approbation of everyone to an amazing degree in these matters. Aristotle, on the other hand, followed Plato in what he wrote on such matters, though he did not speak as distinctly as Plato about them. For instance, in his book *On Divine Things* [that is, the *Metaphysics*],[21] he quotes the famous line of Homer: 'Let there be one king; let there be one ruler.'[22] To take another example, he asserts that God and nature do nothing in vain. Again, in Book VIII of the *Physics* and Book XII of *On Divine Things,* he discusses very briefly the unmoved mover, who is the cause of his own existence. Even if he wrote on these things correctly and wisely, the enormous difference between his statements and those of Plato is easy for anyone to judge.

Chapter 5: My Adversary Has Ineptly Interpreted Aristotle's Words at the Beginning of De Caelo

. . . Everyone knows that Plato was not a Christian and that, consequently, no one who professes to be a Christian should follow in his precise footsteps. To be sure, some signs, marks and traces, as it were, of our faith can be found in Plato's writings. Their presence is due to the natural lucidity of an enlightened mind. It is, however, through the incarnation of his beloved son and the teaching [of the Church] that the creator and master of the universe in the course of time amended and perfected these signs and revealed them more clearly. I am convinced that these hints provide no small help for those who are eager to leave the shores of Platonism and to set sail for the perfection of our faith, for they come very close to the truths proclaimed by our own theology. The similarities are only slightly obscured by the differences. If, therefore, someone turns his back on the divine and perfect teaching of the Holy Scriptures and prefers instead the writings of Plato, the blame must be laid on this person rather than on Plato himself.

Another reason why Plato deserves praise is that those who wish to become Christians cling to his doctrines. Indeed, it would be impossible to profess at the same time both a Platonic and a Christian faith if there were no similarity between the doctrines of Plato and those of Christ which shine through. Whoever strays from the truth wanders more readily towards that which is close to it than towards that which is opposed to it. This explains why those who went astray did not embrace the doctrines of Aristotle, which are completely contrary to our own, but preferred instead those of Plato, who is closer to us and holds opinions that accord better with our own beliefs.[23] Even if, in this respect, they have committed a grave and unforgivable sin – for, being Christians, they can boast both of having the wisdom of God, in whom the treasures of wisdom are hidden,[24] as their teacher and of having a share in the divine revelation – they were nonetheless right to hold the divine utterances of Plato in higher esteem than anything else and, being firmly established in that foundation alongside which no other foundation-stone can possibly be laid, to subject everything else to their duty to Christ. . . .

Here is another example of how Plato accords better with the Church than does Aristotle, or, to be more precise, of how Plato's doctrines accord with those of the Church, whereas similar considerations never even entered into Aristotle's mind. Plato holds faith to be the first and foremost virtue, thus paying eloquent tribute to many supernatural things. Thus, he says in the *Timaeus:*

Concerning the other divinities, to know and to declare their generation is too high a task for us; we must trust those who have declared it in former times: being, as they said, descendants of gods, they must, no doubt, have had certain knowledge of their ancestors. We cannot, then, mistrust the children of gods, though they speak without probable or necessary proofs; when they profess to report their family history, we must follow established usage and accept what they say.[25]

And in Book I of the *Laws,* when speaking of Tyrtaeus's praise of a brave man for defending his city against 'foreign aggressors from abroad', he shows that those who act bravely in a state of civil war (which he calls 'a more bitter war') are far superior and much more valiant, quoting Theognis's saying: 'A faithful man, Cyrnus, is worth his weight in gold and silver in the hour of deadly feuds.'[26] In the explanation which he himself gives of these lines, he says that this type of man is better than the other sort 'to the extent to which justice, prudence and wisdom, combined together and seconded by valour, are better than mere valour by itself. For a man will never prove himself faithful and sound-hearted in times of faction unless he has all the virtues.' And a little further on: 'Obviously our legislator from the school of Zeus, or any other worth his salt, could have no other object in view in his legislation than the supreme virtue. This supreme virtue is what Theognis speaks of as faithfulness in peril, and we may call it complete righteousness.'[27] And in Book XI of the same work, when Plato appoints the guardians and foster-parents for orphans and entrusts them with the care of these children with a view to their becoming, as it were, second parents to the orphans, in no way inferior to their natural parents, he says, in an effort to rally them to his opinion:

I believe that there was something really opportune in all we said before of a power of taking an interest in human life retained by the souls of the departed after death. The tales which convey this moral may be lengthy, but they are true, and we ought to have faith in the general tradition on the subject, when we consider how abundant and how very venerable that tradition is, and we ought particularly to have faith in our legislators, who lend their sanction to such beliefs – unless, indeed, we account them men of no judgement at all.[28]

These words resemble those spoken by the prophet Jeremiah in the Book of Maccabees: after his bodily death, he was seen praying for his people, thus demonstrating his concern for those living on earth.[29] These are the dead in whom Plato, in the passage just quoted, says we ought to have faith. The same holds true for his observations on the subterranean prison cells in the *Gorgias* (a myth according to his exegetes, but a true account if we are to believe his own words): those who have led a righteous life depart in the direction of the Isles of the Blessed, whereas those who have led a criminal and godless life depart in the direction of the prison of retribution and judgement, which is also called Tartarus.[30] And, having added many similar observations, he goes on: 'This is what I have heard, Callicles, and believe to be true.'[31] And towards the end he says, summing up: 'For myself then, Callicles, I am persuaded by these accounts.'[32] Proclus likewise states: 'Those who wish to unite themselves to the good no longer require any kind of knowledge or action, but a grounding [in being], a stable constitution and serenity.'[33] This means:

To sum up, it is belief in the gods which unites all the classes of gods and daemons and the blessed souls to the good. We must not seek the good with the help of knowledge – that is, imperfectly – but rather we must abandon ourselves to the divine light and close our eyes, thus establishing ourselves in the unknown and secret *henad*[34] of beings. For this kind of belief is superior to the operation of knowledge.[35]

. . .

Chapter 8: What Opinions Plato Held on the Soul

We must now examine the soul and the opinions Plato held concerning it. Did he tell fictitious stories and fables about it, as his detractor inanely maintains, or did he discuss it in a way that was both appropriate to the soul's worth and to his own elevated thought and wisdom? Was it not impossible for a Greek philosopher, without any guidance from the light of faith, to speak and to think more suitably under the circumstances?

There are two questions that one must ask with respect to every immaterial being: first, whether[36] it exists; and second, what it is. These two questions are again subdivided. If one asks whether a thing exists, one has to ask whether it is uncaused or caused, that is, whether it derives its existence from itself or from God. If one asks what a thing is, one has to ask whether it is a substance or an accident. Therefore, our first question will be whether there is a soul and whether it derives its existence from God who created it; then we will examine whatever is useful to know about its essence for the benefit of all those who want to give an adequate account of it. We must furthermore enquire whether it belongs to the category of substance, quantity or quality. Once we have found and determined its category – bearing in mind that every category is twofold, that is, in potentiality and in actuality, like animals and plants (for an egg and a seed are an animal and a plant in potentiality, while a bird and a tree are the same beings in actuality) – we will have to consider, after having determined its essence, whether it should be understood as an underlying potentiality naturally suited to receive being, or as something that exists in actuality. We will then have to consider its potentiality and its actuality, since every essence implies a particular kind of potentiality and a particular kind of actuality. Since the soul is the form of the ensouled body,[37] we will also have to enquire whether it exists before the body or after it or in conjunction with it. If it exists before the body, we will have to ask whether it perishes with the body. If it continues to exist, we will have to ask whether it enters many bodies and watches them wear away time and time again until perishing itself after having left the last body, or whether it is completely imperishable and immortal, existing before every body and continuing to exist eternally after every body.

We will also have to enquire whether it has parts or not. If it has parts, we will have to ask whether it can be divided into particles like a body, or whether its parts are like those of an art or a science (for one also speaks of the parts of medicine or the parts of philosophy). If it does not have parts, we will have to ask whether it is a nature which is absolutely simple, of which plurality cannot be predicated, or whether we are unable to discern a plurality of parts even though it has a multitude of potentialities. There is no difference between the former and the latter position, for one part differs from another with respect to the underlying subject, whereas one potentiality differs from another because of the diversity of their actualities. Another question is whether all souls belong to the same species or not; and if they belong to different species, whether they belong to one genus (as, for example, the soul of a man and the soul of a horse). Does a different species of soul imply a different genus as well? For although man and horse both belong to the genus animal, their souls do not belong to one and the same genus. A further question is whether there are many souls in every living being (such as the vegetative, the nutritive, the appetitive and the intellective, on which still other souls depend), or whether the soul is one complete entity with different parts. If we have to assume that there is one soul with different parts, we will have to ask whether these parts differ both in definition and in substance, or in definition only, but not in substance.

These are the main questions that are usually asked in connection with the soul. Those who know the answers to them have a comprehensive knowledge and understanding of it. We must consequently enquire whether the great Plato has dealt with all of them, and whether he has dealt with all of them as well as he could – in accordance with the teachings of the Greek philosophers, that is, for our purpose is to show neither that he was a Christian in an overall sense, nor that he was Christian in this particular respect. We will also have to ask whether his utterances are, within the limits of possibility, for the most part and in the main more compatible with the Christian doctrines on this subject than are those of Aristotle, who my opponent capriciously, idly and falsely struggles to show was in complete agreement with the Church on every point.

First, then, let us see how, in Book X of the *Laws,* Plato tracks down and pursues the question whether[38] the soul exists. This leads him on to the exposition of its essence, after which he sets out the essence of the divine. I shall speak about these things as briefly as possible, referring the diligent reader to Plato's own writings.

It is necessary, says Plato, that among all the things that exist there are some which only move and others which are only moved, while those which are in between both move and are moved. Those belonging to this third category must either be moved by other things and move other things, or else be self-moved. Plato is thus led to assume the existence of these four essences, which follow one upon the other: (1) an essence that is only moved and of which we say that it is acted upon by other causes that are prior to it; prior to this, there is (2) an essence that moves other things, but is itself moved by other things; after these two, there is (3) a self-moved essence that originates in itself and that causes other things to be moved by its own movement; finally, there is (4) an unmoved essence that is the cause of everything which moves or is moved. Plato also shows that everything that is moved by something else depends on the self-moved essence and that the self-moved essence depends on the unmoved essence, since this is the principle of every movement. For if *a* moves *b*, and *b* moves *c*, and so on ad infinitum, there will be no first principle of movement, since everything is moved by something else. Therefore, there must be a first principle of movement, or else we will be faced with an infinite regress. But if *a* moves itself as well as *b*, and if *b* moves *c*, the source of these movements is the movement that sets itself in motion, for otherwise all things would somehow stand still as soon as they had come into existence. What kind of movement, then, must the first among those which we have mentioned be? Can there be a kind of movement prior to that movement which moves itself?[39] It cannot be moved by something else prior to it, because, in the hierarchy of movements, there is none which precedes it. The unmoved essence, by its very nature, cannot be moved; therefore, it cannot be the first to be set in motion. That which is moved by something else, on the other hand, is in need of another force which is moved.

Therefore, it is the force that moves itself and whose activity originates from within itself that is the principle of every movement and is the first movement both in the realms of the unmoved and of the moved. It is also the noblest and worthiest kind of movement. The second type of movement is that which is moved by something else, while it itself moves other things.

Whatever possesses movement that moves itself is said to be alive, and whatever is alive possesses a soul. Therefore, the soul is that essence which moves itself. Now, we must always consider three things: first, the substance; second, the definition of the substance; and third, the concept defined. Sometimes, we set out the concept and seek the definition; sometimes we do it the other way round. But it does not matter whether we seek the concept and answer by stating the definition, or vice versa, since in either case we mean the same thing. For it is the same thing to say, 'An even number is one which can be divided into two equal halves', and to say, 'A number which can be divided into two equal halves is even'. The same holds true for our present enquiry: the substance which is called 'soul' cannot possibly have another definition than the one we have just given, because we call 'soul' that movement which is capable of moving itself, and vice versa. It is also true to say that the soul is the form or actuality of a particular body,[40] but this definition does not apply to every kind of soul, since the intellectual soul is not the actuality of a body. Therefore, the more comprehensive definition of soul is 'that which moves itself'.

Once this has been shown, it can also be demonstrated that the soul is the first principle of becoming and of movement for everything that is, has been and will be, since it has been shown to be the cause of all change and movement for everything. From this it follows that it is also the noblest of all the things which are moved, since it is the origin of movement. It is also nobler than all bodies, since Body holds the second rank and is inferior to Soul, which presides over Body, while Body itself is naturally presided over by Soul. For all bodies are moved only and cannot produce anything by themselves. Indeed, everything that is naturally destined to produce and to move other things produces and moves by virtue of an incorporeal power. Among incorporeal things, some, like those which move other things and are themselves moved by other things, are divisible when they come into contact with bodies, whether they subsist in qualities or in forms that have entered matter; whereas others, like the self-moved essence (which we say is firmly established in itself and not in something else and has no contact whatever with the bodies which derive their movement from it in the first place), are exempt from the division that affects the lowest beings. This is the essence which we have called soul and which is nobler than any body.

This, then, is an abridged account of Plato's argument, showing how the existence of the soul and its essence can be established. It is demonstrated at the same time that it exists in actuality, not in potentiality. . . .

That the soul is imperishable and immortal Plato shows in many places, but above all in the *Phaedrus* and the *Phaedo*. In the former dialogue, the fact that the soul moves itself and is also a principle of movement is used to prove that it is both uncreated and imperishable. He says:

Soul moves itself. What kind of movement this is has been established before: it is an everlasting movement. For that which is always present in itself and never leaves itself is always of such a nature. But if it is of such a nature, it must also be immortal. For how could it be moved eternally if it were mortal? Indeed, whatever is mortal must also be unmoved.[41]

And again: 'If the soul moves itself, it must be the origin and fountainhead of every movement.'[42] Indeed, everything that is moved derives its movement from the self-moved principle in the first place. Since it is the principle of movement, this essence must also be uncreated, for whatever is created cannot possibly be a principle. But if it is uncreated, it must also necessarily be imperishable, at least if Aristotle is right in maintaining that uncreated and imperishable are convertible terms.[43] . . . Those who hold that the universe is eternal, uncreated and imperishable, and who also maintain that no actual infinity exists (as has been convincingly demonstrated in Book III of the *Physics*)[44] must either assume that the soul is immortal and maintain at the same time that all learning is nothing but remembering and that the soul has often been clothed in a different body (which, to my mind, is Aristotle's opinion), or else they must reject these tenets, thereby denying the soul its immortality and coming up with an even stranger doctrine. For in the judgement of the Greeks themselves what was said by Aristotle in his *De anima* on the subject of immortality must be referred to one common intellect – at least if we are to believe the ill-informed explanations of Alexander of Aphrodisias and of the Arab Averroes, who are considered to be among the most famous of Aristotle's exegetes.[45] As Christians we easily avoid all these problems by assuming a beginning and an end for every kind of generation; but it is difficult to see how the Greeks can do without Plato's assumptions if they are to take a justified pride in preferring never-ending generation to everything else. . . .

Contrary to what his detractor claims, there is hardly anything mythical or fictitious to be found in Plato's writings. On the contrary, if one compares him with Aristotle and takes Greek philosophy as a whole into account, all his dialogues seem to be full of wisdom and truth. I can only repeat what I have been saying all along: one must compare a Greek with other Greeks and Plato with Aristotle, since neither belongs to our faith. Our task is to show that Plato agrees with us in some respects, but certainly not in everything. . . .

Translators' Notes

1. For George of Trebizond's preface to his translation of Plato's *Laws* see *Cambridge Translations of Renaissance Philosophical Texts*, II: *Political Philosophy*, ed. J. Kraye (Cambridge, 1997), ch. 9.
2. See Book I of *Against the Slanderer of Plato*.
3. I should like to thank Professor Wolfgang Rösler of the Humboldt Universität (Berlin) for suggesting this translation of Bessarion's Greek pun.
4. See George of Trebizond, *Comparationes philosophorum Aristotelis et Platonis* (Venice, 1523), sigs. Dii^v–Diii^r.
5. Bessarion's interest in Peripatetic philosophy is evidenced by his Latin translations of the *Metaphysics* of Aristotle and of Theophrastus (1447–50).
6. Timotheus of Miletus (c. 450–c. 360 BC), a musician and dithyrambic poet, claimed to have revolutionized music; Phrynis of Mitylene, a virtuoso cithara player and poet, was a key figure in initiating a new style of music in the second half of the fifth century BC.
7. Aristotle, *Metaphysics* II.1 (993^{b}11–19).
8. Bessarion is here stringing together a number of statements about the One from the first antinomy discussed in the *Parmenides*, e.g., 137E–142A.
9. Pseudo-Dionysius the Areopagite (c. 500) was the author of a corpus of mystical theological writings, presenting a Christianized version of Neoplatonism, which was particularly indebted to the thought of the pagan philosopher Proclus (410–85). Until the sixteenth century, his writings were believed to have apostolic authority because he was falsely identified with Dionysius the Areopagite, who was converted by St Paul in Athens (Acts 17:34).
10. Pseudo-Dionysius the Areopagite, *On the Divine Names* I.1.
11. Pseudo-Dionysius the Areopagite, *On the Divine Names* I.5.
12. St Gregory Nazianzenus (329–89) was born in Cappodocia and studied in Athens before adopting the monastic life. Renowned for his eloquent preaching, he was appointed bishop of Constantinople in 381.
13. See Exodus 3.14: 'And God said unto Moses: "I am that I am".'
14. 'Whole being': the Latin, *totum essentiam*, is doubly flawed; *totum* is apparently a typographical error for *totam;* and *essentiam*, while etymologically correct, is not as good a translation of Gregory's *holon to einai* as the medieval scholastic term *esse* because *essentia* can be taken to mean 'essence', whereas *esse* means only 'being' or 'to be'.
15. Gregory Nazianzenus, *Oratio* XLV, in J. P. Migne, ed., *Patrologia Graeca*, 162 vols. (Paris, 1857–66), XXXVI, col. 625C.
16. Ibid., col. 628A.
17. Ignoring the redundant *spiritu* in the *divino afflatu spiritu* of Mohler's text; the Greek reads simply *pneumati theio*.
18. Plato, *Laws* IV (715E7–716B1).

19. Plato, *Philebus* 28C7–8.
20. Plato, *Timaeus* 27D6–28A2.
21. Bessarion's Greek text uses the conventional title, *Metaphysics.*
22. Aristotle, *Metaphysics* XII.10 (1076ᵃ4), quoting *Iliad* II.204. Bessarion adds line 205 ('Let there be one king') to the passage quoted by Aristotle.
23. Bessarion presumably has in mind early heretical sects, many of whose beliefs were close to or inspired by Platonic doctrines.
24. Colossians 2:3.
25. Plato, *Timaeus* 40D–E; F. M. Cornford's translation (London, 1937).
26. Theognis, lines 77–8, quoted by Plato, *Laws* I (630A). This and the following quotations from the *Laws* are adapted from A. E. Taylor's translation (London, 1934).
27. Plato, *Laws* I (630C).
28. Plato, *Laws* XI (926E–927A).
29. See II Maccabees 15:14.
30. See Plato, *Gorgias* 523.
31. Plato, *Gorgias* 524A; T. H. Irwin's translation (Oxford, 1979).
32. Plato, *Gorgias* 526D; Irwin's translation.
33. Proclus, *Theologia Platonica,* ed. H. D. Saffrey and L. G. Westerink (Paris, 1968–), I, p. 109, line 24–p. 110, line 1 (I.25).
34. For the history and meaning of this concept, which was an attempt by late Neoplatonists to bridge the ontological gulf between the One and reality, see Proclus, *The Elements of Theology,* ed. E. R. Dodds, 2nd ed. (Oxford, 1963), pp. 257–60.
35. Proclus, *Theologia Platonica,* I, p. 110, lines 6–13 (I.25).
36. The Latin translation, surprisingly, has *cur* ('why').
37. See Aristotle, *De anima* II.1 (412ᵃ19–21).
38. See n. 36.
39. Reading *hauten* for *auten.*
40. See n. 37.
41. Cf. Plato, *Phaedrus* 245C–D.
42. Plato, *Phaedrus* 245C–D.
43. Aristotle, *De caelo* I.12 (282ᵃ31).
44. Aristotle, *Physics* III.4–8.
45. On the doctrine of one common intellect and its influence in the Renaissance see *CHRP,* p. 489.

Further Reading

CHRP, pp. 16, 23, 36, 67, 82–3, 358, 491, 519, 559, 566–8, 570–1, 809

Fiaccadori, G., ed., *Bessarione e l'umanesimo. Catalogo della mostra* (Naples, 1994)

Hankins, J., *Plato in the Italian Renaissance,* 2 vols. (Leiden, 1990), I, pp. 167–74, 236–63; II, pp. 443–4

Labowsky, L., 'Bessarion Studies 1–5', *Medieval and Renaissance Studies,* 5 (1961), 108–62, and 6 (1968), 173–205

'Bessarione', *Dizionario biografico degli Italiani* (Rome, 1960–), IX, pp. 686–96

Bessarion's Library and the Biblioteca Marciana (Rome, 1979)

Monfasani, J., *Byzantine Scholars in Renaissance Italy: Cardinal Bessarion and Other Emigrés* (Great Yarmouth, Norfolk, 1995)

George of Trebizond: A Biography and a Study of His Rhetoric and Logic (Leiden, 1976), pp. 200–29

Wilson, N. G., *From Byzantium to Italy: Greek Studies in the Italian Renaissance* (London, 1992)

13

Marsilio Ficino

Luc Deitz

Introduction

In his *Platonic Theology* (1474), Marsilio Ficino seeks to demonstrate that rational confirmation of the Christian belief in the personal immortality of the soul can be found in the philosophy of Plato and his ancient disciples. (For another selection, with biographical information, see Chapter 3.) This was part of his overall programme to develop a 'pious philosophy', strongly based on Platonism, which would reduce the conflicts between reason and faith – conflicts that had arisen, in his view, largely because of Aristotle's domination of the philosophical curriculum since the thirteenth century. Like Cardinal Bessarion, Ficino believed that Platonism was much closer than Aristotelianism to Christianity. This was particularly so in relation to the crucial issue of the immortality of the soul, where Aristotle's position was ambiguous at best, while Plato explicitly endorsed the notion of an afterlife.

In the preface, Ficino sets out both the purpose of the book and the method he intends to adopt. He wants to make readers aware of the immortality of their own souls and of the state of eternal bliss which awaits them in the next life, when their souls are finally released from the prison of their bodies. Rather than argue the case on the basis of Christian dogma (Ficino had become a priest at the end of 1473), he will rely instead on Platonic doctrines, in order to convince those perverse intellectuals who are reluctant to yield to religious authority alone. But he makes it clear that, although imitating Plato, he will be doing so in order to serve the true faith. His conviction that Platonism was the closest of all pagan philosophies to Christianity owes a great deal, he tells us, to St Augustine, an important role model for Ficino.

The dedication of the treatise to Lorenzo de' Medici was in recognition of the support which his family, particularly his grandfather Cosimo, had long given Ficino in his Platonic studies. His characterization of Lorenzo as a 'philosopher-king' probably reflects not Ficino's honest assessment of the young ruler, but rather his desire to encourage his former pupil to devote some of his time to the pursuit of philosophical wisdom. The relationship between Ficino and Lorenzo, which came under considerable strain in the late 1470s, was frequently an uneasy one; and although Lorenzo did incorporate some Platonic motifs into his vernacular poetry, he was never a wholehearted supporter of the movement.

Book IV, chapter 2, is a typical example of one of Ficino's arguments in support of the immortality of the soul. Citing various Platonic texts, alongside works by Augustine and Origen, he attempts to prove that the soul has a natural desire to attain knowledge of the highest truth and the greatest good – knowledge, in other words, of God – and that the satisfaction of this desire is the source of our greatest happiness. Since, however, neither this knowledge nor this happiness can be acquired in the present life, it must be achieved in the next. If this were not the case, then the aspiration, implanted in our minds by God, to penetrate to the cause of all causes and thereby achieve happiness would be useless and futile. The soul, therefore, must be immortal.

For the Latin text of the passages from *Theologia platonica de immortalitate animorum* translated here, see Marsilio Ficino, *Théologie platonicienne de l'immortalité des âmes*, ed. R. Marcel, 3 vols. (Paris, 1964–70), I, pp. 35–7; II, pp. 250–6.

The Platonic Theology: Selections

The Preface of the Florentine Marsilio Ficino to his Platonic Theology on the Immortality of Souls, Dedicated to Lorenzo de' Medici 'the Magnanimous'

Plato, the father of philosophers, understood very well, magnanimous Lorenzo, that all intelligences are in the same position with respect to God as our eyes are with respect to the light of the sun and that, therefore, they are unable to understand anything whatsoever without the light of God. Accordingly, he deemed it just and pious that the human mind, which receives everything from God, should give everything back to him. Thus, if we devote ourselves to moral philosophy, he exhorts us to purify our soul so that it may eventually become unclouded, permitting it to see the divine light and worship God. And if we scrutinize the causes of natural things, he exhorts us to enquire into these causes in such a way that in the end we may find the cause of all causes and adore it when we have found it.[1]

But our dear Plato not only exhorts other people to this pious duty, he gives the most shining example of it himself. This is why all nations agree in calling him 'divine' and his teaching 'theology': nowhere does he ever touch on anything related to moral philosophy or to logic or to mathematics or to natural philosophy without soon afterwards referring it most piously to the contemplation and worship of God. Since he holds the soul to be a kind of mirror in which the image of the divine countenance is easily reflected, his scrupulous step-by-step search for God continually prompts him to turn towards the beauty of the soul, understanding the famous oracle 'Know thyself!' to mean above all that whoever desires to know God should first know himself. For this reason everyone who reads Plato's writings, all of which I translated into Latin a long time ago,[2] with the care that they deserve will derive from them every conceivable benefit, but above all these two most important principles: the pious worship of a known God and the divinity of souls. These form the basis for all understanding of things, for every disposition of one's life and for all aspects of happiness. This is especially true in view of the fact that Plato's views on these matters led Augustine to single him out from all other philosophers and to set him up as a model for imitation, maintaining that he had come closest of all to the Christian truth and that the Platonists would be Christians if only they changed a few tiny details of their doctrines.[3]

As for myself, relying on the authority of Augustine and moved by an intense love of humanity, I decided a long time ago to paint a portrait of Plato that would resemble the Christian truth as closely as possible and therefore undertook to study the two issues just mentioned more carefully than any others. This is why I have chosen[4] to give my entire work the title *Platonic Theology on the Immortality of Souls*. My main aim in writing this treatise has been to enable us to explore in the divinity of our own created mind, as if in a mirror placed at the centre of the universe, the works of the creator himself and to contemplate and worship his mind. I believe, and this hope is not a vain one,[5] that divine providence has decreed that the many people who, because of their perverse character, do not easily yield to the authority of the divine law alone should at least give their assent to the Platonic arguments which are brought to the aid of religion; and that those who most impiously separate the study of philosophy from our holy religion should realize at some point that they go astray in the same way as those who would separate the love of wisdom from the honour conferred by wisdom itself, or those who would separate true intelligence from a righteous will. Finally, providence has also decreed that those whose thought revolves only around the corporeal objects of sense-perception and who, to their own disadvantage, prefer the shadows of things to their true reality should in the end be convinced by Plato's arguments and contemplate the sublime instead of the corporeal and, to their own advantage, give precedence to the things themselves over their shadows.

This is the first commandment of almighty God. This is the foremost requirement of the human condition. This is what the divine Plato once effortlessly achieved, with the help of God, for the benefit of his followers. This is, finally, what I myself have tried to achieve in this painstaking work for the benefit of my own followers – imitating Plato, but relying solely on the help of God. I only hope that I have carried out my task with a degree of truth equal to the reverence in which I have held the divine truth while composing it, since I do not wish to approve of anything of which the divine law would disapprove.

I have decided to dedicate this work to you, magnanimous Lorenzo, above all others. In doing so, I do not presume to unfold before you the truths of philosophy. You have been investigating these for a very long time in such a way that it is clearly not for you, but for the rest of mankind, that I am about to publish these mysteries of the ancients, which your remarkable genius has already made its own. The reason I dedicate it to you is because your munificence has permitted me to find the leisure necessary for the unhampered pursuit of philosophy, and because it is our dear Plato, so to speak, who gives thanks to you through my paying off this debt of gratitude. For, what he desired more than anything else in the great men of the past has been achieved by you: the conjunction of philosophy with the highest authority in public affairs.[6]

BOOK XIV, CHAPTER 2

The Fifth Sign of Immortality is Derived from the Fact That the Soul Aspires to the First Truth and the First Good

The foregoing observations[7] will further strengthen our belief in the immortality of the soul if we examine the twelve attributes of God one by one and show that, by naturally seeking them, the soul somehow tries to liken itself to God.

Our soul conceives a universal notion of truth and goodness which prompts it to seek the universal truth and aspire to the universal good. All truths are contained in the universal truth, all goods in the universal good. This explains why the soul naturally seeks all truths and naturally aspires to all goods. There is evidence for this, too: whenever we know one piece of truth about a thing, we do not rest content with it, but go on looking for another one and still another for as long as we think that there remains another truth to be known. The same phenomenon can be observed with respect to the acquisition of goods. Now, the sum of all goods is God himself, who is the first truth and the first good. Therefore, it is God himself whom we seek.

But what is it that we desire above all in him? To become similar to him.[8] For all things strive towards him as their end according to the capacity of their nature, and they long to become similar to him in their own way: inanimate bodies with respect to being alone; animate bodies with respect to life; sensate bodies with respect to sensation; rational bodies with respect to intellect. We can only become similar to God if we make him the object of our thinking, since the intellect becomes similar to other things whenever it makes them the object of its thinking and is thus transformed into images of them. Our goal, therefore, is to see God by means of our intellect and to enjoy the vision of God by means of our will, since our highest good is the highest object of our highest faculty or the most perfect act related to that highest object. Our highest faculties are the mind, the apex of the mind [that is, the intellect] and the will. Their highest object is the universal truth as well as the universal and undivided good, in other words, God.

Let no Arab philosopher object at this juncture that it is enough for us to enjoy an angel,[9] for we have a natural inborn desire always to discover the cause of any given effect, and our enquiry only comes to an end when we have reached the first cause.[10] Consequently, since we wish to understand the cause of every known effect, and since our intellect knows universal being itself, it follows that we have a natural desire to know the cause of being itself, which is God himself. And it is only when our natural desire is entirely appeased that we can claim to have attained our ultimate goal. This is why the ultimate goal of man consists solely in the knowledge or the possession of God, which alone is able to put an end to our natural appetite.[11]

A clear indication of this is the fact that everyone rejoices most when he has attained his own goal. And no possession whatever fills the soul with such ardent, pure and lasting joy as the foretaste, however small, of the contemplation of God. Those who have truly experienced it rate all possessions, the whole world and even their own life as nothing in comparison. Whoever lives piously in the company of God, even if only from time to time, will proclaim that it was only in those moments that he truly lived and was sheltered from evil and had some foretaste of the good – as if it were only in those moments that he had entered into his own proper haven. This is the meaning of Plato's words in his *Book on Knowledge:*

Evil cannot be completely done away with, for the good must always have its contrary. Evil cannot possibly exist, however, in the divine world, so it must haunt our mortal nature and this lower world. Therefore, we should take flight from this world to the other as quickly as possible; and the flight from this world to that means nothing else than becoming like God as far as we are able. This likeness again is achieved through justice and righteousness with the help of prudence.[12]

These are Plato's words. He is right to give such precepts, for it is only where the good that is the source of all goods reigns supreme that we can find a remedy for all our ills.

Nor should we believe Panaetius when he says that we certainly aspire to the divine but are unable ever to attain it completely, since full possession of the divine and a peaceful life are not within reach of the souls of men but are the privilege of angels.[13] Nature itself teaches us the contrary: the elements, which have a natural desire to occupy their proper place, are borne with an ever increasing vehemence the nearer they come to their own place and goal. This is why Aristotle has shown in his *De caelo* that a movement progressing along a straight line cannot go on indefinitely, for otherwise its progress could not be slow at one moment and quick at another.[14] Therefore, everything which is so constituted that it aspires ever more forcefully towards an end does not wander indefinitely but tends towards a well-defined goal. This is exactly what we experience with respect to our desire for knowledge: the more we know, the more ardently we crave to learn what we do not yet know.

The natural desire for knowledge is thus oriented towards a well-defined end. What is this end? It is the cause of all causes, which puts an end to all natural enquiry into causes once it has been found. To dense bodies, nature gave a desire and an inclination for lower places; in addition, it bestowed weight and cold on them, which are the means by which they descend towards their desired place. To subtler bodies, it gave a desire for a higher place; and it added lightness and heat, by means of which they are able to reach their desired end. To brute animals, it gave a desire for food and sexual intercourse; moreover, it imparted bodily parts to them that are fit for the procurement of food and the generation of offspring. To the soul, the master of nature gave a desire for the complete and universal truth and [the complete and universal] good. This is an even more natural appetite than that for food and sexual intercourse inasmuch as it is longer lasting. The body only rarely craves food, and intercourse even more rarely, whereas at every single moment we long for the true and the good. We are always keen to experience new things, to imagine new situations, to think new thoughts. We always open our eyes wide to look at whatever happens. The most extensive and broadest view fills us with the greatest pleasure; indeed, only the boundless satisfies us. We always raise our ears to listen to any kind of sound; this is something done by children and adults alike, by the learned and the ignorant, and by every artisan in whatever craft. In all this, nature is our guide. One should add that sexual desire can be overcome and a ravenous appetite for food weakened, but this is completely impossible with our desire for the true and the good. On the contrary, the former diminish with age, while the latter increases. One should also add that corporeal satisfactions are sought with a view to something else, whereas the desire for the true and the good is an end in itself. Therefore, the desire for the true and the good is more natural than the desire for food and sexual intercourse; and nature, in its provident leadership, has accordingly arranged that it should attain its goal completely. In fact, the best proof for its being more natural is that it is better equipped to reach its goal.

Besides, if the distinguishing property of every species belongs to it of necessity and has been providently put into place by the creator, it follows that the effort of the rational species, directed as it is towards the possession of the whole good as its goal, is capable of reaching its aim. Indeed, if it were impossible to attain the ultimate goal, both the whole species as such as well as every single one of its actions would be contingent, accidental and purposeless. The eye sometimes rests when it beholds a graceful appearance, the ear sometimes rests when it hears a sweet melody, and every other sense's appetite is sometimes satiated and filled with its proper objects. Such is the bliss that nature has given to the senses! Should reason, which reigns over the senses, which is superior to brute animals, although inferior to angels, be in such an unhappy state, should it have been so neglected by the creator of nature that it wanders about endlessly, without ever finding peace? At any rate not in this life.

In this case too, we should not pay any attention to a certain Arab philosopher who imagines that the human intellect is at least capable of achieving in the whole of mankind what it is incapable of achieving in individuals in the course of this life.[15] First, there is no single intellect in the whole of mankind, which consists of utterly irreconcilable individuals, as I shall demonstrate elsewhere.[16] Next, the soul never attains the desired state in all men at the same time; and when it is blind to the presence of the divine in individuals, it is blind to its presence in all individuals taken together in more or less the same way. Furthermore, we should not imagine that we are able to understand the very substances of the divine forms at will simply by comparing them with natural substances: the latter have a propensity towards matter, the former do not. But as long as the human intellect inhabits the body, it somehow leans towards the corporeal in the process of understanding. Besides, natural effects can neither equal nor represent the powers and substances of divine causes. One should also add that divine forms are much further from natural forms than natural forms are from one another. Thus, if colours cannot be known by means of speech, which is evident in the case of blind people, it is even more impossible for divine things ever to be understood by means of the natural, as Plato writes to Dionysius of Syracuse.[17] I do not even mention the fact that divine substance and divine power, inasmuch as they are infinite, cannot be perceived by us at will, unless we have been completely informed by them. This, however, is impossible to achieve while our soul is joined to a body affected in the way it is.

But let us return to the subject matter of this chapter. The capacity and the desire of the mind do not aspire to some truths or some goods, but to the whole and entire truth and the whole and entire good. The reason why it is apparently never able to attain its goal in this life lies in the fact that, as Plato puts it in the *Epinomis,*[18] our intellect is always vacillating and our will never at rest. It is only when the soul has shed its bodily clothing that it will be able to attain its goal. As soon as it acquires the universal good, it will be in full possession of immortality, as great a good as death – which deprives us of all goods – is an evil. But a mind that is able to see every single truth will take no pleasure in any good if it suspects that it will have to die. So, in order for the mind's attainment of its goal to be safe and undisturbed, it must be convinced that the possession of its ultimate goal will be everlasting. St Augustine bears testimony to this in the thirteenth book of his *On the Trinity* in the following words:

Everyone wants to be happy, and the reason why no one wants to die and to be reduced to nothing lies precisely in the fact that they are happy. One can only be happy when one is alive, which explains why no one wants to die. Therefore, those who are truly happy or desire to live in a state of complete happiness want to be immortal. On the other hand, those who do not have what they desire cannot live a happy life. Therefore, a life can only be considered to be truly happy if it is everlasting.[19]

These are Augustine's words.

But in order that the disciples of Panaetius should no longer doubt that a truly happy life is the natural goal of man, let us conclude in the following way: since the proper activity of the intellectual nature consists in tasting every good through the intellect, there can be no doubt that another one of its proper activities consists in feeding on every good, that is, on the good as a whole, through the emotions. Happiness, therefore, is the proper object of the intellectual nature. But the degree of happiness people can achieve is dependent on the kind of intellect they have. Those who have an intellect which concerns itself with the truth and with the forms will attain the true form of happiness. Those, however, whose intellect is concerned with transient shadows will attain a shadowy happiness.

The soul of man, although it is a sort of image of a more divine intellect, contains in itself the true form of mind. This is shown by three signs. First, because it understands a large number of truths according to their true reason. Second, because it understands the true reason of truth itself. Third, because our soul, if it possessed only the shadow of intellect, would never be able to understand or to define the form and the substance of intellect, but would have only a confused perception of its accidents. Accordingly, since our soul not only possesses the shadowy power of intellection, which it shares with some of the more intelligent animals, but also a truly distinct and formal power, it is able to obtain a truly happy life at some stage. No one should be surprised if I posit a shadowy intellect, on the one hand, and a formal one, on the other; for this is, according to Proclus, the fundamental distinction of all things accepted by the Platonists, which applies above all to the One, Mind, Soul and Nature.[20]

But let us leave aside these considerations for the moment and consider how Origen in his work *On First Principles* confirms these points. Seeing that God, the creator of all things, not only takes care in every single object both of the particular and the general requirements of necessity and expediency, but is always equally concerned with the beauty of things and the wonder they provoke in the onlooker, Origen concluded that God had bestowed upon the universe the most exquisite shape, just as a human artisan creates his artefacts as beautifully as he can so that those who look at them will be moved to reflect upon and to admire the skill with which they have been executed.[21] By means of this comparison he wants to show that the investigation of the reasons which underlie everything which exists has been implanted in our minds by the reason of God himself, the creator of everything, and that this explains why our investigation starts afresh every day. For our mind naturally longs to know the causes of things as much as our eyes long to see colours and our palates long to taste food. Origen adds that we have been endowed by God with this desire on the condition that it would be satisfied at some stage, so that he should not appear to have implanted it in vain. Moreover, whoever gives himself up to this passion with all the ardour of his will is well equipped, thanks to this disposition, to understand the fullness of truth in the future, even if he has attained but little truth in this life. And since this kind of preparation comes about with the help of God, it is with the help of God that, at some point, the informing will take place – if it is true to say, that is, that active causes only arrange matter with a view to informing it once it has been arranged.

The truth of this opinion of Origen is briefly confirmed in the following way: as long as we consider the forms of the universe with respect to their effect – that is, whether they are useful or harmful to us – we are apparently led on our way by created nature, and we comply with the life of the body inasmuch as we wish to transform the external forms into our own form according to the criterion of usefulness. But when we investigate the reasons why every single being has been created and disposed in the way that it is (which is a question that occurs to us naturally), that very reason which is the creator of all things draws us towards itself. This is when we not only turn our attention towards eternal life, but also strive to transform our soul on the model of the form of all forms, that is, the creator. This is why the apostle Paul says that the inward man is daily renewed if we contemplate what is invisible and eternal.[22] And again: 'But we all, with unveiled face reflecting as a mirror the glory of the Lord, are transformed into the same image from glory to glory, even as from the Lord the Spirit.'[23]

Translator's Notes

1. See Plato, *Republic* VI (508A–511E).
2. Although Ficino finished the first draft of his complete translation of the Platonic dialogues in 1469, he continued to revise it, and it did not appear in print until 1484.
3. See Augustine, *De vera religione* 4.7 and *City of God* VIII.9.
4. Reading *censui;* Marcel erroneously prints *censuit.*
5. The Latin phrase recalls Virgil, *Aeneid* IV.12: 'Reor equidem, nec vana fides . . . '.
6. See Plato, *Republic* V (473C–E), and, more generally, his seventh *Letter.*
7. That is, that the human soul strives towards assimilating itself to God, which Ficino has shown by means of twelve signs corresponding to the twelve attributes of God.
8. See Plato, *Theaetetus* 176B.
9. See, e.g., Avicenna, *Liber de philosophia prima sive scientia divina* X.1.
10. See Aristotle, *Metaphysics* I.1 (980^{a}21); I.3 (983^{a}25–6).
11. See Thomas Aquinas, *Summa contra gentiles* III.25 *ad finem:* 'man's ultimate goal is to know God'.
12. Plato, *Theaetetus* 176A–B; for the translation, see F. M. Cornford, *Plato's Theory of Knowledge* (London, 1935), p. 87 (with some modifications).
13. Panaetius of Rhodes (c. 185–109 BC) was a Stoic philosopher; cf. his *Fragmenta,* ed. M. van Straaten (Leiden, 1962), frags. 79–89, 96–117, esp. 111 = Aulus Gellius, *Noctes Atticae* XII.5.10.
14. Aristotle, *De caelo* I.8 (277^{a}26–33).
15. See, e.g., Averroes, *Commentarium magnum in Aristotelis De anima libros,* ed. F. S. Crawford, Corpus commentariorum Averrois in Aristotelem 6.1 (Cambridge, Mass.,1953), p. 392, line 158–p. 409, line 653 (III.5).
16. See Ficino, *Theologia platonica* XV.1 = *Théologie platonicienne,* ed. Marcel, III, pp. 8–16.

17. See Plato, *Letter VII* 343A–D.
18. See Pseudo-Plato, *Epinomis* 974A–C.
19. Augustine, *De trinitate* XIII.8.11 (the first sentence appears to be a paraphrase rather than a quotation).
20. See, e.g., Proclus, *In Platonis Timaeum commentaria,* ed. E. Diehl, 3 vols. (Leipzig, 1903– 6), I, p. 444, line 15–p. 445, line 30.
21. See Origen, *De principiis* II.1.1–4.
22. II Corinthians 4:16.
23. II Corinthians 3:18.

Further Reading

Allen, M. J. B., *Icastes: Marsilio Ficino's Interpretation of Plato's Sophist* (Berkeley, Calif., 1989)

   The Platonism of Marsilio Ficino: A Study of His Phaedrus Commentary, Its Sources and Genesis (Berkeley, Calif., 1984)

   Plato's Third Eye: Studies in Marsilio Ficino's Metaphysics and Its Sources (Aldershot, 1995)

CHRP, pp. 67–70, 79–81, 83, 88, 99, 107, 134–5, 237–42, 246, 255, 257–8, 265–7, 270, 272, 274–85, 287–9, 293–6, 299, 398, 312, 377, 428, 461, 469, 498, 500, 568–81, 583–4, 650–1, 673–5, 738, 769, 772, 775, 783–8, 817

Garfagnini, G. C., ed., *Marsilio Ficino e il ritorno di Platone: studi e documenti,* 2 vols. (Florence, 1986)

Hankins, J., 'Lorenzo de' Medici as a patron of philosophy', *Rinascimento,* 34 (1994), 15–53

Kraye, J., 'Lorenzo and the philosophers', in M. Mallet and N. Mann, eds., *Lorenzo the Magnificent: Culture and Politics in Medicean Florence* (London, 1996), pp. 151–66

Kristeller, P. O., *Studies in Renaissance Thought and Letters,* 3 vols. (Rome, 1956–93), I, pp. 35–257

14

Francesco Cattani da Diacceto

Luc Deitz

Introduction

Born into a Florentine family with strong Medicean sympathies, Francesco Cattani da Diacceto (1466–1522) received a solid humanist education and later studied philosophy at the University of Pisa, in the company of Giovanni de' Medici, the future Pope Leo X. In the 1490s he became a disciple of the Neoplatonist Marsilio Ficino; and in 1501 he took up a chair at the Florentine *studio,* where he taught Aristotelian philosophy. Unlike his mentor Ficino, Diacceto's aim was to harmonize Platonism and Aristotelianism; nevertheless, while showing respect for the latter, he clearly favoured the former. He wrote an important vernacular treatise on love (*I tre libri d'amore,* 1508) and also produced a philosophical treatment of beauty *(De pulchro,* first drafted between 1496 and 1499, but not completed until after 1514), in which he dealt with many key issues in Neoplatonic metaphysics. Some of his ideas may have influenced the poetry of Michelangelo, with whom he participated, along with other members of the Sacra Accademia Medicea, in a campaign to have Dante's bones returned to Florence.

The *Panegyric on Love* is strongly influenced by Ficino's commentary on the *Symposium* (1469). Following Plato, as interpreted by Ficino, Diacceto defines love as the desire for beauty; the desire for divine beauty corresponds to Divine and Heavenly Love, that is, a spiritual desire to unite oneself with God; while the desire for bodily beauty corresponds to Vulgar and Common Love, that is, a physical desire to unite sexually with another human. Dividing the cosmos, along Neoplatonic lines, into five levels of being or hypostases (the One, Intelligible World, Soul, Body and Matter), Diacceto argues that neither Matter nor the One possesses any beauty: Matter, because it is deprived of all form and goodness; the One, because it is infinite simplicity, and infinite simplicity, as the cause of beauty, cannot possess beauty itself. Beauty is therefore to be found in Mind, Soul and Body.

For Diacceto, as for Plato, the ancient Neoplatonists and Ficino, beauty always accompanies goodness. Since the body is the true image of the soul, the physical beauty of the body must be the external reflection of the internal perfection of the soul. Consequently, those people endowed with physical beauty must also possess outstanding moral qualities. For this reason, the desire for the physical beauty of an individual body can, and should, be used as a stepping-stone to an appreciation, first, of the superior beauty of the beloved's soul and, ultimately, of the supreme beauty of God. Like Ficino, Diacceto regards Platonic love as an idealized, non-sexual relationship between men, a spiritual friendship which spurs both lover and beloved to ascend to God.

For the Latin text of the *Panegyricus in amorem* see Francesco Cattani da Diacceto, *Opera omnia,* ed. T. Zwinger (Basel, 1563), pp. 130–8. An Italian version was published in Rome in 1526.

Panegyric on Love

Francesco Cattani da Diacceto to Giovanni Corsi and Palla Rucellai: Greetings.[1]

It is a grave sin not to have a correct opinion of the gods;[2] and it is an even graver sin to detract anything from their majesty. Therefore, my dearest friends, you must not find fault with Love, which is surely something most divine, so as not to suffer the same fate as the poet Stesichorus. After he had attacked Helen [of Troy], he was blinded and could not recover his sight until he had placated the offended godhead by means of a palinode.[3] Homer, too, spoke ill of one of the gods and, either because he was unaware of his crime or because he was unrepentant, had to lead his life deprived of his eyesight until he succumbed to old age.[4] Thus, you must not only refrain from criticisms of this kind, but you should also join in my celebration of Love's divine name – if not as befits such an exalted godhead, at least as my talent permits. For it is impossible to conceive of any undertaking that would be more advantageous to us and more agreeable to the gods.

Nothing is so attractive as beauty, nothing so repulsive as deformity. Beauty attracts and delights us; deformity causes us to feel sorrow and withdraw. The reason for this is that the beauty which we perceive on the outside of things is a sign of their inner perfection, which is its source. For there is a certain outward grace attending the perfection of a thing which allows us to infer that it does not contain any inner imperfection. Small wonder, then, if beauty arouses our soul and seems to draw it towards itself: our soul naturally surmises that beauty opens the gates leading towards the limitless perfection of divine goodness. This is why the ancient theologians[5] assert that beauty is, so to speak, the forecourt of divine goodness, as if those who seek the godhead would have to encounter beauty first. It is clear, therefore, that beauty is nothing other than a blossom, a grace, a ray emanating from divine goodness, attracting and drawing all things that are endowed with the faculty of reason towards the good, participation in which is the ultimate perfection of everything.

From this it follows that those beings who possess the faculty of reason are far superior to those who do not, and that among those who strive to know, the ones that have a greater degree of reason also partake of perfection to a greater degree. This is so because those beings which have a greater degree of reason not only have a better understanding of beauty but also partake more fully of the divine, possession of which is identical with perfection. Therefore, the highest degree of reason partakes of the highest degree of perfection, since it inclines towards beauty with more studied and meticulous care than anything else. From those beings, on the other hand, which have no share whatever of the faculty of reason, the splendour of beauty remains likewise hidden, which is why they cannot truly have a share of the divine either and consequently deserve to be considered the most imperfect of all.

Would anyone deny that soulless beings are far inferior to those that have souls? And that among those that have souls, plants and other living beings are clearly inferior to man? Soulless beings, which are completely devoid of reason, are unable to enjoy beauty. Consequently, they have only a small share of perfection, since they are unable to attain divine goodness by means of their own power. Plants, on the other hand, have some kind of reason, as the Pythagoreans maintain.[6] Yet this reason is completely dull and resembles that of a man suddenly roused from a deep sleep: he perceives, but is unable to discern. Animals without reason are able to perceive and to discern; however, since the splendour of beauty is far superior to their capacity for understanding, they are also far removed from true perfection. Among all the beings that live on earth, man alone is capable of apprehending beauty, since he is endowed with the greatest capacity to understand. It follows that he is also able to achieve a high degree of perfection.

The highest degree of perfection can be found in the intelligible realm,[7] since it is filled with the light which emanates from the father of all brightness and which combines the highest degree of understanding with the highest degree of beauty. It is from this beauty that understanding is derived in the things that partake of it, just as whatever brightness is in bodies is derived from the source of light, the sun. Those who are unable to understand that beauty is a true image of the godhead have only to look at the sun and to consider the extent to which its beauty is superior to that of everything else we perceive. It is indeed 'the eternal eye of the world', as Orpheus puts it, which the ancient theologians called 'the visible son of God'.[8] We could go even further and say that its presence in the world is like that of a wondrous statue of God in the most sacred sanctuary. This is why the Egyptians had inscribed in gilded letters on their temple of Minerva: 'I am everything that is, everything that shall be, and everything that has been. No one has ever lifted my veil. The fruit I have borne is the sun.'[9] It is evident from these words that the sun, the most beautiful of all visible things, truly represents divine goodness.

If beauty is such as we have described it here, it is not surprising that it excites rational beings or rather seems to carry them away by force, especially those who have the most abundant share of reason. Or perhaps one should say instead that these beings have an overpowering inborn desire that prompts them to track down beauty and to follow its trail spontaneously, since it is through beauty that they can partake of perfection. This desire neither possesses the beauty towards which it strives, nor is it completely devoid of beauty. Indeed, if it were completely devoid of beauty, it could not derive any knowledge of it from previous experience. Therefore, it would also be unable to desire it, since we usually only desire something because we believe that the object of our desire will be advantageous to us. Otherwise, how could one have any desire at all? Only an utter fool would wish some evil to befall him. Thus, if we do not know what a thing is like, we have no idea whether or not it corresponds to the object of our desire, and therefore we cannot desire it as something that would be advantageous to us.

Accordingly, we must say neither that the desire for beauty is completely devoid of beauty, nor that it possesses the fullness of beauty, since those who possess something are not drawn towards that which they possess but rather enjoy their possessions. Everyone knows that the faculty of motion has been given to things so that they might be able to reach a goal which they have not yet attained; but once they have attained it, they immediately come to a halt. This is why motion counts as something imperfect. But whoever desires [a thing] does not possess [it], for if he possessed [it], his desire would be in vain, since he would already be enjoying his possession. This explains why the desire for beauty lies midway between knowledge and possession: its beginning lies in knowledge, and its end in possession.

Let us call this desire 'love', for then neither man nor god will have any reason to charge us with ignorance. For what else could love be – whether it is of an intelligible or a rational nature – if not the overpowering desire to enjoy beauty as far as possible? Since the realm of the divine overflows with the fullness of beauty, whereas mortal things are completely devoid of it, the ancient theologians distinguished love from both and ranked it among those intermediary beings whose character partakes of both, in other words, daemons. Therefore, Love was called neither a god, nor a mortal, but 'a great daemon'.[10]

Demons occupy the middle rank between gods and mortals, acting as intermediaries: not only do they convey the private and public prayers of men to the gods, they also convey the gods' wishes and their ordinances to men. There is no way, other than through demons, for mortals, either awake or asleep, to be informed of the gods' intentions. In the same manner, Love occupies the middle rank between knowledge and the fullness of beauty. It not only arranges whatever lacks beauty, but is nevertheless able to receive it, in such a way that it is in a position to receive beauty; it also elicits some sparks of light from beauty, with the help of which those beings who already possess beauty are able to attain happiness. This is the meaning of the ancient theologians' saying that Porus and Penia conceived Love immediately after the birth of Venus, and that Love, therefore, was a follower and a worshipper of Venus.[11] Hence, Venus stands for beauty, Porus for resourcefulness and means, and Penia for need and poverty. Thus, Love was conceived from the lack, as it were, of its mother's nature: although it does not yet partake of beauty, it is nonetheless capable of participation in it. Resourcefulness and the means to attain beauty, on the other hand, are said to be Love's father – that is, some sparks of light derived from beauty, which one could with justification call a kind of knowledge and a confirmation of its existence, that prompt the indigent nature to unite itself with beauty. This explains why Love has a share both of need, inasmuch as it strives towards beauty, and of the light of beauty, inasmuch as it is not conceived unless beauty is comprehended and approved of. Therefore, one can legitimately say that Love is a follower and a worshipper of Venus, since Love always eagerly follows beauty. Conversely, beauty always excites Love.

It would take too long to explain what the ancient theologians meant when they said that there were two Venuses: the one a motherless daughter of Uranus [Heaven], named the Heavenly Venus, and born from the foam of the sea and the genitals of Uranus, which were thrown into the sea by his son Saturn, who immediately after his birth castrated his father; the other a daughter of Jupiter and Dione, named the Vulgar or Common Venus.[12] It is sufficient for our present purpose to show that the two Venuses – Heavenly and Vulgar – correspond to a twofold love – heavenly and vulgar – each of which follows its own Venus and its own beauty. Before doing this, however, it will perhaps not be superfluous to set out in what respects the types of beauty, as well as the types of love, differ from one another, since, as has been said, everyone follows his own beauty.

The order of the universe is as follows: the first principle of everything is the One in itself, infinite goodness, infinite simplicity, beginning, middle and end, good of all goods, light of all lights. The One in itself is followed by the Intelligible World, which emanates from the One in itself and therefore retains the first degree of perfection. Following this is the Rational Nature, which is also called Soul. It is less perfect than the Intelligible World, since it is more remote from the first principle. But it does not immediately become so deficient that intelligence, leaving behind the Intelligible World, would be unable to ascend to the boundless expanse of divine light. Soul not only brings forth and governs the body, it also bestows life and movement upon it. For whatever is alive lives only insofar as it has the most noble gift of life bestowed upon it by Soul.

Body as such occupies the fourth rank. It no longer has any connection whatever with the divine realm. There is no truth in body, no solidity; it is all shadow and emptiness. In fact, it is very similar to the phantom images of bodies which appear to those gazing at the endless flow of rivers: they do not even remain the same for a fraction of a second; they merely come to be and immediately cease to exist.

Matter occupies the lowest rank. Its nature entails neither order nor shape; it deserves not to exist more than it does to exist.

There are, then, five levels: the One in itself, the Intelligible World, Soul, Body and Matter.[13] The first and the last of these are so opposed to one another that just as the One in itself (or the Good in itself) is the cause of all goods, Matter is the source of all evils. The One in itself, because it is pre-eminently whatever is, is far superior to anyone's capacity of understanding. Matter, which, because of its deficiency, is not worthy of being said to exist, similarly eludes knowledge by its very nature. So far is it from having any share in beauty that it represents the utmost degree of deformity. Beauty, on the other hand, always accompanies goodness, and it is impossible for beauty to exist without goodness.

We have said that matter does not partake of any kind of goodness since it is evil per se. Nor does the One in itself possess any beauty since it is infinite simplicity, and infinite simplicity, being the cause of beauty, cannot possess beauty itself. Beauty comes to those things that are dependent on the first cause. Thus, the One in itself is so perfect and so pre-eminent that, when we say that it is alive, that it has knowledge, that it is just and beautiful, we should not understand this to mean that it possesses life, wisdom or beauty in the same way as other things, but rather that it is the cause and author thanks to whom wisdom, life, justice and beauty are in these things. This is why Dionysius the Areopagite, the glory of Christian theology,[14] says in his book *On the Divine Names* [1.8] that each name of God denotes a particular property that is divinely bestowed upon the intelligible nature. Therefore, we must conclude that beauty is to be found in the Intelligible World, in Soul and even in Body as such.

Unless I am mistaken, the following observations will make it clear why this is so. Imagine that Minerva was alive among mortals. Imagine also a most exquisitely executed statue of Minerva, like the one by Phidias,[15] and think of its reflected image in a mirror. If someone were to see this image without seeing the statue itself, he would discover in it the artist's uncommon skill. But if he were to look at the eyes and the countenance and the rest of Minerva's body in the flesh, he would not be left in any doubt that the statue itself, as well as the reflected image of the statue, was worth next to nothing, despite his having thought so highly of their beauty just a little while before. Indeed, he would maintain that to the extent that the statue is closer to the true Minerva it is superior to the image. The same applies to the first and true beauty of the Intelligible World: it is the beginning and the measure of all other beauties. Soul itself also possesses beauty – not by its own nature, but in a derivative way, like gold minted with the effigy of a king. This is why it is more properly called a true likeness of beauty than true beauty, since it is in Soul on account of something else. The third type of beauty belongs exclusively to Body. Most certainly, it is not a likeness, but rather a shadow of beauty; and it is much further removed from the beauty of Soul than Soul is removed from the Intelligible World. For Body, as Heraclitus rightly says, has no solidity and no permanence, but is continually changing and in ceaseless flux.[16] This is why bodily beauty is always adulterated by deformity. Among all bodies, the universe is the most beautiful. The whole is always superior to its parts, since it contains without being contained; and no one would surely dispute the fact that other bodies are parts of the universe. Next come the heavenly bodies, from which a clear proof of divine beauty is drawn.[17] Apart from these, there exists a great multitude of other bodies on which I shall not dwell at present. Concerning man, finally, I shall only say that, since he partakes of such perfection and such beauty, the wise men of old called him a microcosm, as if he possessed all the qualities of the universe in readiness.[18]

Since beauty can be found in the Intelligible World, in Soul and in Body, we will call that beauty which belongs properly to the Intelligible World and to Soul the Divine and Heavenly Venus. It is the only beauty that is perceived by the eye of the mind, which is surely something divine. The beauty that belongs to Body, on the other hand, we will call the Vulgar Venus, since it presents itself to the bodily eye. Thus, if every kind of beauty has a kind of love that corresponds to it, and if we say that love is nothing other than an overpowering desire for beauty,[19] it is clear that the desire for divine beauty corresponds to Divine and Heavenly Love and that the desire for bodily beauty corresponds to Vulgar and Common Love. It is evident, moreover, that we would be greatly mistaken if we were to enslave ourselves to corporeal love without using it, so to speak, as a stepping-stone to divine beauty. I will not at this time dwell on all the calamities that befall us when we obey Vulgar Love, since my purpose is to show that the greatest of divine gifts is that type of love under whose leadership we are able to contemplate divine beauty and that, consequently, a true lover is a most sublime thing, a wonder to behold in the midst of other lovers.

Our soul, although full of the divine and the true daughter of God, is so much a prisoner of the body, whose administration it was put in charge of by nature, that, more often than not, it takes on the likeness of the dark jail in which it is imprisoned rather than that of the source from which it emanates. Accordingly, the ancient theologians called the body the tomb of the soul, meaning by this that we have a greater affinity with the realm of death than with that of life as long as the soul is joined to a perishable body.[20] Oblivious of its own beauty and of its divine origin, the soul is assailed by huge and varied swarms of dreams, continually deceiving it during that period of time which the blind and ignorant masses call life. Not everyone can easily remember the divine beauty while still ensnared in a mortal body. There is, however, a very small number of people in whom there remains a spark of the divine splendour, enabling them to conjure up such a happy memory.

Divine beauty shines more radiantly on a person's face than anywhere else; and if a beautiful face is matched by an outstanding body, people are at first thunderstruck when they come across such an uncommon sight. They become speechless and begin to shiver, and when finally they gradually recover and regain some strength, they conclude that this beauty surely deserves divine honours no less than the statues of the immortal gods. Afterwards, by looking more intently, their eyes open up a gateway in their soul through which beauty can flow. They start trembling and sweating all over from this wound and are devoured by an inner burning.[21] From here, excited by this passion, they are raised in a wondrous way; but, weighed down by the stain of corporeality, they tumble downwards. They are like birds devoured by an excessive desire to fly, who audaciously entrust the all too heavy weight of their bodies to their immature wings; since they are not yet strong enough, they fall headlong to the ground when relying on their own strength.

Pulled in opposite directions at the same time, these people labour under an immense burden. Inside their souls, however, the much desired beauty seems to get absorbed, and sorrow is turned into joy. On the other hand, when they are deprived of their usual diet, they become sad and sick, continuously thinking of the beauty of this most resplendent face. Their unquenchable desire makes them behave like madmen. They can neither sleep at night, nor find any rest by day. They run to and fro in search of the divine vision and would doubtless even give free rein to their sufferings and inflict violence upon themselves if they were unable to see it. As soon as they have found it, their hunger is appeased and the burden of sorrow is lifted from their shoulders. They feel that they have been raised beyond themselves to such an extent that they forget their parents, their brothers and the honour of their country, all of which they had once been proud of; they even forget themselves, their only thought being to know how they can enjoy the divine vision. For those who are in its presence enjoy it and derive from it the greatest benefit for their whole state of affairs, both in this life and in the next, as if it were the best healer of mankind's illnesses.

First of all, they ascend from the beauty of one particular perishable body to the beauty of the heavenly bodies and of the whole universe, where they perceive not only the source of corporeal light, but also the sweetest harmonies produced by the order of the heavenly bodies and the regularity of their movements. It thus becomes perfectly clear to them that the heavens are the lyre of God, as the ancient Pythagoreans say, and that everything beneath them dances in a most wondrous way to their music.[22] After this, they encounter the beauty of the soul. It stands to reason that whatever spark of divine goodness inheres in the body (which is itself an image of the soul) was previously in the soul and appears there more conspicuously, for the soul is the ruling principle of the body. One could even say that the body only partakes of divine beauty because of the immense authority exercised over it by the soul. This is why the wise men of old thought that it was almost impossible for those people whose beauty was superior to that of others not also to have outstanding qualities – just as if all those who had a superior and more divine soul also had a more handsome body, the latter being a true image of the soul.

So they gradually ascend until they finally reach the bottomless sea of divine beauty. At the sight of its splendour they start blinking and raising their eyebrows and are able to reason along these lines:

Up to now we have only seen a shadow or a sort of likeness of beauty rather than true beauty itself. But now, sweetest Love, thou who warmest what is cold, who makest bright what is dark, who callest back to life what is dead, now thou hast in thy bounty restored the feathers of our wings, which had been weakened by an excessive desire for procreation. Thou hast exalted our minds and filled them with a burning and unquenchable desire to contemplate the splendour of the divine light. We have been led by a most divine madness to wander throughout the supracelestial region, where we were able to enjoy fully and most wonderfully what no eye has ever seen, what no ear has ever heard and what no mind has ever dared to think.[23]

This is the way that the true lover must go: once he has begun to contemplate divine beauty, he has nearly reached the end of his journey, where all things are at rest and enjoy perfect happiness. Accordingly, whoever contemplates true beauty with the eye of his mind – which alone can see it – does not produce images and counterfeits of virtue, but true virtues. He pleases God and plainly shows that it is because of love that man is a prize possession of the divinity.[25] It is therefore clear to all that it is not only immensely important for everyone in general but even more so for the beloved to value a legitimate lover as highly as possible; and the extent to which divine things are superior to everything else is equally clear to all. Nor can anyone ask or obtain a greater gift from the gods than a beloved who loves him with equal intensity and is prepared to undergo every conceivable danger for the sake of his lover. And it is no less pleasing to the gods to see a lover honoured, extolled and revered by his beloved than if they themselves were praised in solemn worship. For the lover always dwells with his beloved, continuously directed by a divine madness. This is why the beloved must understand that not only in this life, but also in the next, countless favours will be heaped upon him.

If, on the other hand, the beloved[26] rejects his legitimate lover, he is thrown into such calamity that it would be much better for him to be a senseless brute or a stone – unless indeed it were even preferable for him not to exist at all. For surely no greater misfortune can befall us than to hold in contempt the divine entities, which dispense whatever is good and measured to everything below. Not only is such an attitude completely opposed to the divine, it also of necessity entails all that is evil. Thus, anyone who rejects his lover is engaged in battle with the divine, inasmuch as he is obeying contrary forces. In the first place, he becomes a victim of those disturbances which are brought about by unbridled greed, not unlike a plant fixed in the soil which in pushing upwards treats its roots as if they were its head and its branches as if they were its feet. To this is added another evil: tossed hither and yon between false opinions and never-ending insanity, he leads his life as if he were dreaming. Despite all this, he is well aware of the fact that after death he will be severely punished and tortured by the cruellest devils. Some of these terrify our imagination[27] with the most horrendous sights; others torment our body with the most painful wounds. But he will suffer a fate even worse than can be imagined: first, because of the dissolution of his inner harmony, a state which can be compared with that of a sick and prostrate body in which all the parts fight against one another; and, second, because of the omnipresence of God, which is even more painful. For just as an inflamed eye is unable to tolerate the brightness of the sun (which is a continuous source of pleasure to a healthy eye), so the just man greatly rejoices in the presence of God, whereas the unjust is overwhelmed by distress. Such are the calamities – and there are much greater ones as well – with which God pursues those who reject their lover. Nonetheless, we have also seen that the beloved is in a position to enjoy an equal abundance of goods if his only concern, night and day, is to unfold the entirety of virtue by loving in return, so that he can become similar to his lover.

This is our panegyric, most divine Love. These are the thoughts we can conceive and the words we can utter about you without being overwhelmed by the gloom of transitoriness. Anyone who does not pay honour to you in the way you deserve does not understand that everything which is divine and heavenly, as well as everything perishable and transitory, owes its existence to you, and that it is through you that all those things are able to return to their source, in whom they can finally rest and partake of the divine nature, each according to its own capacity.

Translator's Notes

1. The work is dedicated to two pupils of Diacceto, whose fame rests on the roles they played in Florentine politics rather than on their literary achievements. We owe, however, to Giovanni Corsi (1472–1547) the first life of Marsilio Ficino (1506) and a preface to Giovanni Pontano's *De prudentia* (1508), and to Palla Rucellai (1473–1543) an edition of his brother Giovanni's *Le Api* (1539).
2. Reading *de diis <non recte> sentire*. The words in brackets must be added, as is shown by the Italian version of the text, entitled *Panegirico all'amore* (Rome, 1526): 'Grave peccato è non sentire rettamente degli dij . . . '.
3. Originally a palinode was an ode or song in which the author retracted what he had said in a previous poem; it thus came to mean a recantation.
4. See Plato, *Phaedrus* 243A. Helen was thought to have been the most beautiful woman of the ancient world; the offended godhead was Aphrodite, the Greek goddess of love and beauty.
5. As will become clear, Diacceto appears to regard Diotima, the priestess who explains to Socrates the mysteries of love in the *Symposium* (201D–212B), as one of the ancient theologians, that is, the line of (partly mythical) pagan philosophers, beginning either with Hermes Trismegistus or Zoroaster and culminating in Plato, whose doctrines foreshadowed some of the truths of Christianity. See D. P. Walker, *The Ancient Theology* (London, 1972).
6. Diacceto may be alluding to the taboo on eating beans, on which see W. Burkert, *Lore and Science in Ancient Pythagoreanism* (Cambridge, Mass., 1972), pp. 183–5, where all the relevant texts are discussed.
7. That is, the angelic realm.
8. See *Corpus Hermeticum* I.6, and Plato, *Republic* VI (508B–C).
9. See Plutarch, *Isis and Osiris* 9 (354C), where, however, the last sentence of the quotation does not occur.
10. Plato, *Symposium* 202D. Unlike the English word 'demon', the term 'daemon' (from the Greek *daimōn*) does not have the connotation of evil and wickedness.
11. Plato, *Symposium* 203BC.
12. See Plato, *Symposium* 180D–E, and Hesiod, *Theogony* 188–206.
13. On the ancient sources for this five-tiered ontological scheme, which was also adopted by Ficino in some of his works, see M. J. B. Allen, 'Ficino's theory of the five substances and

the Neoplatonists' *Parmenides'*, *Journal of Medieval and Renaissance Studies,* 12 (1982), 19–44.

14. Pseudo-Dionysius the Areopagite (c. 500) was a mystical theologian who adapted the Neoplatonic metaphysics of Proclus to Christian theology; until the sixteenth century, he was wrongly believed to be the convert of St Paul mentioned in Acts 17:34.

15. Among the most famous statues by the renowned Athenian sculptor Phidias (b. c. 490 BC) was a gold and ivory Athena (the Greek goddess of wisdom, known as Minerva to the Romans).

16. See G. S. Kirk, J. E. Raven and M. Schofield, eds., *The Presocratic Philosophers,* 2nd ed. (Cambridge, 1983), pp. 195–7 (fragments 214–16).

17. Reading *sumi* for *summi.*

18. A concept first formulated by Democritus: see H. Diels and W. Kranz, eds., *Die Fragmente der Vorsokratiker,* 5th ed., 3 vols. (Berlin, 1934–7), II, p. 153, 68[55] B 34; it is also found in Aristotle, *Physics* VIII.2 (252ᵇ26). Diacceto may, however, be thinking of Proclus, *In Platonis Timaeum commentaria,* ed. E. Diehl, 3 vols. (Leipzig, 1903–6), I, p. 5, lines 11–17.

19. See Plato, *Symposium* 204D.

20. See Plato, *Gorgias* 493A, *Cratylus* 400C and *Phaedrus* 250C; for Ficino's use of this image in his *Platonic Theology,* see Chapter 4.

21. For the symptoms described here, see Plato, *Phaedrus* 250C–252B.

22. The locus classicus for this notion is Macrobius's *Commentary on the Somnium Scipionis* II.1.1–14; but Diacceto may well have had some other text in mind.

23. See Plato, *Phaedrus* 247C.

24. Psalms 118:24. In the mass, this verse was sung as part of the *graduale* on Easter Sunday and during the week following Easter.

25. For the idea of man being a possession of the gods, see Plato, *Phaedo* 62B and *Laws* X (902B).

26. Reading *amatus* for *amatum.*

27. Reading *phantasiam* for *phantasia.*

Further Reading

CHRP, pp. 312, 348

Diacceto, Francesco Cattani da, *De pulchro libri III . . .* , ed. S. Matton (Pisa, 1986)

Ficino, Marsilio, *Commentary on Plato's Symposium on Love,* trans. S. Jayne (Dallas, 1985)

Kraye, J., 'The transformation of Platonic love in the Italian Renaissance', in A. Baldwin and S. Hutton, eds., *Platonism and the English Imagination* (Cambridge, 1994), pp. 76–85

Kristeller, P. O., 'Cattani da Diacceto, Francesco', *Dizionario biografico degli Italiani* (Rome, 1960–), XXII, pp. 507–9

'Francesco da Diacceto and Florentine Platonism in the sixteenth century', in his *Studies in Renaissance Thought,* 3 vols. (Rome, 1956–93), I, pp. 287–336

Nelson, J. C., *Renaissance Theory of Love: The Context of Giordano Bruno's 'Eroici furori'* (New York, 1958), pp. 108–12

Verde, A., *Lo Studio di Firenze 1473–1503: ricerche e documenti* (Florence, 1973–), III, pp. 1460–3

15

Francesco de' Vieri

JOHN MONFASANI

Introduction

The Italian philosopher Francesco de' Vieri (1524–91) was born in Florence, the scion of a noble family which had produced a long line of humanists, poets, lawyers and doctors. He was called 'il Verino secondo' to distinguish him from his relative, also named Francesco de' Vieri and known as 'il Verino'. Following in the footsteps of his namesake, a distinguished professor of Aristotelian philosophy in the first half of the sixteenth century, de' Vieri taught logic and natural philosophy at the University of Pisa from 1553. And like his forebear, he was actively involved in the Florentine Academy, a Tuscan cultural institute sponsored by Grand Duke Cosimo I de' Medici. The programme of the Florentine Academy centred on the study of Italian literature, but it also promoted the use of vernacular in philosophy and other scholarly disciplines in order to make them more accessible to a wide audience. A number of de' Vieri's extant works, many of which remain in manuscript, consist of lectures written in Italian and delivered to the Florentine Academy. The subjects range from explications of the poetry of Dante and Petrarch to more philosophical topics presented in a simplified manner for popular consumption.[1]

De' Vieri's most important achievement as a university philosopher was to give a course of lectures on Plato – a rare venture in sixteenth-century Italy, where Aristotle continued to monopolize the curriculum. Beginning in 1576, he taught Platonism on so-called festival days, in addition to his normal lectures on Aristotle; but, due to the opposition of staunch Peripatetics at the university, the course was abandoned after three years. Unlike more militant Platonists such as Francesco Patrizi da Cherso, de' Vieri had no intention of substituting Plato for Aristotle. On the contrary, he saw Platonism as a supplement to Aristotelianism, which he envisaged as continuing to occupy the central place in the philosophical syllabus. Inspired by the syncretism of Giovanni Pico della Mirandola, de' Vieri attempted to demonstrate that in many (though by no means all) areas Aristotelianism and Platonism were not only in fundamental agreement with each other but also with Christianity.[2]

De' Vieri nevertheless endorsed the view, put forward in the previous century by Cardinal Bessarion and Marsilio Ficino, that of all pagan philosophical systems, Platonism was the closest to Christianity. In his *Compendium*, written in the vernacular, for a general audience, he carefully lays out the doctrines of Plato which, in his opinion, are in agreement with Christian beliefs.[3] Chapter 8, translated here, deals with the nature of the Trinity, and in it de' Vieri attempts to show that, even in relation to this most profound of religious mysteries, there is a large area of agreement between Christianity and Platonism – and, to a lesser extent, between Christianity and Aristotelianism. In the end, however, de' Vieri makes it clear that Plato, for all the similarity between his teachings and those of Christianity, was denied access to revelation and therefore failed to grasp the essential oneness of the triune God.

For the original Italian text, see Francesco de' Vieri, *Compendio della dottrina di Platone in quello, che ella è conforme con la Fede nostra* (Florence, 1577), pp. 46–63 (pp. 62–3 are misnumbered 46–7).

Compendium of Platonic Teachings Which Are in Conformity with the Christian Faith

CHAPTER 8

God Is One and Triune According to the Christian Faith and, to Some Extent, According to Plato As Well

I have already demonstrated the existence of God according to Plato's teaching and according to the truth which God has revealed to us. So, in keeping with the sequence that I proposed,[4] I now have to show that Plato and the Christian faith also agree in this profound mystery: that God is one and that he is triune; and, furthermore, in regards to the Trinity, that he is not triune in every respect.

To begin our argument then, it is clear that according to faith God is one. Among various other authorities one may see this in Deuteronomy 6[:4]: 'Hear, O Israel: the Lord our God is one Lord'; in Exodus 20[:3–5], where we are commanded to have no other gods before God; and in the Apostles' Creed, where the first article of faith is: 'I believe in one God.' So, too, Plato, in the *Parmenides,* has the multiplicity of things proceed from the first unity which is God; and, in the *Timaeus,* he has God as the first maker of this entire universe. In his *Letters,* he calls God the king of all that is.[5] And Aristotle, in Book XII of the *Metaphysics,* calls God the ruler and governor.[6]

Theologians and philosophers demonstrate this most holy truth by means of a great many proofs. For the sake of brevity, I shall adduce only one, which proceeds by way of division and which incorporates many of the most important proofs.

To make this argument clearer, we have to accept a basic premise granted by Aristotle, Plato and Christian theologians: that God is the cause of all things as formal cause, as efficient cause and as final cause, but not as material cause, since matter, lacking all form and every perfection, receives its perfection from forces which act on it. God, however, who is goodness itself and perfection itself, distributes goodness and perfection to his creatures and receives nothing from them.

Furthermore, we should know that form has three prerogatives. One is giving being to an entity which did not previously exist. For instance, until the soul is introduced into the matter or the blood of a woman, no creature exists; conversely, when the soul leaves the body, the man or woman no longer exists.[7] Moving on, a second prerogative of form is holding together the parts of a composite entity. An indication of this is that when the soul has departed, the humours separate from each other and the limbs break off from one another, as one sees in dead bodies in a state of decay. The third thing that form does in each entity is that, being one itself, it gives unity to them. Everything which exists in some way participates in unity: for example, an army, a house, an animal. Things which lack unity, lack being.

My third assumption is that the task of every efficient cause is to make and produce its effect and products, so that they come into existence. It also has the task of providing for them, so that they continue in existence, as we can see in the case of natural agents, such as animals, which beget offspring and then look after them for as long as they cannot look after themselves. The same thing happens with agents who use reason when they function, such as fathers of families and governors of republics. Thus, a medical doctor, having restored [his patient's] body to health, also sees to it that this condition is maintained.

My last assumption is this: the end is that which everyone desires. Aristotle shows this in Book I of the *Ethics*[8] and Plato in the *Hipparchus.*[9] Furthermore, and more importantly, the end is that for the sake of which other things are sought: riches, for instance, are sought for the sake of the benefits which they confer on the body; and these corporeal benefits, in turn, are sought so that we can attend to virtue and the virtuous operations of the soul.

Taking these assumptions as given, my argument proceeds in the following manner. If we consider the divine majesty, we do so by contemplating it either as perfection and the most perfect form, or as an agent or as an end. In all these ways I understand God to be one pre-eminently. If one of the tasks of form is to give being to a composite entity, how can there not be a first form or a first perfection that gives being to the world, which in Book I of *De caelo* is shown be one.[10] Now, how can the form of the whole world not be one when every form of any composite entity whatever, existing as a particle of this world, is one? Similarly, if other particular forms contain many parts which are united by their unity of essence, power and operation, how can it not be the case even more so that the whole world is contained by one form, which is one in essence, power and operation? Finally, if every other form is one and as one gives being, and if the more united a form is, the greater its power, will not God, who is the supreme form, be one to a greater degree? If then, as Hermes Trismegistus says in his *Pimander,* we concede that there is one sun, one moon, one world, how can we not concede that there is one God?[11]

If we next consider God as an agent, either one who acts or one who exercises providence, he is still one in this guise. To elaborate on this point: if we consider God as an agent and a maker, and if he is not the one maker of all creatures, but there are, for example, two makers, either each can make everything and therefore one of them is superfluous, which is not something admitted in natural nor in artificial things, and therefore much less in divine things; or one of them makes some things and the other makes other things and therefore neither is completely perfect, and they will need above them another God, who is the cause of what both of them make and of everything.

When one thing is more perfect than another, eventually we arrive at the one which is most perfect. Thus, among those things which have greater and lesser degrees of heat, there is one which has the greatest amount, namely, fire, and among luminous things, there is the sun, which is supremely luminous. Similarly, among forms, there is one first form and purest first actuality without any admixture of potentiality or imperfection, and this is God.

To reason in this way about agents is Platonic, similar to the argument Plato used in the *Timaeus* to prove that there is one world and no more than that.[12] It is also partly Peripatetic, similar to the argument Aristotle used in Book I of the *Physics* to prove that there are not more than three first principles of generable things, one being prime matter and the other two the prime contraries, that is, privation and form.[13] It is also partly theological, as is obvious from a consideration of the many arguments St Thomas used in the Book I of *Summa contra gentiles* to prove this conclusion, namely, that God is one.[14]

Likewise, the divine majesty, insofar as it exercises providence and governs all things well, leading them to their end through suitable means and at the opportune time, shares its sovereignty with no companion but is instead the sole ruler, just as Aristotle concludes, in agreement with Homer, at the end of his *Metaphysics*.[15] The basis for this conclusion is that, inasmuch as all things in the universe are governed well, rather than badly, their governor is one and unique. God, as the first principle, through his understanding, directs nature in every natural operation to some determined end; he is therefore one. Just as for sensible things there is one common sense, and for different cases one judge, who keeps all of them in mind, so too there is one will for the good of all things and one power that leads them to their end.

If, finally, God is considered to be the end of ends by virtue of his sovereignty and essence, he is also one, being desired and loved by every single thing, even by prime matter, seeing that prime matter desires the forms, which are perfections that reflect in some small degree the first form and ultimate end.

Furthermore, Plato in his *Second Letter* [312E–313A], which I have cited several times, shows by his use of the singular that God is one as efficient cause, as king, as form and as end. Likewise, the divine Scriptures reveal to us that God is one as creator, in the first verses of Genesis; that he is one as provider, when our Lord Jesus Christ said: 'if ye then, being evil, know how to give good gifts unto your children, how much more shall your Father which is in heaven?';[16] and that he is one as end, when the Scriptures say, also employing the singular: 'Blessed are the pure in heart: for they shall see God.'[17]

According to our religion, therefore, and according to the most excellent philosophers and according to reason using the best means of discourse, God is one in essence and not more than one. And though Plato in the *Timaeus* and elsewhere, and also Aristotle in Book I of *De caelo,* speak of gods in the plural, they are not thinking of him who is rightly God by his nature, but rather of others who are gods through participation, such as the intelligences which move the heavens. In the same way, the Holy Scriptures occasionally call the elect gods and sons of God by adoption and by inheritance from the Father of eternal beatitude.

Nor should we be upset if it seems that there ought to be a plurality of gods, and at the minimum, two: one the cause of good things, the other of evil things. Hence, according to Empedocles, amity was the cause of good and enmity the cause of evil; and the Pythagoreans posited the even number as the cause of good and the odd as the cause of evil.[18] Hence, the Gnostics and the Manicheans maintained that there were two gods: one good and the cause of good, the other evil and the cause of evil.[19] Yet even if the diversity of good and evil effects argues strongly for a diversity of causes from which these effects derive, this does not mean that these causes must be gods, one good and the other evil, since there is only one God, as is proved and written in the Wisdom of Solomon 12[:13], Isaiah 45[:22], I Corinthians 8[:6], Galatians 3[:20], Ephesians 4[:6] and elsewhere. This has been noted by Alfonso de Castro and others who explain and refute heresies.[20] To argue the case, I say that if the evils found in this world are evils of nature, they proceed either: from matter and ill-disposed agents, such as monsters; from a lack or surfeit of matter; or from the weakness of the agent. Natural causes are good, but occasionally they are ill disposed; and, for that reason, they are accidentally the causes of evil. God is that force without whose involvement nothingness, that is to say, evil comes about, because it is outside his primary intention.[21] If there is an evil for which blame can be apportioned, its cause is us as perpetrators, the devil as tempter and the world as that which is ill disposed. If there is an evil that comes about as punishment, God, being most just, is its cause; therefore, he says: 'I am the Lord; I create good and make evil.'[22]

If evil were a natural effect, it would proceed from some determined cause. But this is false because the good is in accordance with nature and design, whereas evil falls outside the intention of nature and design. As Dionysius the Areopagite rightly says in his book *On Divine Names* [4.30–2], the good has a determined cause, while evils have an indeterminate and accidental cause. This is either because the agents are weak in regard to the good, or because what is acted upon is ill disposed, or because of the coming together of many disproportionate and unordered contraries, or because of other similar causes, as Dionysius and Marsilio explain in this passage.[23] In like fashion, if we do something evil, either as natural agents or from design, we do so while desiring the good. No one, says Dionysius, sets out to do something in pursuit of evil.[24]

I next have to show that God is triune, both according to religion and to other authorities. In the first place, Christian theologians, as well as Platonic philosophers, agree that divinity is found in plurality rather than in one alone. The theologians have put forward many reasons, but the three principal ones have been set out by Richard of St Victor in Book III [chapters 11–13] of his *On the Trinity*.[25] He establishes the first of these reasons from a property of charity or love, namely, that it is directed towards others. Charity is a perfection, and no love is greater than charity. Hence, since God is utterly perfect, there is necessarily in him a divine and infinite charity and love; and being infinite, it does not befit God unless it is directed towards another who is similarly infinitely perfect. Consequently, God is a plurality in persons, although in essence he is only one. This great theologian bases his second reason on his theory that God's supreme beatitude must necessarily be accompanied by a supreme joy which is the joy of friendship among equals. If therefore God is utterly happy, he is not one, but a plurality of persons who love each other with a perfect love. Richard takes his third argument from the fullness of glory: the divine majesty would not be completely glorious if it lacked someone to whom it might communicate its perfection and its benevolence thoroughly, rather than partially as it does to creatures; God is worthy of supreme glory and supreme love; therefore, one divine person has communicated all his perfection to another person. So we conclude that God is not one, but a plurality of persons, as is proved by the theological arguments adduced here.

Platonic philosophers have also put forward many arguments, but for the sake of brevity I shall be content here, as earlier, to recite only three. The first of them is as follows. Because he is supremely good, God produced the whole universe. The universe is composed of matter, which consists of the totality of extant sensible bodies, whether simple or mixed; and it is also composed of the most perfect form, the Angelic Mind, which is full of the ideas of everything in the universe. Because this Mind is completely perfect and free of corporeal matter, which is completely imperfect, these two parts – matter and this Mind – are entirely opposite. Consequently, it was necessary to join them together by some intermediate entity. This intermediate entity is the World Soul. As a soul and a divine substance, it is a divine form and an immortal participant in understanding and reasoning. It is also partly material, since it acts in common with the heavens to move the celestial bodies, as well as those things which are here below. Above the World Soul and above the Angelic Mind there is God, through whom they are united, along with matter, to the supreme perfection of the universe. And thus the divine nature is plural rather than singular in God. I have extracted this argument of Plato partly from the *Philebus* and partly from the *Timaeus*.[26]

As for the second argument of the Platonists, we can make use of this one. The deity cannot be one, but is instead to be separated into three because every other form and every other thing has three modes of being. The highest mode is causal being, such as the warmth of the sun; the second mode is formal being, such as the heat of fire; and the third is participated being, such as the warmth of water heated by fire. Thus, divine and intellectual nature, which is the universal principle of the universe, has its causal being in God, its formal being in the Angelic Mind and its participated being in the World Soul. Hence, it was [not] by mere chance that the ancient pagan theologians, concealing profound mysteries under the veil of poetry and fables, called God 'Uranus' on account of his supreme excellence, that they called the Mind 'Saturn' and that they called the World Soul now 'Jupiter', now 'Neptune' and in the next breath 'Pluto'. The Phoenix of past ages, Lord Giovanni, count of Mirandola, in an awe-inspiring manner and with the greatest understanding, has explained this to us in his commentary on that Platonic *canzone* on love by our own Girolamo Benivieni, who was himself a man of great learning and saintly ways.[27]

The last Platonic argument runs as follows. God [can be described as] an intellectual nature without a multitude of intermediary entities, without intellectual species and without discursive reasoning; this is the God whom Plato calls father and maker of the universe. Or, [it can be said that] God has a plurality of intermediary entities and ideas, but lacks discursive reason; this God is the Divine and Angelic Mind. Or, [one can assert that] God has many ideas and also has discursive reasoning; this divine nature is the World Soul. After the latter come the souls of the heavenly spheres, the souls of the daemons and our own souls. The God therefore who is the universal principle of the universe is more than one, that is to say, he is three, as has been explained already by means of three Platonic arguments.

Likewise, according to the theologians, the divine persons are not more nor less than three, that is, Father, Son and Holy Spirit. The holy doctors of our Catholic Church prove this truth using many reasons or persuasive arguments. One such is the following. The first person communicates itself to the Son, imparting to him its selfsame essence and all its perfections by means of intellection. This is why from eternity there occurs a mutual love of the selfsame essence, and this love is the Holy

Spirit. If there were more than three fathers, sons and holy spirits, they would be material, says St Thomas, because the multiplicity of particulars of the same species derives from matter.[28] But God is immaterial and is spirit, as all Christians acknowledge, as the divine Scriptures testify and as the most excellent philosophers – that is, Aristotle in Book VIII of the *Physics*[29] and Plato in the *Republic*[30] and elsewhere – prove.

For all that, we must not consider it an imperfection of the Son that he does not generate nor an imperfection of the Holy Spirit that another divine person does not proceed from it. This is due not to a lack of power but rather to a lack of propriety.[31]

That God is triune in respect to persons – that is, the Father, the Son and the Holy Spirit – according to the teaching revealed to us from above is clear from many passages in the Scriptures. Here I shall make do with just two. One is chapter 3[:17] of Matthew, where it is narrated that when Christ was baptized by John in the Jordan, the Holy Spirit appeared in the form of a dove, and the voice of the Father was heard, saying: 'This is my beloved son, in whom I am well pleased.' If there had not been three persons, how could three have appeared? The other passage comes from the same Gospel of Matthew in chapter 28[:19], where Jesus Christ orders his disciples to baptize all the nations in the name of the Father, of the Son and of the Holy Spirit. If there had not been three persons, he would not have said these words, for he is the teacher of truth – indeed, he is truth itself – as St Augustine says in the first of the *Sixty-Five Questions to Orosius.*[32]

On the other hand, it is not right for us to offer worship to God except as one. As was proved here, we must believe with absolute firmness and must not doubt in any way that God is one in respect to his nature and triune in respect to persons, as St Augustine says in chapter 5 of his book *On Faith to Peter.* To sum up and speak even more clearly, as St Augustine once again says in chapter 11 of the same book, elect and true Christians ought to hold firmly and without incurring any doubts that the nature of the Father, the Son and the Holy Spirit is one and their persons are three;[33] and that it was the Father alone who said: 'This is my son in whom I am well pleased'; and that it was the Son alone upon whom fell the words of the Father when that same Son, who took on human flesh, was baptized in the Jordan. And we must believe that it was the Holy Spirit alone who descended upon Jesus Christ under the appearance and form of a dove and who appeared to the apostles in the form of flames on that supreme day after the resurrection of Jesus.[34]

Similarly, it is clear that according to Plato, God is in some way triune. In the *Timaeus,* he speaks of the father, of the exemplary world, ripe with all the ideas (this is the Angelic Mind) and of the World Soul. The first is called 'Uranus' by the ancient pagan theologians on account of its excellence. The second is named 'Saturn' on account of its contemplation. And the World Soul is called 'Jupiter', inasmuch as it animates, moves and rules the celestial bodies, and 'Neptune', inasmuch as it animates, moves and rules the things of this lower world, which after the manner of water are in continual ebb and flow; and finally it is called 'Pluto', inasmuch as, through its being and operations, it governs those things that are under the earth, the place from which come gems and metals, whose abundance makes us rich. This is the explanation offered by some of the most excellent Platonists and, among others, by the Phoenix of his time, Lord Giovanni Pico, count of Mirandola, commenting on that very erudite Platonic *canzone* of Girolamo Benivieni, a man both learned and of a singularly good life.[35]

That God is triune is also clear from Plato's much cited *Second Letter* [312E–313A], where he talks about the three principles: the First, Second and Third. But Plato did not sufficiently recognize that God is one in nature and essence. He believed that there were three distinct gods, perfect in their nature and operations. For Plato, the father alone is the universal maker of everything, whether or not with an intermediary, but without the mediation of the exemplary world. And, according to many Platonists, the father is the maker of all the intellectual natures, called by him secondary gods, who at his command produced all sensible things in such a way that they are not eternal, as the gods themselves are.

But according to Catholic truth, there are three persons in one essence, and all of them are equal in power. In effect, they act in concert in external operations. Thus, the world was created by the power and operation of the Father, the Son and the Holy Spirit. Likewise, the incarnation of the Son was the work of the three divine persons as efficient cause; but it terminated in the second person alone, as the theologians maintain. And when Jesus Christ occasionally says that the Father is greater than he is, we should understand him to be referring to the human nature which he took as his and not to the divine nature. St Augustine explains this point very well in chapter 2 of his book *On the Trinity and Unity [of God]*.[36] We should note here that in Jesus Christ there are two natures, the human and the divine, in one 'suppositum'[37] and in one person, and there is no confusion between them. In his book *On the Orthodox Faith,* John of Damascus gives a beautiful example, that of a knife made entirely of iron, which is red hot; in it are the nature of fire and the nature of iron, but there is just one 'suppositum'.[38]

In discussing this highest of mysteries, we are all the more readily permitted to use terms coined by theologians rather than Tuscan words, so as not to give occasion for others to go astray, either because we are misunderstood or because we give rise to an impious interpretation of such a profound truth. Furthermore, I call to the attention of your most Serene Highness[39] the fact that I said that the Father, the Son and the Holy Spirit are equal and undifferentiated in respect to their divinity and to their *external* activity, which terminates within the divine essence. I said this because in respect to their *internal* operation: eternal generation belongs to the Father; being generated, to the Son; the 'spiration'[40] of the Holy Spirit, to the two of them, the Father and the Son together; and being 'spirated' and proceeding, to the Holy Spirit. The eternal Father conceives, through his understanding, the Holy Word, which is consubstantial with him. From them both, there then proceeds a love which is similarly consubstantial and which is the Holy Spirit. 'The Father', as Athanasius says in his Creed, 'is neither made nor created nor generated by anyone.'[41] The Son is neither made nor created, but is generated by the Father. The Holy Spirit is neither made nor created nor generated, but proceeds from the Father and the Son.

Finally, in defence of Plato, I say that although he was wise in terms of human wisdom and although he may have read the Old Testament,[42] where these mysteries are enfolded and adumbrated, he deserves to be pardoned [for his inaccuracies] because the mysteries were not explained to him by any member of God's elect. The same can be said of Aristotle, who held God to be one in essence and in person. But there are philosophers and heretics who deserve not only the gravest criticism, but also punishment for refusing to change their views. Claiming the authority of the Holy Scriptures, they wish to maintain that God is [one] in substance as well as in person, or that there are three Gods in person as well as in essence. The Noetian and Sabellian heretics held that there was only one God in essence and in person; this heretical opinion is refuted with a great array of authorities by Alfonso de Castro in his book against heresies.[43] Origen and Arius posit distinct essences in God, along with a distinction of persons, as St Thomas relates in Part I of the *Summa* at question 32, article 1, which consists of scriptural citations plainly asserting that God is one in essence (as I demonstrated here) and triune in persons.[44] Our own Dante gathered this mystery into a few brief lines when he said in his *Paradiso:*

> And I believe in these three eternal persons; and these
> I believe to be an essence so one and so triune
> That it accepts both 'are' and 'is'.[45]

Translator's Notes

1. For a list of his unpublished works see J. Colaneri's introduction to his edition of Francesco de' Vieri, *Lezzioni d'amore* (Munich, 1973), pp. 9–11; for his published works see pp. 12–13.
2. See Francesco de' Vieri, *Vere conclusioni di Platone conformi alla dottrina christiana, et a quella d'Aristotele* (Florence, 1577). The three main areas in which de' Vieri admitted there was a conflict between Plato and Aristotle were the ideas, the creation or eternity of the world and divine providence.
3. He dealt with the disagreements between Platonism and Christianity in an unpublished work entitled *Alcune differenze tra Platone et la fede Christiana* (MS Naples, Biblioteca nazionale, Fondo principale XIII D 96).
4. At the beginning of the book, de' Vieri sets out a chapter-by-chapter 'table of the many, many truths in which Christian doctrine is in agreement with that of Plato', sigs. b6^r–c4^v (for ch. 8 see sigs. c1^v–c2^r).
5. Plato, *Letters* VI (323D).
6. Aristotle, *Metaphysics* XII.10 (1076^{a}4).
7. Following Thomas Aquinas, Christian doctrine regarded the soul as the substantial form of the body.
8. Aristotle, *Nicomachean Ethics* I.2 (1094^{a}18–22).
9. In the *Hipparchus,* which is probably apocryphal, 'the lovers of gain' are discussed; however, it is never asserted that the end is that which everyone desires; but cf. 227C7: 'Well, in that way, everyone seems to be a lover of gain.'
10. Aristotle, *De caelo* I.8–9.
11. *Hermetica,* trans. B. P. Copenhaver (Cambridge, 1992), p. 39 (*Corpus hermeticum* XI.11).
12. See Plato, *Timaeus* 31A–B.
13. Aristotle, *Physics* I.7.
14. Thomas Aquinas, *Summa contra gentiles* I.42.
15. Aristotle, *Metaphysics* XII.10 (1076^{a}4), quoting Homer, *Iliad* II.204. The medieval Latin version of the *Metaphysics* ended at Book XII, rather than XIV, and this tradition was sometimes followed even in the sixteenth century.
16. Matthew 7:11.
17. Matthew 5:8.

18. See J. Barnes, *Early Greek Philosophy* (London, 1987), pp. 166, 168–71, 174–7 (Empedocles); 208–9, 217 (the Pythagoreans).
19. The Manichean sect, founded by Manes (c. 216–76), was a radical offshoot of Gnosticism; its uncompromising dualism posited a primeval conflict between light and darkness.
20. See Alfonso de Castro, O.P., *Adversus omnes haereses libri quattuordecim* (Cologne, 1549), ff. 117ᵛ–119ʳ, on the heresy of *plures dei.*
21. De' Vieri is speaking in terms of the Neoplatonic notion that evil is an absence of being.
22. Cf. Isaiah 45:7. I have moved this quotation from the end of the next paragraph, where it does not fit, to here, where it fits nicely and where the phrase 'he says' is not followed by any quotation.
23. Marsilio Ficino, *Commentarium in Dionysium Areopagitam De divinis nominibus,* in his *Opera omnia,* 2 vols. (Basel, 1576; reprinted Turin, 1962), II, pp. 1086–8.
24. Pseudo-Dionysius the Areopagite, *On Divine Names* 4.19.
25. Richard of St Victor was a twelfth-century mystic and theologian, apparently born in Scotland; he became prior of the Abbey of St Victor in Paris in 1162.
26. The Platonic doctrine of the World Soul had been employed in discussions of the Trinity since the Middle Ages, but its use was controversial; see T. Gregory, *Anima mundi: la filosofia di Guglielmo di Conches e la scuola di Chartres* (Florence, 1955).
27. Giovanni Pico della Mirandola, *Commentary on a Canzone of Benivieni,* trans. S. Jayne (New York, 1984), pp. 83–4 (I.8).
28. This is a very characteristic Thomist doctrine; in addition to the possibly apocryphal *De principio individuationis* see, for a useful list of references, R. J. Defarrari, M. I. Barry and I. McGuiness, *Lexicon of St. Thomas Aquinas* (Washington, D.C., 1948–9), p. 670b, s.v. '(c), *materia communis* and *materia particularis . . . individuans'.*
29. Aristotle, *Physics* VIII.10.
30. Plato, *Republic* II (380D–381D).
31. In other words, the act of generating is not proper to the Son, nor is the act of having a person proceed from it proper to the Holy Spirit.
32. The text of this work, falsely attributed to Augustine, is printed in J. P. Migne, ed., *Patrologia Latina,* 221 vols. (Paris, 1844–64), XL, cols. 733–4 (q. 1).
33. For this Pseudo-Augustinian tract see Migne, ed., *Patrologia Latina,* XL, cols. 769 (ch. 5), 770–1 (ch. 11).
34. See Acts 2:1–4.
35. See n. 27.
36. For this Pseudo-Augustinian tract see Migne, ed., *Patrologia Latina,* XLII, cols. 1194–5 (ch. 2).
37. The scholastic term 'suppositum' refers to a being that subsists by itself.
38. For the Greek text see J. P. Migne, ed., *Patrologia Graeca,* 162 vols. (Paris, 1857–66), XCIV, col. 1024C (III.11).
39. Joan, Queen of Austria and Grand Duchess of Tuscany, to whom de' Vieri dedicated the book.
40. 'Spiration' is the theological term for the procession of the Holy Spirit regarded as an emanation of spirit.
41. See J. N. D. Kelly, *The Athanasian Creed* (London, 1964), pp. 17–20.
42. For the belief, held by certain early Christian writers (e.g., Justin Martyr, Ambrose, Clement of Alexandria), that Plato, during his travels to Egypt, had access to the Old Testament, and in particular to the Pentateuch, see A. S. Riginos, *Platonica: The Anecdotes concerning the Life and Writings of Plato* (Leiden, 1976), p. 65.
43. Reading *Noetiani* for *Noctiani.* According to Castro, *Adversus omnes haereses,* f. 117ᵛ, Noetus, a student of Sabellius, was responsible for the heresy of *plures dei;* for Sabellius, see ff. 120ᵛ–122ᵛ. Both Noetus and Sabellius were, in fact, 'Modalist' Monarchians, who held that the only differentiation in the godhead was a succession of modes; the movement was declared heretical because it failed to do justice to the independent subsistence of the Son.

44. For all its seeming precision, the reference is inaccurate; but for Arius, see Thomas Aquinas, *Summa theologiae* Ia, q. 27, art. 1 and q. 42, art. 1 and 2; for Origen, Ia, q. 42, art. 2.

45. Dante, *Divine Comedy: Paradiso,* Canto XXIV.139–41. In de' Vieri's text 'are' is given as the Latin word *sunt;* modern editions of Dante, however, give the Italian *sono.*

Further Reading

CHRP, pp. 349–50, 352, 357

Del Fante, A., 'Lo Studio di Pisa in un manoscritto inedito di Francesco Verino secondo', *Nuova rivista storica,* 64 (1980), 396–420

Nelson, J. C., *Renaissance Theory of Love: The Context of Giordano Bruno's 'Eroici furori'* (New York, 1958), pp. 147–50

Pintaudi, R., 'Il Platone di Francesco Verino secondo', *Rinascimento,* 16 (1976), 241–4

Purnell, F., *Jacopo Mazzoni and His Comparison of Plato and Aristotle,* PhD thesis, Columbia University, 1971

Schmitt, C. B., 'The faculty of arts at Pisa at the time of Galileo', *Physis,* 14 (1972), 243–72

Verde, A., 'Il "Parere" del 1587 di Francesco Verino sullo Studio pisano', in *Firenze e la Toscana dei Medici nel'Europa del '500,* 3 vols. (Florence, 1983), I, pp. 71–94

Part V.
Stoic Ethics

16

Coluccio Salutati

RONALD G. WITT

Introduction

Coluccio Salutati (1331–1406) was chancellor of the Florentine Republic from 1375 until his death, the first in a distinguished line of humanists to hold that position. He was revered as a father figure by the younger generation of Florentine humanists, including Leonardo Bruni and Poggio Bracciolini, and was responsible for inviting the Byzantine scholar Manuel Chrysoloras to Florence in order to teach Greek, thus inaugurating a new phase in the humanist movement.

For most of his life, Salutati's ethical stance was broadly, though superficially, Stoic, and was based on his reading of the Roman moralists Cicero and Seneca. In the 1390s, however, he gradually moved towards a more Peripatetic outlook, particularly in relation to the emotions. He became increasingly doubtful that the Stoic demand for complete impassivity was feasible, favouring instead the more realistic Aristotelian belief that emotions needed to be controlled and channelled in the proper direction, rather than eradicated. At the same time, Salutati's sincere, if rather shallow, commitment to Christianity began to deepen. The key moment in the development of his own personal brand of Christian Aristotelianism was the death of his beloved son Piero from the plague in May of 1400. The intolerable grief which this event provoked convinced him that human beings were incapable of suppressing such profound emotions and that relief could only be found though faith in the ultimate wisdom and goodness of God's providential plan for mankind.

Soon after the death of Piero, Salutati received a letter of consolation, full of Stoic maxims, from Francesco Zabarella (1360–1417), a professor of canon law at the University of Padua, who had taught in Florence from 1385 to 1390 and who in 1410 was to become bishop of that city. Salutati's reply to this letter was answered by Zabarella, who proceeded to defend three major Stoic consolatory precepts: since vice is the only evil (just as virtue is the only good), death is not an evil; since death is universal, the loss of individuals is not to be lamented; since nothing can be done to reverse the death of a loved one, grief is pointless. In answering Zabarella's second letter, Salutati deployed a combination of Aristotelian and Christian arguments to demonstrate the fundamental weaknesses of each of these precepts.

For the Latin text of the letter to Zabarella see Coluccio Salutati, *Epistolario,* ed. F. Novati, 4 vols. (Rome, 1891–1911), III, pp. 456–79. I would like to thank Raymond Prier for his advice on translating some passages of Salutati's often contorted syntax.

A Letter to Francesco Zabarella: Selections

Outstanding teacher, brother and dearest friend: when I wrote to you I did not think that there would be any dispute between us.[1] In fact, all those contentions of mine seemed so true to me at that time that I never imagined I should at any point be in doubt about them. But as I now feel, and have often felt in the past, no truth is so secure that it cannot be called into question by the rough-and-tumble of debate. It is no surprise to me, therefore, that the studies of the Academy thrived when Greece blossomed with philosophers. The style of philosophizing which originated with Socrates and was taken up by Arcesilaus gained such stature through the authority and energy of Carneades that it lasted for more than three hundred years, almost down to the age of Cicero, who confirms that in his own times, to use his words, it was without offspring in Greece itself.[2] Certainly, as Cicero himself testifies, some falsehoods are so close to the truth that they offer no criterion on which to base our judgement and assent.[3] Nevertheless, I want to see – and it will be helpful to do so – whether my discussion can bring us to a demonstration that what I wrote (as I believe, most truthfully) remains firmly and irrefutably valid. If I at least manage to defend my ideas from those profuse and subtle criticisms which you made,[4] I will regard myself as having more than satisfied your objections. . . .

Coming now to what you attack, I will discuss with you in a friendly manner whether the remedies provided by Cicero and other philosophers for bringing consolation to those who are in mourning actually deliver what they promise. I will proceed according to your main points, or rather those of Cicero, so that we can see whether what you defend so subtly and assert so tenaciously is in fact true. But to tell you frankly what I think, it seems to me that you were moved by the desire to argue and to display your learning rather than by the pursuit of truth.

I have said – and I think it really is very true – that death is an evil of nature, not one of wrongdoing. Granted that Silenus said that it is best for men not to have been born and next best for them to die as soon as possible.[5] And (if I may be allowed to speak in a pagan manner, citing the words of pagans) someone else said that by a singular gift of the gods, it was decreed that the chains of the soul, that is, our bodies, would be mortal and not eternal.[6] But they will never change the fact that death is an evil. The authority of Christian truth and Holy Scriptures carries more weight with me than the ravings of those who imagined that souls were placed in the stars and that they were eternal, having been created from eternity in order to descend into our bodies. As Virgil says:

> When they have all rolled the wheel of time for a thousand years,
> The god calls the assembled masses to the river Lethe,
> In order that, bereft of memory, they may see again the vault of heaven
> And begin to desire to have bodies.[7]

If this were true, then all those things [the pagans] dream up would undoubtedly be true.

Nowadays, however, we know that God created man to be immortal and created him in his image and likeness.[8] Death, however, entered into the world due to the devil's envy.[9] For it was originally ordained that mankind was to be immortal, without mediation – a condition that we were deprived of by the transgression of our first parents. So, if it had been best not to have been born, or to die as soon as possible, or for us to have been wholly mortal, as those pagans lay down, God, who is goodness and who sees that whatever he has made is very good,[10] would not have formed man at all and would not have designated him to be immortal from the beginning. Nor would he have wanted him, complete in the possession of a body and soul, to be in a perpetual state of immortal beatitude after the resurrection. So, however much blind paganism, in disdaining death, flatters itself about the goodness of that release which we call death, the unchangeable, honest-to-goodness truth and the supreme authority of divine majesty, which is superior to everything else, regard it as an evil and think that the immortality of bodies is preferable to a state of corporeal decay. The Lord said to Adam: 'Of every tree of the garden thou mayest freely eat; but of the tree of knowledge of good and evil, thou shalt not eat of it; for in the day that thou eatest thereof thou shalt surely die.'[11] And who would say that God established death as the punishment and penalty for the sin of disobedience and transgression if it were not an evil?

Death is without doubt an evil; but, as I have said elsewhere, it is an evil not of wrongdoing, but of punishment.[12] Morally, death is neither a good nor an evil. In regard to nature, however, it is absolutely an evil, inasmuch as it is a privation of the goodness of life. Life is activity and, in a certain sense, being; its privation, death, is without doubt not good, because it is not being, but a sort of privation of being and goodness, which is indisputably an evil. Setting against me Cicero, Seneca, the Stoics and many others, you say that they maintain that nothing is evil except vice and that nothing is good except virtue. I know that this is the unwavering opinion of Cicero and other Stoics; and, as you would have it, anyone who reads my writings will be able to find me adhering to this view on many occasions.[13] For I have always held this position along with them, and I continue to do so – when it is a question of *moral* good and evil. Now, death well met is a moral good for the good man; faced badly, it is an evil for the evil man. As I have written to you on another occasion, the person who seeks his own glory by fighting or dying for the fatherland is not fighting for his country but rather seeking his own glory.[14]

But what, I ask, has virtue or vice to do with asserting the goodness of death? If nothing is considered to be a good except virtue, death itself cannot be a good. It is not a virtue, which is a disposition; it is rather a privation. Nor is death something that is in itself voluntary – which is the nature of a virtue – no more than birth, which certainly does not depend on our will. We can want to die, but our will alone is not enough to bring about our death. Virtue, on the other hand, is something voluntary, which is achieved by the will alone. Although the virtue of an act or a virtuous act is accomplished by another power, the fact that it is a virtue or is virtuous comes from the will alone. Any act, a vice as well as a virtue, is good, since it possesses some being and God concurs [*concurrit*] with it, or rather, to speak more accurately, he anticipates [*precurrit*] it, in making it possible. He also anticipates and cooperates in the form and appearance of virtue; but he does not cooperate at all in the deformity of an act which is sinful, since deformity is nothing. A sinful act does not have an efficient cause but rather a deficient one; and whatever defect is caused in deviating from what the eternal law commands – to which not God, but man is under obligation – is brought about by the corruption of the will, which neither observes the proper measure nor seeks the appropriate end. Therefore, death is not, as you argue, a good, since it is not a virtue, which according to you is the only good. . . .

Remember that Aristotle maintains that death is the most frightening thing of all and that men are frightened by evil things, not good ones. So that you do not think I am alone in regarding frightening things as evil, listen to what the Philosopher says in the *Nicomachean Ethics:* 'We fear those things which are frightening. Speaking without qualification, these are evils; for this reason, fear is defined as the anticipation of evil. Therefore, we fear all evil things, such as disgrace, poverty, disease and death.' And a little later on: 'The most frightening thing, however, is death, for it is the end.'[15] These are the words of the prince of philosophers in the *Ethics.* Shout, if you like; and let the whole school of Stoics shout. That truth which appears plainly to the senses carries more weight with me than the opinion, not to say the raving, of the Stoics. They sought a kind of virtue which has not been observed in the past and is not to be observed now, and they looked for acts and virtues which are impossible to find in the weak flesh of mortal men. The authority of Aristotle and the moderation of the Peripatetics are superior to the sternness or, to be more precise, the cold-heartedness and unattainable logic of the Stoics. . . .

Even speaking in a moral sense and understanding good as an ethical concept, what you take over from Stoic doctrine as the foundation of your argument (that is, that nothing is good except virtue) does not, despite what you claim, seem right to me. Beatitude, which is the end of virtue, is clearly not itself a virtue; it is nevertheless a good thing and superior to virtue. Are not peace among mankind and political security, to which political virtues and legal justice are in all respects directed, good and indeed better than virtue? Finally, [there is the Stoic belief that] virtue is a disposition. Surely, a virtuous activity is not a disposition, but an act? Tell me then, is such an activity not morally good? I do not believe that you or anyone else would deny this. Therefore, virtue is not the only thing which, even in moral terms, is good, since virtuous activity, peace among mankind, political security and the beatitude which comes from virtue are goods which are not encompassed by the [Stoic] definition of virtue. And what about friendship, which in the opinion of many, and in my judgement as well, is not a virtue but an emotion? Surely it is a good, even though it is not a virtue but rather the result of virtue and, as Aristotle says, involves virtue?[16]

To conclude, finally, and leave moral matters behind: all that we see and all that we cannot see, because it is not accessible to the senses – everything, in short, that was created by God – is good, for it is written in the Bible: 'And God saw everything that he made and behold it was very good.'[17] Although these things are not virtues, will you, seduced by your Stoics, deny that they are goods? Finally, look, if you will, at the saviour of the human race. See how passionately he refused the chalice prepared for his death; how devoutly he prayed that the cup would pass him by; with what sadness of soul he said: 'My soul is exceedingly sorrowful, even unto death';[18] and see what kind of sweat he sweated when contemplating his future passion.[19] Would this summation of all goodness, wisdom and courage have asked for and desired these things and sweated blood on account of death, if it were not an evil, as you seem to want to argue? Or was it because this man who was incapable of error knew that death was the worst evil? Nor can we say of him that he feared the danger of a second death; for he had said: 'the prince of this world cometh, and hath nothing in me'.[20] Nor, in that bond of divinity by which Christ was both God and man could he not have known (what he had predicted earlier): the glory of his resurrection. And even though he had said to Martha as she wept and prayed: 'Thy brother shall rise again,'[21] he groaned and wept when led to the sepulchre,[22] showing that it is not irrational for men to mourn the death of their friends.[23]

Go then and say with the Stoics that virtues are the only good. Say that not only is death not an evil but a good: that it is not to be feared, but desired; not to be contemplated with horror, but delight; not to be lamented, but despised. Nature will tell against you; and, if other arguments do not make the point, the example of Christ will stand in opposition to you. Your senses too will affirm the same thing. And those nitpicking and, to repeat my own words,[24] sophistical disputations, of which nothing sensible or substantial remains when the sound of the words has faded away, will be left far behind. Since death is patently an evil, a show of reason will never extort consent to the view that it is a good. Because this belief in the goodness of death is false, it can never bring the balm of true consolation to the dying nor to those they leave behind.

I think that I have sufficiently demonstrated, using clear and valid arguments, that death is not only an evil but also a legitimate source of sorrow. This shows that the first precept of Ciceronian consolation by no means delivers what it promises. . . . Let us now see how you would demolish what I have said against the second precept of consolation and how this subject can be treated more fully. I said that although it is a characteristic of the human condition that we all at some point die, meditation on this fact does not fulfil the task of consolation, since the length or brevity of our life has not been fixed equally for all alike. Consequently, although no individual should lament the common condition of dying, which is the same for everyone, the inequality of the lifespan allotted to us is not unreasonably a cause for sorrow.

Take a look, if you will, at the way in which you contradicted my objections to this consolatory precept and at the grounds on which you would demolish them. In the first place, you bring up against me that proverbial saying of Terence: 'time is the great healer'.[25] But what, I ask you, does this have to do with the point that I attacked? Does it add anything to the contemplation of death? Does it reduce the grief we feel on account of the suddenness of death? I admit that time takes away all sorrow; nothing, as the saying goes, dries so quickly as tears.[26] Certainly, as you go on to maintain, it may perhaps be of some help to have mentally anticipated something before the misfortune occurs, so that one is prepared for the arrival of death. When we are touched by its effects, however, it is difficult to keep in mind what we have persuaded ourselves through reading or what we have given out as advice when attempting to console others. Contemplation of death differs from the actuality of dying as much as bloodless knowledge of fighting differs from bloody gladiatorial combat. All skill in this art is forgotten when a battle is about to take place. While the fighting remains far away, there are exercises, instruction in how to hurt the enemy and a prudent and easy alacrity in parrying blows. Thought responds to the will in such cases; and when danger is at a distance, boldness readily promises that it will do everything, and courage makes pledges which, melting away, so to speak, at the moment of truth, it cannot fulfil.

Well now, do you think that Nestor, after his first hundred years, after so many wars, so many reversals of fortune and the death of so many leaders and heroes, was unaware that he had fathered a mortal son, Antilochus, and that, amidst the deaths of others, he had not many times considered his own fate and that of his son? Nestor was a man of such a calibre that the king of kings, Agamemnon, did not want ten Ajaxes to conquer Troy, but six Nestors.[27] And yet in the experience of his old age and in the enlightenment of his grey-haired wisdom, Nestor

> if we can believe the great Homer,
> Was an example of longevity second only to the crow,
> Happy no doubt to have postponed death for so many generations,
> To have drunk new wine so many times and to have lived to be over a hundred.
> But wait a moment: look at the way he complains about the decrees of fate
> And about the excessive length of the thread of his life when he sees
> The eager Antilochus, with his beard in flames [from the funeral pyre].
> He asks all his fellow-mourners why he has survived for so long a time,
> What crime he has committed to deserve such longevity.[28]

. . . Do please stop [trying to attain Stoic wisdom], Francesco; and do not think that the contemplation of death so steels men's minds that its arrival is not disturbing or that it is possible not to be distraught about the death of our loved ones, unless contemplation can tear out the whole essence of humanity from our minds – something which our friend Cicero thought impossible. And do not say that things to which we have become accustomed do not produce emotion, if they are the sort of things which naturally have the power to upset us. Say instead that what is natural in us is not accustomed to act in an unnatural manner. Can anyone, by running frequently, however much he does it, reach the point where he is not tired and does not pant and sweat? Can anyone be wounded so frequently that he learns, by becoming used to receiving blows, not to die from loss of blood or not to feel pain?

Consider Hecuba: having seen so many of her loved ones die and the disasters that befell her country in that mournful decade, was she ever able to refrain from grieving? Or did she not rather finally go mad in an excess of grief, after hearing of the death of her beloved Polydorus and, forgetting that she was a woman, did she not gouge out with her savage hands the eyes of the grieving king she hated?[29] And finally, is she not portrayed in fiction as being turned into a dog, because of the custom of uttering cries of grief as if one were barking?[30] And what of Niobe? After the deaths of her children in succession – twelve in number, according to Statius and Homer before him, or fourteen, as Ovid has it – did she grieve less for the last of them than for the earlier ones?[31] Or did she not instead become stiff at that point and turn into weeping stone? Need I say more? Do you think that by contemplating something we can learn what the actual presence, knowledge and experience of it has not been able to teach us? . . .

Indeed, because a concentrated, genuine and efficacious pre-meditation on death cannot occur without sorrow and the greatest mental agitation, I am not sure that it induces less emotion than it takes away. In truth, the slow torture of contemplation over a long period of time provides relief from momentary grief and transient emotion. Before making a hasty judgement on this matter, remember that when Christ, greatest of all philosophers, to whom no man can be compared, thought about death, he broke out into a bloody sweat, as I mentioned, and did not pass over in silence the sadness that afflicted his mind, saying: 'My soul is exceedingly sorrowful, even unto death.'[32] So, if you measure this mental anguish properly, there is more sorrow in meditating in advance on death and in dying than an unforeseen death has the power to stir up or to bring with it. . . .

In addition to the points already made I would like to say that those emotions which are movements of the mind, such as fear and sadness, are one thing, while those of the body, which when injured is agitated by physical pain, are another. Certainly the latter are not removed or diminished by contemplation or habit. As for emotions of the mind, whatever philosophy promises with its lessons on consolation, these are not removed, but are instead relieved by the passage of time or else by another method. Nor does it seem to me that any habit of contemplation, though practised over a long period of time, allows us to face things which are contrary to nature, such as death, without feeling the sadness and grief which are stirred up in us by nature itself.

You put forward as a consolation the young man who says to himself: 'I will not see old age, but how many old men will I triumph over by the extent of my fame!' What kind of consolation, I ask you, is this? It was the preoccupation of the pagans to seek fame. They considered nothing more beautiful than the celebrity conferred by a name which lived on. The desire for this fame raged, without the restraint of moderation, to such a degree that they would procure this renown for their name even by means of sacrilegious crime: the man we read about, for instance, who burned down the remarkable shrine and temple of Diana at Ephesus so that his name might reach future generations on account of this foul deed. Those who are right thinking should keep their distance from such a foolish thought, for, as Ecclesiastes states: 'There is no remembrance of the former generations; neither shall there be any remembrance of the latter generations that are to come, among those that shall come after.'[33] Those of us who are guided by Christian sentiments should also keep away from such an erroneous belief, so that we do not, by wishing to acquire a reputation even for virtuous deeds, become like those [hypocrites] about whom it is said in the Gospels: 'Verily I say unto you, they have received their reward.'[34] We should not live or work in order to attain fame, perhaps not even to gain eternal life; our actions should instead be directed towards God, who is the end of all things. Anyone who proposes another end for himself, even beatitude, will never act properly, whatever he does. Finally, believe me, Francesco, it has always been the same with these ostentatious displays of philosophy, these magnificent words: although they promised the greatest things, they failed utterly to deliver them.

But you will object: so many philosophers, so many wise men, so many leaders and so many princes, acting in accordance with ethical precepts, have not only been unwilling to reject death, but, regarding it with contempt, have accepted it with the greatest courage when it was inflicted on them or have voluntarily brought it on themselves, when both cause and occasion were presented to them. Think carefully about this, for all these men who died or spurned death were frightened or even frantic with fear, despairing of their causes, or else were bewildered by shame or terrified by the magnitude of the approaching evil. They thought, however, as we read, that they died gloriously and that dying of their own free will, they merited the renown of eternal fame. Nor is this my interpretation. Listen to St Augustine, who, in Book V [chapter 12] of *The City of God,* states:

The earliest of the ancient Romans, according to what is said about them by historians, like other nations, with the sole exception of the Jews, worshipped false gods and sacrificed victims not to God, but to daemons. Nevertheless, they were 'very desirous of praise, generous with their money, and wanted to attain great fame and morally respectable wealth'.[35] They passionately desired glory; it was their reason for living, and they were willing to die for it as well. It was this all-consuming passion for glory which kept their other appetites under control.

This is what Augustine wrote. And do not think that this passion was felt only by the Romans. Clearly, it was felt by all pagans. Corrupt nature, having forgotten its origins, directs itself towards things other than God. But if from the beginning it had remained in the dignity of its original condition, it would rightly lead us to him and would incline us towards our proper end. We are seduced by our senses, which are the instruments of corrupt nature; and these men were seduced all the more since they had less knowledge of God and of the true end of all things. But above all they were seduced by glory, flattering themselves that through it they would attain a sort of immortality and celebrity for their name. It was neither philosophy nor anything other than glory alone that led them to despise death and made them so willing to endure sorrows and suffering (which Cicero defines as 'a newly formed belief of present evil, in which it seems to be right to feel depressed and saddened').[36]

But how, Francesco, do you defend Solon's consolation,[37] since I have claimed that he was motivated not by the desire to console himself but rather by envy? Tell me, please, is it not a sign of the greatest malice to be consoled in one's own grief by the evils and sorrows of others? I do not see the justification for this type of consolation. Born in the city of Rome, will I grieve less that my son fell at Cannae with so many thousands of citizens than I would if he were killed in that fortunate battle in which, under Pompey's leadership, Mithridates was conquered, when the Roman army lost only twenty soldiers and two centurions, although forty thousand of the enemy were killed?[38] On the contrary, I would think that if we want to follow reason, which unites the human race in a sort of natural fellowship, not only will we be vexed by our own misfortunes, we will also sympathize with all those whom we see dying or about to die along with our own people. We will not alleviate our own pain by gazing at the disasters which befall others; nor will we be able to avoid suffering along with those who suffer, or be able to hold back our tears when we see others crying, or be consoled by the weeping of others. We will instead be reminded of the stinging memory of our own sorrow.

Do not deny what we see before our eyes every day, what the ancients did and what even in more recent times reason, warnings and examples have been unable to control. Observe in Statius how the circle of mourners helps Lycurgus and his wife Eurydice, and you will find amidst the group that grief is unbridled and tears are flowing in abundance.[39] Observe in the same author how inconsolably all the women wept over the multitude of heroes, for whom they piously performed funeral ceremonies, and this even after Creon was killed, over which they should have exulted, rejoiced and been consoled. And see how madness gripped Evadne, who threw herself on the burning funeral pyre of Capaneus.[40] Believe you me, the grieving throng did not extinguish or diminish the suffering, but rather encouraged, roused and augmented it. If the presence of weeping mourners does this, the thought of them ought to do the same, because thought represents to the mind whatever the senses are capable of receiving and of transmitting, after it has been received, to the imagination and common sense, so that from there the intellect can grasp it. Do you not recall how the Cyrenaic Hegesias imprinted the evils of life on the minds of his listeners with such powerful compassion that he was forbidden from lecturing by Ptolemy, since many resolved to commit suicide after listening to this philosopher's arguments?[41]

Perhaps the same thing happens to minds that we see happening to bodies, inasmuch as a medicine which is fatal to one person, another finds very salubrious; and something which is avidly consumed by one person, another not only spurns but finds repugnant. [We read of] 'two wise men, one of whom used to laugh every time he left his house, while the other used to weep'.[42] Small wonder then that while some people find these consolations acceptable and are healed by them, in like manner, as I believe, there are many who would have the greatest difficulty in putting up with these remedies which you recommend for reducing sorrow and would actually find that their suffering is increased. . . . Enough then of the second precept, which in my judgement, if I am not mistaken, does not fulfil the task of consolation. . . .

Let us now deal with the third precept, which in my view has perhaps more validity, since we are advised that it is foolish to be overcome with sorrow when we know that this accomplishes nothing at all. Those, therefore, who weep for the dead can be told what we read in Terence: 'he will never come to life again now'.[43] But against this I have said: 'Despair over what you have lost increases and aggravates your suffering.'[44] In other words, what really stings and torments is having lost the thing which you mourn not for a limited time, but forever. Is this not very true, Francesco? Surely, you will feel more grief if a son or friend leaves you never to return than if you hope that he will come back after many years, even if he stays away for a long time? I do not believe that you would deny this, although you seem very keen to contradict me. Can anyone be so insane that he would not admit this point without dispute?

What more can I say? Imagine, if you will, that the son of your friend is killed in a battle, from which it is reported that a very few soldiers escaped alive. Having been present, you go to the father in order to console him. Will you not base your consolation on the fact that he can hope that his son did not die but may have escaped and will return in a little while, or that, having been taken prisoner, he is still alive? Will you not enjoin him to hope for better things? Although you are certain of his son's death, which he appears not to know about, will you not maintain a solemn silence about what he has lost forever? Will you not indulge his hope and, taking advantage of his lack of knowledge, prevent him from despairing about his son's safety? Or will you instead confirm for him his son's death, about which he is unsure? I do not believe that you would upset your distraught and unhappy friend, making him even more miserable. These examples and arguments make it clear that hope alleviates the heaviest sorrows and, conversely, that despair aggravates even the lightest ones. . . .

I think you will admit that offering the third precept of consolation to someone can give offence, because one is saying that the person's loss is without remedy, that what cannot be recovered should be endured and that it is foolish, as you yourself say, to beat your head against a wall and kick against the pricks.[45] Even though these words might persuade some people, they are like puncture wounds to those who are in deep mourning, either when they consider things they are already aware of, or when such things, if by some chance they are not already thinking about them, are brought to their attention. Such observations do not lighten their burden but rather add weight to it, and, penetrating deeper, prepare the way for a loss of control.

Tell me your reaction to this story, Francesco. A friend gets sick and, seized by a serious illness, is confined to bed. The doctors arrive and investigate the man's condition, life-style, temperament and age; and at length they diagnose the illness. They bid him to hope for a return to health. Will you not, happily offering congratulations, encourage the invalid? But if they predict death or a long-lasting and incurable ailment, will you not suppress your response and simulate hope on your face,[46] thereby creating the opposite impression, so that you do not add to the patient's suffering? I would like to see you on that occasion, my dear Francesco. I would like the whole crowd of Stoics to be present. I would like Cicero to be there and Seneca of Cordova, so that I might see what you would take as the guiding principle of your consolation and what foundation you would construct, in the face of the certainty of his death and the incurability of this serious illness. I would ask the sick man and those relatives of his who were present what weighs most heavily on them, what vexes them the most and upsets them most deeply. I know that they would reply that what afflicts them the most is seeing that there is no remedy and that the disease is incurable. Take it from me, if in the midst of suffering you release the reins of emotional restraint, fine words will not cure you, nor will they take away or heal your pain.

To sum up everything together, with a kind of epilogue: at what time will you have recourse to these precepts of consolation? Before the pain is felt? I admit that thoughts, as I have said before, respond to the will; and when danger is far away, boldness readily promises to do everything, and courage makes pledges which, melting away, so to speak, at the moment of truth, it cannot fulfil. Reason is drowned out by the pressing commotion of mental disturbance, and words do not bring peace of mind when sorrow, standing in opposition, bears down hard on us and rages furiously. It is therefore futile at that point to attempt to console anyone or to expect someone who is tortured beyond reason to act rationally. Cicero may tell us that Posidonius cried out against pain: 'You can do nothing, pain! Even though you cause distress, I shall never admit that you are an evil'.[47] Nevertheless, the type of distress which carries the mind along with it, disturbing its vision and not permitting it to judge rightly and freely, is sufficient to prevent reason from being heard. Although physical pain produces less of this effect, mental anguish, such as that which comes from the death of loved ones, is extremely effective in bringing about this result.

But even if, after the sorrow has passed, these precepts work and are admitted to be a remedy for grief, it is due to the power of time, not to the force and efficacy of the consolation offered by philosophical reason. And since time by itself, without any help from these precepts, cures even those who are most out of control – something which reason is unable to do when an emotion first comes into being – it cannot be denied that whatever the effect of these arguments seems to be, it comes not from their own power but from time.

My consolation, however, is in God alone, who governs all things and disposes everything beneficently and agreeably, and who in his wisdom – his great wisdom – foresees everything. This consolation is known beforehand, felt at the relevant time and strengthened afterwards by previous experience and the constancy of faith. In him, from whose hand we have received so many goods, we must also patiently endure evils. This is all the more true since he is the height of goodness, and therefore he alone knows how to extract good things not only from the evils of nature and fortune but also from those of wrongdoing. We ought therefore to endure without sorrow or annoyance both death and anything else which we are in the habit of weeping over, even though these things are evils. Looking with the eyes of our mind on that goodness which does nothing that is not good and fitting, we ought not to condemn in a foolish and wicked manner what he does, but rather wisely and equitably endure it *because* he has done it. Indeed, we ought to regard with fear and trembling those things which beguile us, for they might be lures of the devil, and we must ensure that they do not captivate and delight us, making us forget the author of all things which are good.

This view of divine goodness means that no one should be distressed by human frailty and that it is a matter of no importance or moment whether we die later or sooner. Since it is agreed that the goal of life is to return to that highest principle, the dying are to be congratulated, not pitied, especially those who are snatched quickly from a brief life. Whatever this goodness accomplishes – and it is responsible for everything – cannot be unlike its maker, nor can it be anything other than good. Also, it cannot be the case that God wanted us to be upset by what is irrevocably lost, since in our blindness we must be certain that, if something were good, God would have made it in such a way that it was possible for it to be restored. All these things, if you weigh them up correctly, were highly valued by those philosophers whom you think so much of, and these consolatory precepts must stand in need of them.

Let this suffice, then, regarding those points to which you wanted me to reply, forcing me to discuss what I had written in greater detail. I leave the determination of the truth of all these matters to you and, so to speak, your muses. But your attempt to show – I have no idea how – that Cicero and other pagan thinkers believed that true consolation lay in God is such that I am unwilling to dispute with you, hoping that you are aware how far from the truth it is. . . . Farewell, and in future please do not push me to such a point that I am under similar constraint. Florence, 21 February 1401.

Translator's Notes

1. See Salutati's letter to Zabarella of 30 August 1400: Salutati, *Epistolario,* III, pp. 408–22, which was a reply to a letter of Zabarella written shortly before: ibid., IV, pp. 347–9.
2. Cicero, *De natura deorum* I.5.11; see also Cicero, *Academica* I.4–13. Arcesilaus, head of the Platonic Academy in the middle of the third century BC, initiated the sceptical orienta-

tion of the school, which was strengthened in the second century BC by Carneades, founder of the so-called New Academy.

3. Cicero, *De natura deorum* I.5.12.

4. See Zabarella's letter to Salutati, probably written in September 1400: Salutati, *Epistolario*, IV, pp. 350–61.

5. Cicero, *Tusculan Disputations* I.44.114. See his earlier (and more positive) reference to this maxim: Salutati, *Epistolario*, I, pp. 9–12, at 11 (letter to Luigi de' Gianfigliazzi, 26 December 1365).

6. Salutati may be alluding to Seneca, *Epistulae* LVIII.27–9; for Seneca's reference to bodies as chains of the soul see, e.g., *Ad Marciam De consolatione* 24.5.

7. Virgil, *Aeneid* VII.748–51.

8. Genesis 1:27.

9. Wisdom of Solomon 2:24.

10. Genesis 1:31.

11. Genesis 2:16–17. Salutati quotes two different Latin versions of the first part of verse 17.

12. Salutati, *Epistolario*, III, p. 417.

13. See, e.g., Salutati, *Epistolario*, I, p. 19; for his praise of the Stoics see his *De laboribus Herculis*, ed. B. L. Ullman, 2 vols. (Zurich, 1951), I, pp. 311–12; see also R. G. Witt, *Hercules at the Crossroads: The Life, Works, and Thought of Coluccio Salutati* (Durham, N.C., 1983), pp. 63–5.

14. Salutati, *Epistolario*, III, p. 415.

15. Aristotle, *Nicomachean Ethics* III.6 (1115ª7–11, 26). Salutati quotes two different Latin translations of the passage.

16. Aristotle, *Nicomachean Ethics* VIII.1 (1155ª4).

17. Genesis 1:31.

18. Matthew 26:38; Mark 14:34.

19. Luke 22:44: 'and his sweat was, as it were, great drops of blood falling down to the ground'.

20. John 14:30.

21. John 11:23.

22. John 11:33–5.

23. Almost a decade earlier, when Salutati still adhered to an essentially Stoic conception of ethics, he had suggested that while the ideal of complete emotionlessness was out of reach for virtually all human beings, it had been attained by Christ: see Salutati, *Epistolario*, II, pp. 307–12, at 310 (letter to Antonio de Cortona, 10/14 March 1392).

24. See Salutati, *Epistolario*, III, p. 417.

25. Terence, *Heautontimorumenos* III.422.

26. Pseudo-Cicero, *Ad Herennium* II.31.50.

27. Cicero, *De senectute* 10. Antilochus, son of Nestor, an aged advisor to the Greek side during the Trojan War, died while defending his father against Memnon, who was later slain by Achilles.

28. Juvenal, *Satires* X.246–55.

29. After the Thracian king Polymestor murdered Hecuba's son Polydorus during the Trojan War, she and her female entourage killed his children and blinded him.

30. Ovid, *Metamorphoses* XIII.423–577; Cicero, *Tusculan Disputations* III.26.63.

31. Statius, *Thebaid* VI.124–5; Homer, *Iliad* XXIV.602–4; Ovid, *Metamorphoses* VI.182–3.

32. See n. 18 above.

33. Ecclesiastes 1:11.

34. Matthew 6:2.

35. Sallust, *Bellum Catilinae* VII.6.

36. Cicero, *Tusculan Disputations* IV.7.14.

37. Valerius Maximus, *Facta et dicta memorabilia* VII.2.ext.2, where Solon attempts to console a friend by urging him to think about the myriad tribulations which afflict others, so that he will not regard himself as alone in his sorrows.

38. Cannae, in Apulia, was the site of Hannibal's great victory over the Romans in 216 BC. Pompey defeated Mithridates, king of Pontus, in 66 BC at the battle of Nicopolis.
39. Statius, *Thebaid* V.605–60. Lycurgus, king of Nemea, and his wife Eurydice were mourning the death of their child, who was killed by a serpent while in the care of his nurse Hypsipyle.
40. Statius, *Thebaid* XII.768–81, 800–9. After the defeat of the Seven Against Thebes, the corpses of the dead heroes were given to their womenfolk to be buried. Their opponent Creon was defeated by Theseus, king of Athens. Evadne threw herself on the burning pyre of her husband Capaneus.
41. Cicero, *Tusculan Disputations* I.34.83.
42. Juvenal, *Satires* X.28–30, referring to the laughing philosopher, Democritus of Abdera, and the weeping one, Heraclitus of Ephesus.
43. Terence, *Hecyra* III.465.
44. Salutati, *Epistolario,* III, p. 419.
45. Cf. Terence, *Phormio* I.77–8.
46. Cf. Virgil, *Aeneid* I.209.
47. Cicero, *Tusculan Disputations* II.26.61.

Further Reading

CHRP, pp. 365, 368, 835

King, M. L., *The Death of the Child Valerio Marcello* (Chicago, 1994)

McClure, G. W., 'The art of mourning: autobiographical writings on the loss of a son in Italian humanist thought', *Renaissance Quarterly,* 39 (1986), 440–75

Ullman, B. L., *The Humanism of Coluccio Salutati* (Padua, 1963)

Witt, R. G., *Hercules at the Crossroads: The Life, Works, and Thought of Coluccio Salutati* (Durham, N.C., 1983)

Zonta, G., *Francesco Zabarella (1360–1417)* (Padua, 1915)

17

Angelo Poliziano

JILL KRAYE

Introduction

Angelo Ambrogini (1454–94), known as Poliziano or Politian from his birthplace of Montepulciano (Mons Politianus) in Tuscany, was sent to live with cousins in Florence around 1469, after the death of his father in a vendetta. In 1473 he entered the household of Lorenzo de' Medici, to whom the precocious young scholar and poet dedicated his partial Latin translation of the *Iliad.* Two years later he became tutor to Lorenzo's three-year-old son Piero. Between 1475 and 1478 he composed the *Stanze,* perhaps his most famous Italian poem. This peaceful and poetically productive period came to an end in 1478 with the conspiracy of the Pazzi family against Medici rule in Florence, in which Lorenzo was wounded and his brother Giuliano murdered. In the tense atmosphere which followed this traumatic event, Lorenzo's highly strung wife Clarice ejected Poliziano from the Medici household. In the second half of 1479 he travelled around various northern Italian cities and during this period composed the *Orfeo,* a dramatic work, written in the vernacular, dealing with a classical subject.

When he returned to Florence in 1480, Lorenzo arranged for him to get the chair of Latin and Greek eloquence at the *Studio,* where over the following decade he lectured on literary and historical texts (Statius, Quintilian, Persius, Ovid, Suetonius). In 1489 he published the *Miscellanea,* a landmark in fifteenth-century humanist philology. With the arrival in Florence of Giovanni Pico della Mirandola in the same year, Poliziano's interests turned towards Aristotelian philosophy: in 1490–1 he lectured on the *Nicomachean Ethics* and in 1492 the *Prior Analytics.* He launched the latter course with an inaugural lecture, entitled the *Lamia* ('The Vampire'), in which he defended his philological approach to Aristotle against those traditional philosophers who resented this humanist invasion of their intellectual territory. He died suddenly of a fever in 1494, aged forty, leaving behind a further, unfinished collection of *Miscellanea.*

It was during the aftermath of the Pazzi conspiracy that Poliziano translated into Latin the *Enchiridion* ('Handbook' or 'Manual') of the Stoic philosopher Epictetus (c. 55–c. 135), dedicating it to Lorenzo. The austere but practical advice which this brief treatise provided on controlling the emotions and responding rationally to all life's disappointments seemed the perfect antidote to the anxiety, stress and insecurity which both Poliziano and his patron were undergoing at the time. In the dedication, Poliziano explained that he had supplemented and corrected the readings in the two Greek manuscripts at his disposal by consulting the commentary on the *Enchiridion* by Simplicius, a sixth-century Aristotelian commentator. Not only did he make philological use of Simplicius, he also followed his interpretation of the work, in particular the belief that it was inspired by Plato's *First Alcibiades.* Poliziano cleverly exploited this Platonic view of Epictetus in order to defend the Stoic philosopher from the attacks of Bartolomeo Scala, one of the less distinguished humanist chancellors of Florence and, like Poliziano, a client of Lorenzo.[1] Scala found Epictetus's precepts to be unclear, untrue and inhumane. Using Simplicius, as well as drawing on his own vast knowledge of classical literature, Poliziano constructed an eloquent and cogent defence of Epictetus and his Stoic philosophy of resignation.

The Latin text of Poliziano's letter is printed in his *Opera . . . omnia* (Basel, 1553), pp. 405–9. See also the edition and facing Italian translation in E. Garin, ed., *Prosatori latini del Quattrocento* (Milan, 1952), pp. 912–25. For Poliziano's Latin translation of Epictetus's *Enchiridion* see his *Opera,* pp. 393–405; and Epictetus, *Manuale,* ed. G. De Ruggiero (Milan, 1971), pp. 69–104.

A Letter to Bartolomeo Scala in Defence of the Stoic Philosopher Epictetus

Not content, my dear Scala, to carry out the duties of a brave soldier and a very valiant general, you, with your usual diligence in all matters, do not even allow your trainees to languish in leisure and idleness, but instead call them away from the shady tent to the dusty field, to sweaty exertion and fighting-practice, believing as you do that you have sole responsibility for the entire corps of soldiers.

I for my part thought that I had done enough by translating Epictetus from Greek [into Latin]. But now you rouse me, with a trumpet-call to battle, to defend him as well. Therefore, as Horace says, 'this and every other war will be gladly fought in the hope of winning your favour'.[2] You attack the very citadel and what is in truth the stronghold of the entire city by wiping out the first chapter of Epictetus, which is like the centre of the entire circle, or rather the sphere, the most perfect figure. You make three objections, although those things to which you object are actually totally at variance with the principles of his teaching: you say that his precepts are obscure, that it is beyond human powers to follow them and that they are false. His precepts are obscure, inasmuch as you deny that he has explained what, in the final analysis, our responsibilities are. They are beyond human powers, inasmuch as you assert that nature commands us to express our grief; and the dominion of nature, you maintain, surpasses all human capacities in efficacy and power. His precepts are false, inasmuch as you allege that, contrary to Epictetus, our body is part of us, since, in your view, we are composed of a body and a soul. It is now up to me to refute these points, as you ask, and also to say a few things of my own. Certainly not in order to instruct you, for that would be like teaching my grandmother to suck eggs.[3] Nor because I regard myself as a legitimate champion of Epictetus against you, for I am neither worthy of such an honour nor am I as well disposed towards him as I know you to be. But since you have assigned this role to me, I will play it as well as I am able.

I shall begin by making a few points, sowing the seeds, so to speak, from which will arise the fierce and well-equipped troops of our author Epictetus – like the men of Thebes and Colchis who, according to myth, sprang from dragon's teeth scattered on the ground. But just as Homer placed Ajax of Salamis in the way of Hector when he was attacking the Greek camp,[4] so I will place the Athenian Plato in your way. Plato, in the dialogue entitled *On Human Nature,*[5] has Socrates disputing with Alcibiades, nicknamed 'Good Looking'. He there proves that man – the subject of our discussion – consists of nothing more than a rational soul, for he says that a man uses his hands to act in the same way that a shoemaker uses an awl. That point granted, he makes another claim: the user of a thing, he says, is different from the thing which is used, for the latter is a tool. Then, he advances the view that the person who uses his body as if it were an instrument is the one who truly deserves to be called a man. It is precisely the rational soul which uses the body as if it were an instrument, either when it is making things or when it is engaging in other activities. On these grounds, he next asserts that the rational soul both uses the body and rules over it.

Dividing the possible alternatives into three, he then states that man must consist either of a soul or of a body or of a combination of the two. If man is in control of his body, but the body is not even in control of itself, it cannot be that man consists of a body. Nor can he consist of a combination of body and soul, for if it is man who is in control of the body, and the body is not even in control of itself, it certainly cannot be a combination of body and soul which is in control. Furthermore, if the body is by its very nature immobile, it must be the soul which moves. In fact, we see in the case of the various crafts that it is the craftsman who moves and the tools which are moved; and there is no doubt that the body has the role of a tool in relation to the soul. Man therefore consists of a soul, and anyone who has concern for man cares for his soul; those, however, who care for money or other such things, not only have no concern for man, they do not even care for the tool used by man.[6] Therefore, either by virtue of Plato's authority, which is so great that, like Rumour in Virgil, 'its head is hidden by the clouds',[7] or on the basis of his iron-clad, rock-solid arguments, I think it has been proved beyond question that the body is not part of us. Let us, however, move on.

There are three levels of virtues according to Plato.[8] The highest of all are called exemplary virtues; these we look for in the wise man and attribute to God. Those which follow are called the virtues of a purified soul; we believe these to exist in the philosopher who has withdrawn himself from any stain or contagion of the body. It is for this reason that Plato, whose delicious name I savour as it rolls off my tongue, states in the *Protagoras* that in order to become a philosopher one must die.[9] The third class of virtues are those which are called cleansing; we assign these to the continent man but deny that they exist in the temperate one. The person who can justly claim these virtues is someone who has persuaded himself that man truly consists of a rational soul. He does not judge the body to be the equal of the soul, nor does he think that it contributes to man's perfection, but has resolved that the soul should use the body as its instrument. A person who regards his body as equal or superior to his soul does not deserve the name of man any more than those brute beasts, the animals, 'whom nature has fashioned to lie face down, slaves to their bellies', as Sallust admirably puts it. 'Therefore', as he says, 'we use the mind to rule, the body to serve'.[10] So let us preserve our freedom by means of that which alone distinguishes us from the beasts and that which alone constitutes man's essential nature. Let us use our body not as some part of us, joined to the soul, but rather as an instrument.

It is such a person that Epictetus undertook to teach. A wise man would have had no need for these precepts, having long ago asserted his claim to freedom and

Cast all fear beneath his feet, along with inexorable fate
And the din of the greedy underworld.[11]

And Epictetus did not think that there was anything to be done with a person who had degenerated so far below human nature that he could be ranked with the beasts.

Once you understand that Epictetus's teaching was aimed at such a person, I think you will no longer be in the dark as to what man's responsibilities are. Epictetus, having stated that instinct – you could also call it desire, since the Greek term is *hormē*,[12] or equally appetite, opinion or inclination – is one of the things which is part of us, immediately adds: 'and whatever else is our responsibility'. This undoubtedly shows that he defines the things which are our responsibility as those which derive from what is part of us. The question of whether what we term emotions or emotional disturbances (the Greek *pathē*) come from the body or from the soul is too large to be dealt with here. Nevertheless, no one would deny that all emotions are related to the soul. But they are related to it in the same way that good or bad health is related to the body, for they are as beneficial or harmful to the soul as good or bad health is to the body. Therefore, whatever the emotions do wrongly – whatever indeed they do – is our responsibility.

In a well-adjusted body good health is produced by the disposition we call equilibrium, and it is destroyed when the balance is tipped in the direction of either excess or deficiency. The same thing undeniably happens in relation to the emotions. When they are unrestrained and violent, they make a man miserable, but when moderate and orderly, they make him happy. The soul, as Plato wrote with divine inspiration, is like a charioteer or a horseman:[13] if it spares the whip and makes more vigorous use of the reins, it will run the course successfully and easily arrive at the finishing-line. If, on the other hand, it holds the reins too loosely or applies the whip more violently than is reasonable, then, like Phaethon or Bellerophon, it will inevitably come crashing down to earth. In this way, it is in our power to determine whether we turn out miserable or happy.

You will easily gather what our responsibilities are when you consider those things which pertain to us. Everything which Epictetus teaches in the entire book concerns what is part of us; it would have been foolish to teach us about what was not so. Was then our author Epictetus obscure and muddled? You could not hope to find anything plainer, more precise or more lucid, so that even those with the dimmest sight – not to speak of your own lynx-like vision – can clearly see what he intended.

But you say that what he teaches is too demanding and beyond human powers. What is it, at the end of the day, that you object to? 'If you love your son or your wife, tell yourself that you love a human being, then you will not be upset when they die.'[14] Is it what he teaches or what he promises that you find fault with because it is difficult to do? If it is what he teaches, then you regard as difficult things which we see going on every day in ordinary life, things in the marketplace and on street corners. Who does not from time to time consider what might happen in the future? The slave in Terence says: 'Ah, my friend, that is wisdom: to see not only what is in front of your face but also to foresee what the future will bring.'[15] And, remaining in the theatre, listen to the old man in another of Terence's plays:

I don't know what to do, because what has happened to me is unexpected and
   unbelievable.
I am so annoyed that I cannot get my mind to function.
This is why, when things are going especially well for us,
We ought all to rehearse how to bear affliction when we encounter it.
Returning from abroad, you should always be thinking about lawsuits and losses,
About an offence committed by your son or your wife's death or your daughter's illness.
If you reflect that these are common occurrences which could happen to you, nothing will
   catch you unawares;
And anything which turns out better than you expected should be regarded as pure
   profit.[16]

And then there are those impressive lines of Virgil:

> The mind of man does not know what fate has in store,
> Nor is it able to exert restraint when uplifted by good fortune.[17]

As you see, these things are not hidden away but are everywhere on view. Both poets
praise the anticipation of future events to the skies, while damning the failure to do
so.

Since there is no need for me to come up with showy arguments to prove an
obvious point, I shall proceed with my analysis of your objection. As I understand it,
you rebuke not so much what Epictetus teaches as the extravagant promises he
makes, that is, his claim that we will not be upset by the death of our wife or children
if we have contemplated these events in advance. In opposition to this precept you
thrust forward, as if it were the shield of Ajax, the august name of nature (which
according to the physicians plays a role of the greatest importance in all the emotions), when you maintain that it is nature which commands us to express our grief.
But is it actually true that our author forbids us to weep? On the contrary, he teaches
us that when the occasion calls for it, we should groan and let our tears flow, even if it
is someone else's grief.[18] Nor does Juvenal insist that we accept his statement that it
is the command of nature which forces us to weep at the death of our children.[19] No
one resists the force of nature: to oppose nature would be to follow the example of the
giants and wage war against the gods.[20] We read, however, that many people have
abstained from tears and weeping at the death of their loved ones: Solon the Athenian, for instance, and Cato the Censor – two men who were not only wise but also
had a reputation for being so.[21] It is certainly not easy to do these things, but it is not
beyond human powers. If you concede that one or two persons have done it, then you
will surely concede that it can be achieved by many people. To demonstrate this point
I shall use the type of argument which the logicians call induction,[22] and which is
frequently employed by Socrates in the dialogues of Plato, the prince of philosophers. When you concede that something actually exists in one or two people, you
cannot deny that the potentiality and capability exists throughout the entire human
race.

You see now that our Stoic's line of reasoning is consistent. You see that he speaks
very clearly and distinctly, both in explaining throughout the book what our responsibilities are – for it is from them that he draws his individual precepts – and in
enumerating those emotions which are the fountainhead of all our responsibilities.
You see, then, how much Plato's discussion, when understood in a discerning man-

ner, helps us to comprehend his meaning. You see that our body is not part of us. Good heavens, how true and how strong are the arguments with which he defends himself! What a champion he has! Were we to contend stubbornly that he was retailing falsehoods, he would launch against us the majesty of Plato and the entire Platonic school. So far from his teachings being beyond what human nature can achieve, our author Epictetus seems even to be over-indulgent, since he only allowed himself to teach things which not merely had the potential to exist but which actually occurred and examples of which can be found here and there.

If you concede these points, I shall demolish with no difficulty at all the other criticisms you have formulated in your letter. I do not understand, for instance, why you attack as arid and slack the way in which Epictetus succinctly, skilfully and carefully divides everything which exists into units. You yourself do not deny that nothing escapes this division, nor that there is no need for a further division, since each unit is of a single kind, so that if you try to divide it further, you will smash and tear it to pieces. This is not arid, but very substantial and full of vigour. There is nothing wanting in this division and nothing surplus to requirements; no element is without value. He uses words which lend themselves readily to comprehension, so that nothing could be devised in a more considered fashion.

But someone might perhaps ask: why did Epictetus not make clear right at the beginning what sort of person he was undertaking to teach? He did in fact indicate this, though rather succinctly. Did he not show that it was the person who maintained that the body itself and other things of this kind are not part of us? But perhaps he should have done so more explicitly and expansively? Yet this point was not hidden away; it was there in the storeroom, ready and waiting for anyone who wanted to take it up.

Is there anything more famous than what Plato himself wrote? Nevertheless, you say that Epictetus could have briefly set out Plato's arguments. He could have done so, but it would not have been appropriate. In this little book he was handing down precepts, promulgating laws, so to speak, not disputing contentious points. There are boundaries which circumscribe every profession; and if you exceed these limits and trespass into the territory of another discipline, you will be called to account to fight over its possession. You observe that mathematicians do not present proofs of the principles on which their demonstrations are based, entrusting this instead to metaphysicians, since those things which we call universals are their concern. A point, according to Euclid, is that which cannot be divided into parts. If someone denies this, the mathematician is struck dumb, but the philosopher is there to rescue him. What then does the philosopher say? That which forms the boundary of any given thing has one dimension fewer than that which is bounded by it. After exacting agreement to this, he continues: a body, which has three dimensions, is confined by a surface, which has only two dimensions: length and width. A surface does not possess depth, which is the one thing that it lacks in relation to a body. A surface, which has two dimensions, is terminated by a line, which has only one dimension, length. Finally, a line is bounded by a point, which indisputably lacks any dimension, since the dictum which states that every terminus has one dimension fewer than that which it terminates is quite true.[23] Therefore, Epictetus organizes this little book so that what has already been proved by Plato is regarded as given, and his entire series of precepts is uniformly interwoven with this material. Just as in Homer Teucer defended himself with the shield of Ajax,[24] so our Stoic fights boldly, using Platonic arguments as his shield. Epictetus thus determined not to transgress the boundaries which he set for himself, so as to avoid being forced, as they say, to dance outside the ring.[25]

This is all that occurs to me at present to say in support of Epictetus. I am well aware that it goes far beyond what is required of a letter. Nevertheless, I think that I have not explained more than was necessary, nor done so in greater detail than was called for. If you accept what I have said, my dear Scala, let us shake hands on it. If, however, you reject it, come then and show yourself to be as good a defender of Epictetus as you have been an opponent of his. Everyone says that he was a great man, and it gives me pleasure to repeat it a hundred times in succession. I'm afraid, however, that my translation of Epictetus is rather flattering to me, like a clever little son, and this makes me favourably disposed to the author of the work. I am grateful to you, all the same, for stirring me to fight this battle; for contentious disputation, as Aristotle says, is profitable to the intellect.[26] And the divinely inspired Homer calls that battle which renders men illustrious *kudianeira* [bringing glory or renown],[27] while our author, no less admirably, says that inactivity is inglorious.[28] Therefore I ask you to provoke me to action frequently and repeatedly. We must struggle against the turmoil of these times, Scala, defending ourselves as far as we are able by studying literature and philosophy. When the time comes for the effort which you have promised, with your usual generosity, I will make use of it with as much confidence as I have done in the past. Farewell. 1 August 1479.

Translator's Notes

1. For a translation of Scala's *Dialogue on Laws and Legal Judgements,* see *Cambridge Translations of Renaissance Philosophical Texts,* II: *Political Philosophy,* ed. J. Kraye (Cambridge, 1997), ch. 12.
2. Horace, *Epodes* I.23–4.
3. Poliziano refers to the Greek proverb, *hē hus tēn Athēnan,* which in Latin became *sus Minervam* (a sow to Minerva); it was used of an ignorant person who presumed to teach someone who by rights should be teaching him: see Sextus Pompeius Festus, *De significatu verborum,* ed. W. M. Lindsay (Leipzig, 1913), p. 408; for a Renaissance discussion see Erasmus, *Adages* I.1.40.
4. See Homer, *Iliad* XIV.402–41.
5. That is, *Alcibiades I* 129C–130C.
6. That is, the body.
7. Virgil, *Aeneid* IV.177.
8. This doctrine is not found in Plato, but in Plotinus, *Enneads* I.2, and Macrobius's *Commentarium in Somnium Scipionis* I.8, in which, however, four levels of virtues are set out: political, cleansing, purified and exemplary.
9. This statement does not occur in the *Protagoras;* see, however, *Phaedo* 65A–67D.
10. Sallust, *Bellum Catilinae* 1.
11. Virgil, *Georgics* II.491–2.
12. Poliziano uses the Latin word *conatus* (impulse) to translate *hormē* in chapter 1 of the *Enchiridion:* see his *Opera,* p. 394. In Stoic terminology, *hormē* signified any form of desire, from rational choice to irrational impulse.

13. Plato, *Phaedrus* 246A–B.
14. See Epictetus, *Enchiridion* 3; in Poliziano's translation it is chapter 5: see *Opera,* p. 395.
15. Terence, *The Brothers* III.386.
16. Terence, *Phormio* II.239–46.
17. Virgil, *Aeneid* X.501–2.
18. See Epictetus, *Enchiridion* 16.
19. See Juvenal, *Satires* XV.138–40.
20. According to Greek mythology, the giants attacked the gods and were roundly defeated; they were believed to be buried under various volcanoes.
21. Solon, an Athenian statesman and poet of the late seventh and early sixth century BC, was regarded as one of the Seven Sages of antiquity. Contrary to what Poliziano maintains, Plutarch (*Life of Solon* 6) describes an episode in which he was transported with grief upon hearing a (false) report of his son's death. The Roman statesman Marcus Porcius Cato (234–149 BC) wrote treatises on agriculture, rhetoric and other subjects; for later writers, he embodied the high moral values of early Rome; Plutarch (*Life of Marcus Cato* 24) states that he bore the loss of his son with the equanimity of a philosopher.
22. Induction (*epagogē* in Greek) is a type of argumentation which proceeds from known particulars to general principles by means of analogy: see, e.g., Cicero, *Topics* 10.42; and Quintilian, *Institutio oratoria* V.10.73.
23. See Aristotle, *Metaphysics* III.5.
24. See Homer, *Iliad* VIII.266–72.
25. According to Erasmus, *Adages* II.6.67, the Greek proverb *ektos chorou orcheisthai* (to dance outside the ring) refers to a person who says or does something foreign to his purpose. Staying within the ring entails obeying the rhythms and limits of the other dancers in the group, rather than doing as one pleases.
26. See Pseudo-Aristotle, *Problems* XVIII.2.
27. See Homer, *Iliad* IV.225.
28. See Epictetus, *Discourses* IV.4.1–3 and 23–4.

Further Reading

Branca, V., *Poliziano e l'umanesimo della parola* (Turin, 1983)

Brown, A., *Bartolomeo Scala 1430–1497, Chancellor of Florence: The Humanist As Bureaucrat* (Princeton, N.J., 1979)

CHRP, pp. 80, 131, 194–5, 364, 582, 730, 773–4, 782, 833

Grafton, A., 'The scholarship of Politian and its context', in his *Defenders of the Text: The Traditions of Scholarship in an Age of Science, 1450–1800* (Cambridge, Mass., 1991), pp. 47–75

Hadot, P., 'La survie du commentaire de Simplicius sur le Manuel d'Épictète du XVᵉ au XVIIᵉ siècles: Perotti, Politien, Steuchus, John Smith, Cudworth', in I. Hadot, ed., *Simplicius: sa vie, son oeuvre, sa survie. Actes du colloque international de Paris (. . . 1985)* (Berlin, 1987), pp. 326–67

Oliver, R. P., 'Politian's translation of the "Enchiridion"', *Transactions of the American Philological Society,* 89 (1958), 185–217

18

Justus Lipsius

ROBERT V. YOUNG

Introduction

The Flemish humanist Justus Lipsius (1547–1606) first gained prominence through his commentaries on classical culture and literature and his editions, especially of Tacitus and Seneca.
Lipsius was educated by the Jesuits at Louvain and studied under the patronage of Cardinal
Granvelle at Rome. During important periods of his academic career, however, he adopted the
Protestantism of the universities of Jena (1572–4) and Leiden (1579–90). Reconciled at last to
the Catholic Church in 1590, he spent his final years teaching at Louvain. The constant in his
life was an avid enthusiasm for Christian Neostoicism, to which he made a significant and
widely translated contribution with *De constantia* (1584). His treatise on politics, *Politicorum
libri sex* (1589), was also influential and rather controversial. His last books were *Physiologia
Stoicorum* and the work excerpted here, *Manuductio ad Stoicam philosophiam* (1604). The
Manuductio is essentially a compendium of arguments and illustrations from various Stoic
writers, above all Seneca. Scriptural and patristic citations are adduced to show the general
compatibility between Stoicism and Christianity.

The work technically takes the form of a philosophical dialogue between 'Lipsius' and a
'listener', but the pretence of dialogue crops up only infrequently as a device to resume the
argument at the beginnings of some chapters. The first of the chapters translated here (II.8) sets
out a description of the ideal sage or wise man (*sapiens*), as conceived by Stoic philosophy.
The second (II.20) argues that virtue is the only good and is itself sufficient to produce
happiness. And the third (III.6) explains the Stoic paradox that the wise man is happy even in
anguish or torment.

The Latin text of *Manuductio ad Stoicam philosophiam* translated here is based on the first
edition (Antwerp, 1604), collated with the revised posthumous edition (Antwerp, 1610) and
the version printed in Lipsius's *Opera omnia* (Lyons, 1613). The only significant difference in
the chapters given here is explained in n. 39. Most of the notes are taken from the margins of
the early editions, though I have silently expanded or added to Lipsius's references.

A Guide to Stoic Philosophy in Three Books: Selections

BOOK II, CHAPTER 8

*The True Wise Man of the Stoics Is Described by Them in Ideal Terms and
Therefore Has Never Been Found; Nonetheless, Their Description of Him Is
Neither Unreasonable Nor Useless*

Lipsius: Well then? Are you already in your mind raising an objection against me: all
this effort to know the wise man?

200

Listener: Certainly I had an objection. In fact, I was near to giving up, overcome by desperation. Has anyone ever known everything, divine or human? No one ever has, nor ever will; and for that reason I feel justified in shrinking from this high-sounding wisdom, pitched on a precipice where no one ever goes.

Lipsius: Perhaps I may be able to comfort you with the words of Aristotle, who maintains that 'the wise man knows everything, as far as it is possible, without having knowledge of each thing individually', being content, as he later adds, 'with a knowledge of universals'.[1] Take comfort also in the words of Demetrius the Cynic, as quoted by Seneca: 'It is more advantageous if you hold fast to a few precepts of wisdom that are nevertheless readily available and in use, than if you learn many but do not have them to hand. In the same way, a great wrestler is not one who has acquired a knowledge of all the numerous holds, which are rarely of use against an opponent, but rather one who has trained competently and scrupulously in a few of them; for it does not matter how much he knows, providing he knows enough to gain victory. The same is true in this endeavour: many things provide delight, but few bring victory.'[2] He adds a number of points that seem to move in the direction of a contempt even for natural science, encouraging us to concern ourselves solely with the knowledge of life, that is, of good and evil. But I have no use for these solaces and evasions; and we have said well and truly that the wise man knows everything.

But which wise man? Undoubtedly the Stoic one, that is, the perfect and consummate man, who is lacking nothing good and has nothing evil about him. He stands out from everyone else:

> . . . like the lofty summit of Mt Olympus,
> Which leaves the winds and the clouds in the distance.[3]

And as another poet writes:

> . . . from the lofty citadel of the mind
> He looks down on our wanderings and laughs at human joys.[4]

'Like light in the darkness, he blazed forth and drew the minds of all men towards himself.'[5] In the words of Plutarch, he has a 'godlike character'.[6] Or, in the words of our Seneca, he has 'the weakness of man, the assurance of God'.[7] Finally, 'as he goes through the city they gaze upon him like a divinity'.[8] Is there no end to these utterances? But look, in this last remark I have not been entirely honest. I made out that he was gazed upon as he went through the city. This is false, for these words do not refer to an actual wise man but merely (to put it briefly) to a hypothetical description of him. Plutarch says candidly of the Stoic wise man: 'he exists nowhere amongst nations or on earth',[9] nor has he existed. According to Cicero, 'the Stoics interpret wisdom as something which no mortal has yet attained'.[10] And again in another place: 'Who the wise man might be, or might have been, the Stoics themselves are not accustomed to say.'[11]

I think – no, I know – this to be truer than what our Seneca writes, which sounds more agreeable and pleasant, for at times he makes it out that the wise man has occasionally existed – occasionally, to be sure, but nevertheless he has existed. 'Do you know', he remarks, 'what I mean now when I refer to a good man? Someone who belongs to the second level', that is, outside the class of proficients, about which he speaks immediately after, 'for the other sort', namely, someone who belongs to the first level, 'like the phoenix is perhaps born once every five hundred years.'[12] And while here he is somewhat undecided, elsewhere he argues more forcefully: 'There is no reason', he asserts, 'for you to say, in your usual manner, that this wise man of ours is nowhere to be found. We have not imagined some insubstantial ornament of human character, nor do we conceive a lofty image of a false thing; rather, we have presented and shall present him just as we fashion him. Seldom perhaps, and at great intervals of time, is he discovered; for magnificent things which go beyond the normal and ordinary do not frequently come into existence. Be that as it may, I suspect that Marcus Cato, the mention of whom sparked off this dispute, surpasses our model.'[13]

Oh dear, Seneca, my friend, even you yourself, though well intentioned, go astray – or you lead us astray. Are you so credulous? God forbid. We know that no Stoic claimed that a wise man such as you have described has ever existed, though they all say that one could exist. Posidonius even concluded, using this argument, that since 'Socrates, Diogenes and Antisthenes made such great progress', they stood not far from the summit.[14] Consequently, someone who strives very intently, by means of good character, good discipline and unremitting effort, can arrive at this level. We Christians deny this and agree with Plato that anyone who would truly be a philosopher must never and under no circumstances suppose that he will achieve pure wisdom other than among the gods of the underworld,[15] that is, in those pure and blessed places, in the presence of the author of all wisdom and his flock.

What, then, is the point of describing someone who is denied existence by nature? I would say: as an example. Some idea and semblance of that highest excellence ought to be set forth, by means of which we may strive, not to attain it, but to approach it; not to equal it, but to imitate it. Similarly, Cicero and Quintilian fashion an orator who never was and never will be; nonetheless, that perfection ought without doubt to be expressed. It is the same with our wise man. Quintilian himself writes: 'To anyone asking whether such an orator ever existed, I shall answer in the same way as the Stoics would reply if they were questioned whether Zeno or Cleanthes or Chrysippus was a wise man. I shall say that they were great and deserving of respect, but they did not reach the heights to which human nature can aspire.'[16] And certainly the wise man inspires us to lofty discourse and stimulates honourable souls to achieve honourable deeds. At this point I might fittingly quote the words of Seneca: 'Is it any wonder if they do not ascend to the heights, having taken the steep path? Look up to those who attempt great things, even if they fail. It is a noble thing, taking into account not one's own strength but that of nature, to strive, to aim at the heights, to conceive in one's mind greater undertakings than even those endowed with immense spirit could achieve.'[17] Here he despairs of or rejects what he had previously asserted.

*Virtue Alone Is Sufficient for Supreme Happiness; That Which Is Extraneous
or Accidental Is Unnecessary*

Observe the trunk that grows out of the root of precepts which we have planted: the
supreme good is located in virtue alone, or rather, virtue alone is good. This is the
pronouncement which distinguishes this vigorous, manly school from others which
are softer and more indulgent. It leads away from the earth, the body – everything
extraneous – towards the soul, towards what is intrinsic and eternal. Good lord, how
much discord and contention there is on this subject! The philosophers charge forward with their entire army, especially the ancient Academics, among whom on this
issue Aristotle belongs. I of course leave aside the Epicureans and that whole group:
even hearing about this doctrine is fatal to them. To us, taken in a good sense, it seems
good – indeed, excellent – whether in the formulation of Seneca, that 'virtue is the
chief means to a happy life',[18] or that of Cato, as quoted by Cicero, that 'it is the
essential factor in our lives and fortunes no less than in Stoic philosophy'.[19]

In the first place, let us consider this point, presenting it straightforwardly, without
gloss or approval: 'The supreme good is that which is honourable; and, what you may
find more remarkable, that which is honourable is the only good.'[20] Here you have
both principles: the first, which I have proposed and affirmed, and the second, which
follows automatically from it. I have said that happiness consists in virtue alone.
Why not? 'Let us place the supreme good in the soul. If it passes from our best to our
worst part, it becomes tarnished. The sum total of our happiness must not be placed in
the flesh.'[21] Do you not see that 'everything else has its own particular good? The
vine is valued for its fertility, wine for its flavour, the stag for its speed. What is man's
best feature? Reason, in which he surpasses the beasts and comes second to the
gods.'[22] Here, therefore, is man's good: in virtue. And so, let us judge a man correctly
by the only part of him which makes him a man; and, in this tribunal, let us take small
account of his other features, or disregard them entirely.

In the second place, the good to be sought and conferred is something which is in
our control and which is neither given nor taken away by chance. Such a description
fits only virtue. 'For a person who regards anything else as good comes under the
power of fortune and becomes subject to another's control.'[23] Just as those who
move about in hostile territory look all around fearfully, eager to strike or anxious
about being exposed, so those who seek this good elsewhere live, so to speak, with
their insides in turmoil, either nervously on the look-out or constantly on guard. And
what sort of good would I regard as mine yet not ascribe to my own exertions? What
sort of good has not been produced by my effort, knowledge or skill? 'There is
nothing more foolish than complacency about something one has not oneself
accomplished.'[24]

In the third place, those things which we are given do not last. They are, one might
say, lodged with us and will leave in due course. The true good, however, is fixed and
solid: no force can shake it loose; no accident or guile can steal it away. Look at the
anguish we suffer if our happiness comes from external things: we busy ourselves

trying to possess things that make us feel bad if we do not obtain them and apprehensive if we do; we are upset by those things which are taken away from us, and we worry about those which might be taken away. 'Like birds who are frightened at the sound made by an empty sling, these men become agitated not only by the blow but even by the noise.'[25] Good heavens, where are the liberty and security promised to the wise man? They are never there when the maxim of Epictetus is overthrown: 'Some things are in our control, some outside of it. In our control are desire and aversion, virtue and vice. Outside our control are the body, ownership, glory and authority.' And he adds: 'Things in our control are by nature free, unhindered and unimpeded. Things outside our control are feeble, servile, subject to hindrance and do not belong to us.'[26] How much he conveys in so few words, in the manner of the Holy Scriptures! Look closely, and you have in these words the fountainhead of wisdom. Among adults, the wise man is the one who is pleased by peace and security; it is boys who run after games and the prizes thrown to the crowd there. Fortune stands upright, scattering external things: one person is trampled, another crushed, another cast out; few collect them without suffering injury, nor are the things themselves intact and undamaged.

In the fourth place, how often do these things go to those unworthy of them, even in their own judgement? The pimp has wealth, the whore beauty, the rascal government office, the thief health and strength. Shall I call those things goods that often – indeed, more often than not – are bestowed upon the wicked?

In the fifth place, other animals are happier than we are, if we are judged on the basis of external things. Surely we observe in them bodily endowments which are more numerous, more impressive and more solid than ours. And how about the fact that they enjoy food, drink and sexual pleasure more easily and in a more forthright manner than we do, without fear of shame or remorse?

In the sixth place, if the view that these things are goods survives, then virtue dies. Shall I cultivate loyalty, justice and courage, and leave behind things considered to be goods, such as wealth, fame, popular favour and life itself? Such situations do occur, and often it is a choice between giving up the latter or abandoning the former. In this case, virtue will be cultivated with little enthusiasm and with one eye always looking backwards, as if, for the sake of a greater good, things were being discarded which, though less good, were nevertheless goods.

In the seventh place, if such things are goods, we must necessarily hold God himself and providence in low esteem: 'since many troubles befall the just man; and again, since whatever he has given us is transient and slight, if you compare it to the age of the universe'.[27] Shall we therefore interpret God's gifts with ingratitude, asking why he has given or denied this thing to this person? Someone who possesses the highest good, however, also has the only good. He stands firm and, being replete, is at peace, because there is nowhere else to go.

Finally, arguing from our ultimate goal, we want to follow nature, that is, God. But it is only in terms of virtue (I speak here as a Stoic) that God is measured; he certainly does not possess these external things. If, however, they are good, do we not attribute them to God, who is the Good Itself? Or is man, to whom we attribute both virtue and external goods, happier than God?

I know that much more could be said and various points could be introduced; but my objective was to explain principles rather than to assert them. And yet why am I in doubt here? Just as we see the sun, after it has risen, 'cover and suffuse everything with its light'[28] – cover but also caress – so here I might have said that the light of this conviction immediately penetrates and persuades all the more virtuous souls. This conviction, therefore, is old, not new. The Brahmins in India (who have survived as a race with the same name to this day) used to maintain that 'what happens to mankind has nothing to do with good or evil, for otherwise it would not be the case that the same things caused anguish to some, joy to others, both having dream-like thoughts'.[29] What about the Cynics? They say openly that virtue is sufficient for a happy life and requires nothing except the vigour of Socrates.[30] I interpret this small qualification to mean that the only thing required is a steadfast wisdom and a wise steadfastness, following the example of that remarkable man. Plato himself seemed to some to hold this view; and 'Ariston the Stoic', says Clement, 'once wrote a three-book work entitled *According to Plato, Only That Which Is Honourable Is Good.*'[31]

What is more, the Jews, and we ourselves, think the same. Was this not the opinion of the royal author of the Psalms? 'Blessed are they that are perfect in the way';[32] they are united to virtue, strangers to vice. And what of his son? 'But with her [that is, wisdom] there came to me all good things together and in her hands innumerable riches.'[33] It is very clear that this saying is the aim even of our comic playwright: 'Virtue comprises all things; all good things belong to the virtuous man.'[34] And elsewhere the Hebrew sage says: 'Blessed is the man that shall meditate in wisdom.'[35] Among Christian authors, let Clement be heard: 'That only what is honourable is good was known even to barbarian philosophy', that is, our [Stoic] philosophy and that of the Jews, 'and, likewise that virtue is sufficient for happiness, where God said: "I have set before thee this day life and good, and death and evil . . . choose life."'[36] Now, he calls life here good and the choice of it virtuous. The goal of both, however, is the same: to love and revere God.' Finally, Clement adds: 'The Stoics continually boast about these things.'[37] See how he equates the Scriptures with our philosophers. And what does Ambrose say? He too is often a Stoic, as I have noted, here at any rate explicitly: 'The Scriptures', he says, 'maintain that nothing is good except virtue and judge virtue to be blessed in every state of affairs. It can neither be increased by bodily goods nor diminished by adversity.'[38] Could Zeno have expressed these life-and-death principles more clearly? And so you see what our Christian thinkers maintain and what they agree with.[39]

BOOK III, CHAPTER 6

The Fourth Paradox: That the Wise Man Experiences Happiness Even When He Is in Torment

The fourth unexpected doctrine I put forward is that the wise man experiences happiness even when he is in torment. We advance this notion forcefully, however much the Pythagoreans, Academics and Aristotelians assail us in battle. 'For what can be more certain, according to the reasoning of those who consider pain to be an evil, than that the wise man tortured on the rack cannot be happy?' On the contrary, however, 'the reasoning of those who do not consider pain to be an evil', that is, the Stoics, 'is compelling: despite all torments, the happy life is preserved'.[40] Indeed, even when the comparison is made, 'Zeno denies that the life of Metellus is happier than that of Regulus'.[41] An unexpected point of view, alas, and one which has provoked opposition! 'How can these things be equivalent', the critics say, 'when some should be chosen, others avoided?'[42] And even the Stoa[43] does not altogether deny that the life of Metellus is preferable and should be adopted. They insist, nevertheless, that these things are equivalent because they are both good, and there is no distinction among goods (as taught earlier).[44] Therefore, 'joy and a courageous, determined endurance of torments are equivalent goods, for in both there is the same greatness of soul: relaxed and light-hearted in one, aggressive and ready for action in the other.'[45] Our Seneca dwells upon this kind of distinction in another passage: 'It is not that you should assume that any virtue is acquired without effort, but rather that some virtues require the spur, others the bridle. In the same way that a body needs to be held back on a downward slope, and driven upwards on an incline, so some virtues are on a downward slope, others ascend a difficult incline.' In the former class are generosity, temperance, gentleness; in the latter, patience, courage, perseverance and 'whatever virtue opposes hardships and subdues fortune'.[46]

Well then, you ask, are sorrow and torment not contrary to nature? We admit they are. And 'is something contrary to nature therefore good? Hardly. But at times good emerges from something which is contrary to nature; for being wounded or wasting away over a fire is contrary to nature, but preserving an invincible spirit in the midst of those adversities is in accordance with nature. To express what I mean briefly, the circumstances which surround a good are sometimes contrary to nature, but a good itself never is, since there is no good which is not reasonable, and reason is in accordance with nature.'[47] It is very true to say, then, that these things are so good that we ought sometimes to choose them. How should this be done? In this way: 'so that it is not the hardships which are desirable, but rather the virtue by means of which the hardships are endured'. Here is an example: 'I might wish to be free from torments, but if they must be endured, I shall desire to conduct myself bravely, honourably and courageously.'[48] A soldier does not wish for battle or wounds for their own sake, but rather because they are combined with glory or victory. And so 'the brave man will not deliberately expose himself to dangers, but nor will he fear them; he will, instead, avoid them. Caution suits him, fear does not.' He knows that all these external things which are called evils are fearsome only to the fearful. He feels them, nevertheless, and he also suffers pain: 'For no human virtue is devoid of feeling; but he is not afraid and, unconquered, beholds his sufferings from on high.'[49] You have read that Mucius Scaevola endured, or rather gloried, in the fire, his spirit not crushed by his wound[50] – it is like this with the wise man. And yet Mucius would have preferred to make his hand whole rather than to suffer mutilation. 'The wise man despises the entire realm of fortune; and yet, if given the choice, he would select those things which are more tolerable.'[51]

To understand the matter in its entirety, this distinction must also be brought to bear: 'There are three kinds of goods', says Seneca. 'Certain things seem to us', that is, the Stoics, 'to be primary goods, such as joy, peace and the safety of one's country. Others goods are secondary and are shaped out of unfortunate material: patience, for instance, in the face of torments and self-control during serious illness. The former goods we straightforwardly wish for ourselves; the latter, only if necessary. In addition, there is a third class of goods, such as a dignified manner of walking, a trustworthy face and a bearing befitting a prudent man.'[52] Goods of whatever kind, you see, are still goods – indeed, they are equivalent to those that have a pleasing appearance. I have touched on this already, but it is worth repeating: 'What then? Are reclining at a banquet and being tortured equally good? Does this seem astonishing to you? This may astonish you even more: reclining at a banquet is an evil, while being tortured on the rack is a good, if the former is done in a disgraceful manner, the latter in an honourable one. It is not the material condition which makes those actions good or evil; it is the virtue. All actions in which virtue is revealed are of the same measure and value.'[53]

And why is it surprising for us to say that there is no evil outside the soul? Consider the words uttered by Epicurus, the teacher of pleasure and the enemy of pain: 'If a wise man is being burned, if he is being tortured, if he is inside the bull of Phalaris, he will say, "How sweet this is! How little I care about it!" '[54] And Epicurus himself behaved in this way when he was near death, according to Seneca: 'What is more, does it not seem equally unbelievable for someone in the throes of extreme suffering to say, "I am happy?" And yet this utterance was heard in the very workshop of pleasure. "I regard this day and one other," said Epicurus, "as the happiest of all," even though in the one case he was afflicted by urinary disease, and in the other by the incurable pain of an ulcerated stomach. Why then are such things incredible among those who cultivate virtue, when they are found even among those ruled by pleasure?'[55]

There is, you can be sure, spite, or rather feebleness, in the mind of those who belittle these things: 'And so they think that whatever they themselves cannot do is impossible; they pass judgement on virtue on the grounds of their own weakness.'[56] But listen to the voice of Solomon: 'For when they heard that through their own punishments the others had been benefitted, They felt the presence of the Lord.'[57] It is the cause and the end which render these things mild, or even sweet: 'Although the body, brimming over with a good conscience, trickles away, it will take pleasure in the fire by means of which its good faith shines forth.'[58] Do you hear, too, 'it will take pleasure'? This is so; and according to the poet, Cato proclaims:

> . . . patience finds pleasure in hardships,
> Virtue is happy when it pays a high price for its existence.[59]

But with a clear conscience, to be sure. The Church Father Ambrose attests to this: 'The wise man is not broken by bodily pains nor troubled by discomforts, but even when afflicted remains happy. For happiness does not consist in bodily delights but rather in a conscience entirely free from the stain of sin.'[60]

Translator's Notes

1. Aristotle, *Metaphysics* I.2 (982ª8–10, 22).

2. Seneca, *De beneficiis* VII.1.3–4. Demetrius the Cynic lived in Rome in the first century AD; exiled to Greece under Nero, he returned during the reign of Vespasian.

3. Claudian, *Panegyricus dictus Manlio Theodoro Consuli* 206–7.

4. Statius, *Silvae* II.2.131–2.

5. Seneca, *Epistulae* CXX.13.

6. Plutarch, 'Conspectus of the Essay: "The Stoics Speak More Paradoxically Than the Poets"', in his *Moralia* 1058B. Plutarch, an inveterate enemy of the Stoics, is naturally ironic here. Lipsius, who does not identify the work he is quoting, may be indulging in irony of his own at Plutarch's expense.

7. Seneca, *Epistulae* LIII.12. For similar comparisons by Seneca of the wise man to the gods, see *Epistulae* LXXIII.12–16 and XCII.27–31.

8. Homer, *Odyssey* VIII.173.

9. Plutarch, *Against the Stoics on Common Conceptions* 1076B.

10. Cicero, *De amicitia* 5.18.

11. Cicero, *Academica* II.47.145. Following older editions Lipsius cites Book IV.

12. Seneca, *Epistulae* XLII.1.

13. Seneca, *De constantia sapientis* 7.1. Marcus Porcius Cato of Utica (95–46 BC) was regarded by Seneca, Cicero and other ancient Latin authors as a type of the Stoic sage.

14. Diogenes Laertius, *Lives of the Philosophers* VII.91 ('Life of Zeno').

15. Plato, *Phaedo* 66B–67B. Socrates here argues that pure knowledge can only be attained when the soul is free of the body. Lipsius does not quote verbatim.

16. Quintilian, *Institutio oratoria* XII.1.18. Cicero fashions his ideal orator in *De oratore*.

17. Seneca, *De vita beata* 20.2. Where modern texts read *naturae suae* ('of one's nature'), Lipsius writes *naturae* ('of nature').

18. Seneca, *Epistulae* LXXIV.1.

19. Cicero, *De finibus* III.7.26.

20. Seneca, *Epistulae* LXXI.4.

21. Seneca, *Epistulae* LXXIV.16.

22. Seneca, *Epistulae* LXXVI.8–9.

23. Seneca, *Epistulae* LXXIV.1.

24. Seneca, *Epistulae* LXXIV.17–18.

25. Seneca, *Epistulae* LXXIV.5.

26. Epictetus, *Enchiridion* 1.1–2.

27. Seneca, *Epistulae* LXXIV.10.

28. Lucretius, *De rerum natura* II.148.

29. Strabo, *Geographia* XV.1.59 (C713).

30. Diogenes Laertius, *Lives of the Philosophers* VI.11 ('Life of Antisthenes').

31. Clement of Alexandria, *Stromatum* V.14: see J. P. Migne, ed., *Patrologia Graeca,* 162 vols. (Paris, 1857–66), IX, cols. 144B–145A. Lipsius's text reads 'Ariston the Stoic' rather than 'Antipater the Stoic'.

32. Psalms 119:1. King David is regarded as the author of this book of the Old Testament.

33. Wisdom of Solomon 7:11. Solomon was the son of David.

34. Plautus, *Amphitrion* 651.

35. Ecclesiasticus 14:20.

36. Deuteronomy 30:15, 19.

37. Clement of Alexandria, *Stromatum* V.14: see Migne, ed., *Patrologia Graeca,* IX, col. 144A–B.

38. St Ambrose, *De officiis ministrorum* II.3: see J. P. Migne, ed., *Patrologia Latina,* 221 vols. (Paris, 1844–64), XVI, col. 112C.

39. In the 1610 and all subsequent editions, the final sentence of the chapter replaces the following from the first (1604) edition: 'In addition, Nemesius, bishop of Emesa in that era, says [*De natura hominis* XLIV.66]: "The virtues, both by themselves or joined together with other things, render a man happy – with other things in a broad sense, by themselves in a strict sense. Now, some things are understood in a strict sense – two cubits,

say; others in a broad sense, as for example a heap: if you take two measures from a heap, what remains is still a heap. And so happiness understood in the broad sense remains happiness, even if you take away bodily and external goods and leave only the virtues.'"

40. Cicero, *De finibus* III.42. See also Seneca, *Epistulae* LXVI.18.
41. Cicero, *De finibus* V.83. In the previous paragraph, Cicero describes Quintus Caecilius Metellus Macedonicus (d. 115 BC) as having 'left his four sons alive and well and three daughters married, having himself been consul, censor and augur and having had a triumph'. Marcus Atilius Regulus (mid third century BC), by contrast, 'died a captive in the hands of the enemy [i.e., the Carthaginians], from starvation and sleep deprivation'.
42. Seneca, *Epistulae* LXVI.6.
43. That is, the portico or colonnade in Athens where Zeno taught and founded the Stoic school of philosophy.
44. Lipsius is probably referring to Book III, chapter 4: 'The second paradox: that all virtues are equal and likewise are individual'.
45. Seneca, *Epistulae* LXVI.12.
46. Seneca, *De beata vita* XXV.5–6.
47. Seneca, *Epistulae* LXVI.38–9.
48. Seneca, *Epistulae* LXVII.4.
49. Seneca, *Epistulae* LXXXV.26, 29.
50. According to legend, Gaius Mucius Scaevola, after being arrested in the Etruscan camp, responded to threats of torture and burning at the stake by thrusting his right arm into a fire. Porsenna, the Etruscan king, was so impressed by this act he ordered Scaevola to be set free.
51. Seneca, *De beata vita* XXV.5. Modern editions give *meliora* ('the better part') rather than Lipsius's *molliora* ('those things which are more tolerable').
52. Seneca, *Epistulae* LXVI.5.
53. Seneca, *Epistulae* LXXI.21.
54. Cicero, *Tusculan Disputations* II.7.17. See also Seneca, *Epistulae* LXVI.18. Phalaris was a sixth-century BC Sicilian tyrant, who killed his victims by roasting them in a brazen bull.
55. Seneca, *Epistulae* XCII.25–6.
56. Seneca, *Epistulae* LXXI.22. Lipsius mistakenly cites LXXII.
57. Wisdom of Solomon 11:13.
58. Seneca, *De beneficiis* IV.21.6. Lipsius cites chapter 23, and where his text reads *corpus* ('body'), modern editions give *cor* ('heart').
59. Lucan, *Pharsalia* IX.403–4.
60. St Ambrose, *De Jacob et vita beata* I.7; see Migne, ed., *Patrologia Latina,* XIV, col. 639C.

Further Reading

CHRP, pp. 370–3, 445, 774, 779, 824–5

Grafton, A. T., 'Portrait of Justus Lipsius', *American Scholar* (1987), 382–90

Halsted, D., 'Distance, dissolution and Neo-Stoic ideals: history and self-definition in Lipsius', *Humanistica Lovaniensia,* 40 (1991), 262–74

Lagrée, J., *Juste Lipse: la restauration du Stoïcisme* (Paris, 1994)

Morford, M., *Stoics and Neostoics: Rubens and the Circle of Lipsius* (Princeton, N.J., 1991)

Oestreich, G., *Neostoicism and the Early Modern State* (Cambridge, 1982)

Osler, M. J., ed., *Atoms, Pneuma and Tranquillity: Epicurean and Stoic Themes in European Thought* (Cambridge, 1991)

Saunders, J. L., *Justus Lipsius: The Philosophy of Renaissance Stoicism* (New York, 1955)

19

Francisco de Quevedo

LUC DEITZ AND ADELHEID WIEHE-DEITZ

Introduction

Don Francisco de Quevedo y Villegas (1580–1645) is chiefly known nowadays (as he was in his own time) for his picaresque novel *The Petty Thief* and his satirical *Dreams*. He deserves to be remembered, however, not only as a prolific poet and moralist, but also as an amateur translator and dilettante philosopher.

Stoic Doctrine – the title commonly given to the work translated here – first appeared in 1635 as part of a volume which contained Quevedo's translation of Epictetus and Phocylides into Spanish verse and his defence of Epicurus (see Chapter 23); the full title of the volume is *Epicteto y Phocilides en español con consonantes, con el Origen de los estoicos, y su defensa contra Plutarco, y la Defensa de Epicuro, contra la común opinion.* Epictetus's *Enchiridion*, with which this work starts, had been translated into Spanish twice before: by Francisco Sánchez in 1600 and by his successor in the chair of Greek and rhetoric at Salamanca, Gonzalo Correas, thirty years later. Although the Spanish speaking world of the Golden Age was thus well acquainted with the most comprehensive ancient text expounding Stoic moral philosophy, it was not until 1616, when Justus Lipsius's *De constantia* appeared in a Spanish translation (under the title *Libro de la constancia*), that readers without Latin were able to peruse a fully fledged introduction to Neostoicism. Surprisingly, the translation of Lipsius's treatise remained the only Spanish account of Neostoicism available for almost twenty years. Quevedo's *Stoic Doctrine* was the second defence of Christian Stoicism to appear in the vernacular.

Christian Stoicism is a contradiction in terms only if the metaphysical tenets of Stoicism – the imperturbability of God, the never-ending cyclical recurrence of the same events, and so on – are taken into account. The Neostoic movement, however, was less concerned with metaphysics than with ethics. And in this respect, it was not too difficult to see in the Stoic sage's moral integrity and unflinching courage in the face of adversity an anticipation of the Christian saints' resistance of temptation and the martyr's fortitude when shedding his or her blood for the love of Christ. Quevedo clearly felt that these obvious and well-worn parallels were not engaging enough to justify a Christian's recourse to pagan philosophy in matters ethical. Accordingly, he went one step further and, with the help of a highly original historical reconstruction the ingeniousness of which is matched only by its absurdity, would have us believe that the moral teachings of the Stoa derive directly from the Book of Job. (He seems to have been unaware of the fact that, as early as Justin Martyr, many Christian apologists with more than a passing interest in Plato had been engaged in an analogous enterprise and had tried to derive all or part of his philosophy from the teachings of Moses.)

It should be noted that the *Stoic Doctrine* depends largely on Lipsius's 1604 treatise *A Guide to Stoic Philosophy in Three Books* (see Chapter 18). It is perhaps a fitting tribute on the part of Quevedo to the memory of the Fleming whom he so much admired that he should have contributed to the diffusion of his teaching by incorporating it into his own works.

For the Spanish text of *Nombre, origen, intento, recomendación y decencia de la dotrina estoica* see Francisco de Quevedo, *Obras completas,* 3rd ed., ed. L. Astrana Marín and F. Buendía, 2 vols. (Madrid, 1945), I, pp. 872–9. We have checked it against the editio princeps of 1635, and whenever a variant reading has been followed, this has been recorded in the notes. We would like to record our thanks to Roberto Casazza, whose help with the subtler points of Spanish grammar has been invaluable.

Stoic Doctrine

Name, Origin, Aim, Commendation and Descent

For the Learned and Erudite Licentiate Rodrigo Caro, Judge of Testamentary Provisions in the City of Seville[1]

> *Let us study something*
> *for those who*
> *study; let us write*
> *for those who write.*

When an ignorant man talks to an educated person, he does so in order to gain credit for himself, not in order to put an obligation on his interlocutor. Therefore, my dear sir, I would not wish that this book and everything in it which may seem strained should be defended solely on account of my friends' charity. I dedicated the treatise to Don Juan de Herrera.[2] To your grace I dedicate the questions which have arisen from it. They would be more learned if I had adapted them from his comments instead of writing my own; however, in the present state of my work, this is the only token of my sincere friendship that I am able to provide. I shall write about things which your grace knows better than I do. I shall therefore be content if my discourse is tolerated, not expecting it to win approval.

The Stoics, whose doctrine has been transmitted to us in an easily comprehensible manner and for our benefit by Epictetus, derived their name from the portico where they used to meet.[3] One can read in the third book of Athenaeus: 'those puny quibblings from the Painted Portico'.[4] For this reason, in Book XIII of the same author, they are called 'Stoacs'[5] by a comic poet, who jokingly says: 'Listen to the Stoacs, the merchants of dreams, the judges and censors of words.'[6] It is clear from this that, as in our own day, the merchants and businessmen of antiquity used to assemble in the porticos which we call marketplaces.

This insult from the comic poet, who called the Stoics merchants of lies because of their portico, was answered by Tertullian in his *Praescriptio.* As a Christian, he took pride in making a connection between himself and the Stoics and therefore said: 'Our doctrine is derived from the portico of Solomon.'[7] This provides authoritative support for the argument of my discourse concerning the origin of the name Stoic, which will be my second topic. For the Peripatetics and the Stoics named their sects after the garden and the place where they used to meet, and not after the heads of the schools which were associated with these doctrines. This remark deserves consideration. There is no one else whom I can follow in this opinion of mine, and it is of no great importance whether I deserve to be followed by anyone else.

Philosophers have always held the place which offered them the opportunity to talk and the person who offered them the leisure to remain there in higher esteem than the masters by whom they were taught. Seneca prompted me to observe this. The words are his, but the interpretation is mine; Seneca speaks them in *Letter* LXXIV, but I make use of them:

It seems to me erroneous to believe that those who have loyally dedicated themselves to philosophy are stubborn and rebellious and scorners of magistrates and kings and of those who control the administration of public affairs. For, on the contrary, no class of man is so popular with the philosopher as the ruler is; and rightly so, because rulers bestow upon no men a greater privilege than upon those[8] whom they allow to enjoy peace and leisure. Hence, those who profit greatly, as regards their purpose of right living, from the security of the state, must needs cherish as a father the author of this good.[9]

That place which preserved for them solitude in the turmoil of the cities; that site which welcomed[10] their leisure devoted to intellectual activity; that garden which, with the help of some walls, brought together scholars while excluding busybodies; that portico which preserved the seclusion to be enjoyed at any hour of the day, without which teachers would not be able to teach and students would not be able to learn – all these have well deserved to have their names inscribed in the coat of arms of the professions. This is the reason for the reputation of the founding-fathers and the recognition given to them – the ministers and kings who, in their states, provide the leisure which these places achieve and preserve.

David, in Psalm 84[:1], regards as sacred the gates and the courts in the house of God: 'How amiable are thy tabernacles, O Lord of hosts!' And in verse 10: 'For a day in thy courts is better than a thousand. I had rather be a doorkeeper in the house of my God, than to dwell in the tents of wickedness.' Infinite reverence is due to divine tents, courts and houses. Great love and recognition are due to the porticos and the virtuous places of withdrawal, whereas all the places and all the schools in which evildoers and sinners assemble deserve our greatest abhorrence. David begins the first Psalm with this doctrine: 'Blessed is the man that walketh not in the counsel of the wicked, nor standeth in the way of sinners, nor sitteth in the seat of the scornful.'[11] I only wish that the *Letter* to Lucilius of our Seneca cited earlier might count as an epistle commending scholars to princes, for those who are in power often scowl at their pursuits,[12] abusing the superiority of their position and their misguided opinions to spy on them and bring them to court! We know full well that Seneca wrote his letter with this aim in mind, but we know equally well that he did not achieve his aim.

The origin of the Stoics is more ancient than their name. It is both different from and nobler than what many people have assumed – these two beneficial points, I maintain, they owe to me.

The sect of the Stoics, which, in comparison with all the others, had a keener appreciation of virtue, deserves for this very reason to be called earnest, manly and resolute. Such is its closeness to Christian courage that it could boast of a privileged relationship with it if it did not sin by an excess of insensitivity. On this account the Stoic sect is criticized and refuted by St Thomas, using actions taken from the life of Christ our Lord, God and true man, as well as by many other doctors of the Church, especially Petrus Comestor in his *Ecclesiastical History,* in those passages in which Christ, the eternal wisdom, is afflicted, distressed, angry, afraid and tearful.[13] To this very day the origin of this doctrine is a matter of dispute, since it does not have the source it deserves and is worthy of.[14] Such naked truths about the world could not have been derived unsoiled by earth and dust from any other source than the Holy Scriptures. I would even venture to maintain that they are derived from the sacred Book of Job and are a literal translation into precepts of his actions and words. I will prove this by means of demonstrations and on the basis of the chronology of the first leaders of the school.

The whole of Stoic doctrine is based on the following principle: that things can be divided into those that belong to us and those that do not; that those that belong to us are in our power and that those that do not belong to us are in someone else's power; that the former affect us, whereas the latter do not, and that, therefore, they should neither upset nor distress us; that we should not worry about whether things conform to our desires, but rather about adjusting our desires to the outcome of things; that in this way we will enjoy freedom, peace and tranquillity, whereas otherwise we will always be full of sorrow and restlessness; that we should not say that we lose our children or our property, but rather that we repay the one who lent them to us; and that the wise man should accuse neither someone else nor himself for whatever happens to him and should not complain about God.[15]

Job lost his children, his house, his property, his health and his wife, but not his patience. And he did not reply to those who brought him the news that his herds of cattle had been stolen, that fire had burnt his servants and that his house had been destroyed by the wind, with complaints about thieves, fire or wind.[16] He did not say that they had taken them away from him, but rather said that he who had given them to him had recovered them: 'The Lord gave, and the Lord hath taken away; blessed be the name of the Lord.'[17] Nor did he merely give them back, he also thanked God for having recovered them, and in order to show that he considered these things to be someone else's possessions, he said: 'Naked came I out of my mother's womb, and naked shall I return thither.'[18] Job neither blamed the thieves nor himself. His wife tried to persuade him to complain to God, and seeing a knot of worms in a dunghill, where the manure made her feel sick, she said to him: 'Dost thou still hold fast thine integrity? Praise God, and die',[19] thus ironically reproaching Job for praising God and for not voicing any complaint against him. To this Job replied: 'Thou speakest as one of the foolish women speaketh. What? Shall we receive good at the hand of God, and shall we not receive evil?'[20] Would anyone deny that this action and these words, taken literally in their straightforward sense and without any attempt to distort their meaning, correspond to the source of Stoic doctrine and are justified by the incomparable simplicity of that man whose like does not exist on this earth? It is not I who is exaggerating, but the divine voice of the text. God said to Satan: 'Hast thou considered my servant Job? For there is none like him in the earth, a perfect and an upright man, one that feareth God, and escheweth evil?'[21]

In this single chapter we can read everything which Epictetus took over into Stoic doctrine from the tradition of his predecessors. We read about the subdivision of those things that are in our power – that is, the opinions we hold about things, and whether they should be avoided or sought after – and about the indifference towards those things that are irrelevant for our salvation – life, property, wife and children. Epictetus devotes the first, second and third chapters, as well as the fourth to the ninth, to repeating these tenets; and he does not write down one single precept that was not already put into practice by Job. The last chapter that I have just mentioned teaches us that it is not things in themselves that trouble us, but the opinions we hold about them: we think they are frightening, even though they are not.

Epictetus takes death as an example and says that if it were something abominable, it would have seemed so to Socrates.[22] How much better is this point exemplified by Job, from whom Socrates derived this truth! He showed that neither poverty, nor the greatest of disasters, nor the loss of one's children, nor the persecution of one's wife and friends, nor illness – even a disgusting disease that was worse than death – were exasperating evils per se. Not only did he himself find something positive to say about those things, a matter which was entirely in his own hands, but he also taught his wife to find something positive to say about them. And his whole book has no other purpose than to teach his friends that what he has suffered is not itself bad, but rather that their mistaken opinions about his afflictions make them appear to be bad. Not only did Job preserve an indomitable spirit amidst all his calamities, but he showed that he was thirsty for even greater ones, in the following words of chapter 6[:9–10]: 'Even that it would please God to crush me; that he would let loose his hand, and cut me off! Then should I yet have comfort; yea, I would exult in pain that spareth not.' Epictetus translated these brave utterances as well as he could: *Plue, Domine, super me calamitates,* 'O Lord, let calamities pour down upon me!'[23]

Chapter 13 of the *Enchiridion* shows that Epictetus is a disciple not only of the precepts of that sacred book, but also of its very words. For he says, in the sequence of chapters that corresponds to the division of Simplicius in the Greek original and the Latin text,[24] and in Gonzalo Correas's Spanish translation (the arrangement of chapters by Sánchez is different from the one by Correas, and I follow the former's division):

Never say about anything, 'I have lost it', but only 'I have given it back.' If your child dies, do not say, 'I have lost it', but 'I have paid it back.' Have they cheated you out of your inheritance? You will still say that you have given it back. 'Yet he is a rascal and a scoundrel who cheated me out of it.' Why do you bother about the collector sent by the creditor to collect your debts?[25]

I have already quoted the Holy Scriptures and the way in which Job reacted to these problems, for when he was told that the fire had burned up his sheep and the herdsmen, that the wind had smitten his house and that his children had been buried under its ruins, that the Sabeans had taken away his oxen and his asses and that the Chaldeans had carried away his camels,[26] he made no distinction between the thieves and the fire and the wind, but saw them all as collectors sent by God to recover the goods that he had given him. He did not say: 'Thieves have robbed me', but rather said: 'The Lord gave, and the Lord hath taken away. As it was agreeable to the Lord, so it hath happened; blessed be the name of the Lord.'[27] And in order to see that he literally interpreted the thieves as the sort of collectors whom God is accustomed to send, he said in chapter 19, verse 12: 'His troops come on together and cast up their way against me, and encamp round about my tent.' Finally, Epictetus took over the following words of Job literally: *Sicut Domino placuit, ita factum est* [As it was agreeable to the Lord, so it hath happened],[28] by saying in his last chapter: *Si Deo ita visum fuerit, ita fiat* [If it is pleasing to God so, let it be so].[29]

The origin of Stoic doctrine, then, has been made nobler since we have derived it from the Holy Writ, where we read that their doctrine was practised, and all its words have been given a greater fullness of meaning. It remains to prove this origin from a chronological perspective.

Everyone calls Zeno of Citium the founder of this school, his name being derived from his home town in Cyprus. He was a disciple of Crates the Cynic, but although he followed the tenets of the Cynics, he was thoroughly convinced[30] of the value of decorous and urbane modesty and therefore cleaned his body of all the filth which they were so fond of and got rid of the contempt that followed their dirty way of life. We can therefore conclude that the doctrine of the Stoics, who began to be called by this name with Zeno, derived from that of the Cynics, and that Zeno added the element of cleanliness in order to prevent their degrading squalor from bringing the doctrine into disrepute. Humility is not equivalent to shabbiness; it consists rather in disdain for what is precious.[31] Filthiness is not a sign of wisdom, but a blemish. Wisdom may be poor, but it must not be disgusting. Zeno added a great deal to the doctrine by taking away from it. He was not the first to discover it, but he was the first to dress it in clean clothes. The appearance [of the Cynic Crates] was such that people did not listen to his wisdom because they could not see it; whistles were the only kind of applause he could win for it, and the taunts to which he was exposed made him withdraw.[32]

Strabo, discussing Cyprus and the town associated with Zeno, says in Book XIV: 'Citium has a harbour that can be closed; and here was born Zeno, the original founder of the Stoic sect.'[33] According to Diogenes Laertius: 'Zeno was a native of Citium, a Greek village in Cyprus, which was inhabited by the Phoenicians.'[34] Suidas likewise states: 'Zeno was also called "the Phoenician" because the Phoenicians inhabited his native town.'[35] Cicero says in Book V of the *Tusculan Disputations* that 'the inhabitants of Citium were Phoenicians'.[36] We read in Diogenes' *Life of Zeno:* 'The men of Citium living in Sidon also held Zeno in high esteem.'[37]

On the basis of all the authorities just quoted we conclude that the Cynics and Zeno, who was their disciple and the leader of the well-groomed and well-dressed Cynics who called themselves Stoics, prided themselves on being inhabitants of the lands bordering on Judaea, from which the wisdom of all nations is derived. Not only is it possible, it is also easy to believe and even necessary to assume that the Cynics and the Stoics had seen the Holy Scriptures, since they shared their lives with the Jews, who never had the Bible out of their hands. What can be gathered from the authorities is proved by what I have said about the doctrine of Stoics and by the text of the Book of Job.

The aim of the Stoics was to count as nothing whatever was in someone else's power and to do this without counting themselves as nothing through taking on an air of dirtiness and shabbiness; to pursue virtue and to enjoy it both for its own sake and as a reward; to put reason beyond the reach of disturbances; to put man above adversities, although, being human, he cannot be completely without them; to establish peace of mind by disregarding the emotions, irrespective of external help and internal seditions; to live with the body, but not for the body; to value the life that is good, not the one that lasts for a long time; to value years highly only when they are blameless. They would consider a lifetime to consist of only those years during which they managed to live well. They lived in order to die, like those who live and die at the same time. They kept in mind the long period of time when they did not exist, knowing that they had only existed for a short while. They saw that they were insignificant beings, who only survived for an insignificant amount of time, and they believed that they could cease to exist at any moment. They did not despise death because they considered it to be the highest good in nature; they were not afraid of it, because they saw it as a haven of rest and knew it was inescapable.

I have now arrived at the scandal of this sect. The paradox of the Stoics can be seen in the following statement: 'The philosopher may sometimes kill himself: this is what is proper for him, this is what he must do.'[38]

Socrates courageously drank his own death. Seneca courageously sweated to death in his bath. Socrates was a member of the Ionian school, a disciple of the Athenian Arcesilaus, as everyone, with the exception of Sidonius, holds. Indeed, the opinion expressed by Sidonius in his verses is itself discredited by the contradictions contained in these very verses.[39] And if it is true that Socrates was a member of the Ionian sect (which Sidonius calls Socratic), it is also true that he was the first to improve the study of astrology and ethics by taking into account mores and manners. It is for this reason that I number Socrates with Seneca: Seneca was a Stoic, while Socrates was a Stoic *avant la lettre.* Yet neither Socrates drinking his poison nor Seneca bleeding to death in his bath justified the paradox that the wise man could and indeed should inflict death upon himself. Both were condemned to death. They did not choose death, but they did choose what kind of death they wanted, since they were forced to suffer it anyway. I report, not without pain, Seneca's words in *Letter* LXXIX: 'There is no difference whether death comes to us, or we go to death. Make yourself believe that the following words are the utterance of an ignorant man: "It is a beautiful thing to die one's own death."'[40] Even pagan philosophy could not hear such reasoning without criticism, and the sacrosanct truth of Christianity condemns it outright. But not only does Seneca state this view, he even recommends suicide and tries to persuade us to pursue this course of action. *On Anger,* Book III, chapter 15:

In whatever direction you turn your eyes, there lies the means to end your woes. Do you see that precipice? Down it is the way to liberty. Do you see that sea, that river, that well? There sits liberty – at the bottom. Do you see that tree, stunted, blighted, and barren? Yet from its branches hangs liberty. Do you see that throat of yours, your gullet, your heart? They are ways to escape from your servitude. Are the ways of exiting I show you too laborious, do they require too much courage and resolution? Do you ask what is the highway to liberty? Any vein in your body![41]

Neither the fact that Seneca was a native of Cordova, nor the fact that his writings are of such quality could induce me to keep quiet. And I have to say at this juncture that it is Timon rather than Seneca whom we meet in those words, and they are all the more poisonous the more alluring they sound.[42] It is Timon, I maintain, who was condemned as an enemy of mankind, who asked and actually persuaded people to hang themselves from a tree which he had dedicated to this fruit. How, noble Seneca, could you be unaware that it is ignorant cowardice to let oneself be overcome by the fear of hardship? That it is lunacy to commit suicide in order to avoid death? It was to you, not to Fannius, that Martial spoke when he said: 'Because he was flying from an enemy, Fannius slew himself. Is not this, I ask, madness – to die to avoid death?'[43]

I have made up for one Spaniard with the help of another.[44] I find it surprising that our Seneca, despite admiring the courage with which his Epicurus called the very day on which he died happy, even though he was fighting against the excruciating pain caused by his bladder and his ulcerated intestines,[45] can still recommend violent death in a situation of despair in order not to have to endure it.

It should also be noted that just because Seneca was of the opinion that it is permissible to commit suicide this does not mean that this is a Stoic opinion; rather, it is the opinion of one particular Stoic. Let us listen to our Epictetus: 'Men, wait upon God. When he gives the signal and sets you free from this service, then you shall depart to him; but for the present be equanimous and endure to abide in this place, where he has stationed you. Short indeed is this time of your abiding here, and easy to bear for men of such convictions.'[46] Because these words contain so much truth and are so pious that they might have been spoken by a Christian, we praise them and hold them up against those Stoics who maintained the contrary. Compare the subtle indictment of Augustine, *The City of God* XIX.4: 'Now I am amazed that the Stoic philosophers have the nerve to argue that there are no ills, though they admit that, if they should be so great that the wise man cannot or ought not to endure them, he may inflict death on himself and depart from this life.'[47] Let Stoic doctrine acknowledge that it is I who am defending it against this hideous error of which some Stoics were guilty!

The great Plutarch attacked the Stoics and ridiculed their doctrines on many counts and with great venom, although all his ethical treatises are in fact Stoic. He wrote a book which he called *Against the Stoics on Common Conceptions*. Being human, Plutarch had to go astray in his judgement of some matters; and if he did go astray, it was in this respect. I am convinced that everything he wrote about the Stoics was written on the spur of the moment and not after mature reflection. One is only justified in contradicting Plutarch in order to come to the defence of Stoic doctrine. The innocence of the accused is the excuse for my insolence, for I not only attack the book just mentioned, but also two others. One is called *Conspectus of the Essay, 'The Stoics Talk More Absurdly Than the Poets'*, and the other *On Stoic Self-Contradictions*. Exaggeration and excess are the signs of anger, not of equanimity. Although I have good reason to answer all three of these books, I have neither the time nor the space to do so in this introductory note. Let me only deflect Plutarch's strongest attack, by means of which he tries to prove that the Stoics talk more absurdly than the poets.

These are his words, and for every single one of them I will provide an answer by administering an antidote. 'When the Stoic sage is imprisoned, he is not confined.'[48] It is not the better part of him, because it is his body which is locked up in prison; it is not his mind, nor his judgement, nor his good intentions, nor the motions of his understanding, nor the acts of his free will that are imprisoned. No tyrant has ever been able to devise a prison for the faculties of the soul, and no tyrant's cruelties have been able to affect anything but the senses. His power does not go beyond the body.

'Flung down a precipice, he does not suffer violence.' The sage only suffers violence in his body. If the fall kills him, it is not the sage who suffers, but his life. The sage does not refer to that which flings him down the precipice as violence, because he knows how easy it is to fall by oneself and that many have fallen when they were going upwards in joy, or downwards in grief, or even when they were walking securely. He knows that the blow takes away from him the life[49] which was bound to end even without such a blow and that the soul is not flung down a precipice when it does not sin. Whoever assists those who are falling to fall and those who are dying to die cannot possibly inflict any violence on them while he is helping them. If he were able to hold on to them or to heal them without wanting to do so, he would display greater weakness in what he omitted to do than strength in what he did do. The wise man would rather die deserving to live than live[50] an unworthy life. He defends the light of his soul with the shadow of his body. He staves off the vengeance of the tyrant with earth and dust, satisfying him with the ashes that deceive him.

'When on the rack, he does not suffer.'[51] No, because torture and tyrants are themselves the victims of those who have to endure them. If, speaking like Plutarch, it were possible to relate how much greater were the torments endured by the tyrants when they were faced with the firmness of the martyrs than those endured by the martyrs themselves while they were being tortured, the Spaniard St Lawrence[52] would be a case in point to illustrate this opposition. When he was roasting on the grill, the saint said: 'Tyrant, pray, turn me over on the other side, for this one is well done.' These words served as a grill for the tyrant. But I must not have recourse to a saint of the Church; let Plutarch therefore be answered by Anaxarchus.[53] When Nicocreon had him pounded to death with iron pestles, he pounded Nicocreon himself when he said: 'Pound, pound my haunch, for Anaxagoras is in a place where your hand cannot shatter him.' Can there be a better reply than this? The wise man is on the rack, but he does not suffer. The tyrant has put him on the rack, and he is the one who suffers. Christ our Lord, truly God and truly man, said: 'Be not afraid of them which kill the body.'[54] Will anyone deny that Anaxarchus obeyed (although without having the true faith) this precept which he had not heard of and that Plutarch doubts what he sees, contradicting what he knows to be true?

'When set ablaze,[55] he does not burn.' The sage in flames does not burn; what does burn is the clothing of his life in his body, which, as no one will deny, is part of the man. Tyrants burn a statue of the man whom they cannot burn. They tell vainglorious lies when they say that they are burning him, for it is only his statue that they are burning. When directed against the sage and the wise man, their power does not reach beyond the statue. The sage is not overtaken by the flames, for he is far away from the furies of mankind. He will only meet with his punishment and his pyre beyond the body in the place where souls can be burnt. What tyrants burn here is the mortal part of the sage, not the sage himself.

Although it is leading us astray slightly, the saying of a French nobleman living under Henry IV ties in with our present discussion. He had fled Turin and crossed the

Alps during the heaviest snowfalls of winter. Later, when he heard that a statue of himself had been burnt on the very day when he was crossing the glaciers of the Alps, he said: 'In my whole life, I never froze so much as on the day when they were burning me.' What was so truly said by a criminal of his statue can be said even more truly by the sage of his body, and gloriously and triumphantly by the victorious martyr of Christ.

'Knocked down in wrestling, I remained invincible.' The sage does not wrestle, says Epictetus; he does not enter competitions; he does not descend into the arena. Thus, he will remain invincible if he neither wrestles nor quarrels. Nobody can win a contest, unless someone opposes him. The sage has no opponent, except vices and base feelings. If they are victorious, he is not a sage. If he is victorious, he is invincible.

'When surrounded by walls, he is not blockaded.' No, for the same reason that, as I have shown, he is not confined when he is imprisoned. It is his body that is block-aded, which is the tightest blockade that the sage undergoes. And since when he is surrounded by his body, his soul is not blockaded as far as its voluntary actions are concerned,[56] then this is even less so when he is surrounded by walls.

'When his enemies sell him, he cannot be a slave.' No, because his enemies sell his body, which is the slave of the sage. They do not sell the sage, who can neither be sold or be a slave. The sage is only a slave if he serves his body. If he makes use of his body, he is always free and reigns even in captivity. Therefore, his enemies sell the slave of the sage, not the sage himself.

'The disciple who learns virtue from the Stoic school may say: "Wish for whatever you like, so that all may be yours."'[57] I will not reply to these words myself, because Epictetus refutes them in chapter 13 of his *Enchiridion:* 'Do not seek to have everything that happens happen as you wish, but if you are a wise man, wish for everything to happen as it actually does happen.'[58] This flatly contradicts Plutarch's false imputation, for he says that the Stoic should wish for what he likes, and that he will attain it all. Epictetus says that one should not seek to have something happen according to one's wishes, but that one should accommodate one's wishes to what-ever happens. It is now incumbent on me to show that Plutarch lacks reason and the Stoics lack truth.

'Virtue brings them wealth, conquers kingships for them, grants them good for-tune, makes them happy, prosperous and free from all other wants, though they do not have a penny of their own.'[59] This ironical statement of Plutarch is true in spite of himself: virtue is said to give the Stoic sage this wealth, this kingship, this happiness and this prosperity. Will anyone, apart from those who are ignorant about the riches of virtue, deny that it is virtue alone that can provide these things? I am the first to admit that crooks seem to possess all these things by breaking the law and commit-ting the worst offences, and that these goods are more often a reward for crime than a distinction for merit. When, however, they are given by an unjust hand, they lose their innocence; and when they are received by a greedy hand, they lose their usefulness. Thus, fish are also fed by the hand that throws food into the water while hiding the hook by which they will be caught: one hand brings them death, the other gives them food. Sin and crime provide wealth, kingship, happiness and prosperity:

they catch people with a hook without actually giving them anything. Virtue alone gives these things without reserve or deceit. If justice owes them to virtue alone, why is Plutarch so convinced that justice will deceive virtue and that the very justice that punishes others for not doing what they ought to do will not do what it itself ought to do? I would not have dared to contradict Plutarch if I had dared, at this juncture, to accuse the Stoics.

The main tenet of this sect was apathy or insensibility, which completely excluded any kind of feeling. Both the Pythagoreans and the Peripatetics were opposed to this overall condemnation of the passions. Among the more recent critics, Lactantius says in Book VI: 'The Stoics are raging mad; they do not temper the passions but eliminate them and somehow want to deprive man of something that naturally forms a part of him.'[60] St Jerome says in the first book of his *Against the Pelagians:* 'According to the Stoics, one must not have any passions in order to attain perfection; according to the Peripatetics, this is difficult and even impossible, and this opinion is favoured by the whole authority of the Holy Scriptures.'[61] This holy doctor of the Church himself, who approves, as do the Holy Scriptures, of the teaching of the Peripatetics, disapproves of the teaching of the Stoics on apathy and condemns it as heretical in the following words from his *Against the Pelagians:* 'One can get rid of all the passions and all their roots; the Pelagians learnt this from Pythagoras and Zeno.'[62]

Justus Lipsius, an eminently learned man, says in his *Guide to Stoic Philosophy* that he is willing to accept that the Pelagians learnt this from Zeno. It is surprising that St Jerome should say that they learnt this from Pythagoras, since it is contrary to the truth, as Lipsius never tires of proving. I wish that the same piety with which Lipsius emended and corrected Plautus, Martial, Varro and generally all the profane authors in order not to admit that they committed errors would now assist him in his dealings with this most holy and learned Church Father; for he had better reason to presume and find errors in all these writers than in St Jerome, particularly concerning something of which he could not possibly be ignorant. I am as grateful to Lipsius for having left me this emendation as I am reproachful towards him for not having corrected the error himself. The Latin text of St Jerome sounds strained: *Omnes affectus tolli posse, omnesque eorum fibras, a Pythagora, et Zenone, Pelagianos*[63] *hausisse.* I maintain that we must read: *Omnes affectus tolli posse, omnesque eorum fibras apathia e Zenone Pelagianos hausisse* [One can get rid of all the passions and all their roots with the help of impassivity; the Pelagians learnt this from Zeno].[64] This is an emendation in which all the signs and all the letters are contained in the error, for *Pythagora* contains, in its orthography, all the letters of *apathia* in an inverted order. The scribe or printer would have found it easy to recognize all the distinctive letters of 'Pythagoras' in an inverted order in the word *apathia,* which he could not understand on account of it being in Greek. The context seemed to imply that it was philosophers who were being talked about; and since there is no philosopher called 'Apathia', the close resemblance to 'Pythagoras' would have prompted him to change the word accordingly. My emendation, therefore, is necessary: the word *apathia* is the one that must be read in this passage, since it was the formal cause of this error.

St Thomas, the 'Angelic Doctor', and with him all the other doctors [of the Church], reject this insensibility so categorically that it seems impossible to say anything in its defence. However, in order to show that they have not spoilt my affection for the Stoics, while conceding that it would be heretical nowadays to hold an opinion that has been proved by everyone to have been an error in the past, I will nevertheless try to interpret their doctrine. They say that we must not have any feelings: this is what they teach; this is what they command. I am convinced that some people understand the verb 'to feel' to mean 'to be overcome[65] by feelings', since it is from experiencing feelings that virtues such as mercy, pity and commiseration arise, whereas being overcome by them is tantamount to being too fainthearted to produce any sort of virtue.

If we want now to listen carefully to some of those who managed to bring all their undertakings to a good end, this will not be a form of misplaced courtesy. We owe them many things; let them owe one thing to us. The Stoics' descent and genealogy is linked from the beginning to the Cynics, through Zeno.[66] He was followed by Cleanthes, Chrysippus, Zeno of Sidon, Diogenes the Babylonian, Antipater, Panaetius, Posidonius, Persaeus, Herillus, Ariston of Chios,[67] Athenodorus, Sphaerus, Zenodotus, Apollonius, Asclepiodotus, Archidemus or Arched[68] and Sotion. I include among the Stoics the fountainhead of all knowledge, Homer. Seneca, himself a Stoic, denied him this honour at the beginning of *Letter* LXXXVIII;[69] but the very reasons for which he was led to deny that Homer should be included among the Stoics can be used to grant admission to him. Seneca was not motivated by blameworthy envy, but by overzealous severity. Socrates was not a Stoic, but he professed some of their doctrines. I say the same about Sophocles and Demosthenes – indeed, about no one with better reason than Sophocles. Philo said of himself that he was a Stoic in his *Every Wise Man Is Free.*[70] Plato cannot deny that he was a Stoic, for this is proved by his very works.

Among the Romans,[71] there were the Tuberos, the Catos, the Varros, Thrasea Paetus,[72] Helvidius Priscus, Rubellius Plautus, Pliny, Tacitus, Emperor Marcus Aurelius and all those mentioned by Sextus Empiricus. Virgil was a Stoic and followed the doctrine of impassivity, as he himself plainly teaches in the second book of the *Georgics:* 'He knows naught of the pang of pity for the poor, or of envy of the rich.'[73] There were some Christians in antiquity who thought well of the Stoics. Among them were Arnobius, Tertullian to a larger extent and the great Pantaenus, who was a doctor [of the Church] in Alexandria where he taught the Holy Scriptures. St Jerome says of him: 'Pantaenus, a philosopher of the Stoic sect, because of the immense fame of his erudition was sent to India in order to preach the gospel of Christ to the Brahmins and to the philosophers of those nations.'[74] Clement of Alexandria approved of Stoic doctrine, as anyone who peruses his admirable writings can see. St Jerome, in his *Commentary on Isaiah,* chapter 20, characterizes them in the following words: 'The Stoics agree in many points with our own doctrine.'[75] As a shining ornament of the Stoics in our days, Lipsius adduces St Carlo Borromeo,[76] although he was more than a Stoic, since the teaching of this sect could not include all that was contained in his Christian holiness. I add the blessed Francis of Sales, because, in his *Introduction to the Devout Life,* he expressly includes the *Enchiridion* of Epictetus, as can be seen in the chapters on humility.[77] I also add Justus Lipsius: he was a Christian Stoic, a defender of the Stoics and a master of this doctrine. Francisco Sánchez de las Brozas, the glory of Spain at the University of Salamanca, prided himself on being a Stoic in the commentary he wrote in chapter 6 of his *Epicteto*.[78] He has said it; I dare not repeat his words.

I would not myself boast of being a Stoic, but I hold them in high esteem. Their doctrine has served me as a guide in moments of doubt, as a comfort in adversity, as a defence in persecution – all of which have formed so great a part of my life. I have studied their doctrines continually; I do not know whether, in me, they have had a good pupil.

Translators' Notes

1. Reading *en la ciudad de Seuilla* with the 1635 edition. Rodrigo Caro (1573–1647) was the foremost Spanish antiquarian of his time as well as a distinguished poet; see D. Santiago Montoto, *Rodrigo Caro. Estudio biográfico-crítico* (Seville, 1915), and for his role as a judge of testamentary provisions, pp. 36–41.
2. That is, the verse translations of Epictetus's *Enchiridion* and of Pseudo-Phocylides, published in the same volume as the *Stoic Doctrine* in 1635. Juan de Herrera (b. 1583) was a stableman of Gaspar de Guzmán (1587–1645), the favourite of Philip IV.
3. The school was named after the Stoa Poikile, 'the Painted Portico'.
4. Theognetus fragment 1: R. Kassel and C. Austin, eds., *Poetae comici Graeci*, 7 vols. (Berlin, 1983–9), VII, p. 697, quoted by Athenaeus, *Deipnosophistae* III (104B). Quevedo took this information from Justus Lipsius, *Manuductio ad Stoicam philosophiam* (Antwerp, 1604), p. 47 (I.14).
5. The Greek term *stoakes* was a nickname given to the Stoics. Quevedo has *portaleros* ('belonging to the Porch'), which seems to be a word of his own invention.
6. Hermeias of Curium, *Collectanea Alexandrina*, ed. I. U. Powell (Oxford, 1925), p. 237, quoted by Athenaeus, *Deipnosophistae* XIII (563D). Quevedo took the quotation from Lipsius, *Manuductio*, p. 47 (I.14).
7. Tertullian, *De praescriptione haereticorum* 7.10, quoted in Lipsius, *Manuductio*, p. 48 (I.14).
8. Reading *más que aquellos* with the 1635 edition.
9. Seneca, *Epistulae* LXXIII.1–2; the translation is adapted from that of R. M. Gummere, 3 vols. (London, 1917–25); the passage is quoted in Lipsius, *Manuductio*, p. 51 (I.15). Quevedo apparently misread LXXIIII for LXXIII, since Lipsius gives the correct reference.
10. Reading *hosbedaua* with the 1635 edition.
11. Psalms 1:1.
12. Reading *obras* for *horas*.
13. See, e.g., Thomas Aquinas, *In decem libros Ethicorum Aristotelis ad Nicomachum expositio*, ed. A. M. Pirotta (Turin, 1934), I.16, nos. 195–6; II.3, no. 272; IV.13, no. 804; and Petrus Comestor, *Historia Scholastica – In Evangelia* 118.156, in J. P. Migne, ed., *Patrologia Latina*, 221 vols. (Paris, 1844–64), CXCVIII, cols. 1599–1601, 1632.
14. Reading *y de la que es decente.*
15. See Epictetus, *Enchiridion* 1, 8, 11 and 31.
16. See Job 1:14–19.
17. Job 1:21.
18. Job 1:21.
19. Job 2:9. In the Revised Version Job's wife says 'Renounce God', but Quevedo is translating from the Vulgate, which reads *Benedic Deo*. The worms and the dunghill referred to

here are not mentioned in the Bible, where Job is smitten 'with sore boils from the sole of his foot unto his crown' (2:7).

20. Job 2:10.
21. Job 1:8.
22. See, e.g., Epictetus, *Discourses* I.4.24; IV.1.159–69.
23. This is not a quotation from Epictetus, but from Francisco Sánchez, *Vida de Epicteto,* the preface to his *Doctrina del estoyco filosofo Epicteto* (Pamplona, 1612), f. 10ᵛ.
24. Simplicius, a sixth-century Greek philosopher, wrote a commentary on the *Enchiridion,* which was used by Angelo Poliziano in his Latin translation of the treatise and in his defence of Epictetus (see Chapter 17).
25. See Epictetus, *Enchiridion* 11; adapted from W. A. Oldfather's translation (Cambridge, Mass., 1978). The reference is to Sánchez, *Doctrina,* f. 30ʳ. The following quotation from the Book of Job occurs in the *Annotación* to chapter 13 of Sánchez's translation.
26. See Job 1:15–19.
27. See Job 1:21.
28. This line is a variant reading in the Vulgate text of Job 1:21; it is not included in the Revised Version of the Bible.
29. Epictetus, *Enchiridion* 53 (adapted from Plato, *Crito* 43D). K. A. Blüher, *Séneca en España* (Madrid, 1983), p. 462 n. 137, points out that the use of this particular Latin translation of Plato's famous line proves that, besides the translations of the *Enchiridion* by Francisco Sánchez (Madrid, 1600) and Gonzalo Correas (Salamanca, 1630), Quevedo was also aware of the one by Hieronymus Wolf (Basel, 1563).
30. Reading *persuadido muy* with the 1635 edition.
31. Reading *precioso* with the 1635 edition instead of *no preciso* ('unnecessary').
32. The translation of this sentence and the insertion of the reference to Crates are an attempt to make sense of the almost unintelligible original.
33. See Strabo, *Geography* XIV.6.3, quoted by Lipsius, *Manuductio,* p. 30 (I.10).
34. Diogenes Laertius, *Lives of the Philosophers* VII.1, quoted by Lipsius, *Manuductio,* p. 30 (I.10).
35. See *Suidae Lexicon,* ed. A. Adler, 5 vols. (Leipzig, 1927–38), II, p. 507, lines 11–12 (Z 79), quoted by Lipsius, *Manuductio,* pp. 30–1 (I.10).
36. See Cicero, *De finibus* IV.20.56. Quevedo's mistaken reference is explained by the fact that he linked this quotation to the reference for the quotation following this one in Lipsius, *Manuductio,* p. 31 (I.10).
37. Diogenes Laertius, *Lives of the Philosophers* VII.6.
38. Lipsius, *Manuductio,* p. 199 (title of III.22).
39. Quevedo is referring to Sidonius Apollinaris, *Carmen* 15.89–97, cited by Lipsius, *Manuductio,* p. 24 (I.8), where it is stated that the 'Socratica secta' derived its existence from Arcesilaus, head of the Athenian Academy in the middle of the third century BC.
40. The passage comes, in fact, from Seneca, *Epistulae* LXIX.6, and is quoted by Lipsius, *Manuductio,* p. 199 (III.22). 'To die one's own death' presumably means dying when one's time has come, as opposed to committing suicide.
41. Seneca, *On Anger* III.15.4, adapted from J. W. Basore's translation (London, 1928); the passage is quoted by Lipsius, *Manuductio,* p. 200 (III.22).
42. Timon of Athens, the subject of a play by Shakespeare, was a famous misanthrope, who reputedly lived in the era of Pericles.
43. Martial, *Epigrams* II.80; W. C. A. Ker's translation (London, 1919).
44. Both Seneca and Martial were born in Spain.
45. See Seneca, *Epistulae* XCII.25–6.
46. Epictetus, *Dissertation* I.9.16–17; W. A. Oldfather's translation (London, 1926).
47. Adapted from W. C. Greene's translation (London, 1960). The text is quoted by Lipsius, *Manuductio,* p. 207 (III.23).
48. This and the following paradoxes are all taken from the first chapter of Plutarch's *Conspectus* (*Moralia* 1057E).

49. Reading *lleva la vida* instead of *le da la vida;* although this seems an unlikely misreading, it is the only way to bring this phrase into line with Quevedo's argument.
50. Reading *vivir* with the 1635 edition.
51. For Lipsius's discussion of this paradox see his *A Guide to Stoic Philosophy in Three Books* III.6 in Chapter 18.
52. The legend of St Lawrence's Spanish origin derives from the *Passio Polychronii.*
53. Quevedo's text has 'Anaxagoras' instead of 'Anaxarchus' whose name occurs a few lines later. The story told here can be found in Diogenes Laertius, *Lives of the Philosophers* IX.59.
54. See Matthew 10:28.
55. Quevedo seems to have read *puroumenos* instead of *peroumenos* ('mutilated'), which is the commonly accepted reading nowadays. Both words are pronounced the same in modern Greek.
56. Reading *no está cercado el alma* with the 1635 edition.
57. See Plutarch, *Conspectus* 4 (*Moralia* 1058C).
58. Epictetus, *Enchiridion* 8; Oldfather's translation. The printer seems to have misread VIII for XIII, which is a common mistake.
59. Plutarch, *Conspectus* 4 (*Moralia* 1058C); adapted from H. Cherniss's translation (Cambridge, Mass., 1976).
60. Lactantius, *Divinae institutiones* VI.15.3, quoted by Lipsius, *Manuductio,* p. 160 (I.7).
61. See Jerome, *Against the Pelagians* II.6, quoted by Lipsius, *Manuductio,* p. 160 (I.7).
62. This text is quoted by Lipsius, *Manuductio,* p. 151 (I.7), with a marginal gloss identifying its provenance as *Against the Pelagians,* but it is to be found neither in this treatise nor in any other work of Jerome.
63. This is the correct reading as found in the 1635 edition; Astrana Marín's edition has *Pelagianus.*
64. This sentence is mistakenly omitted in the edition of Astrana Marín.
65. Reading *dexarse* with the 1635 edition.
66. The following list is derived from Lipsius, *Manuductio,* pp. 30–42 (I.10–12).
67. Reading *Aristo de Chío;* the 1635 edition reads *Aristodechio,* and Astrana Marín's *Aristodequio.*
68. Lipsius, *Manuductio,* p. 41 (I.12), reads: 'ARCHIDEMUS, or ARCHED. as it is most often written.' A marginal gloss explains: 'At any rate by the Greeks, for the Latins as a rule write Archidemus.' Quevedo evidently did not understand that 'Arched.' was meant to be an abbreviation for Archedemus; hence this odd name in his list of the Greek Stoics.
69. See Seneca, *Epistulae* LXXXVIII.5.
70. See, e.g., Philo, *Quod omnis probus liber sit* 3–8, where Philo defends a number of Stoic paradoxes.
71. This list is derived from Lipsius, *Manuductio,* pp. 55–6 (I.17).
72. In Quevedo's text Thrasea Paetus and Rubellius Plautus are each mistakenly treated as two people.
73. Virgil, *Georgics* II.498–9; H. R. Fairclough's translation (Cambridge, Mass., 1978).
74. See Jerome, *De viris illustribus* 36, quoted by Lipsius, *Manuductio,* p. 56 (I.17).
75. Jerome, *Commentarii in Isaiam prophetam* IV.11, quoted by Lipsius, *Manuductio,* p. 56 (I.17).
76. Lipsius, *Manuductio,* p. 56 (I.17).
77. See chapter 3.4–7, where, however, Epictetus is not referred to by name. Quevedo's translation of the *Introduction* was published in Madrid in 1634, one year before the *Stoic Doctrine.*
78. Sánchez, *Doctrina,* ff. 19ᵛ–20ʳ.

Further Reading

Blüher, K. A., *Seneca in Spanien. Untersuchungen zur Geschichte der Seneca-Rezeption in Spanien vom 13. bis 17. Jahrhundert* (Munich, 1969); there is also a revised Spanish translation: *Séneca en España* (Madrid, 1983)

Burns, J. H., ed., *The Cambridge History of Political Thought 1450–1700* (Cambridge, 1991), p. 690

CHRP, pp. 372–3, 381, 383, 834

Ettinghausen, H., *Francisco Quevedo and the Neostoic Movement* (Oxford, 1972), esp. pp. 26–42

Mérimée, E., *Essai sur la vie et les oeuvres de Francisco de Quevedo (1580–1645)* (Paris, 1886)

Part VI.
Epicurean Ethics

20

Petrarch

Luc Deitz

Introduction

Petrarch (Francesco Petrarca; 1304–74), who was crowned poet laureate in 1341, is deservedly regarded as the founding father of Italian humanism. Yet despite his groundbreaking contributions to almost every facet of the study of classical antiquity, he hardly deserves to be reckoned among the most original of moral philosophers. His most substantial and influential work in this field, *On the Remedies for Both Kinds of Fortune* (1366), is a vast encyclopedia of morally uplifting dialogues between Reason and the four emotions condemned by the Stoics: Joy and Hope, Sorrow and Fear. It contains a good deal of Stoic material taken from Seneca and Cicero, which is combined, often in a somewhat uneasy synthesis, with traditional Christian attitudes.

Petrarch's unfinished *Memorable Matters,* written between 1343 and 1345, was planned as a systematic and comprehensive account of the four cardinal virtues, illustrated by classical, medieval and contemporary *exempla.* Of this ambitious programme, however, only one-quarter was actually carried out: what we have deals exclusively with prudence and its triple role as the memory of the past, the knowledge of the present and the foreknowledge of the future. We do not know what authorities Petrarch would have invoked to illustrate justice, courage and temperance.

The main interest of the text translated here resides in the fact that it is the first defence of Epicurus written by a Renaissance author. Petrarch was far from an enthusiastic supporter of Epicurus, regarding with contempt his belief that pleasure was the highest good and condemning the subordination of virtue to pleasure which this entailed. Yet Petrarch, as a careful and sensitive reader of Seneca, recognized that many of the statements of Epicurus quoted by the Roman Stoic were of considerable ethical value and not without relevance to his own moral struggles – no matter who had originally spoken them. Petrarch even devised ways of adapting Epicurus's maxims to a Christian context. In this way, he initiated the trend – later developed by Lorenzo Valla, Francesco Filelfo, Erasmus and Francisco de Quevedo – of transforming Epicureanism into a philosophy which was broadly compatible with Christianity.

For the Latin text see Petrarch, *Rerum memorandarum libri,* ed G. Billanovich (Florence, 1943), pp. 166–9. The notes to this translation are heavily indebted to the exemplary commentary of Billanovich.

Memorable Matters

Book III, Chapter 77

Epicurus

Now let Epicurus stand amidst his enemies. Everyone tears him to pieces; everyone cries out against him; everyone attacks him; every philosophical school conspires

229

against him – and quite rightly, too! For he is the man about whom Cineas said to Fabricius: 'He has placed the highest good in pleasure in the same way as he would bury a piece of gold in mud.'[1] He even made virtue itself subject to pleasure, as if placing the lady of the house under the control of a dirty little maid; and he stated that every single action men perform should be measured according to the standard of pleasure. What an unmanly creed this is, and what a disreputable one, too, which does not see the slightest difference between man and beast.

But if we could approve of some of the maxims of haughty emperors and kings, why should we not also applaud some of the sayings uttered by a philosopher, albeit an infamous one? For Epicurus expressed so many wise thoughts in so many sweet words that even the great Seneca deemed it appropriate to cram and adorn his *Letters* with them. Leaving aside what is known to everyone, I decided to turn to these, rather than to the author's writings themselves, and to put together some reflections of a more elevated moral character, regardless of what may have been said in the others. They are 'all the more noteworthy', as Seneca himself says, 'because it is surprising that brave words should be spoken by a man who made himself an advocate of effeminacy'.[2] And again:

I think we ought to do in philosophy as they are accustomed to do in the Senate: when someone has made a motion, of which I approve to a certain extent, I ask him to make his motion in two parts, and I vote. For this reason I am all the more glad to repeat the distinguished words of Epicurus, in order that those who have recourse to them through a bad motive, who think that they will serve as screens for their own vices, should acknowledge that, wherever they turn, they must live honourably.[3]

So much for Seneca's fine characterization of Epicurus. I now turn to the man himself about whom we are speaking.

'I have never sought to cater to the crowd', says Epicurus.[4] No Stoic, no Peripatetic could devise anything more manly, more high-minded, more worthy of a wise man. Nor does the reason he adduces carry less weight: 'For the things I know are not approved of by the crowd, while the things they approve of are unknown to me.'[5] Marvellous, if only this was said by a lover of virtue, not of pleasure! For the crowd always loves the latter, while it hates the former. Indeed, what is it that you claim yourself ignorant of, Epicurus? Are you not the only one among all the troops of philosophers to defend the madness common among the masses and to recommend in your sober lectures the very things that unlearned sots belch forth in their cups? But let us disregard the man and assume that whatever he said was said by someone else.

Epicurus says: 'If you live according to nature, you will never be poor; if you live according to opinion, you will never be rich.'[6] Since I myself have experienced both these riches and this poverty, I am in a better position than most to appreciate the truth of this statement. It is my armour against the attacks of my friends, whenever they reproach me for my sloth or my lack of ambition: they say that with only a little effort I could have risen to a higher position and accuse me of consciously despising a fate that was offering me more than I was willing to accept. I truly need eternal patience when they take eternal pleasure in upbraiding me. I hardened my ears when they would not hold back their tongues, and I clad myself in callousness in order to avoid suffering from the wounds caused by their words or getting angry with them in the purity of my faith.[7] But, unless I am mistaken, I can assure those who admonish me with perverse and unholy counsel of one thing: their efforts are futile. The more I advance in years, the more firmly I cling to my resolutions. I feel neither shame nor guilt at my career; on the contrary, I feel pity and disgust at the sight of the foolishness of my friends, whom neither time, nor reason, nor just and friendly admonition, nor example, nor shame, nor loathing, nor fear, nor the proximity of death can call away from the error of their ways. I would be delighted if I could speak in this way about myself to my friends, but since I am unable to give satisfaction to every single one of them without great difficulty, let me tell all of them at once to keep their mouths shut, to mind their own business and to cease, for my own good, to be concerned about my own good. I have decided with Epicurus to scorn fashionable opinions and to follow nature instead, for it promises riches without sorrow or disturbance. Indeed, how could I possibly change when I am not even aware of having sinned in this way? Rather, I would rejoice in this error – if it is an error – and be proud of it, which is the very opposite of contrition, without which the sinner hopes in vain for salvation. Therefore, one cannot but admire the wealth of wisdom contained in the following saying of Epicurus: 'The knowledge of sin is the beginning of salvation.'[8]

I find myself similarly unable to pass over the following saying from the same source which Seneca enjoins us to engrave on our hearts: 'Choose some man of high character and keep him ever before your eyes, living as if he were watching you, and ordering all your actions as if he beheld them.'[9] In another passage, speaking of this imaginary witness, Epicurus put forward his own name: 'For you should do everything as if Epicurus were watching you.'[10] Commenting on both these passages, Seneca recommends choosing Scipio or Cato or, if Cato should seem to be too severe, Laelius;[11] in short, someone whose speech, manners and integrity are a source of pleasure to you. Thus, Epicurus's suggestion has been taken up in a most congenial and profitable way by Seneca. For there can be no doubt that the intervention of illustrious men – or, failing this, the very memory of them – acts as a curb on the soul, preventing it from rushing headlong into the abyss of sins that beset it from all sides. Whenever a person who has become acquainted with this mental exercise starts to slide towards sin, the recollection will bring about a feeling of shame, and he will be held back as if someone were physically present. Not only will his actions blush, but his thoughts will blush as well. Thus, the disturbances of our soul will be appeased, and our imagination will create the witness whom nature has denied us and introduce him into the innermost recesses of our heart. As for me, I welcome both Cato and Laelius and, above all, Scipio. But since we ought now to ask our own kind [that is, Christians] for advice, choose a John or an Antony for yourself. If their saintliness seems too harsh,[12] choose one of those who, having experienced both sin and forgiveness, has learnt to pray for the sinners: Paul or Augustine, whose unwavering virtue and whose judgement are beyond suspicion.[13] Yet what need have we of these figments of the imagination, we who revere neither silent statues – those man-made idols – nor hollow spectres, nor the impious shadows of thieves and adulterers, but rather worship the one truly immortal God who lives without end? It will be enough for us to remember that he is present at all our actions and all our thoughts, not only as a witness, but as a judge in whom supreme justice and supreme mercy are invested.

There are many more sublime sayings by Epicurus which it would take too long and be utterly pointless to list in detail. There is, however, one rule that applies to all of them: while we like the judgement expressed, we dislike the author expressing it. It may well be true that, as Cicero puts it, 'he was a good man, polite and humane',[14] but no one would maintain that he was a good philosopher – no one, that is, who has not been brought up in the same school of pleasure. For he may well overflow with the most celebrated sayings, but he directs them all, as I have said, towards the most unworthy end.

Translator's Notes

1. See Cicero, *De senectute* 13.43; Valerius Maximus, *Facta et dicta memorabilia* IV.3.6.
2. Seneca, *Epistulae* XXXIII.2. Here and in other quotations from Seneca's *Epistulae* I have followed, often with slight modifications, the translation of R. M. Gummere, 3 vols. (London, 1917–25).
3. Seneca, *Epistulae* XXI.9.
4. Seneca, *Epistulae* XXIX.10 = *Epicurea,* ed. H. Usener (Leipzig, 1887), fragment 187.
5. Seneca, *Epistulae* XXIX.10–11.
6. Seneca, *Epistulae* XVI.7 = *Epicurea,* ed. Usener, fragment 201.
7. Cf. Psalms 94:8; 56:5.
8. Seneca, *Epistulae* XXVIII.9 = *Epicurea,* ed. Usener, fragment 522.
9. Seneca, *Epistulae* XI.8 = *Epicurea,* ed. Usener, fragment 210.
10. Seneca, *Epistulae* XXV.5 = *Epicurea,* ed. Usener, fragment 211.
11. Seneca, *Epistulae* XI.10; XXV.6. The Roman general Scipio Africanus (236–184 BC) was the subject of Petrarch's unfinished Latin epic poem, the *Africa;* both he and Marcus Porcius Cato (234–149 BC) were highly regarded for their exemplary behaviour, especially by the Stoics. The Roman statesman Gaius Laelius (c. 190–after 129 BC) was named Sapiens (The Wise) on account of his Stoic learning.
12. St John the Baptist and St Antony of Egypt both lived as hermits in the desert and were renowned for their severe asceticism.
13. St Paul was a Pharisee who persecuted Christians before his conversion on the road to Damascus (Acts 9:1–19, 22:5–6, 26:12–18). St Augustine, in his autobiographical *Confessions,* presents an exceptionally vivid account of his sinful past before his baptism in 387, when he was in his thirties.
14. Cicero, *De finibus* II.25.80.

Further Reading

CHRP, pp. 15, 36–7, 59–60, 62–3, 81, 105, 115, 123, 125–30, 176–7, 306, 321, 361, 364, 368, 378, 411–16, 420, 545–6, 557–8, 644–5, 672, 727, 730, 747–8, 771, 779, 786, 831

Foster, K., *Petrarch: Poet and Humanist* (Edinburgh, 1984)

Kristeller, P. O., *Eight Philosophers of the Italian Renaissance* (Stanford, Calif., 1964), pp. 1–18 ('Petrarch')

Mann, N., *Petrarch* (Oxford, 1984)

Petrarch, *Remedies for Fortune Fair and Foul: A Modern English Translation of 'De remediis utriusque fortunae',* trans. and comment. C. H. Rawski, 5 vols. (Bloomington, Ind., 1991)

Rabil, A., ed., *Renaissance Humanism: Foundations, Forms, and Legacy,* 3 vols. (Philadelphia, 1988), I, pp. 71–137 ('Petrarch and the Humanist Traditions')

Trinkaus, C., 'Petrarch and Classical Philosophy', in *Francesco Petrarca: Citizen of the World. Proceedings of the World Petrarch Congress, Washington, DC, 1974,* ed. A. S. Bernardo (Albany, N.Y., 1980), pp. 249–74

21

Francesco Filelfo

Luc Deitz

Introduction

The Italian humanist Francesco Filelfo (1398–1481) was born in Tolentino, in the Marches, and spent his early years studying in Padua and Venice. From 1421 to 1427 he was in Constantinople, where he acquired a Byzantine wife, an impressive haul of manuscripts of Greek classical works and a solid knowledge of the Greek language. On his return to Italy, he taught first in Bologna and then moved, in 1429, to Florence, from which he was exiled in 1434 because of his quarrels with Cosimo de' Medici. After a four-year stint at the University of Siena, Filelfo moved to Milan, where he was based for the rest of his long life, aside from a brief period (1475–6) as a highly paid lecturer at the Sapienza in Rome. His long-desired return to Florence was finally achieved in 1481, just a few weeks before his death. Filelfo wrote poetry in Latin, Greek and Italian, produced a number of Latin translations of Greek works (including Xenophon's *Cyropaidea,* the pseudo-Aristotelian *Rhetorica ad Alexandrum* and various writings by Plutarch) and was the author of prose dialogues and treatises respected for their humanist erudition and their impressive display of classical Latin style.

Filelfo's Latin correspondence is composed of letters of three kinds: first, those addressed to his peers and colleagues, which discuss matters of ephemeral and anecdotal interest; second, those addressed to princes and patrons, which mostly consist of general reflections on the course of human affairs; and third, those mainly written for posterity, which discuss literary or philosophical issues and are meant to be showpieces of their author's learning and mastery of the Latin language.

The letter to Bartolomeo Fracanzano belongs to the third group. Its addressee – a Benedictine monk, who seems to have taken his vows shortly before this letter was written – would be completely unknown to us but for this and two other letters (dated 5 and 31 December 1428) which Filelfo wrote to him. Filelfo's concern in sending them was evidently not the welfare of his correspondent, but the defence of Epicurus and his theory of pleasure. Although Filelfo states, wrongly, that Epicurus upheld a distinction between bodily and spiritual pleasure, what is important is his insistence on the fact that pleasure is not an evil per se for the Christian.

For the Latin text of the letter see Francesco Filelfo, *Epistolarum familiarium libri XXXVII* (Venice, 1502), f. 6ʳ. Whenever a reading printed in an earlier edition has seemed preferable, this has been recorded in the notes. A partial edition of the Latin text can also be found in D. Robin, *Filelfo in Milan: Writings 1451–1477* (Princeton, N.J., 1991), pp. 174–5.

A Letter to Bartolomeo Fracanzano

Francesco Filelfo to Bartolomeo Fracanzano: Greetings.

The most eminent philosophers have taught that there are three types of life which men ought to seek above all: the contemplative, the active and the pleasurable.[1] The contemplative life belongs solely to the rational soul; its guide is wisdom. The active life is mainly of service to the body; it is ruled and governed by prudence. The life, however, that strives for enjoyment is connected with pleasure, whose nature is difficult to ascertain. This is not surprising, since it is beleaguered by valiant assailants. Indeed, the person who declares that pleasure is completely alien to reason is no better than a feeble brute. The kind of pleasure which conforms to decency is, in my opinion, hardly inferior to decency itself: it is a question of correctly deciding what kind of pleasure is true and Christian. Such pleasure is founded and established in that calm composure of the mind that is free from torments, free from disturbing passions and free from unsettling emotions. The Greeks call this state of the mind *alupia,* which we could conveniently translate into Latin as *indolentia* [freedom from pain].

There are, however, people who insinuate that pleasure is only related to the body and that it is also a shameful thing; as if, when we say, 'Your letter gave me extraordinary pleasure', we were to mean by this that it was not our mind that was filled with joy, but our body – and shamefully, to boot. Let us firmly reject all these perverse explanations, for pleasure is related both to the mind and to the body. Nor does the word *voluptas* [pleasure] have any other meaning in Latin than *hēdone* in Greek. *Hēdone,* too, is experienced both by the mind and by the body; and it can be respectable or disgraceful according to the degree of thoughtfulness or thoughtlessness involved. Moreover, Aristotle ranks pleasure, just like prudence and virtue, among the goods of the mind.[2] Besides, I do not think that the objections raised against Epicurus are well-founded. It is said that he was addicted to pleasure, lewd and lascivious, whereas it is an established fact that he was sober, learned and venerable. The only flaw, in my view, that one might find in his character is that he scoffed at the other philosophers too frequently and too abrasively.[3] Be this as it may, there can be no doubt that this man referred to and expounded the pleasure not of the body, but of the mind.

But let us not dwell on Epicurus and on the other philosophers of those old and primitive times who had no knowledge whatever of the true God. I for my part am of the opinion that the kind of pleasure which is praiseworthy and eminently desirable is that which results from understanding the truth and leading an entirely respectable life. Truth, I believe, has its dwelling-place among those things that are unchangeable and eternal. What else could this be except the one and immortal God? I am certainly unable to conceive of any other possibility.

Accordingly, our actions should, I think, be adjusted to the understanding of the truth in such a way that we never lose sight of the fact that they are all subject to the authority of wisdom. Wisdom alone, like a queen or an empress, rests contentedly in itself and has given up all concern for lower and temporal things in order to be able to direct her eyes towards the light of that highest good, and never to let them stray again. Wisdom has set prudence over the other moral virtues in order that it should, like a steward, dispense to everyone in any given circumstance knowledge of the action required of him in accordance with his position. Therefore, it is necessary that we subject all the moral virtues to prudence, the virtue of the rational soul. Again, prudence is governed by wisdom, which, taken as a whole, is identical with reason.[4]

Now, if someone were to live such a life,[5] anyone who would dare to deny that this person not only leads the most pleasurable life of all, but is also perfectly blessed and happy, would, in my opinion, have to be considered not merely stupid, but positively idiotic and insane. For there could not conceivably be any obstacle that would prevent such a person from always being his own master. Not only would he never be subject to any kind of disgrace, he would always think, speak and act in a becoming way.

I therefore congratulate you, my dear Fracanzano, on the very commendable decisions you have made for your life. You submit yourself to the rule of the contemplative life in such a way that you never shrink from the virtues of sustained action, or indeed from the moral virtues, so that your life does not lose its unity.[6] You help everyone else with your advice and your support in the same way as you help yourself; and you consider it to be your greatest pleasure to let everyone who chooses to be a man rather than a beast share in your goodness. Whenever I hear these reports about you – and not a single day passes without some of them reaching me – I am filled, on account of our long-standing friendship, with such overflowing joy that I seem to be in a state of rapture and to walk on air.

Assuming that more time is given us, do you think that we shall be able to meet? Since it is impossible to do so at the moment, it will require either your kindness or your sense of duty to remove our physical separation entirely by an exchange of letters. This will be, for both of us, not only an easy task, but a very pleasurable one as well. Farewell. Bologna, 1 August 1428.

Translator's Notes

1. See, e.g., Aristotle, *Nicomachean Ethics* I.5.
2. See Aristotle, *Nicomachean Ethics* VII.12–15; X.1–5.
3. Diogenes Laertius, *Lives of the Philosophers* X.1–34, esp. 7–8. Filelfo owned a manuscript of Diogenes Laertius: see his Greek letter to Giovanni Aurispa dated 9 January 1431. The first complete Latin translation of this text was not finished until 1433; see M. Gigante, 'Ambrogio Traversari interprete di Diogene Laerzio', in G. C. Garfagnini, ed., *Ambrogio Traversari nel VI centenario della nascita* (Florence, 1988), pp. 367–459, at 371–2.
4. See Aristotle, *Nicomachean Ethics* VI.12 (1145^a6–9).
5. Reading *vixerit* (found in the 1485 and 1492 editions) for *vinxerit*.
6. Reading *quin* (in the 1485 and 1492 editions) for *qui*.

Further Reading

Allen, D. C., 'The rehabilitation of Epicurus and his theory of pleasure in the early Renaissance', *Studies in Philology*, 41 (1944), 1–15

CHRP, pp. 329, 382, 728, 817–18

Francesco Filelfo nel quinto centenario della morte. Atti del XVII convegno di studi maceratesi (Tolentino . . . 1981) (Padua, 1986)

Jones, H., *The Epicurean Tradition* (London, 1989), ch. 6, esp. pp. 148–50

Rosmini, C. de, *Vita di Francesco Filelfo da Tolentino,* 3 vols. (Milan, 1808)

Saitta, G., *Il pensiero italiano nell'Umanesimo e nel Rinascimento,* 2nd ed., 3 vols. (Florence, 1961), I, pp. 186–9

Sheppard, L. A., 'A fifteenth-century humanist, Francesco Filelfo', *The Library,* ser. 4, 16 (1935), 1–26

22

Cosma Raimondi

MARTIN DAVIES

Introduction

Very little is known about Cosma Raimondi. He calls himself a native of Cremona in Lombardy and a pupil of the well-known humanist teacher Gasparino Barzizza, probably at Milan in the 1420s. His life seems to have been dogged by ill fortune: he was forced to seek employment abroad, as a teacher of law at Avignon, where he appears to have emigrated about 1430. His efforts to return to a post in the Milanese dominion were rebuffed, and he hanged himself in 1436.

His only significant work, apart from decipherment of the newly discovered manuscript of Cicero's rhetorical works (1421), is the epistolary treatise in defence of Epicurus translated here. It is addressed to an unknown Ambrogio Tignosi, perhaps a student at the Milanese university at Pavia, and seems to date from before Raimondi's departure for France, probably about 1429. Its importance lies in the fact that it is the only thoroughgoing espousal of Epicurean ethical doctrine of the Quattrocento, preceding not only the widespread dissemination of the ancient sources on Epicureanism (Book X of Diogenes Laertius's *Lives of the Philosophers* and *De rerum natura* of Lucretius) but also the popular dialogue of Lorenzo Valla, *On Pleasure* (1431). Raimondi argues for a human good, one which takes account of the whole parcel of body and mind which we are; and he finds it in the pleasure (*voluptas*) of Epicurus, a pleasure not opposed to virtue but both guided and produced by it. Neither the barren end-in-itself virtue of the Stoics nor disembodied Peripatetic contemplation can bring the tranquillity which Raimondi supposes, with Epicurus, to be the true end of human life. This refinement of the crude and widespread notion of Epicurus the voluptuary represents a long step towards recovery of the historical figure.

For the Latin text of Raimondi's letter see my critical edition in 'Cosma Raimondi's defence of Epicurus', *Rinascimento,* 27 (1987), 123–39.

A Letter to Ambrogio Tignosi in Defence of Epicurus against the Stoics, Academics and Peripatetics

I have very little leisure at the moment to argue my views on the subject which your letters raise, being taken up with more weighty and much more difficult matters – I do not mind saying that I am very much occupied with my studies in astrology. But since I have always followed and wholly approved the authority and doctrine of Epicurus, the very wisest of men, and now see his standing bitterly attacked, harassed and distorted by you, I have taken it upon myself to defend him. It is only right that tried and true pupils (as I have proved myself in all fields of learning) should defend their master's teaching when it is attacked. Otherwise when teachers are criticized, the pupil's studies may themselves seem to be under attack: the great pains you have taken to gather material against Epicurus seem directed not so much at refuting him but me, his follower and disciple. But I shall pay you back as you deserve.

It is not just a dispute between ourselves, for all the ancient philosophers, principally the three sects of Academics, Stoics and Aristotelians, declared war to the death against this one man who was the master of them all. Their onslaught sought to leave no place for him in philosophy and to declare all his opinions invalid – in my view, because they were envious at seeing so many more pupils taking themselves to the school of Epicurus than to their own. So I shall now set about doing within the limits of a letter what I had meant to do at greater length elsewhere and defend him as fully as I can. And if the defence appears rather long-winded, it might well seem too short when you consider that debate on this topic could fill not just a longish letter but thick books. The subject – what is the supreme good – is important and difficult; and it requires lengthy exposition: it is an investigation that attracted a good deal of discussion among the ancients, and many books survive on either side of the question.

To show how unjustly you have attacked Epicurus and to make plain what he thinks is our ultimate goal, I shall therefore begin by treating the topic in some depth. Then I shall answer your letter and explain the whole matter in such a manner that you may actually be glad to return to the Epicurean camp you abandoned. Those who are not involved will say that it would be better first to refute the opponent's position and then state one's own. Yet the subject is so complex and obscure that I think it will perhaps be granted that we should first explain it as a whole, so that it becomes clearer what it is we are seeking.

Epicurus is criticized, then, because he is thought to have taken too effeminate a view on what the supreme good is, by identifying it with pleasure and using that as the standard to measure everything else. But the more closely I consider the proposition, the more right it seems to be, as though it were something decreed not by a man but by Apollo or some sort of higher being. Epicurus scrutinized the force of nature in everything and grasped that nature has made and formed us in such a way that nothing suits us more than having and keeping our bodies sound and whole and remaining free from afflictions of mind or body. And so he laid down that the supreme good was located in pleasure. And how wise he was! What more can be said on the matter? What else can human happiness consist of? A man whose soul is in turmoil cannot be happy, no more than someone whose body is in pain can fail to be miserable. In case anyone thinks I am unaware of the temper of the times in which I discuss such things, I wish it to be understood that I am not now considering that absolute and true philosophy which we call theology. This entire enquiry concerns the human good of humankind and the various competing views of ancient philosophers on the matter.

Though this was Epicurus's judgement, the Stoics took a different view, arguing that happiness was to be found in virtue alone. For them the wise man would still be happy even if he were being tortured by the cruellest butchers. This is a position I most emphatically reject. What could be more absurd than to call a man 'happy' when he is in fact utterly miserable? What could be sillier than to say that the man being roasted in the bull of Phalaris,[1] and subject to the most extreme torment, was not wretched? How again could you be further from any sort of happiness than to lack all or most of the things that themselves make up happiness? The Stoics think that someone who is starving and lame and afflicted with all the other disadvantages of health or external circumstances is nonetheless in a state of perfect felicity as long as he can display his virtue. All their books praise and celebrate the famous Marcus Regulus for his courage under torture.[2] For my part I think that Regulus or anyone else, even someone utterly virtuous and constant, of the utmost innocence and integrity, who is being roasted in the bull of Phalaris or who is exiled from his country or afflicted quite undeservedly with misfortunes even more bitter, can be accounted not simply not happy but truly unhappy, and all the more so because the great and prominent virtue that should have led to a happier outcome has instead proved so disastrous for them.

If we were indeed composed solely of a mind, I should be inclined to call Regulus 'happy' and entertain the Stoic view that we should find happiness in virtue alone. But since we are composed of a mind *and* a body, why do they leave out of the account of human happiness something that is part of mankind and properly pertains to it? Why do they consider only the mind and neglect the body, when the body houses the mind and is the other half of what man is? If you are seeking the totality of something made up of various parts, and yet some part is missing, I cannot think it perfect and complete. We use the term 'human', I take it, to refer to a being with both a mind and a body. And in the same way that the body is not to be thought healthy when some part of it is sick, so man himself cannot be thought happy if he is suffering in some part of himself. As for their assigning happiness to the mind alone on the grounds that it is in some sense the master and ruler of man's body, it is quite absurd to disregard the body when the mind itself often depends on the state and condition of the body and indeed can do nothing without it. Should we not deride someone we saw sitting on a throne and calling himself a king when he had no courtiers or servants? Should we think someone a fine prince whose servants were slovenly and misshapen? Yet those who would separate the mind from the body in defining human happiness and think that someone whose body is being savaged and tortured may still be happy are just as ludicrous.

I find it surprising that these clever Stoics did not remember when they were investigating the subject that they themselves were men. Their conclusions came not from what human nature demanded but from what they could contrive in argument. Some of them, in my view, placed so much reliance on their ingenuity and facility in debate that they did not concern themselves with what was actually relevant to the enquiry. They were carried away instead by their enthusiasm for intellectual display and tended to write what was merely novel and surprising – things we might aspire to but not ones we should spend any effort in attaining. Then there were some rather cantankerous individuals who thought that we should only aim for what they themselves could imitate or lay claim to. Nature had produced some boorish and inhuman philosophers whose senses had been dulled or cut off altogether, ones who took no pleasure in anything; and these people laid down that the rest of mankind should avoid what their own natural severity and austerity shrank from. Others subsequently entered the debate, men of great and various intellectual abilities, who all delivered a view on what constituted the supreme good according to their own individual disposition. But in the middle of all this error and confusion, Epicurus finally appeared to correct and amend the mistakes of the older philosophers and put forward his own true and certain teaching on happiness.

Now that the Stoics have, I hope, been comprehensively refuted, I shall set about confirming his views as clearly as I can, which will at the same time rebut those of the Peripatetics and of the Academics too. On these last, though, I shall not need to dwell at length, as for them everything is uncertain. What sort of philosophy is it that denies that anything is certain? I do not think that even the Academics themselves understood what they were saying. If the Stoics are madmen, the Academics seem to me quite insane.[3]

There remain the Peripatetics, and they are more difficult to refute. Not only do they have a standard of certainty, but they argue in such a way that there seems to be some substance to what they are saying. But these philosophers too have in my judgement gone wholly astray. That will be more clearly grasped later on, once I have explained the main points of Epicurean doctrine. It will then be apparent to everyone that any others who lay claim to supremacy in philosophy and try to dislodge Epicurus from that position are utterly wrong, and that Epicurus's teaching on happiness is entirely correct.

To show that this is so, there is no better place to begin than with nature herself, the sole mistress and teacher of everyone, whose judgement on each and every matter we must take to be absolutely true. When she was fashioning man, she polished her creation with so many little touches that he seems to have been made purely for enjoyment and to take advantage of every sort of pleasure. She endowed him with senses so distinct, varied and useful that though there were many different types of pleasure, there was none in which he could not share. First she gave him eyes, whose outstanding characteristic is that they shrink from looking on anything ugly or disgusting. We love to look at things of beauty, and not by any conscious or rational decision but because nature impels us to do so. Which of us, even if we are hurrying off elsewhere, does not stop to look if we catch a glimpse of some attractive sight? This effect is so marked that I think man would have been a poor thing indeed if nature had taken away from him the ability to gaze on all the many lovely and beautiful objects she had created. Is there anyone, again, who does not thoroughly enjoy hearing singing and the sweet sounds of music? The lyre and other such instruments seem to have been invented for the specific purpose of charming our souls. The same can be said of smell and the other senses, which the mind uses as its servants in sensing and grasping pleasure. I do not see what sort of pleasure can be found without the aid of the senses, unless perhaps it lies in study of the deep mysteries of the universe, which I do not deny can be a source of great mental delight. Of all the pleasures that there are, in fact, this is the greatest; and this is where the Peripatetics see true felicity, in examining and contemplating those hidden things which are most worth knowing. But our enquiry is into man as a whole, and not just a part of him: the Peripatetic thinker, no matter how profound, cannot be happy without external and bodily goods.[4]

Epicurus was right, then, to call pleasure the supreme good, since we are so constituted as almost to seem designed for that purpose. We also have a certain inherent mental disposition to seek and attain pleasure: as far as we can, we try to be happy and not sad. No one who ponders how much nature has produced for the sake of man alone, the quantity and copiousness and variety of her bounty, can doubt that pleasure is the greatest of all goods and that it should direct all our aims. We see a vast array of fine things on land and sea. Many of them are necessary to support life, but most are simply pleasurable – they are of such a sort that nothing but pleasure is to be gained from them. Nature would certainly not have created such objects of pleasure had it not intended man to enjoy them and concern himself with them.

The passions and activities of mankind themselves make plain that everything is done for the sake of pleasure. Why on earth should we spend anxious nights and days involved in such great struggles to find and keep what we need for daily life unless we were sustained by the hope that some day we should be able to live a life of pleasure and enjoyment? If that hope were gone, our minds would be decidedly less inclined to take those pains and less keen and steadfast in enduring them. Why are scholarship and the disciplines of arts and letters thought so desirable unless there is some special natural enjoyment in acquiring them, besides the help they afford in gaining the wherewithal to pass our lives in pleasure? Nor should we be so keen on honours and glory, on kingdoms and empires, to acquire and defend which great battles and disputes often arise, if these were not objects of the utmost delight. Decisions on war and peace alike are taken on the basis of keeping, protecting and increasing those things by which we live and in which we take pleasure.

Virtue, finally, is both the cause and guide of pleasure: it constrains us and warns us that we should pursue each thing within those same limits by which virtue itself is circumscribed. Why then should virtue be desired if not to allow us to lead an enjoyable life by avoiding those pleasures we should not seek and seeking those we should? If virtue brings no pleasure or delight, why should we want it or make so much of it? But if it does, why not concede that the greatest of all goods – what we should seek above all – is that for the sake of which virtue itself is desirable? We can see that man's whole constitution is geared towards the perception of pleasure, that nature carries us towards it, that a great many important things exist for the sake of pleasure, that all our actions are measured against its standard so that in the end our lives may be free of care, in short that everything is desired purely on account of the pleasure it will give us. In these circumstances, now that Epicurus's case has been conclusively proved by these rigorous and convincing arguments, who could still be so hostile to him as not to assent to his doctrine and admit that the highest felicity is to be found in pleasure?

But the Peripatetics do deny his doctrine and cannot bear the thought that pleasure is the supreme good, placing it rather in virtue. I should like to ask them: if virtue itself is going to bring in its train sadness, grief, pain and fear, is it still to be desired? That, I think, they will not agree to. Since, then, virtue is sought for the tranquillity it brings to life (in which, under the name of pleasure, Epicurus identified the supreme good), again I ask the Peripatetics why they are unwilling to place the greatest good in pleasure. If perhaps some think that by this Epicurus meant that we should spend our days wallowing in feasting and drinking, in gambling, games and the pleasures of sex, such a wastrel Epicurus would hardly deserve our praise. His teaching would indeed be lamentable if he wanted us to be gluttonous, drunken, debauched, boastful and promiscuous. But that is not what Epicurus in his wisdom said or recommended. In fact, so far was he from wanting us to live without virtue that virtue is actually essential for living up to his teaching, since it constrains and directs, as it were, all the bodily senses (as we argued already) and does not permit us to make use of them except when needed. Epicurus does not slide into pleasure in the manner of animals, without the exercise of judgement and when necessity does not require it, but rather enjoys it with restraint when it is right to do so. His theories, therefore, should not be neglected, nor should they be treated as condemned; and it is clear that the Peripatetics have not sufficiently understood what it is they are saying.

I have run through these matters briefly and cursorily even though I do not suppose they necessarily respond to your letter directly. The discussion here will have answered it in full measure, or very largely. Yet I should still like to complete this refutation by touching on each single point you raise. You think that we should not let pleasure direct all our aims. That, I think, has been demolished at length, and with some elegance, by what I have said: it has been shown that pleasure is the standard to which everything must be referred. As for your adding that Epicurus likened us to animals,[5] in that you seem to be not merely not attacking him but actually supporting his case. Since pleasure is endowed with such power that it is sought even by animals – brutes bereft of reason whose impulses are entirely guided by nature – Epicurus could draw from that fact the very firm conclusion that what all beings seek is the greatest of all goods. When I wrote that the severe Catos of old would on occasion take ample refreshment of wine, and you thought that a matter for criticism, it is in fact wholly admirable if a sage (as the Catos were taken to be)[6] sometimes engages in conviviality of a rather exuberant sort. Your following remarks, whose drift is that if we embrace Epicurus we should be obliged to live like beasts, have, I think, been dealt with by what I said before: since Epicurus does not suppose that life should be lived without virtue, I do not think he leads the life of animals. So he is not to be shunned like some traitor who would overthrow or pervert human society. He does not corrupt public morals; his whole doctrine is instead directed at making us as happy as we can be.

You must at length give up your attacks on Epicurus, then: reform yourself and return to the camp in which you once fought with distinction. You have now turned against him, under the spell of Stoic subtlety of argument and seduced by the majesty and splendour of the Academics and Peripatetics. But you may be forgiven for that, since you are a younger man not yet of an age to form a proper judgement on these very difficult matters, with the indulgence granted to youth. But now that you have been fully instructed in the arguments of Epicurus, if you persevere in your hostility towards him, you will be thought intolerably arrogant, and not a little stupid.

Turn then to embrace Epicurus, whose teaching I shall perhaps expound at more length if ever I have greater leisure (this letter took me just two days to write, though I fear it may still be rather prolix). Shortage of time did not allow me to pursue all those aspects of the controversy which I feel could still benefit from clear exposition and discussion. I have had to leave many important points untouched, which someone who wanted to take an opposing view could seize upon to rebut my arguments, either from disinterested love of truth or as an intellectual exercise. And that is not something which I should find unwelcome: I encourage any one who wants to contribute to the debate to enter the fray.

You have had a pretty long letter which sets out the whole truth about Epicurus. You must either find it convincing or refute it by contrary arguments, so that if you come up with something better, I in turn may be persuaded by that. Farewell.

Translator's Notes

1. Phalaris was a sixth-century BC Sicilian tyrant who killed his victims by roasting them in a brazen bull.
2. Marcus Regulus was a Roman general captured by the Carthaginians, who was supposedly tortured to death on his return from a mission to Rome, where he advised his countrymen against peace with his captors (c. 250 BC). The examples of Phalaris and Regulus are used *against* Epicurus by Cicero, *In Pisonem,* 42–3, to which this passage is an answer.
3. Raimondi has in mind such thinkers as Arcesilaus (third century BC), founder of the New Academy, which derived its radical Scepticism from the tradition of Socrates.
4. See Aristotle, *Nicomachean Ethics* X.7 (1177^a20–1) and X.8 (1178^b33–5).
5. Epicurus pointed to the animals to show that the primary aim of all creatures was pleasure (*hēdone*): see *Epicurea,* ed. H. Usener (Leipzig, 1887), fragment 398.
6. Both Cato the Censor (Marcus Porcius Cato; 234–149 BC) and his great-grandson and namesake, Cato of Utica (95–46 BC), were noted for their severe Stoic morality.

Further Reading

CHRP, pp. 361–2, 381–2

Garin, E., *La cultura filosofica del Rinascimento italiano* (Florence, 1979), pp. 72–92

Jones, H., *The Epicurean Tradition* (London, 1989), ch. 6, esp. pp. 150–2

Saitta, G., *Il pensiero italiano nell'umanesimo e nel Rinascimento,* 3 vols. (Bologna, 1949–51), I, pp. 233–6

Santini, G., 'Cosma Raimondi umanista ed epicureo', *Studi storici* [Pisa], 8 (1899), 153–68

23

Francisco de Quevedo

Luc Deitz and Adelheid Wiehe-Deitz

Introduction

The *Defence of Epicurus against Commonly Held Opinions* was originally intended as an introduction to Quevedo's *Stoic Doctrine* (see Chapter 19). The earliest draft of the treatise consisted of little more than a string of quotations about Epicurus and Epicureanism taken from the works of the Roman Stoic Seneca.[1] The sympathetic treatment accorded to Epicurus by Seneca formed the basis of Quevedo's view that the authentic principles of Epicureanism, as opposed to the slanderous misrepresentations of this philosophical system put forward by certain classical authors, were fundamentally the same as those of Senecan Stoicism. It was for this reason that Quevedo regarded a defence of Epicurus against his detractors as an appropriate way to introduce his detailed account of Stoic philosophy.

In expanding the draft to its present state, Quevedo added material from a number of authorities – classical, Christian and contemporary – to the Senecan core of the treatise: Juvenal, Petronius, Diogenes Laertius, Sextus Empiricus, Jerome, Augustine, Francisco Sánchez de las Brozas and Michel de Montaigne are cited as witnesses for the defence by Quevedo. His purpose throughout is to undermine the 'commonly held opinions' about Epicurus and his sect which had circulated since antiquity and which had so damaged the reputation of his philosophy. He tackles the widely held view that Epicureans were shameless hedonists, single-mindedly devoted to bodily pleasures, by referring to the many testimonies to Epicurus's almost saintly abstemiousness and his incredible bravery in the face of painful illnesses. He shows, moreover, that virtue was the necessary concomitant to Epicurean pleasure and that Epicurus aimed to convince his disciples that happiness was the result of controlling and limiting, rather than indulging, their desires. In addition, he maintains that the notoriety associated with Epicureanism was due to the behaviour of those who claimed to be adherents of the philosophy but who in reality distorted and perverted the tenets laid down by its founder.

Just as Quevedo, following in the footsteps of Justus Lipsius, attempted to demonstrate in his *Stoic Doctrine* that Stoicism was in large measure compatible with Christianity, so in this work he makes a similar case for Epicureanism, arguing that the bad name which Epicureanism had always enjoyed among Church Fathers was the result of the inaccurate and spiteful reports found in classical authors such as Cicero (whom Quevedo regarded as more of a lawyer – a profession which he despised – than a philosopher). Quevedo maintains, for instance, that Epicurus did not actually deny divine providence nor was he opposed to the immortality of the soul. Epicureanism was, of course, a pagan system of thought and therefore inevitably inferior to Christianity. But, like Stoicism, it contained much that was admirable and that could be utilized by present-day Christians.

For the Spanish text see Francisco de Quevedo, *Defensa de Epicuro contra la común opinion,* ed. E. Acosta Méndez (Madrid, 1986); the introductory essay (esp. pp. L–LXX) offers the most comprehensive account to date of Quevedo's attempts to make Epicurus acceptable to a

Catholic public. The text is also published in Francisco de Quevedo, *Obras completas,* 3rd ed., ed. L. Astrana Marín and F. Buendía, 2 vols. (Madrid, 1945), I, pp. 879–91.

Defence of Epicurus against Commonly Held Opinions

There remains the defence of Epicurus. I am not conducting it myself; I am rather giving an account of the defence put forward by great men. In this case, too, I am not the first to take pity on his name. Arnaud printed such a defence in the book which he called *Pastimes;* but he left some things out, so that I will not waste my time if I now write a defence of my own.[2]

It is not the fault of the moderns if they think of Epicurus as a glutton and use his name as a synonym for debauchery and shameless lasciviousness; this was the commonly held opinion before Seneca. Despicable wickedness characterized those who first made his name synonymous with depravity, thus setting the tone for those who would necessarily follow them in later times. It is easier to believe that other people have a bad reputation than to establish it, and – what is worse – something is always added along the way. Diogenes Laertius says that Diotimus the Stoic forged many scandalous and slanderous books out of sheer jealousy and that he ascribed others to Epicurus and published them in order to discredit his school.[3] There are few people who, when they hear others being vilified, would not accept a little of the vilification they hear and believe it to be true. This was the fate of Epicurus in relation to other philosophers – due to the intervention of ignominy and jealousy.

Epicurus placed happiness in pleasure and pleasure in virtue, which is such a Stoic doctrine that even the absence of this label does not render it unrecognizable. He freed the attention of his disciples from the stranglehold of the sophists' dialectic, as if it were a load of rubbish; and if he mentioned dialectic, he did so only because in the classroom it is a large and important part of theology. This rejection of dialectic (by which one should understand that of the sophists), which was the greatest source of pride for other philosophers, was the reason why Epicurus was loathed and discredited.

In the first fragment of Petronius Arbiter, Epicurus's position is defended most eloquently (those who compel me to translate his words lose a great deal):

These things might be endured if they smoothed the path of aspirants to oratory. But nowadays, the sole result of this bombastic matter and this noise of empty phrases is that, when they step into a court, they think that they have been carried into another world. I therefore believe that schools make complete fools of young men because they see and hear nothing of ordinary life there.[4]

A few elegant voices are raised in defence of this view; let us listen to a voice that is elegant, eminently learned and sacred. St Jerome writes in his *Commentary on the Epistle of St Paul to Titus:* 'The dialecticians, whose prince is Aristotle, are used to traps composed of arguments and to restraining the rambling freedom of rhetoric in the thickets of their syllogisms. If this is the occupation of those whose own proper skill is controversy, what must a Christian do, if not avoid controversy?'[5] St Ambrose in the *Hexameron:* 'In the same way that the water (as they say) is able to remain above the firmament while the firmament revolves, so dialectic is full of cunning. Give me something to which I can reply, for if you do not give it to me, I shall not answer a single word.'⁶ St Augustine, in his *Against the Grammarian Cresconius:* 'This skill which they call dialectic does nothing but demonstrate, with the help of the conclusion, either truth for the sake of truths, or falsehood for the sake of falsehoods.'⁷ St Ambrose, *On Faith, to Gratianus:* 'The heretics found the whole power of their poison in the art of dialectic, which is considered by the philosophers to be an art that has no capacity to foster studies, but only to destroy them.'⁸ There were no other philosophers besides the Epicureans who would have maintained that dialectic destroys learning rather than fostering it.

So, because Epicurus rightly rejected the dialectic of the sophists and because all philosophers were outraged by the truth he proclaimed, they used the word pleasure, on which he grounded happiness, to discredit the most sober and severe of philosophers, without mentioning the virtue which he said was the foundation of pleasure.

That Epicurus said that there is no pleasure without virtue is stated by Seneca in Book IV, chapter 2 of his *On Benefits:* 'Virtue is the handmaid of pleasures; there can be no pleasure without virtue.'⁹ The same is found in his book *On the Happy Life,* chapter 12: 'It is not Epicurus who has driven them to debauchery, but they, having previously surrendered themselves to vice, hide their debauchery in the lap of philosophy and flock to the place where they may hear the praise of pleasure, and they are not after this pleasure of Epicurus – for, in all truth, this is what I think – because it is sober and abstemious.'¹⁰ And in chapter 13: 'Personally I hold the opinion – I shall express it even though the multitude may protest – that the teachings of Epicurus are upright and holy and, if you consider them closely, austere.'¹¹

How sublime these words are in the mouth of our Seneca! With what high esteem do they vindicate Epicurus! With what just indignation do they rouse us against those ignoramuses who slandered his name! And in particular against Cleomedes (an author whose memory should be damned) for the book in which he called Epicurus the 'Thersites of philosophers'.¹² While studying, to his own discredit, every opprobrium he can voice against the great philosopher, he wastes his ink in digressions born of envy. While this useless Greek author treats Epicurus so ignominiously, Lucretius, giving comfort to man in view of his inevitable death by pointing out that princes and wise men have to die as well, says in his verses by way of the ultimate praise of the power of death: 'Epicurus himself died when he had finished the course of his life, he whose intellect surpassed the whole of humankind, who outshone all the others just as the heavenly sun outshines the stars.'¹³

My beloved Juvenal, who, in my opinion, wrote (and not without care) about politics in verse in a number of satires – for this kind of philosophy demands the satirical rather than the hortatory genre, since the good is more often to be found in that which one does not do rather than in that which one does – when he attacks gluttony and debauchery, sets up Epicurus as the most perfect example of sobriety and abstinence: 'And one who neither reads the Cynics, nor studies the doctrines of the Stoics – who are distinguished from the Cynics only by their cloaks – nor of Epicurus, contented with the vegetables in his humble garden.'¹⁴ And in his fourteenth *Satire:* 'If anyone should ask me what measure of fortune is enough, I will tell him: as much as thirst, cold and hunger demand; as much as satisfied you, Epicurus, in your little garden.'[15] It is an established fact that Epicurus lived on a diet of water and herbs. In one of his letters, which is quoted by Diogenes Laertius, he says that he is sustained by bread and water and that he requires only a morsel of cheese for a treat.[16] Pliny says that he was the first to introduce gardens into the city.[17]

Seneca lavishes the warmest praise on Epicurus, and he deserves credit for the fact that he does not speak of him in the fourteenth chapter of his book *On the Happy Life* in the way that the useless and raving Cleomedes does: 'I do not say, as do most of our school, that the sect of Epicurus is an academy of vice, but this is what I say – it has a bad name, is of ill repute, and yet undeservedly.'[18] Seneca knew what Diogenes Laertius related in his life of Epicurus in the following words: 'Diotimus the Stoic abhorred him so much that he viciously slandered him by publishing five hundred lascivious and scandalous letters as if they were written by Epicurus, as well as ascribing to him those that are attributed to Chrysippus.'[19]

At all times there have been infamous men who preferred to slander the famous instead of becoming famous themselves, infamous as they were. We have already seen this in the case of Epicurus; in the case of Homer, it was true of Zoilus, who would have been the vilest of ignoramuses if Julius Scaliger, who followed him, and other abominable idiots who followed Scaliger, had not surpassed him in opprobrium.[20]

What supreme spite it is to make Epicurus's name a synonym for depravity instead of virtue, for debauchery instead of self-restraint, for gluttony instead of abstinence, for drunkenness instead of sobriety, for reprehensible pleasures instead of a melancholy retreat into studies devoted to the teaching of an honourable doctrine! Many learned men, many saints and Church Fathers understood his name in this way – not because Epicurus was debauched and depraved, but only because his name had become a synonym for depravity and debauchery. It was not they who were ignorant; the fault lay with those who, with their slanders, were at the origin of this rumour.

Seneca, whose words all great men take over into their writings like so many gems, took over Epicurus's words into his own works, where we see them sparkling like stars. Among Epicurus's writings, Cicero said of the one called *Kanon* that it was a book which has fallen from heaven.[21] He wrote so many books that Diogenes Laertius said that it was impossible to count them and that their number surpassed those of all other philosophers.[22] All the titles of his works are useful, modest and – insofar as it is permitted to say such a thing of a pagan – saintly. Among other works, he wrote a book called *On Preferring and Avoiding,*[23] which contains the whole of Stoic teaching and which Epictetus summed up in the two words *sustine et abstine* [bear and forbear].[24] This prompted Seneca to say in the thirtieth chapter of his book *On the Happy Life:* 'In this matter the two sects, the Epicureans and the Stoics, are at variance, but they both direct us to leisure by a different road. Epicurus says: "The wise man will not engage in public affairs except in an emergency." Zeno says: "The wise man will engage in public affairs unless something prevents him." The one valued leisure on account of its purpose, the other on account of its cause.'[25] Both Zeno and Epicurus felt sorry for the wise man when they burdened him with political responsibilities. It seems that he cannot get involved in politics without running a risk: public posts are coveted by the crafty rather than by the wise.

Epicurus can be found more often in Seneca's works than Socrates, Plato, Aristotle and Zeno. Seneca is very fond of quoting him and gives the reason for this in his eighth *Letter:* 'It may be that you will ask me why I quote so many of Epicurus's noble words instead of words taken from our own school. But why should you regard these sayings as belonging to Epicurus, and not as common property? Many poets say what has been said or what should have been said by philosophers.'[26] This is why Seneca quotes him in twenty letters whenever he needs help with the ethical matters with which he deals. He says in the seventh *Letter:* 'It was not the classroom of Epicurus that improved Metrodorus, Hermarchus and Polyaenus (these great men!), but their daily dealings with him.'[27] A telling praise of the life of Epicurus: to improve by example rather than by teaching.

In the ninth *Letter,* he states that Epicurus said: 'If someone does not regard what he possesses as sufficient wealth, he is unhappy, though he be the master of the whole world.'[28] Can anyone but a wise man utter such words? Anyone but a good man perform such deeds? In the twelfth *Letter:* 'You say that Epicurus said: "Why do you trouble yourself with another's property?" Whatever is true is my property; I shall continue to introduce you to Epicurus.'[29] Those whom Seneca wants to improve he helps by means of Epicurus.

In the thirteenth *Letter:* 'What is more shameful than the old man who starts to live? I would not have added the author of this maxim if it had not been taken from the sayings of Epicurus, which I pride myself on praising and on making my own.'[30] Magnificent Seneca! You pride yourself on that which improves you, and you name the unknown author of the maxim which makes you famous. You are what one so rarely finds: an honest and learned man.

In the eighteenth *Letter:* 'That teacher of pleasure, Epicurus, used to observe certain special days during which he barely satisfied his hunger in order to see whether he thereby fell short of full and complete happiness, and by what amount, and whether this amount was worth compensating at the price of great effort. Metrodorus, who had not attained the same degree of perfection, spent less than tuppence on his entire living expenses.'[31] Such behaviour is more characteristic of fasting than of stuffing oneself. It shows Epicurus and Metrodorus as penitents rather than as revellers.

And in the nineteenth *Letter:* 'According to the necessities of our argument, we have to seek the help of Epicurus, who says: "You must reflect carefully beforehand with whom you are to eat and drink, rather that what you eat and drink."'[32] He wants to be sure about the manners of his company before he satisfies his appetite at table.

Twenty-first *Letter:*

I shall mention the example of Epicurus. He was writing to Idomeneus and trying to recall him from the broad path (this is how I understand the text – neither a showy [*speciosa*] life [*vita*] nor a showy path [*via*], but a broad [*spaciosa*] path) to stable and permanent fame. Idomeneus was at that time an austere minister of state and involved in important affairs. He said to him: 'If you are attracted by fame, my letters will make you more famous than all these things which you cherish and for which you are cherished.' Did he perhaps tell a lie? Who would have known of Idomeneus had not Epicurus made him famous with his letters? All these magistrates and satraps, and even the king himself, from whom Idomeneus sought this title, are buried under deep oblivion.[33]

It is a powerful virtue which, with one single letter, recalls a tyrant from the abuse of power to the safe fame of virtue, and which, with one sentence in which he is named, bestows on him the renown that his own king could not preserve from oblivion.

In the same *Letter:* 'It is to him that Epicurus addressed that noteworthy saying, urging him to make Pythocles rich, but not in the vulgar and dubious way. If you wish, said he, to make Pythocles rich, you must not add to his wealth, but subtract from his desires.'[34] What a great soul – and a marvellously learned one – to give birth to such judicious thoughts! What human mind could bring such honest wealth to the spirit without the light of faith? Our Seneca was full of admiration for these words, for he says in what follows: 'This saying is so clear that it needs no interpreter; so learned that it needs no effort [to be understood].'[35] And a couple of lines further down, Seneca says with reference to Cleomedes and other such owls who are unable to see this light of Epicurus: 'For this reason I am all the more glad to refer to the admirable sayings of Epicurus, in order that those who take refuge in this reviled name, having been led by a bad motive and thinking that they will have a screen for their own vices, should learn that, no matter what school they follow, they must live honourably.'[36]

It is with this very aim in mind that I am relating all the sayings of Epicurus; it is with this same aim in mind that I am defending him. My wish is that no one should seek refuge for his own shamelessness in such an admirable man: I am claiming back from the power of vice the admirable achievement that springs from virtue. A man of such elevated character could not be completely given over to abominations. Nor was he given over to them – reprehension was his concern, upbraiding was his concern. In the twenty-third *Letter:* 'I can answer you with a saying of your friend Epicurus and thus ennoble this letter: "It is bothersome always to be beginning life." Or another, which will perhaps express this meaning better: "They live badly who are always beginning to live."'[37] These words could not gush forth from a throat stuffed with food and drink; they are not open to interpretations justifying gluttony. Whoever said that those persons lived badly who always began to live could not live like someone who does not think that he himself will die.

In the twenty-fourth *Letter:* Epicurus upbraids those who crave, as much as those who shrink from, death: 'What is so absurd as to seek death, when it is through fear of death that you rob your life of peace?'[38] In a few words and with the utmost elegance Epicurus rejects the opinion of certain Stoics (which we will be discussing),[39] who maintained that the wise man can and should inflict death upon himself. Seneca forgot that he was quoting these words against his own interest. But rather than a failure of memory this is an excess of candour. He did not refuse to quote the truth even when it went against his own interest. By maintaining that the wise man must inflict death upon himself, he proved himself to be a Stoic, and by contradicting himself, he proved himself to be a good Stoic. Magnificent Seneca, how well you are able to hit the mark, even when you contradict yourself!

In the twenty-fifth *Letter:* 'Nature craves only bread and water. No one is poor according to this standard; when a man has limited his desires within these bounds, he can challenge the happiness of Jupiter himself, as Epicurus says. I will insert some other saying of his in this letter: "Do everything," he says, "as if someone were watching you."'[40]

And some lines further down: 'Epicurus suggests the same: "The time when you should most of all withdraw into yourself is when you are forced to be in a crowd."'[41] When he was on his own, Epicurus knew that within himself his conscience and above himself God were witnesses of his actions. He wanted men to behave on their own just as if they were watched by everyone. He recommended as the most important kind of solitude the one that is to be found in the midst of the crowd. No one before Epicurus said that the best hermit was the one who knew how to be alone when surrounded by people.

In the forty-sixth *Letter,* treating of a book that Lucilius had sent him, he says by way of high praise: 'Quam disertus fuerit ex hoc intelligas licet, levis mihi visus est, cum esset nec mei, nec tui temporis, sed qui primo aspectu, aut Titi Livii, aut Epicuri posset videri' [You may understand from this fact how learned I thought it was; for it seemed to be written in the smooth style, and yet did not resemble my time or yours, but at first sight might have been ascribed to Livy or to Epicurus].[42] I have transcribed the Latin words since they cannot stand as they do, as every scholar with some degree of intelligence will see. I read and emend as follows: 'Brevis mihi visus est, nec esse mei, nec tui temporis' [It seemed to be written in the brief style, neither being of my time nor of yours]. This reading is confirmed by the *sed* which indicates that, by comparison, he judges the book worthy of Livy or Epicurus. For *levis mihi visus est,* I read *brevis:* the best sign of a book's being good is that it seems to be short; and the mistake is easily accounted for. This is the translation of the passage as I have read it: 'You may understand from this fact how learned I thought your book was; for it seemed to be brief, neither of your time nor of mine, but at first sight might have been ascribed to Livy or Epicurus.' What an abiding tribute to the lofty spirit of Lucilius, which allows us to know the sublimity of Epicurus's style, since, in Seneca's own judgement of its rhetorical qualities, it ranks directly after Livy.

In the fifty-fourth *Letter,* Epicurus says:

There are certain men who have worked their way to the truth without anyone else's assistance, carving out their passage by themselves for the benefit of themselves. [Epicurus] gives special praise to these men, for their impulse has come from within, and they have forged to the front by themselves. There are others who need outside help, who will not proceed unless someone leads the way, but who will follow faithfully. Metrodorus was one of these, he says.[43]

Epicurus does not waste words on anything other than virtue, the virtuous and the truth.

In the sixty-seventh *Letter:*

I will show you in the writings of Epicurus a division of goods just like our own. For there are some goods, he declares, which he prefers should fall to his lot, such as bodily rest free from all inconvenience and relaxation of the soul as it takes delight in the contemplation of its own goods. And there are other things which, though he would prefer that they did not happen, he nevertheless praises and approves – for example, the absence of good health, to which I have already alluded, and the suffering resulting from excruciating pain and disabling illnesses in which Epicurus found himself on that last and most blessed day of his life. For he tells us that he was suffering from his bladder and from an ulcerated stomach – so acutely that the pain did not admit of any increase, and yet he calls this 'a happy day'.[44]

Seneca considers Epicurus to be a Stoic with respect to the division of goods; I consider him to be the best of all Stoics with respect to the tolerance of the most excruciating pain. Has anyone ever – of all the days of his life – called only that day happy on which he died, overcome by intolerable pain? How was it possible to think of stomach disorders as bliss? Magnificent Epicurus neither despised death, nor was he afraid of it, and the pain led him neither to covet nor to loathe it. His acts matched his words: he died as he said one ought to die; he lived in such a way as to be able to die as he said one should. Ninety-third *Letter:* 'Furthermore, does it not seem just as incredible that any man in the midst of extreme suffering should say, "I am happy?" And yet this voice was heard in the very factory of pleasure: "Happy is this day on which I am dying," Epicurus said when bowel ulcers and the invincible pain of strangury tormented him.'[45]

The fact that Seneca refers to this action and these words of Epicurus four times in his *Letters* is not a sign of prolixity, but rather of admiration. It is not for lack of knowledge of another example; it is for lack of another example in someone other than Epicurus. It is true that he is saying the same thing, but the more frequently something is repeated, the more conviction it carries. Seneca is not content to state the fact; he comes back to it time and again in order to convince us of it. One has to repeat many times those things which a few people do from time to time and which all people ought to do frequently.

In the book *On Poverty, to Luceius,* Seneca states, in order to give it a majestic opening: 'Epicurus says that contented poverty is an honourable thing.'[46] Could Epicurus say anything more honourable? Could one hear anything with greater satisfaction? Seneca quotes Epicurus in many other passages which I will leave aside, in order to prevent these notes from turning into a book. Besides, what has been said of Epicurus by Diogenes Laertius, Seneca, Petronius and Juvenal shows his great erudition, his praiseworthy virtue, his sublime eloquence, his rich poverty, his abstinence and perseverance, and at the same time provides the reason why other philosophers were jealous of him to the point of inventing scandalous and slanderous books and publishing them under the name of Epicurus.

It was sufficient to name Seneca to produce a strong defence of Epicurus. I have produced an even stronger defence by relating his doctrine and his words as they are quoted by Seneca. The authority of the lord of Montaigne will conclude this defence. The work which he wrote in French and whose title is *Essais* or *Discourses* is such a great book that anyone who neglects to read Seneca and Plutarch because he has seen this book will nonetheless read Plutarch and Seneca. In Book II, chapter 11, 'Of Cruelty':

For it seems that virtue presupposes difficulty and opposition, and cannot be exercised without a struggle. That is doubtless why we can call God good, mighty, bountiful and just, but we cannot call him virtuous: his works are his properties and cost him no struggle. Among the philosophers take the Stoics, and even more so the Epicureans – and I borrow that 'even more so' from the common opinion, which is wrong, despite the clever retort which Arcesilaus made to that philosopher who reproached him with the fact that many people crossed over from his school to the Epicurean one, but never the other way round: 'I am sure that is so', he said; 'you can make plenty of cocks into capons, but never capons into cocks' – for in truth the Epicurean school in no wise yields to the Stoic in firmness of opinion and rigour of doctrine.[47]

And in the same book, chapter 10, 'On Books': 'Plutarch holds to Plato's opinions, which are gentle and well-suited to public life; Seneca's opinions are Stoic and Epicurean, farther from common practice, but in my judgement more suited to the individual and firmer.'[48]

Cicero, in the first book of his *De natura deorum,* enjoins that Epicurus should be revered. These are his words: 'He alone was the first to see that there are gods whose reason, power and usefulness we can learn about from his heavenly book *On the Rule and the Judgement* [that is, the *Kanon*].'[49] And in Book I of his *Tusculan Disputations,* he said: 'Not only Epicureans, whom I do not despise; rather, I do not know why they are despised by learned men.'[50] The severe Lord of Montaigne judges that in truth, rigour and firmness the doctrine of Epicurus is equal to that of the Stoics. He does not say that the former surpasses the latter – not because such a claim is untrue, but because it was not easy to believe. He says that Plutarch was a Platonist and that his opinions are opposed to those held by the Stoics and the Epicureans. In this way he explains why such an eminent man as Plutarch opposed the Stoics with such vehemence: he was a victim of the passions of his own sect.

It has been my endeavour to discharge myself of the promise I made – namely, to introduce the *Stoic Doctrine.*[51] The sect is outside commonly accepted feelings, or rather, opposed to them; the terms with which it expresses itself are unfamiliar to the common mind, more elevated than what the ear can perceive. This is why Seneca says in his thirteenth *Letter:* 'I am not speaking with you in the Stoic language, but in another, lower style.'[52] The language of truth is not only different, it is a foreign tongue; it is bitter (let it be known!) and is not studied, but rather feared. This is the language in which Epictetus wrote, this is the language in which Epicurus wrote – not in the one used by those who, knowing themselves to be guilty of disobeying the language of truth, accused him of debauchery and drunkenness. It was the vile idolatrous philosophers who slandered him. Seneca admired him, indeed truly admired him. Thus, whoever does not believe and does not follow the great Cordovan [that is, Seneca] in this respect heaps disgrace on him. It is not I who defend Epicurus (for such a thing would be beyond my powers). I am joining in his defence because I could not believe that it was an error for such an admirable philosopher to have been a follower of Epicurus.

Epicurus's faults were those of a pagan, not those of an animal. On account of the former, he was condemned by the Christians; the latter were attributed to him by the envious. And since the doctors of the Church found him already singled out as someone commonly and proverbially used as a synonym for vice, they pointed at him as an object of scandal. St Peter Chrysologus, *Sermo* 5: 'They give themselves up to Epicurus, the foremost author of despair and luxuriousness.'[53] It is commonly held that he denied the immortality of the soul. This abominable error could be inferred neither from his life nor from his words nor from the fact that he called the day on which he died happy, while being tortured by immense pain. His death is instead a proof of the contrary, according to the description given by the Holy Spirit in the Book of Wisdom of those who do not believe in another life.[54] The man without God is characterized by the fact that he enjoys all [earthly] pleasures and joys because he does not believe that any others exist; whereas not enjoying any pleasures, refraining from all of them and calling the day of one's death happy characterizes those who believe in another life.

They accuse him of denying divine providence. I treat this matter in the book which I call *Historia teologética, política de la divina providencia.*[55] It may be that he was mistaken in this respect, but the great Church Father Augustine gives the reason for it in his book *The Eighty-Three Questions,* where he proves that the mind in a state of blindness is unable to see God: 'Just as the eyesight, when it is impaired, concludes that that which it cannot see does not exist (for the presence of an image within the eyes is useless when they suffer from cataracts), God, who is everywhere, cannot be seen by those souls who suffer from mental blindness.'[56] This is why Epicurus could not see God and his Providence: his mind was unable to see that vision which faith allows us to see. And because it is through God's compassion that we are in possession of the light which he and all other pagan philosophers were lacking, let us praise them for what they saw rather than criticize them for what they failed to see. When passing sentence on him, we will not slander his memory if we contradict his writings.

Let us listen to what Aelian has to say of Epicurus in Book IV of his *De varia historia,* under the title 'A saying of Epicurus, and his happiness': 'Epicurus of [the deme of] Gargettus said: "Whoever is not satisfied with little is satisfied with nothing." The same Epicurus said that he would dare to compete with the happiness of Jupiter when he had water and bread. Since these were the feelings of Epicurus, we shall say some other time what he had in mind when he praises pleasure.'[57] Aelian does not omit anything that speaks in Epicurus's defence; and although he does not specify, as he promises to do, what kind of pleasure he was speaking of, this can be gathered from many passages in Cicero. *De natura deorum,* Book I: 'We Epicureans place the happy life in tranquillity of the soul and freedom from all obligations.'[58] And in the third book of the *Tusculan Disputations:* 'Epicurus says a pleasurable life is impossible unless accompanied by virtue; he says that fortune has no power over the wise man; he prefers a plain to a rich diet; he says there is no season when the wise man is not happy.'[59] And in the first book of the *Tusculan Disputations:* 'Crowds of opponents are coming, not merely Epicureans – whom for my part I do not despise, though somehow or other all the best philosophers are contemptuous of them.'[60]

I am surprised at Cicero's surprise in the second book of his *De finibus:* 'Epicurus always says that the wise man is happy: his desires are kept within bounds; death he disregards; he has a true conception, untainted by fear, of the immortal gods; he does not hesitate to depart from life, if that would better his condition. Thus equipped, he enjoys perpetual pleasure.'[61] And in *De finibus,* Book II: 'Epicurus denies (for this is your strong point) that anyone who does not live morally can live pleasantly.'[62] And in the [fifth] book of the *Tusculan Disputations:* 'Not without reason did Epicurus venture to say that the wise man always has the enjoyment of many goods because he always has pleasure.'[63] And in the third book of the *Tusculan Disputations,* Cicero says, speaking about the *Principal Doctrine* on providence for which Epicurus was attacked: 'Indeed, Epicurus was perfectly right to speak the following words: "whatever is eternal and blessed knows no trouble itself nor causes trouble to any other."'[64] If there is to be some truth in these words, we must adapt them to the holy Catholic faith by understanding that God, although he looks after everything, remains unaffected and unperturbed by the entirety of his providence. He does not suffer any embarrassment or awkwardness, all of which are defects which men call movements, affections and perturbations.

I am fully aware of the fact that Cicero also indicted Epicurus on many charges and contradicted many of his opinions. It was not unheard of for Cicero to contradict himself, as Quintilian says in Book III, chapter [18]: 'Even Cicero is a little at odds with himself in this matter.'[65] But, with the respect due to such a great man, I dare say that Cicero was very interested in [Epicurus's] opinions and that he showed in his defence the ethical indifference of a lawyer who, for a price, not only excuses crimes but also defends virtues and merits. Besides, it is beyond dispute that Cicero's philosophical books show him to be a lawyer rather than a man of discernment. Anyone who reads him will forgive me on the basis of what he reads and will see that these words flow less from my own quill than from Cicero's. In the first book of *De natura deorum,* he says: 'Indeed, I do not understand why Epicurus chose to say that the gods were similar to men rather than that men were similar to the gods.'[66] I find it surprising that Cicero did not understand a problem which any ignoramus is able to solve, as I can verify in my own case. The reason was that since the nature of God can neither be seen nor grasped nor understood, whereas the nature of man can be seen and understood, the rules of scientific observation demanded that the unknown should be explained by the known. For this is how we understand; the contrary view [that is, that the known should be explained by the unknown] was an oft-repeated axiom devoid of reason. It is Christian to say: 'It is through created things that we can see things perceptible to the mind.'[67] This is what the Catholic Church teaches us with its sacred adoration of God the Father and of the Holy Spirit and of the souls and angels, whom it depicts in human likeness in order to enable our senses to grasp the incomprehensible according to our mode of understanding.

In another passage Cicero says that he is appalled that Homer prefers to depict the gods in the likeness of men rather than men in the likeness of gods.[68] Since Cicero repeats this warning (as he sees it), he was either presumptuous or else determined to make us believe it – something difficult to achieve even for his elegant powers of persuasion.

I am not the one who provides Epicurus with his claim to fame. I am merely relating the descriptions of his learning that I find written in the works of the greatest men among the pagans. Diogenes Laertius, Aelian, Seneca and Cicero were the first to investigate these accounts so diligently. In our times it was Arnaud.[69] And I am now joining this group as the sixth member: since I cannot add any authority to this defence of Epicurus, I increase the number of those who have undertaken it by one. Let me, however, add two things which I would wish the reader to consider. First, in order to attack the doctrine of Epicurus, Cicero in some passages uses those writings which Epicurus's envious slanderers circulated under his name with the help of forged letters. Second, one frequently reads that the Epicureans were banned from several republics, but never that Epicurus himself had to go into exile. On the contrary, Cicero says that his memory was held in such veneration that his picture was worn on rings;[70] and Diogenes Laertius states that they erected statues in his honour and commemorated his name with celebrations.[71]

This is the reason why Epicurus called virtue pleasure: in order to lure people effortlessly to virtue, for pleasure is a word that stirs up greater sympathy in our natures than virtue or the authority of philosophy. The dissolute (who were identical with the exiled Epicureans) assembled when they heard the word pleasure in order to bestow authority on their vices and deprive Epicurus of authority. They achieved this through no fault of those who made him a proverbial figure of gluttony and infamy. Exactly the same thing happened in our Spain to Juan del Encina.[72] He was an erudite and exemplary priest, prudent and pious, as his published writings reveal; in these one finds many proofs of serious erudition. The most excellent marquis of Tarifa made him one of his company when he vowed to visit Jerusalem. Not only did the marquis honour him with his protection, he also had a versified version of the journey, written by the priest Juan del Encina, published in the very book which His Excellency wrote about his journey.[73] It is only because, among all his other works in verse, del Encina published a lighter piece which he called *Nonsense*[74] that the tyranny of the populace has unjustly condemned his name to the fate of becoming a proverbial synonym for nonsense. This association is so commonly accepted that, whenever we accuse someone of foolishness, we invariably say: 'This is nonsense by Juan del Encina.' To my mind, the cases are so similar that the one can seek comfort from the other; and it can teach all of us about the injustices done to both without the slightest justification.

Clement of Alexandria, in the first book of the *Stromata,* calls Epicurus the prince of impious authors.[75] The same holds true of many passages in St Augustine.[76] But the Epicurus they were speaking about was the one whom they found to be a proverbial synonym for wickedness and for the impious doctrine that Diotimus had wrongly attached to the name of Epicurus.[77]

I'm afraid – experience has taught me this – that some people who make a living nowadays by confusing learning with the stage and whose only qualification is their proficiency in producing grimacing gesticulations will snap at me because I have dared to criticize Cicero's pretensions in philosophical matters. Let me sharpen their teeth with the following words from the *Dialogue on Orators.* (Whether Tacitus or Quintilian wrote it is a matter of dispute, for it is printed with the name of the one among the works of the other.) Speaking of Cicero, the author says as follows: 'As to his earlier speeches, they are not free from the old-fashioned blemishes. He is tedious in his introductions, long-winded in the narrative parts and wearisome in his digressions. He is slow to rouse himself and seldom warms to his work.'[78] Although these accusations are neither small in number nor insignificant, he adds many more.

These doctors in the art of abuse should ponder over the fact that if Cicero was so vulnerable to criticism in the art of oratory (which was his pride, his trade and the source of all his vanity), it does not come as a surprise that he should also be so in philosophical matters. Nor am I the only one who does not admire him in this respect. One should read Ortensio Landi in his *Paradoxes;*[79] and one should read Majoraggio when he strenuously attacks Cicero's paradoxes.[80]

And if these vinegary critics, claiming legitimacy for their lies on the basis of raising their eyebrows, had read Cicero himself, and especially the whole first book of his *About the Ends of Goods and Evils,* they would hold their tongues when they heard the following words: 'An elaborate defence of the hedonistic theory of Epicurus was once delivered by Lucius Torquatus, a student well versed in all systems of philosophy.'[81] Despite themselves, they would be forced to recognize how ancient the defence of Epicurus is and what great men have undertaken it. And if they read the whole book until the end, they would see that the defence of Epicurus, as presented by Cicero, is learned, rigorous, honest and truthful, very unlike the doctrine with which the envious men who published profligate and slanderous treatises under his name defiled themselves. And even if, in the second book, Cicero contradicts the defence of the doctrines of Epicurus attributed to Torquatus in the first, these are replies which, read with intelligence, serve only to condemn the person who makes them.

There are many references to Epicurus in the works of Sextus Empiricus. In the beginning of *Against the Professors,* he says: 'The Epicureans and the Pyrrhonists seem to belong to the same species, although they behave in different ways.'[82] And a couple of lines further down: 'In many matters Epicurus is held to be ignorant, and even in ordinary conversation his speech was not correct. The reason for this may be his hostility towards Plato and Aristotle and their like who prided themselves on their wide learning.'[83] Sextus Empiricus does not say that Epicurus was held to be ignorant because he actually was ignorant, but rather because he thought that Plato and Aristotle were ignorant.

In the same book, chapter 3, the title of which is 'What is grammar?', he begins by stating: 'Since, according to the wise Epicurus, it is not possible either to enquire or to doubt without a preconception, it will be as well first of all to consider what grammar is.'[84] And in chapter 13, he says: 'Epicurus has been detected as guilty of having filched the best of his dogmas from the poets.'[85] This he proves with the help of Homer and Epicharmus. And in the same chapter he says:

Epicurus did not take from Homer the saying that the end of intensity was pleasure. For there is a vast difference between saying that certain persons ceased eating and drinking and satisfying their appetite (for that is the meaning of: 'When they had put aside all longing for eating and drinking')[86] and saying that the end of the intensities of pleasures is the removal of what is painful.[87]

This doctrine finds a more benign expression in Sextus Empiricus than in Cicero. This was the way in which Aelian promised to state it.[88] Three lines further down, Sextus carries on: 'That death is nothing was said by Epicharmus but was proved by Epicurus. What was admirable was not the statement but the proof.'[89] In Book VII of *Against the Professors,* he says: 'They set Epicurus beside him [that is, Archelaus] as someone who rejects the study of logic. But there have been others who said that he did not reject logic as a whole but merely that of the Stoics.'[90] And in Book X, page

466: 'Epicurus declared that philosophy is an activity which secures the happy life by arguments and discussions'.[91] He did not say drunkenness or wantonness, but philosophy. These were the merits recognized by the following verse which can be read in Petronius: 'The learned Epicurus himself, the father of truth in philosophy'.[92] Although this praise is taken from Petronius, it is not invalidated.[93] Its irony, however, prompted Cleomedes to call him the inventor of truth when, as he said, Epicurus wrongly maintained that the sun is extinguished in the sea with a sizzle, just like a chandelier.[94] And yet Epicurus is so unique among the pagans that there is no other man apart from him whom these misguided souls, stained by idolatry, called the father of truth. The sheer fact that they gave him this name is a proof of their acclaim. I find the reason for this in Sextus Empiricus, *Against the Professors,* p. 197: 'like Epicurus, because those who agree about him that he has found the truth are many in number'.[95] I find that Lactantius, *De divino praemio,* Book VII, chapter 1, says the following words: 'Only Epicurus, according to Democritus, was truthful in this respect, since he says that the world had a beginning and will have an end.'[96] I know full well that he did not find the truth and that the truth is found only by those who find our lord Jesus Christ, who is the truth, the way and the life.[97] I know full well that Epicurus was not the father of truth, because I know that only God is truth, and that he is the true God from the true God. I know this through the words of the Apostle: 'Let God be found true, but every man a liar; as it is written.'[98] I condemn in Epicurus all the words and opinions that are condemned by the only true Holy Roman Catholic Church.

It is not with my own words that I defend his doctrine, which has been slandered by the envious, but with those, as they have been read, of Diogenes Laertius and L. Torquatus, with some words of Cicero, those of Aelian and with the whole work of our magnificent Seneca, with the authority of Juvenal, the elegant and admirable weight of the lord of Montaigne and the diligence of Arnaud. The interested reader should therefore note that if, in his stubbornness, he does not give back to Epicurus what is his due, he will be judging all those writers to whom I have referred to be worse than Epicurus, since he also accuses them at the same time. He should restore Epicurus to the place which he deserves in the name of venerable Seneca, whom I have used in this defence. He should revere in his writings all the majesty of pagan philosophy, for no criminal could possibly commit a more heinous crime than to unite irreverence with imbecility.

And in order to make it known that the opprobrium attached to Epicurus's name by those who slander him is of ancient date, let me quote the words with which Diogenes Laertius refutes all those whose views he reports. It was said of Epicurus that he was a drunk, that he found happiness in pleasure and that his pleasure consisted in stuffing himself with food and drink and sleeping with whores. In the beginning of Book X, Diogenes says as follows:

Sed hi profecto insaniunt [But these people (that is, the detractors of Epicurus) are stark raving mad].[99] Surely these people do not know what they are talking about. For our philosopher has an abundance of witnesses to attest to his unsurpassed goodwill towards all men: his native land, which honoured him with statues in bronze; his friends, so many in number that they filled all the cities; the disciples who never left his side, spell-bound as they were by the siren-charm of his doctrine, save Metrodorus of Stratonicea, who went over from him to Carneades, being no doubt burdened by the excessive goodness of this incomparable man; the Epicurean school itself which, while all the others have died out, continues alone through successive reigns of leaders. He showed great piety towards his parents; he was generous to his brothers and very gentle to his servants, as evidenced by the terms of his will and by the fact that they were members of the school, the most eminent of them being the aforesaid [Mys].[100] His benevolence towards all mankind was unsurpassed. No words can describe his piety towards the gods.[101]

These words are a faithful rendering of this passage in Diogenes Laertius. We can see what reasons moved our dear Seneca to praise this doctrine as much as he did and to take such pride in it. Reading the last words which describe Epicurus's piety towards the gods, I am reminded of Seneca's words in *On Benefits,* Book IV, chapter 4: 'God does not give benefits, but, free from all care and unconcerned about us, he turns his back on the world, and either does something else, or – that which Epicurus counts supreme happiness – does nothing at all.'[102] For this reason everyone is convinced that Epicurus thought that there was no providence. But if, as Diogenes Laertius said, he was observant in his piety towards the gods, it would seem that, as I have pointed out before, he did not want to say that God did nothing at all, but rather that he acted without being subjected to anxious concern or embarrassing solicitude while doing so. The way we express ourselves in Spanish teaches me this: we say of someone that he does something *sin cuidado* [without concern] when he seems to be doing nothing, because doing it is nothing to him.

These are the words of Seneca in *On Benefits,* Book IV, chapter 2: 'On this point we are in arms against the effeminate and shade-loving troop of the Epicureans. At their banquet, attended by those who philosophize about the Epicureans, virtue is the handmaid of pleasure, which she obeys and serves and sees to be above herself. "There can be no pleasure," he says, "without virtue".'[103] This sentence is not a slight against Epicurus, but against the troop of Epicureans. We have already said how different they are. I point out, however, that the Epicureans say: 'Virtue is the handmaid of pleasure.' This is what Seneca attacks. The words of Epicurus are as follows: 'There can be no pleasure without virtue.' Cicero said as much in the passage which we have already quoted.[104] It is only reasonable to infer from this that, if there can be no pleasure without virtue, the pleasure which one feels must be virtuous. Seneca, who displays greater subtlety than reliability in this passage, says against the Epicureans: 'Virtue does not exist if it is possible for her to follow; her main role is to lead, to command, to have the supreme position; you bid her to follow.'[105] And a few words further down:

The only point in question is whether virtue is the cause of the highest good, or is itself the highest good. Do you suppose that the answer to this question turns upon merely making a shift in the order? It does indeed show confusion and obvious blindness to give preference to last things over first things. But what I protest against is, not that virtue is placed second to pleasure, but that virtue is associated with pleasure at all.[106]

Let me take advantage of two passages in Aulus Gellius which fit this context very neatly. He there defends Epicurus against Plutarch, who had accused him of the same juxtaposition of terms in his syllogisms. It is legitimate to answer Seneca with the answer and the reprimand given to Plutarch for [his criticism of] the teaching of Epicurus. Aulus Gellius, Book II, chapter 8:

Plutarch, in the second book of his essay *On Homer,* asserts that Epicurus was ignorant of the [laws of the] syllogism and used it in an inconclusive manner, and he quotes Epicurus's own words: 'Death is nothing to us, for what is dissolved is without perception, and what is without perception is nothing to us.' 'Now Epicurus', says Plutarch, 'omitted what he ought to have stated as his major premise, that death is a dissolution of body and soul, and then, to prove something else, he goes on to use the very premise that he had omitted, as if it had been stated and conceded. But this syllogism', says Plutarch, 'cannot validly conclude, unless that premise is first presented.' What Plutarch wrote as to the form and sequence of a syllogism is true enough; for if you wish to argue and reason according to the teaching of the schools, you ought to say: 'Death is the dissolution of soul and body; but what is dissolved is without perception; and what is without perception is nothing to us.' We cannot, however, suppose that Epicurus, being the man he was, omitted that part of the syllogism through ignorance, or that it was his intention to state a syllogism complete in all its members and limitations, as is done in the school of the logicians; but rather, since the separation of body and soul by death is self-evident, he of course did not think it necessary to call attention to what was perfectly obvious to everyone. For the same reason, too, he put the conclusion of the syllogism, not at the end, but at the beginning; for who does not see that this also was not due to ignorance? In the writings of Plato too you will often find faulty syllogisms.[107]

And in chapter 9, Aulus Gellius says as follows:

In the same book, Plutarch finds fault with Epicurus once again for using an inappropriate word and giving it an incorrect meaning. Now Epicurus wrote as follows: 'The definition of the utmost height of pleasure is the removal of every pain.' He ought not to have said 'of every pain', but 'of everything that is painful and distressing'; for it is the removal of pain, he explains, that should be indicated, not of that which causes pain. In bringing this charge against Epicurus Plutarch is splitting hairs almost with frigidity; for far from fancying such verbal meticulousness and such refinements of diction, Epicurus condemns them.[108]

These are the words of Aulus Gellius. They constitute my answer to the strong opposition of our Seneca to the Epicureans, and they add another name to the list of champions of Epicurus from antiquity.

I observe that Seneca, speaking of the troop of Epicureans, calls them *delicata et umbratica* [effeminate and cloistered],[109] which are terms of abuse, as can be seen from Petronius: *Nondum umbraticus doctor ingenia deleverat* [No cloistered pedant had yet ruined their brains].[110] As for Epicurus himself, we have already seen that Seneca calls him a wise man and his teachings holy.[111]

Lactantius says in Book III, chapter 7, of *De falsa sapientia:* 'Epicurus maintained that the highest good consisted in the pleasure of the soul; Aristippus maintained that it consisted in the pleasure of the body.'[112] Thanks to this passage, we know that Epicurus did not place happiness in the pleasure of the body. Apparently, we have to emend this passage in Lactantius and must read 'Chrysippus' instead of 'Aristippus', for it is clear from the *Life of Epicurus* in Diogenes Laertius that he wrote lascivious and frivolous letters which Diotimus ascribed to Epicurus,[113] and that he died in a drunken stupor after having intoxicated himself.[114] On the other hand, it is true that Aristippus was an utterly contemptible character and that, according to Diogenes Laertius in his *Life,* Xenophon hated him and wrote a book against pleasure because Aristippus was a champion of pleasure[115] — which tallies with the characterization of

Lactantius, thus supporting the reading in his text, and also constitutes an argument in favour of Epicurus. But if an emendation is required, I myself would rather emend Diogenes Laertius and read 'Aristippus', thereby taking account of his known sayings and the intemperance of his actions, which correspond to those Epicurus was accused of and are not attributed to Chrysippus.

I am not the only person to think that the doctrines of the so-called Epicureans are different from those of Epicurus, and that those of the latter were admired, whereas those of the former were condemned. The eminently learned Spaniard Francisco Sánchez de las Brozas says as much in the prologue to his *Epicteto,* in which he very strenuously defends, in the following words, the teaching of Epicurus as well as his virtue, which he prefers to that of the Stoics and the Peripatetics:

Others, such as the Epicureans, maintained that since there was only birth and death, one should indulge in every physical pleasure. I would like to examine those three opinions which came closest to the truth, and then we shall see which one was followed by Epictetus. The first and best of all was that of Epicurus, the philosopher, if it is understood correctly. He was the one who placed happiness and bliss in pleasure and contentment. Aristotle refers to this tenet in Book X of the *Nicomachean Ethics* and speaks very highly of it, saying that this happiness and satisfaction are to be understood as belonging to the soul, because, he says, the gods in heaven are properly called *makares* [blissful],[116] which means very happy. Thus, it is the pleasure of the soul which is conferred by bliss. The reason why this doctrine of Epicurus earned such scorn is explained by the fact that it was misunderstood by his successors and taken to refer to the pleasures of the body, which was an insult to its inventor, because Epicurus himself was very abstemious and a man of exemplary character.[117]

Master Gonzalo Correas, in his notes on the *Tabula Cebetis,* is of the same opinion and expresses it in the following words: 'We call Epicureans the followers of Epicurus, who placed happiness in pleasure, by which he meant the pleasure of the soul, even if the common herd understood him to mean bodily pleasure.'[118]

Jean Bernaerts is a learned man and the only judicious commentator of our times. He paid attention to the meaning and the philosophical content of an author's text, while all the others busy themselves with confounding their authors with the help of manuscripts and blurring their meaning with emendations of points which, if ignored, would be completely irrelevant for the understanding of their teachings. Without paying the slightest attention to the meaning of the text, they discuss whether someone was called Liberius or Niberius or Linerius, just as if they had to give him their daughter in marriage, which merely increases the volume of their notes. In his commentary on Boethius's admirable book *On the Consolation of Philosophy,* Book III, prose 2, Bernaerts champions the following opinion concerning the innocence of Epicurus: 'Epicurus is thought to be the father of outrageous conduct. One may well ask whether this is true, since the pleasure of Epicurus refers to small and ephemeral things, and what is called virtue by us is called pleasure by him.'[119] Bernaerts answers the questions raised in this clause with the words of Seneca in *On the Happy Life,* chapter 13,[120] and he goes on to add the passage of Aelian which I have already quoted.[121]

In his letter to Johannes Sambucus, Hubert van Giffen says of the way Lucretius wrote about the soul and its relationship to pleasure and the vices:

Lucretius writes so much and with such chastity about these things [i.e., bodily pleasures and the way to hold them at bay] that Diogenes Laertius's account of Epicurus seems to correspond to the truth: that some people wrongly accused Epicurus of subjecting everything to pleasure and that those who maintained that what this great man had intended to be understood in relation to the tranquillity of the soul was to be referred to the pleasures of the body were deliberately slandering him. Our poet also deals with this subject at the beginning of Book II in verses full of elegance and splendour.[122] Again, the famous general Cassius,[123] who was a student of Epicurean philosophy, writes to Cicero: 'Those whom we call "friends of pleasure" are also friends of beauty and friends of justice, and they cultivate and hold fast to every kind of virtue'; indeed, 'it is impossible to live well without living in beauty and justice', as Cassius reminds us in the same passage, using the very words of Epicurus.[124] Although Cicero himself was very strongly opposed to this philosophical school, he nevertheless declares in many passages that the Epicureans are honest men and the least knavish of philosophers.[125]

If only a few of those people who awarded themselves academic degrees could be convinced that van Giffen is speaking with the authority that befits him, confounding the gossip which they listened to and which they sought to justify using the words of Cicero, whose statements about Epicurus contradict one another, I would not consider that I had wasted my time (though, in my opinion, it is an ungrateful task to convince academic bigwigs of their own ignorance, especially when they present their amateurishness as professionalism without having any other talent than the ability to condemn and to reprimand). If they, however, scorn the authority of so many eminent writers and stubbornly persevere in slandering Epicurus, those who scorn them in turn cannot possibly be blamed. And in my desperation to convince them, I can only recommend that they should stop blaming on Epicurus the manners that the envious Greeks ascribed to him, so that they do not inadvertently condemn their own manners, from which they may well expect prestige, but for which there is no excuse.

Licentiate Rodrigo Caro: your grace has vigorously defended the tenets of Flavius Dexter and opposed erudition to the understanding of the common herd.[126] Your own experience has taught you mercy, and you are very familiar with calumny. You will therefore expect me to defend myself from the mouths of those whose rottenness keeps them barking and biting: chasing books like bloodhounds, their recompense consists of their rage against learning, and their competence lies in the venom of their teeth. Truth, the only effective healer, kills them with a mere puff of breath.

Clement of Alexandria, *Stromata,* Book I, says: 'For I think that there is no piece of writing which is lucky enough to be of such surpassing excellence that no one ever opposes it; rather, we must reckon that those pieces of writing which no one can with justification oppose are in accordance with reason.'[127]

Whatever I have written in this book I submit to the correction of the one and only true Holy Roman Church, with Catholic devotion; and I am prepared to confess to my ignorance in everything which might not agree with the truth of the faith or might set a bad example.

Translators' Notes

1. In his copy of the first volume of the 1555 Lyons edition of Seneca's works, Quevedo carefully annotated all the references to and quotations from Epicurus; it is these passages

which he cites in the *Defence.* See H. Ettinghausen, *Francisco Quevedo and the Neostoic Movement* (Oxford, 1972), p. 45.

2. The reference is to the *Apologiae* contained in André Arnaud, *Ioci* (Avignon, 1600), pp. 169–90.
3. Diogenes Laertius, *Lives of the Philosophers* X.3.
4. Petronius, *Satyricon* 1.2–3; adapted from M. Heseltine's translation (London, 1913).
5. Jerome, *In Epistolam ad Titum* 3.9.
6. See Ambrose, *Hexameron* II.3.9.
7. See Augustine, *Contra Cresconium Donatistam* I.20.25.
8. Ambrose, *De fide* I.5.42.
9. Seneca, *De beneficiis* IV.2.1; adapted from J. W. Basore's translation (London, 1935).
10. Seneca, *De vita beata* 12.4 = *Epicurea,* ed. H. Usener (Leipzig, 1887), fragment 460; adapted from J. W. Basore's translation (London, 1932).
11. Seneca, *De vita beata* 13.1 = *Epicurea,* ed. Usener, fragment 460; adapted from Basore's translation.
12. Cleomedes, *De motu circulari* II = *Epicurea,* ed. Usener, p. 89. Thersites, the ugliest of the Greeks who sailed to Troy (Homer, *Iliad,* II.216), railed against Agamemnon until he was beaten up by Ulysses; his name is synonymous with ugliness, cowardice and meanness of spirit.
13. Lucretius, *De rerum natura* III.1042–4.
14. Juvenal, *Satires* XIII.121–3.
15. Juvenal, *Satires* XIV.316–19; G. G. Ramsay's translation (London, 1918).
16. Diogenes Laertius, *Lives of the Philosophers* X.11 = *Epicurea,* ed. Usener, fragment 182.
17. Pliny the Elder, *Natural History* XIX.51.
18. Seneca, *De vita beata* 13.2 = *Epicurea,* ed. Usener, fragment 460; adapted from Basore's translation.
19. See Diogenes Laertius, *Lives of the Philosophers* X.3.
20. Zoilus 'the Homer-basher' was a fourth-century BC philosopher belonging to the sect of the Cynics. He was particularly notorious for the bitterness of his attacks on Plato, Isocrates and Homer. Julius Caesar Scaliger was the author of *Poetices libri septem* (1561); showing little taste for, and even less understanding of, poetry, he proclaimed the superiority of Latin literature over Greek in general and of Virgil over Homer in particular.
21. Cicero, *De finibus* I.19.63 = *Epicurea,* ed. Usener, fragment 34, p. 104, line 25.
22. Diogenes Laertius, *Lives of the Philosophers* X.26.
23. See Diogenes Laertius, *Lives of the Philosophers* X.27.
24. See Aulus Gellius, *Noctes Atticae* XVII.19.6.
25. Seneca, *De otio* 3.2–3 = *Epicurea,* ed. Usener, fragment 9*; adapted from Basore's translation (London, 1932).
26. See Seneca, *Epistulae* VIII.8 = *Epicurea,* ed. Usener, fragment 199. This and the following quotations from Seneca's *Epistulae* are adapted from R. M. Gummere's translation, 3 vols. (London, 1917–28).
27. Seneca, *Epistulae* VI.6.
28. Seneca, *Epistulae* IX.20 = *Epicurea,* ed. Usener, fragment 474.
29. Seneca, *Epistulae* XII.11 = *Epicurea,* ed. Usener, fragment 487.
30. Seneca, *Epistulae* XIII.17 = *Epicurea,* ed. Usener, fragment 494.
31. See Seneca, *Epistulae* XVIII.9 = *Epicurea,* ed. Usener, fragment 158.
32. Seneca, *Epistulae* XIX.10 = *Epicurea,* ed. Usener, fragment 542.
33. See Seneca, *Epistulae* XXI.3–4 = *Epicurea,* ed. Usener, fragment 132.
34. Seneca, *Epistulae* XXI.7 = *Epicurea,* ed. Usener, fragment 135, p. 143.
35. Seneca, *Epistulae* XXI.8.
36. Seneca, *Epistulae* XXI.9.
37. Seneca, *Epistulae* XXIII.9 = *Epicurea,* ed. Usener, fragment 493.
38. Seneca, *Epistulae* XXIV.23 = *Epicurea,* ed. Usener, fragment 498.

39. The *Defence* was originally planned as an introduction to the *Stoic Doctrine* (see Chapter 19); Ettinghausen, *Francisco de Quevedo,* pp. 43–4.
40. See Seneca, *Epistulae* XXV.4–5 = *Epicurea,* ed. Usener, fragments 602, 211.
41. Seneca, *Epistulae* XXV.6 = *Epicurea,* ed. Usener, fragment 209.
42. Seneca, *Epistulae* XLVI.1.
43. See Seneca, *Epistulae* LII.3 = *Epicurea,* ed. Usener, fragment 192.
44. Seneca, *Epistulae* LXVI.47 = *Epicurea,* ed. Usener, fragment 449.
45. See Seneca, *Epistulae* XCII.25 = *Epicurea,* ed. Usener, fragment 138.
46. Pseudo-Seneca, *De paupertate* = *Epistulae* II.6 = *Epicurea,* ed. Usener, fragment 475; see Seneca, *Opera quae supersunt. Supplementum,* ed F. Haase (Leipzig, 1902), p. 56.
47. See Michel de Montaigne, *Essais* II.11; *The Complete Essays,* ed. and trans. M. A. Screech (London, 1993), pp. 472–3.
48. Montaigne, *Essais* II.10; *Complete Essays,* ed. and trans. Screech, p. 464.
49. See Cicero, *De natura deorum* I.16.43; see *Epicurea,* ed. Usener, fragment 255.
50. Cicero, *Tusculan Disputations* I.31.77. The full text and a slightly different translation of this truncated quotation are provided later in this chapter (at n. 59).
51. This sentence seems to have introduced the last paragraph of the original draft of the *Defence;* see n. 39.
52. Seneca, *Epistulae* XIII.4.
53. Petrus Chrysologus, *Sermones* 5; see J. P. Migne, ed., *Patrologia Latina,* 221 vols. (Paris, 1844–64), LII, col. 199A.
54. See Wisdom of Solomon 3:1–3: 'But the souls of the righteous are in the hand of God, and no torment shall touch them. In the eyes of the foolish they seemed to have died; And their departure was accounted to be their hurt, And their journeying away from us to be their ruin: But they are in peace.'
55. According to E. Acosta Méndez, in his edition of Francisco de Quevedo, *Defensa de Epicuro contra la común opinion* (Madrid, 1986), p. 35 n. 90, a reference to the first draft of his posthumously published *Providencia de Dios* (1713). Instead of the untestified word *teologética,* the title should perhaps read *Historia apologética.*
56. Augustine, *De diversis quaestionibus* I.12.
57. Aelian, *De varia historia* IV.13 = *Epicurea,* ed. Usener, fragments 437, 602.
58. Cicero, *De natura deorum* I.20.53.
59. Cicero, *Tusculan Disputations* III.20.49; J. E. King's translation (London, 1927).
60. Cicero, *Tusculan Disputations* I.31.77; King's translation.
61. Cicero, *De finibus* I.19.62; adapted from H. Rackham's translation (London, 1914); see *Epicurea,* ed. Usener, fragment 397, p. 273.
62. Cicero, *De finibus* II.22.70; adapted from Rackham's translation.
63. Cicero, *Tusculan Disputations* V.38.110; adapted from King's translation. Quevedo mistakenly refers to the third book.
64. This passage, in fact, comes from Cicero, *De natura deorum* I.17.45. The reference is to Epicurus, *Principal Doctrine* 1.
65. Quintilian, *Institutio oratoria* III.11.18. Quevedo mistakenly refers to chapter 13.
66. Cicero, *De natura deorum* I.32.90.
67. See Romans 1:20.
68. See Cicero, *De natura deorum* I.16.42; II.28.70.
69. See n. 2.
70. Cicero, *De finibus* V.1.3.
71. See Diogenes Laertius, *Lives of the Philosophers* X.9, 18.
72. Juan del Encina (1469–c. 1530), poet, dramatist and pioneer of the popular theatre in Renaissance Spain.
73. The reference is to D. Fadrique Enríquez de Rivera, marquis of Tarifa, *De el viaje que hize a Ierusalem; de todas las cosas que en el me pasaron* (Seville, 1606), in which del Encina's version of the *Viaje de Jerusalem* in 'coplas de arte mayor' appears on pp. 187–226.

74. See the *Disparates* in his *Cancionero* (Salamanca, 1496), ff. lvii^v–lviii^r.
75. Clement of Alexandria, *Stromata* I.1.1.2.
76. This is a general characterization rather than a specific reference to a particular passage; but see, e.g., Augustine, *Contra Academicos* III.10.23.
77. Diogenes Laertius, *Lives of the Philosophers* X.3.
78. Tacitus, *Dialogus de oratoribus* 22.3; W. Peterson's translation (London, 1914).
79. Ortensio Landi, *Paradossi, cioè, sententie fuori del comun parere, novellamente venute in luce* (Lyons, 1543).
80. M. A. Majoraggio, *Antiparadoxon libri sex, in quibus M. Tullii Ciceronis omnia paradoxa refelluntur* (Lyons, 1546).
81. Cicero, *De finibus* I.5.13; Rackham's translation. Quevedo quotes the passage in Latin.
82. Sextus Empiricus, *Adversus mathematicos* I.1 = *Epicurea*, ed. Usener, fragment 227. This and the following quotations from Sextus Empiricus are adapted from R. G. Bury's translation, 4 vols. (London, 1933–49).
83. Sextus Empiricus, *Adversus mathematicos* I.1–2 = *Epicurea*, ed. Usener, fragment 227.
84. Sextus Empiricus, *Adversus grammaticos* I.57; see *Epicurea*, ed. Usener, fragment 255, p. 188.
85. Sextus Empiricus, *Adversus grammaticos* I.273.
86. Homer, *Iliad* I.469.
87. See Sextus Empiricus, *Adversus grammaticos* I.283.
88. Aelian, *De varia historia* IV.13 = *Epicurea*, ed. Usener, fragments 437, 602.
89. See Sextus Empiricus, *Adversus grammaticos* I.284.
90. Sextus Empiricus, *Adversus logicos* I.14–15; see *Epicurea*, ed. Usener, fragment 242, p. 177.
91. Sextus Empiricus, *Adversus ethicos* 169 = *Epicurea*, ed. Usener, fragment 219. The page reference is to the editio princeps of the Greek text (Paris, 1621).
92. Petronius, *Satyricon* 132.
93. Reading *no está profanado.*
94. See Cleomedes, *De motu circulari* II.1 = *Epicurea*, ed. Usener, fragment 346b, p. 354.
95. See Sextus Empiricus, *Adversus logicos* I.328; the actual sentence, in full, runs as follows: 'If, for instance, we name Epicurus because those who agree about him that he has found the truth are many in number, why Epicurus rather than Aristotle, since those who side with the latter are no less numerous?' For the page reference see n. 91.
96. Lactantius, *De vita beata* VII.1.
97. See John 14:6: 'Jesus saith unto him, I am the way, and the truth and the life.'
98. Romans 3:4.
99. Quevedo quotes from Ambrogio Traversari's Latin translation of the *Lives of the Philosophers,* completed c. 1433.
100. Quevedo omits the name Mys, although it occurs in the Latin translation he was using.
101. Diogenes Laertius, *Lives of the Philosophers* X.9–10; adapted from R. D. Hick's translation, 2 vols. (London, 1925).
102. Seneca, *De beneficiis* IV.4.1 = *Epicurea*, ed. Usener, fragment 364; Basore's translation.
103. See Seneca, *De beneficiis* IV.2.1; adapted from Basore's translation.
104. See n. 59.
105. Seneca, *De beneficiis* IV.2.2; adapted from Basore's translation.
106. Seneca, *De beneficiis,* IV.2.3–4; Basore's translation.
107. Aulus Gellius, *Noctes Atticae* II.8.1–9; adapted from J. C. Rolfe's translation, 3 vols. (London, 1927–8).
108. Aulus Gellius, *Noctes Atticae* II.9; adapted from Rolfe's translation.
109. Seneca, *De beneficiis* IV.2.1.
110. Petronius, *Satyricon* 2; adapted from Heseltine's translation.
111. See n. 11.
112. Lactantius, *Divinae institutiones* III.7.7; see *Epicurea*, ed. Usener, fragment 452.
113. See Diogenes Laertius, *Lives of the Philosophers* X.3.

114. Diogenes Laertius, *Lives of the Philosophers* VII.184.
115. Diogenes Laertius, *Lives of the Philosophers* II.65, where a slightly different account is given.
116. See Aristotle, *Nicomachean Ethics* X.8 (1178^{b}7–9).
117. See Francisco Sánchez, *Doctrina del estoyco filosofo Epicteto* (Pamplona, 1612), ff. 6^v–7^r.
118. G. Correas, *Ortografia Kastellana, nueva i perfeta. Dirixida al Prinzipe Don Baltasar N.S. I el Manual de Epikteto, i la Tabla de Kebes, filosofos estoikos* (Salamanca, 1630), p. 115 n. 5.
119. Boethius, *De consolatione philosophiae libri quinque*, ed. and comment. J. Bernaerts (Antwerp, 1607), p. 281.
120. Seneca, *De vita beata* 13.1–2 = *Epicurea*, ed. Usener, fragment 460. See nn. 11 and 18.
121. See n. 57.
122. See Lucretius, *De rerum natura* II.20–36.
123. Gaius Cassius Longinus, the tyrannicide.
124. See Cicero, *Epistulae ad familiares* XV.19.3, and Epicurus, *Principal Doctrine* 5.
125. Lucretius, *De rerum natura libri sex*, ed. and comment. H. van Giffen (Leiden, 1595), sig. *5^{r-v}. The quotation is given in Latin by Quevedo. The commentary on Lucretius by the Flemish scholar Hubert van Giffen (Obertus Giphanius; c. 1534–1604) was first published in Antwerp in 1566. Johannes Sambucus (Janos Zsamboky; 1531–84) was a Hungarian humanist and physician.
126. The reference is to Rodrigo Caro's edition of Pseudo-Flavius Lucius Dexter, *Omnimodae historiae quae extant fragmenta* (Seville, 1627), in which Caro (to whom both Quevedo's *Stoic Doctrine* and his *Defence* are dedicated) vindicated the authenticity of the *Chronicon Dextri*. In fact, this text is a forgery by the Spanish Jesuit J. R. de la Higuera (1538–1611), who himself wrote the manuscript of the lost chronicle. It was published after his death by the Franciscan J. Calderón (Saragossa, 1619), but was almost immediately suspected of being a fake. Dexter's authorship was attacked with much venom and erudition by Gabriel Pennot in his *Generalis totitus ordinis clericorum canonicorum historia tripartita* (Rome, 1624), pp. 168–173 (Book I, chapter 52: 'De fragmento assertae historiae Lucij Dextri Sancti Paciani filij Iudicium'). For the text of the *Chronicon*, see Migne, ed., *Patrologia Latina*, XXXI, cols. 49–572.
127. Clement of Alexandria, *Stromata* I.1.17.2; quoted in Latin in Quevedo's text.

Further Reading

CHRP, pp. 372–3, 381, 383, 834

Ettinghausen, H., *Francisco Quevedo and the Neostoic Movement* (Oxford, 1972), esp. pp. 43–56

Iventosch, H., 'Quevedo and the defense of the slandered: the meaning of the *Sueño de la muerte*, the *Entremés de los refranes del viejo celoso*, the *Defensa de Epicuro*, etc.', *Hispanic Review*, 30 (1962), 94–115, 173–93.

Mérimée, E., *Essai sur la vie et les oeuvres de Francisco de Quevedo (1580–1645)* (Paris, 1886)

Bibliography of Renaissance Moral Philosophy Texts Available in English

Anthologies

Cassirer, E., Kristeller, P. O., and Randall, J. H., Jr., eds., *The Renaissance Philosophy of Man* (Chicago, 1948)

Schneewind, J., ed., *Moral Philosophy from Montaigne to Kant: An Anthology,* 2 vols. (Cambridge, 1990), vol. I

Texts by Author

Alberti, Leon Battista, *The Family in Renaissance Florence,* trans. R. Neu Watkins (Columbia, S.C., 1969)

Bembo, Pietro, *Gli Asolani,* trans. R. B. Gottfried (Bloomington, Ind., 1954)

Bruni, Leonardo, *Dialogues,* in G. Griffiths, J. Hankins and D. Thompson, trans., *The Humanism of Leonardo Bruni: Selected Texts* (Binghamton, N.Y., 1987), pp. 63–84

Bruno, Giordano, *The Heroic Frenzies,* trans. P. E. Memmo (Chapel Hill, N.C., 1964)

Calvin, Jean, *Commentary on Seneca's 'De clementia',* ed. and trans. F. L. Battles and A. M. Hugo (Leiden, 1969)

Castiglione, Baldesar, *The Book of the Courtier,* trans. G. Bull (Harmondsworth, 1986)

Charron, Pierre, *Of Wisdome* (London, 1608; reprinted New York, 1971)

Du Vair, Guillaume, *A Buckler against Adversity,* trans. A. Court (London, 1622)

Holy Philosophy, trans. J. Hawkins (Douai, 1636; reprinted Menston, 1976)

The Moral Philosophie of the Stoicks, trans. T. James (London, 1598; reprinted, with introduction and notes by R. Kirk, New Brunswick, N.J., 1951) [selections in J. Schneewind, ed., *Moral Philosophy from Montaigne to Kant: An Anthology,* 2 vols. (Cambridge, 1990), I, pp. 201–15]

Ebreo, Leone, *The Philosophy of Love (Dialoghi d'amore),* trans. F. Friedberg-Seeley and J. H. Barnes (London, 1937)

Erasmus, Desiderius, 'The Epicurean (*Epicureus*)', in *The Colloquies of Erasmus,* trans. C. R. Thompson (Chicago, 1965), pp. 535–51

Ficino, Marsilio, *Commentary on Plato's Symposium on Love,* trans. S. Jayne (Dallas, 1985)

'Letter 115: what happiness is', in M. Ficino, *The Letters* (London, 1975–), I, pp. 171–8

Phaedrus Commentary, in *Marsilio Ficino and the Phaedran Charioteer,* ed. and trans. M. J. B. Allen (Berkeley, Calif., 1981)

The Philebus Commentary, ed. and trans. M. J. B. Allen (Berkeley, Calif., 1975)

Hall, Joseph, *The Works,* ed. P. Wynter, 10 vols. (Oxford, 1863)

Lipsius, Justus, *Two Bookes of Constancie,* trans. Sir John Stradling (London, 1594; reprinted, with introduction by R. Kirk, New Brunswick, N.J., 1939)

267

Manetti, Giannozzo, *On the Dignity of Man* [selections], in B. Murchland, trans., *Two Views of Man* (New York, 1966), pp. 61–103

Montaigne, Michel de, *The Complete Essays,* ed. and trans. M. A. Screech (London, 1993)

More, Thomas, *Utopia,* ed. E. Surtz and J. H. Hexter, in *The Complete Works* (New Haven, Conn., 1963–), vol. IV

Petrarch, *Letters on Familiar Matters: Rerum familiarium libri I–XXIV,* trans. A. S. Bernardo, 3 vols. (Albany, N.Y., 1975; Baltimore, 1982–5)

    Letters of Old Age: Rerum senilium libri I–XVIII, trans. A. S. Bernardo, S. Levin and R. A. Bernardo, 2 vols. (Baltimore, 1992)

    Remedies for Fortune Fair and Foul: A Modern English Translation of 'De remediis utriusque fortunae', trans. and comment. C. H. Rawski, 5 vols. (Bloomington, Ind., 1991)

    Secretum, ed. and trans. D. A. Carozza and H. J. Shey (New York, 1989)

Pico della Mirandola, Giovanni, *Commentary on a Canzone of Benivieni,* trans. S. Jayne (New York, 1984)

    Oration on the Dignity of Man, in E. Cassirer, P. O. Kristeller and J. H. Randall, eds., *The Renaissance Philosophy of Man* (Chicago, 1948), pp. 215–54

Pletho, Gemistus, *De differentiis,* in C. M. Woodhouse, *Gemistos Plethon: The Last of the Hellenes* (Oxford, 1986), pp. 191–214

Poggio Bracciolini, *On Avarice,* in B. Kohl and R. G. Witt, eds., *The Earthly Republic: Italian Humanists on Government and Society* (Manchester, 1978), pp. 231–89

Valla, Lorenzo, *On Pleasure. De voluptate,* ed. and trans. A. K. Hieatt and M. Lorch (New York, 1977)

Vives, J. L., *A Fable about Man,* in E. Cassirer, P. O. Kristeller and J. H. Randall, eds., *The Renaissance Philosophy of Man* (Chicago, 1948), pp. 385–93

    De institutione feminae Christianae, liber primus, ed. and trans. C. Matheeussen and C. Fantazzi (Leiden, 1996)

Index Nominum

Abel, 111
Abu Faris, 5, 16n
Acciaiuoli, Donato, 47–58
Achilles, 190n
Adam, 15, 181
Aelian, 254–5, 257–8, 261, 264n, 265n
Agamemnon, 184, 263n
Agathon, 96, 105n
Agathonius, *see* Agathon
Agesilaus, 26, 27n
Aglaus, 96, 105n
Ajax, 184, 193, 196, 198
Albertus Magnus, 47, 83, 86n
Albinus, 86n
Alcalá, 37
Alcibiades, 193
Alcinous, 85, 86n
Alexander of Aphrodisias, 73, 79n, 144
Alexander of Hales, 83, 86n
Alexander the Great, 26, 27n, 96, 104n
Alexandria, 221
Allucius, 118n
Almain, Jacques, 103, 107n
Alps, 219
Ambrose, St, 95, 175n, 205, 207, 208n, 209n,
    246–7, 263nn
America, 37
Anaxagoras, 30, 36n
Anaxarchus, 218, 224n
Antilochus, 184, 190n
Antipater, 208n, 221
Antisthenes, 202, 208n
Antony of Egypt, St, 231, 232n
Aphrodite, 164n
Apollo, 104n, 239
Apollonius of Tyre, 221
Apulia, 191n
Arcadia, 105n
Arcesilaus, 180, 189n, 216, 223n, 244n, 253
Archedemus, 221, 224n
Archelaus, 257
Archidemus, *see* Archedemus
Archytas of Tarentum, 70, 78nn
Argyropulos, Johannes, 47
Aristides, 26, 27n, 98, 105n

Aristippus, 30, 36n, 260–1
Ariston of Chios, 205, 208n, 221
Aristophanes, 104n
Aristotle, 26, 28n, 37, 43n, 47–129, 133–7, 139–
    40, 142, 144–5, 145nn, 146nn, 147, 151,
    154nn, 165n, 166–9, 172, 174, 174nn, 175n,
    182, 190nn, 192, 198, 199n, 201, 203, 207n,
    235, 236nn, 244nn, 246, 249, 257, 261, 265n,
    266n
Aristotle, Pseudo-, 66n, 199n, 234
Arius, 174, 176n
Arnaud, André, 246, 255, 258, 263n
Arnobius, 221
Asclepiodotus, 221
Athanasius, 173
Athena, 165n, 191n
Athenaeus, 211, 222nn
Athenodorus of Tarsus, 221
Athens, 104n, 105nn, 137, 145nn, 209n
Augustine, St, 14, 16nn, 47, 52, 57n, 66nn, 71,
    78n, 83, 91, 95, 104n, 118, 118n, 199n, 127,
    135, 147–8, 152–3, 154n, 155n, 172–3, 186,
    217, 231, 232n, 245, 247, 254, 256, 263n,
    264n, 265n
Augustine, Pseudo-, 175nn
Augustus, Emperor, 36n, 96, 104n
Aulus Gellius, 154n, 259–60, 263n, 265nn
Auost, Hièrosme d', 38
Aurispa, Giovanni, 236n
Averroes, 144, 154n
Avicenna, 154n
Avignon, 238

Barzizza, Gasparino, 238
Basel, 91
Basil the Great, St, 135
Basil the Great, Pseudo-, 118, 119n
Bathsheba, 118n
Bellerophon, 195
Benivieni, Girolamo, 171, 173
Bernaerts, Jean, 261
Bernard, St, 37
Bessarion, Cardinal, 133–46, 147, 166
Beza, Theodore, 120
Bezalel, 128

Index Rerum